ZATCH BELL! ™

15

STORY AND ART BY
MAKOTO RAIKU

KIYO TAKAMINE

Kiyo is a passive student with a keen intellect. When Kiyo meets Zatch he assumes ownership of the "Red Book" and starts to grow up.

ZATCH BELL

A mamodo who can't remember his past. When Kiyo holds the "Red Book" and reads a spell, lightning bolts shoot from Zatch's mouth. He is fighting to be a "kind king."

 # THE STORY THUS FAR

The battle to determine who will be the next king of the mamodo world takes place every 1,000 years in the human world. Each mamodo owns a "book" which increases its unique powers, and they must team up with a human in order to fight for their own survival. Zatch is one of 100 mamodo chosen to fight in this battle, and his partner is Kiyo, a junior high school student. The bond between Zatch and Kiyo deepens as they continue to survive through many harsh battles. Zatch swears, "I will fight to become a kind king."

The battle rages on and now the number of the remaining mamodo is less than 40. Meanwhile, something evil has been brewing. Zofis, who's determined to become the next king, manipulates a group of mamodo from 1,000 years ago and brings them back to life. Zatch and Kiyo, along with their friends, storm into Zofis's castle stronghold. However, their team gets split in three and each group is forced to fight against different enemies!

KAFK SUNBEAM

Ponygon's book owner who somehow completely understands Ponygon's emotions...! He works as an engineer in Japan.

KEDO

He's a mamodo who believes whatever Dr. Riddles tells him.

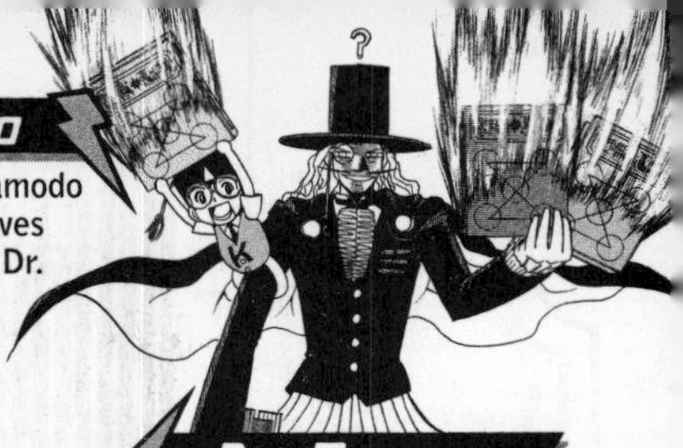

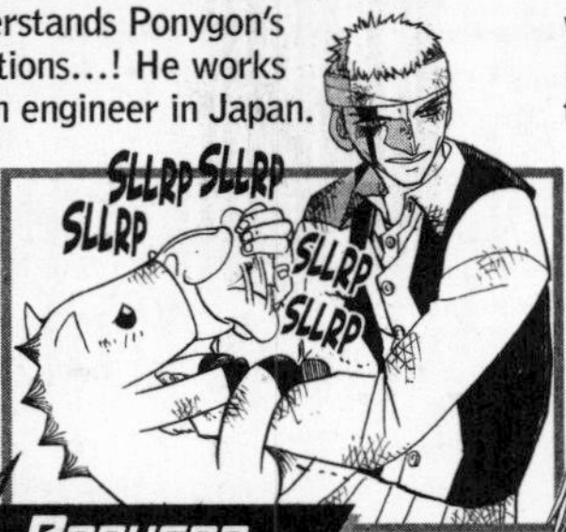
SLLRP SLLRP
SLLRP
SLLRP
SLLRP

DR. RIDDLES

He knows everything...or not. He's also Kedo's book owner.

PARCO FOLGORE

He's an Italian superstar and Kanchomé's book owner. He loves girls.

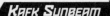

PONYGON

A mamodo who stays at Kiyo's house. He finally found a book owner!

MEGUMI

She's a popular pop idol and Tia's book owner.

ZOFIS

A mamodo with the power to control people's hearts, his mission is to become king by using the strength of the mamodo from 1,000 years ago.

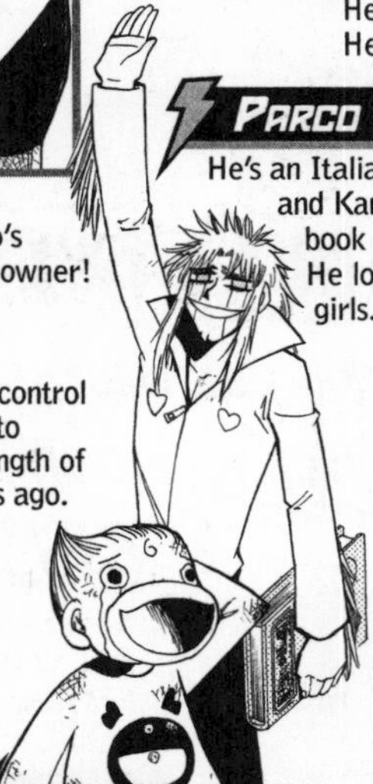

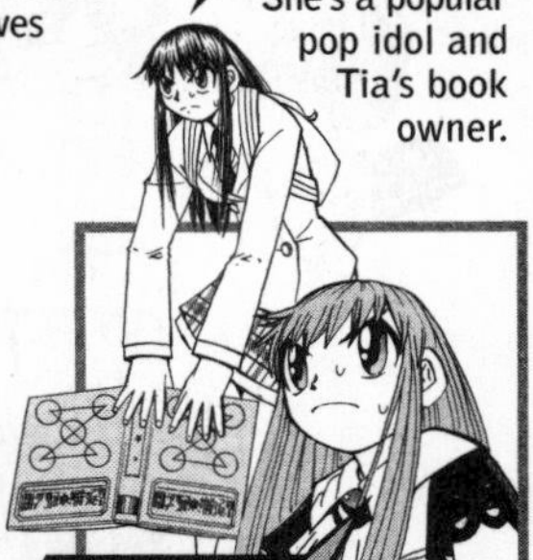

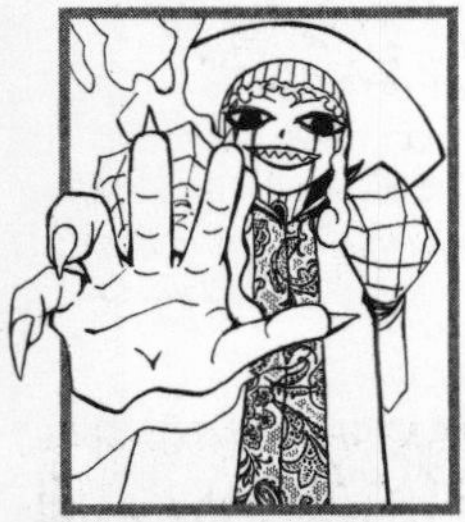

TIA

She's a mamodo who's friends with Zatch. She's a tough cookie.

KANCHOMÉ

He was a failure in the mamodo world. He's a happy-go-lucky mamodo who makes mistakes all the time, but...

SHERRY

Brago's book owner. She's searching for her best friend Koko.

LI-EN

Wonrei's book owner. Kiyo and Zatch helped her out a little while ago.

WONREI

A mamodo who's a kung fu master.

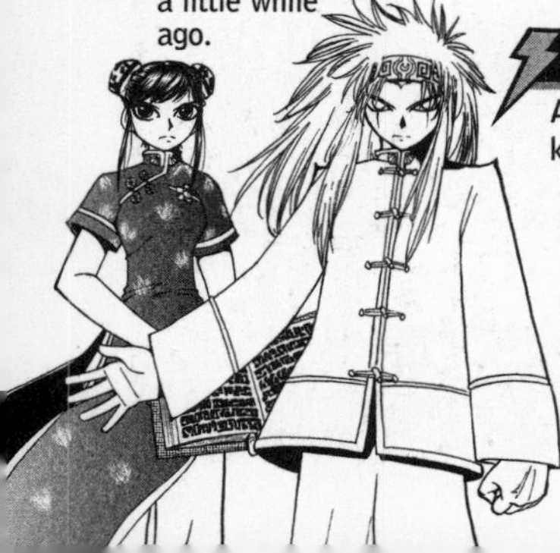

BRAGO

A mamodo who has the power to control gravity, he has a black book and is always very cool.

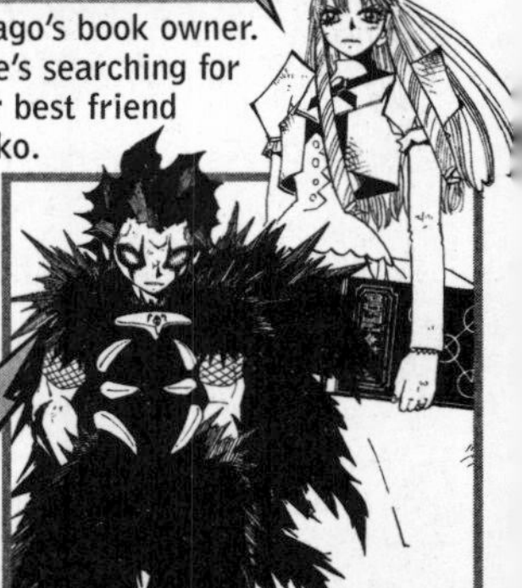

ZATCHBELL!™ 15

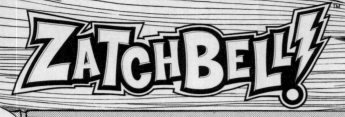

CONTENTS

LEVEL 134: Let's Sing Together

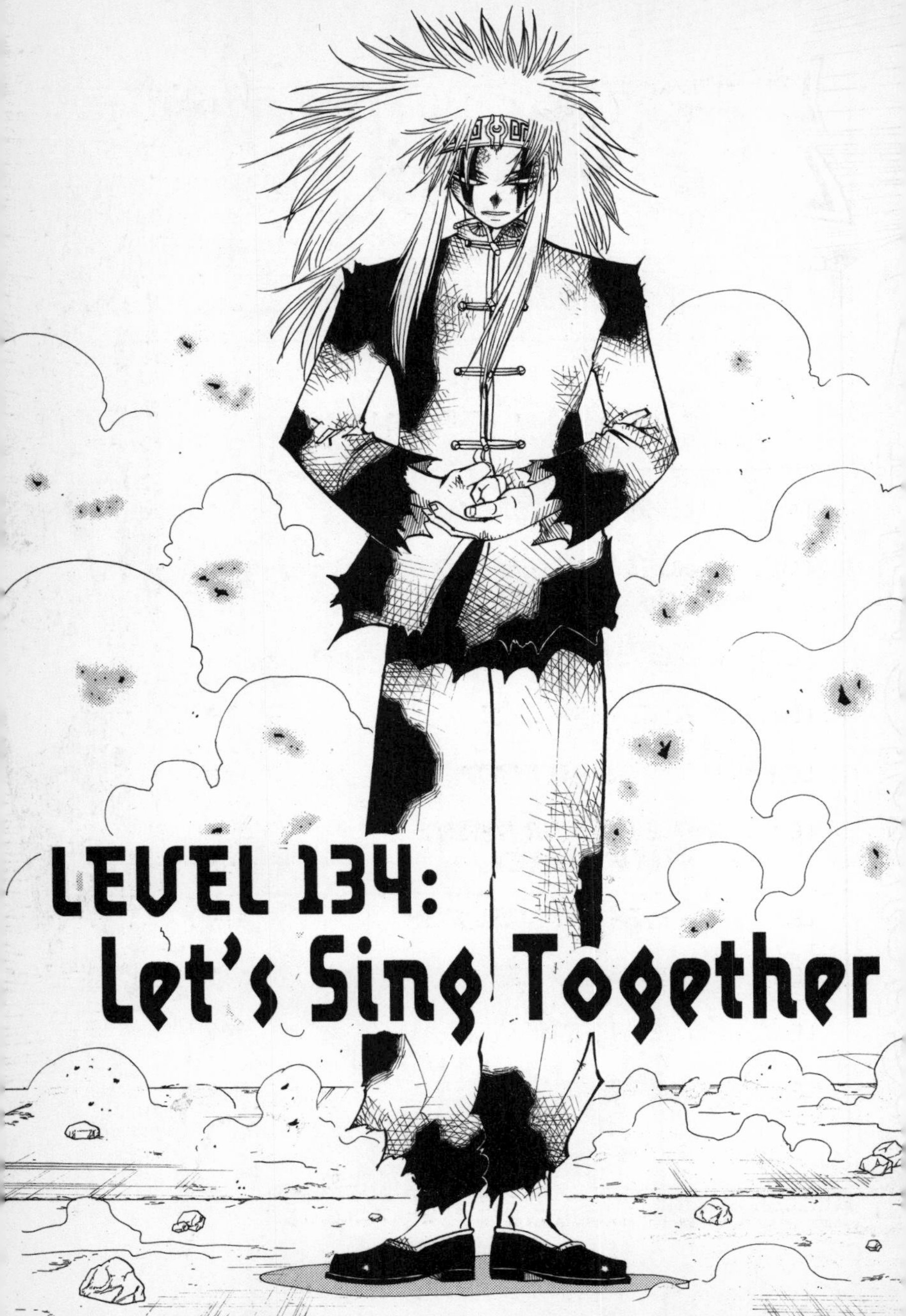

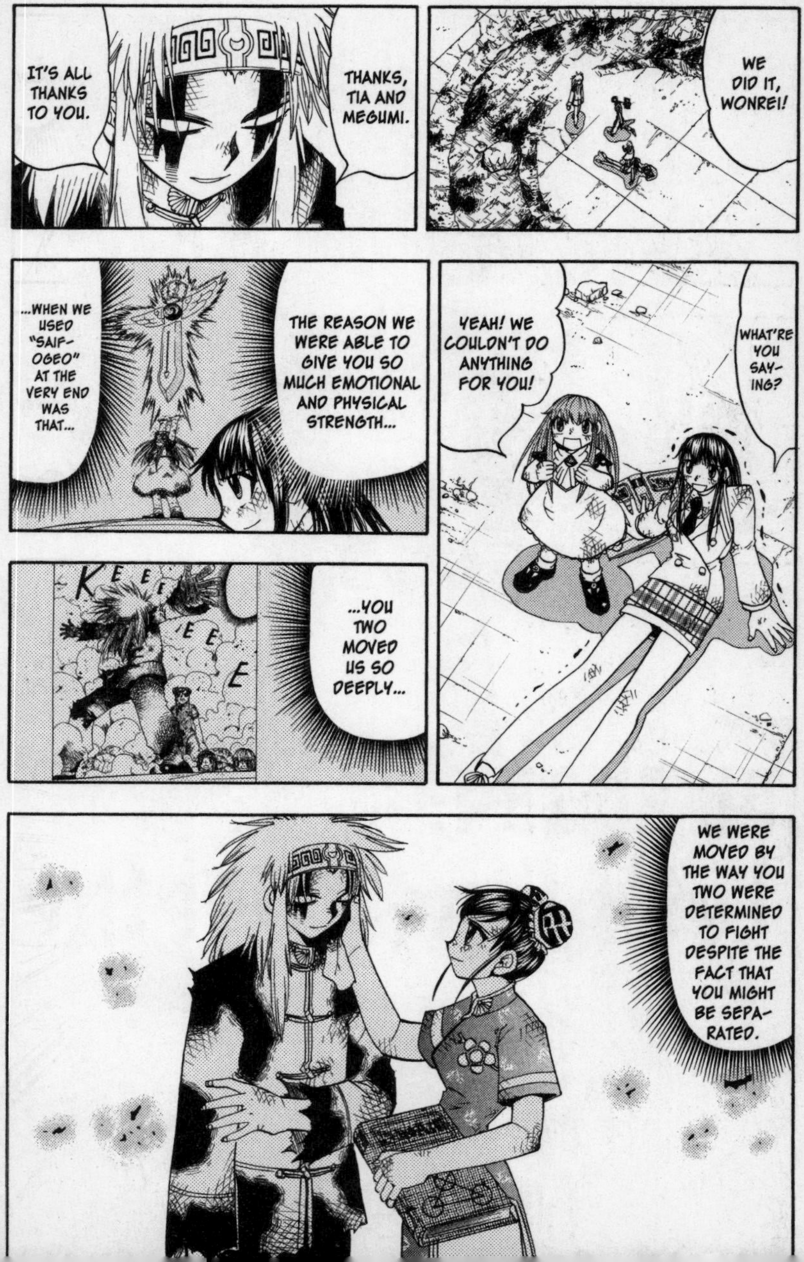
WE DID IT, WONREI!
THANKS, TIA AND MEGUMI.
IT'S ALL THANKS TO YOU.
WHAT'RE YOU SAYING?
YEAH! WE COULDN'T DO ANYTHING FOR YOU!
THE REASON WE WERE ABLE TO GIVE YOU SO MUCH EMOTIONAL AND PHYSICAL STRENGTH...
...WHEN WE USED "SAIF-OGEO" AT THE VERY END WAS THAT...
...YOU TWO MOVED US SO DEEPLY...
KEEEEEE
WE WERE MOVED BY THE WAY YOU TWO WERE DETERMINED TO FIGHT DESPITE THE FACT THAT YOU MIGHT BE SEPARATED.

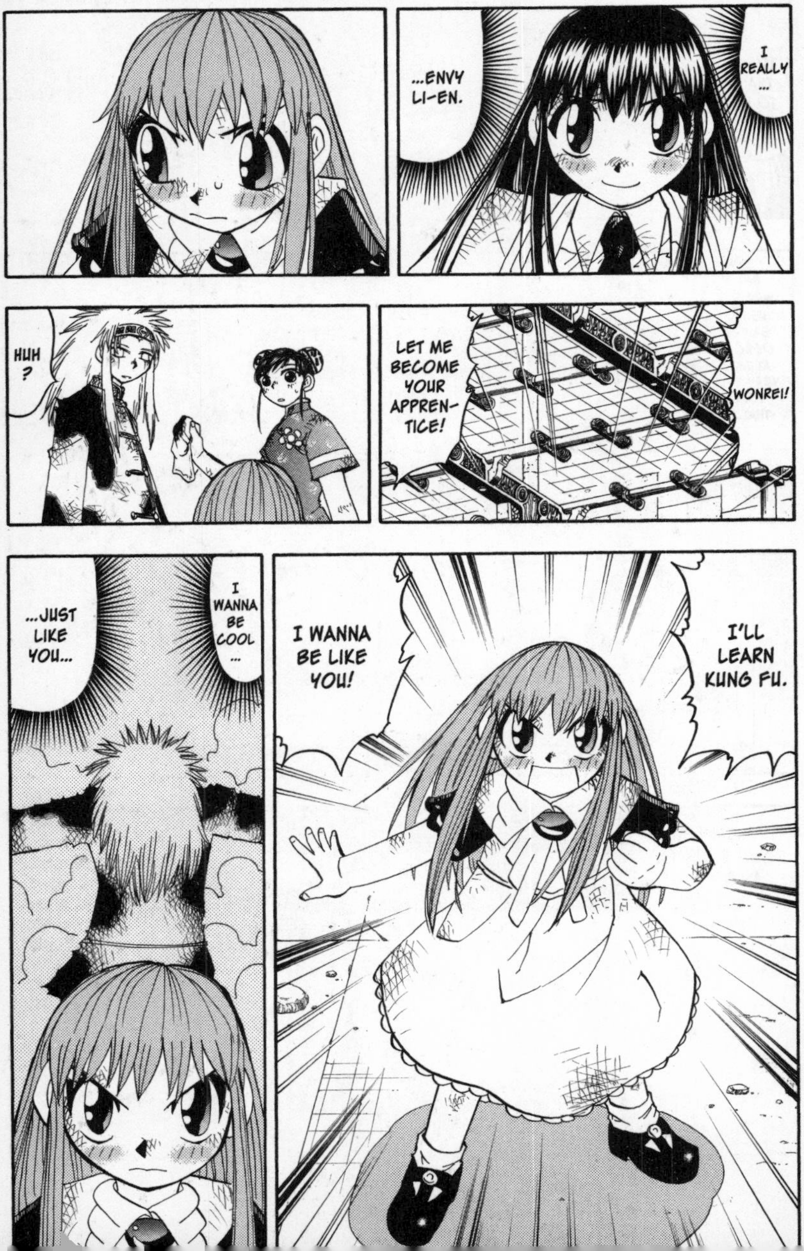
I REALLY ...
...ENVY LI-EN.
WONREI!
LET ME BECOME YOUR APPRENTICE!
HUH ?
I'LL LEARN KUNG FU.
I WANNA BE LIKE YOU!
I WANNA BE COOL ...
...JUST LIKE YOU...

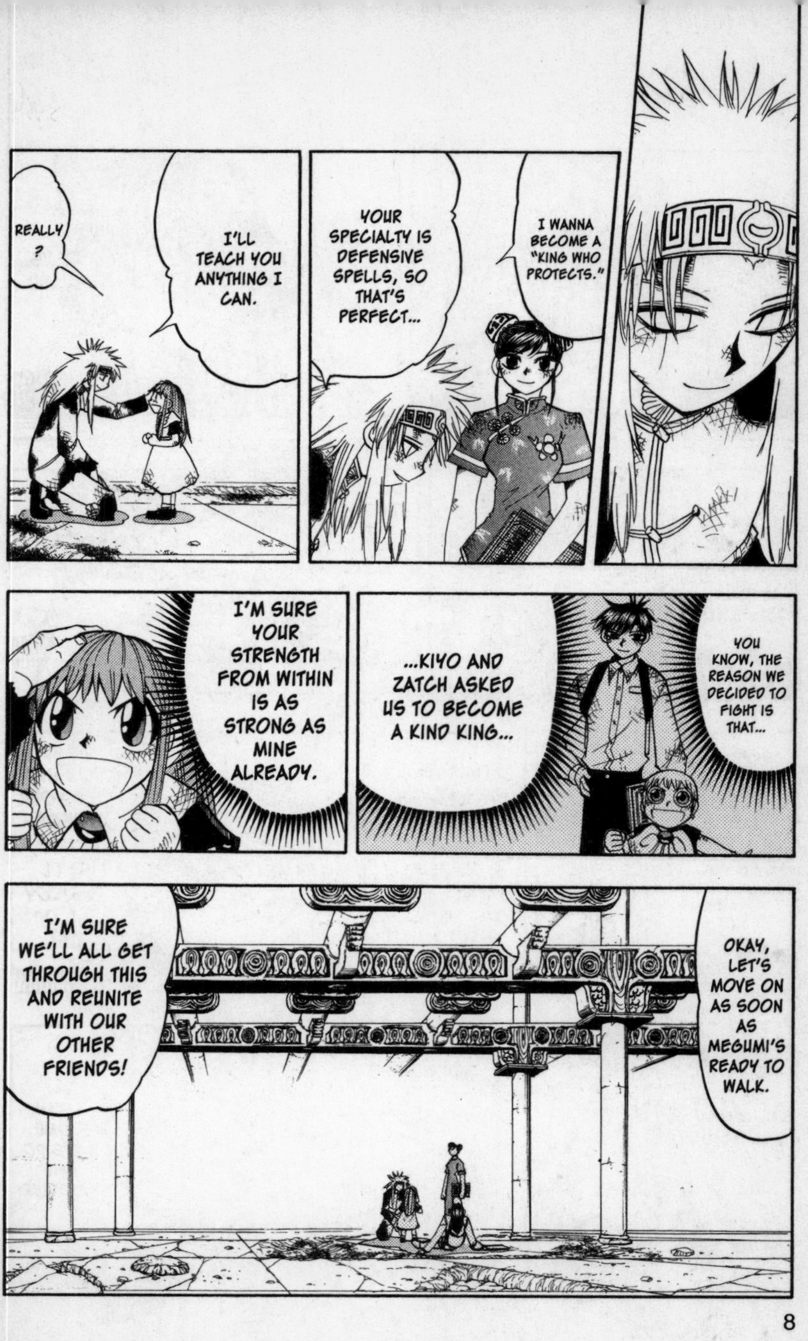

I WANNA BECOME A "KING WHO PROTECTS."
YOUR SPECIALTY IS DEFENSIVE SPELLS, SO THAT'S PERFECT...
I'LL TEACH YOU ANYTHING I CAN.
REALLY?
YOU KNOW, THE REASON WE DECIDED TO FIGHT IS THAT...
...KIYO AND ZATCH ASKED US TO BECOME A KIND KING...
I'M SURE YOUR STRENGTH FROM WITHIN IS AS STRONG AS MINE ALREADY.
OKAY, LET'S MOVE ON AS SOON AS MEGUMI'S READY TO WALK.
I'M SURE WE'LL ALL GET THROUGH THIS AND REUNITE WITH OUR OTHER FRIENDS!

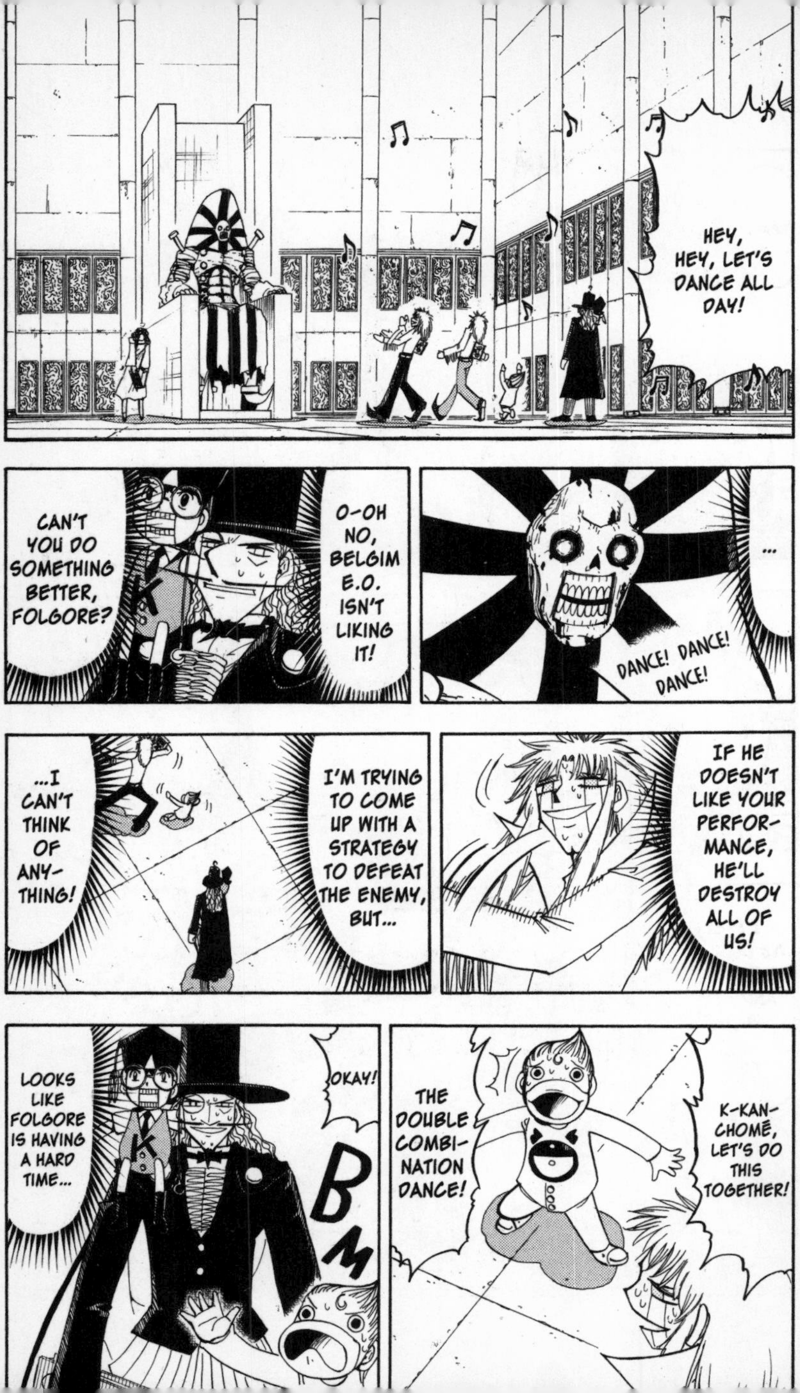
HEY, HEY, LET'S DANCE ALL DAY!
...
DANCE! DANCE! DANCE!
O-OH NO, BELGIM E.O. ISN'T LIKING IT!
CAN'T YOU DO SOMETHING BETTER, FOLGORE?
IF HE DOESN'T LIKE YOUR PERFORMANCE, HE'LL DESTROY ALL OF US!
I'M TRYING TO COME UP WITH A STRATEGY TO DEFEAT THE ENEMY, BUT...
...I CAN'T THINK OF ANYTHING!
K-KANCHOMÉ, LET'S DO THIS TOGETHER!
THE DOUBLE COMBINATION DANCE!
OKAY!
BM
LOOKS LIKE FOLGORE IS HAVING A HARD TIME...

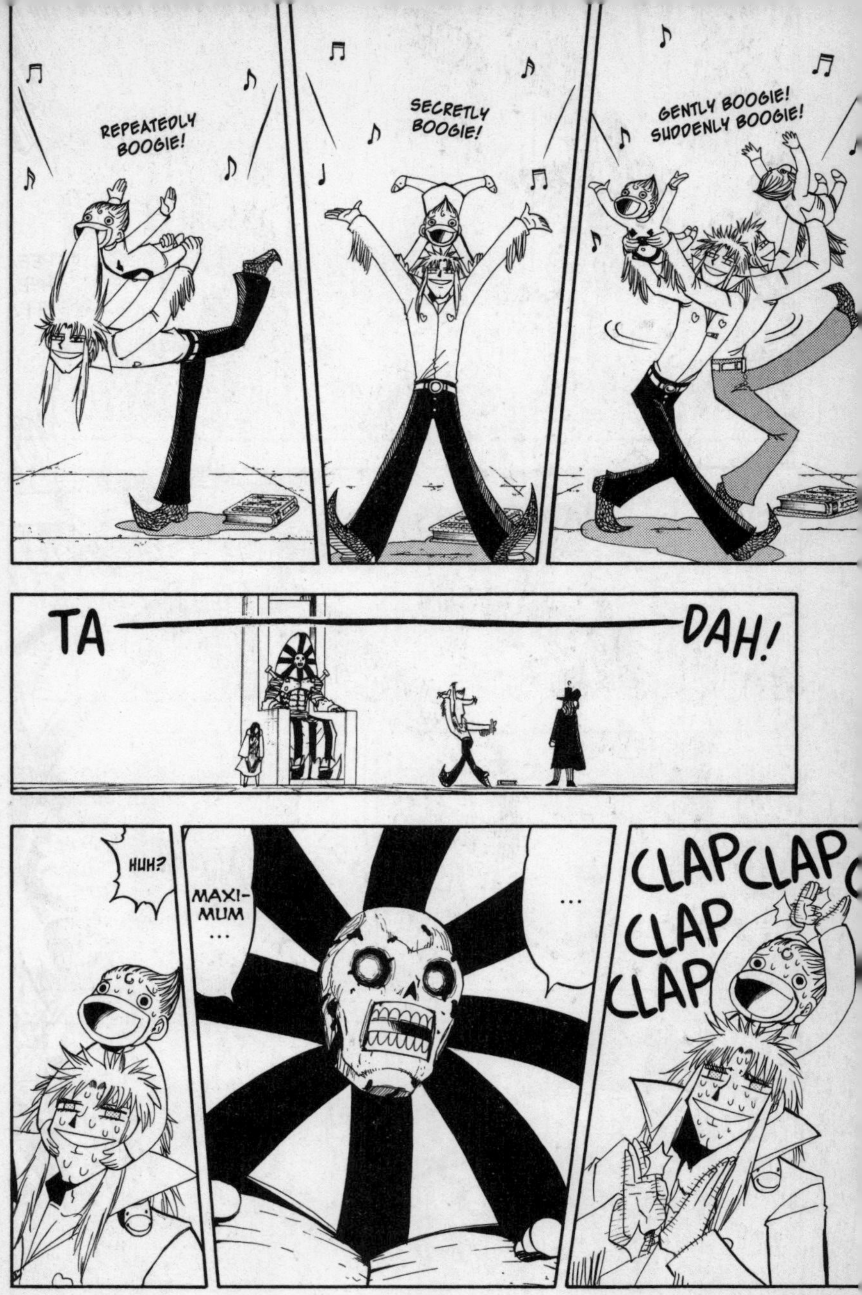
GENTLY BOOGIE! SUDDENLY BOOGIE!
SECRETLY BOOGIE!
REPEATEDLY BOOGIE!
TA——DAH!
CLAPCLAP CLAP CLAP
...
MAXI-MUM ...
HUH?

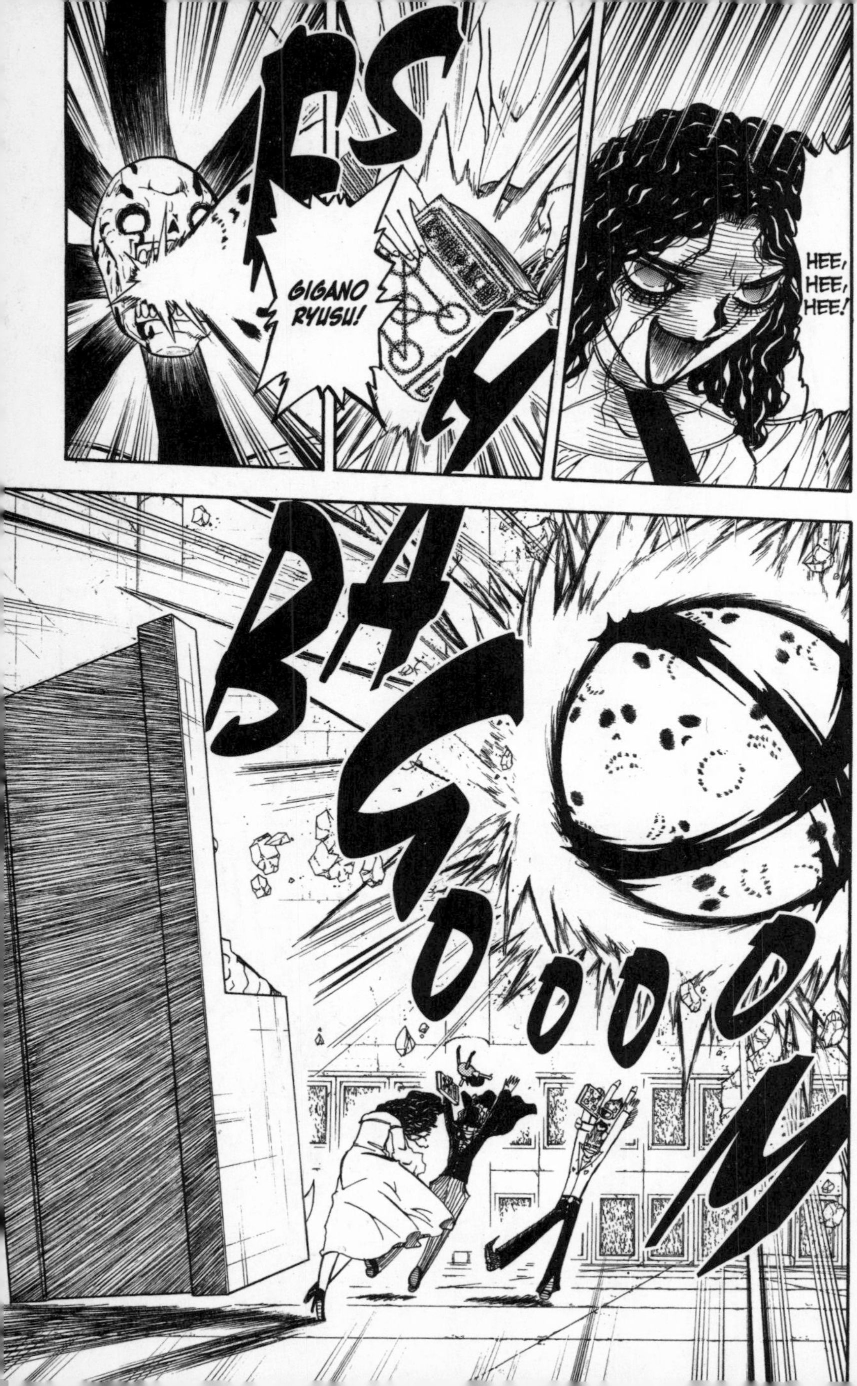
HEE, HEE, HEE!
GIGANO RYUSU!

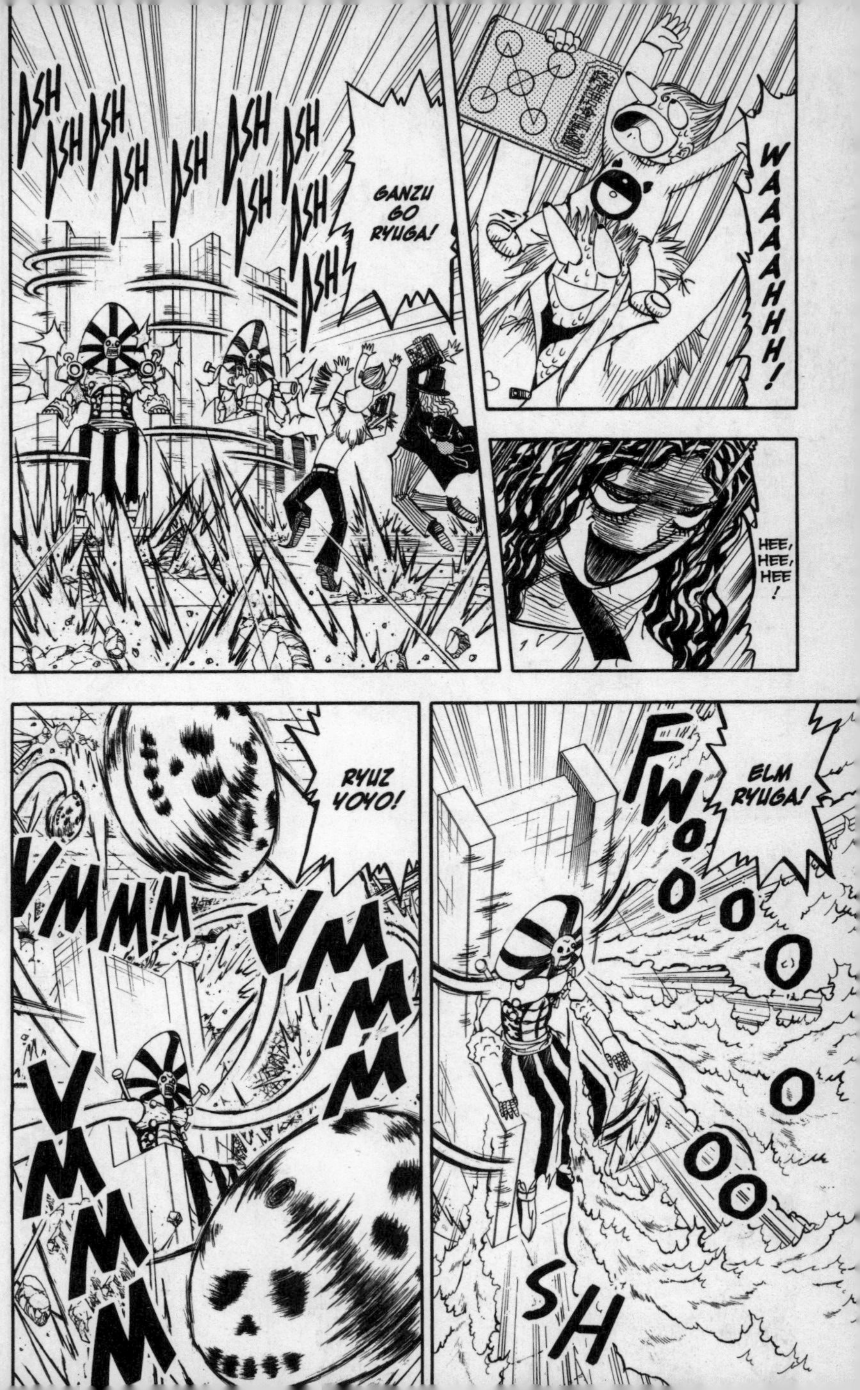
WAAAAAHHH!
HEE, HEE, HEE!
DSH DSH DSH DSH DSH DSH DSH DSH DSH DSH DSH
GANZU GO RYUGA!
ELM RYUGA!
FWOOOOOOOOSH
RYUZ YOYO!
VMMM
VMMMM
VMMMMM

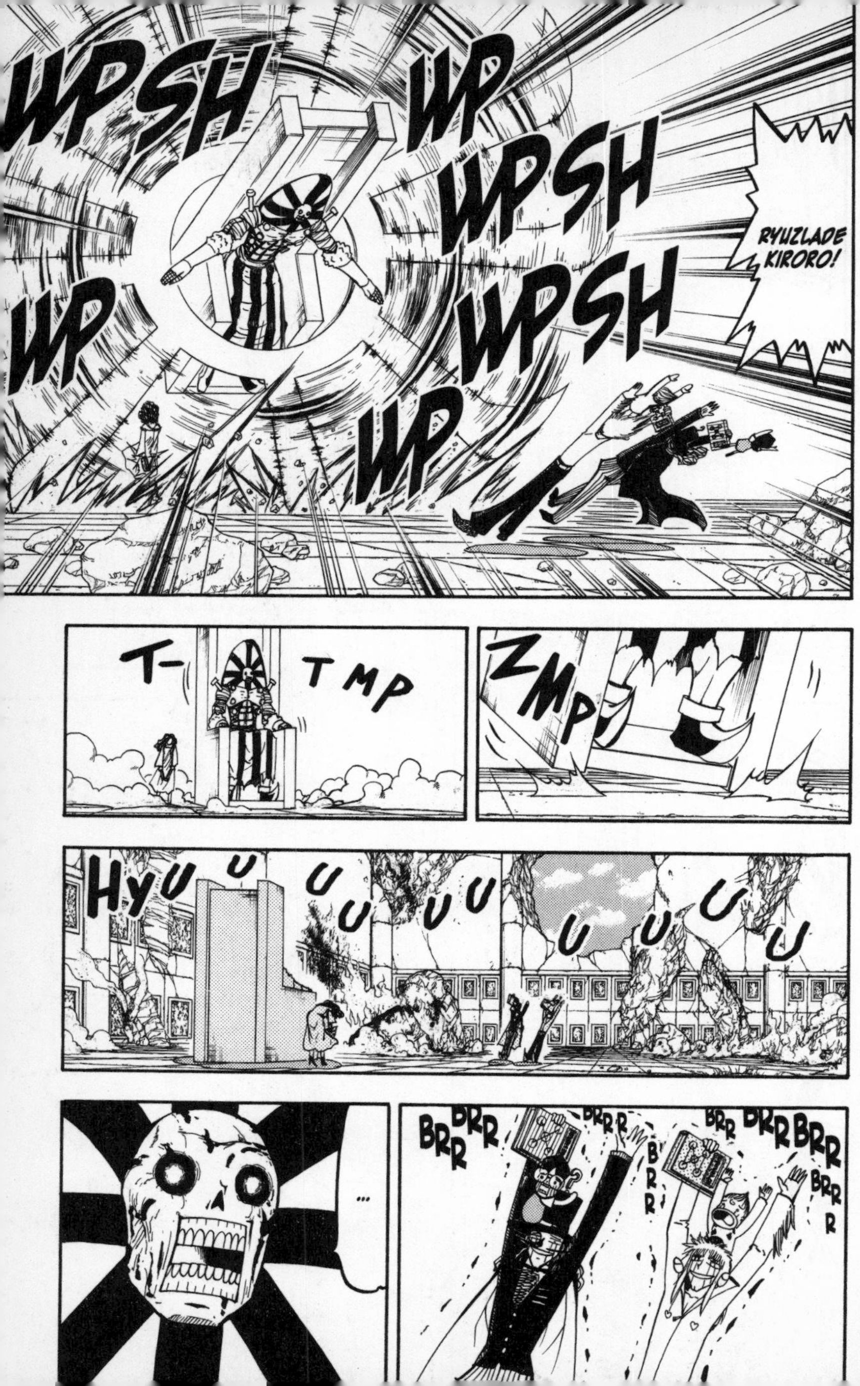
RYUZLADE KIRORO!
WP
WPSH
WPSH
WP
WPSH
WP
ZMP
T—
TMP
HyUUUUUUUUUUUUU
BRR BRRR BRRR BRRR BRR BRRR BRRR BRRR
...

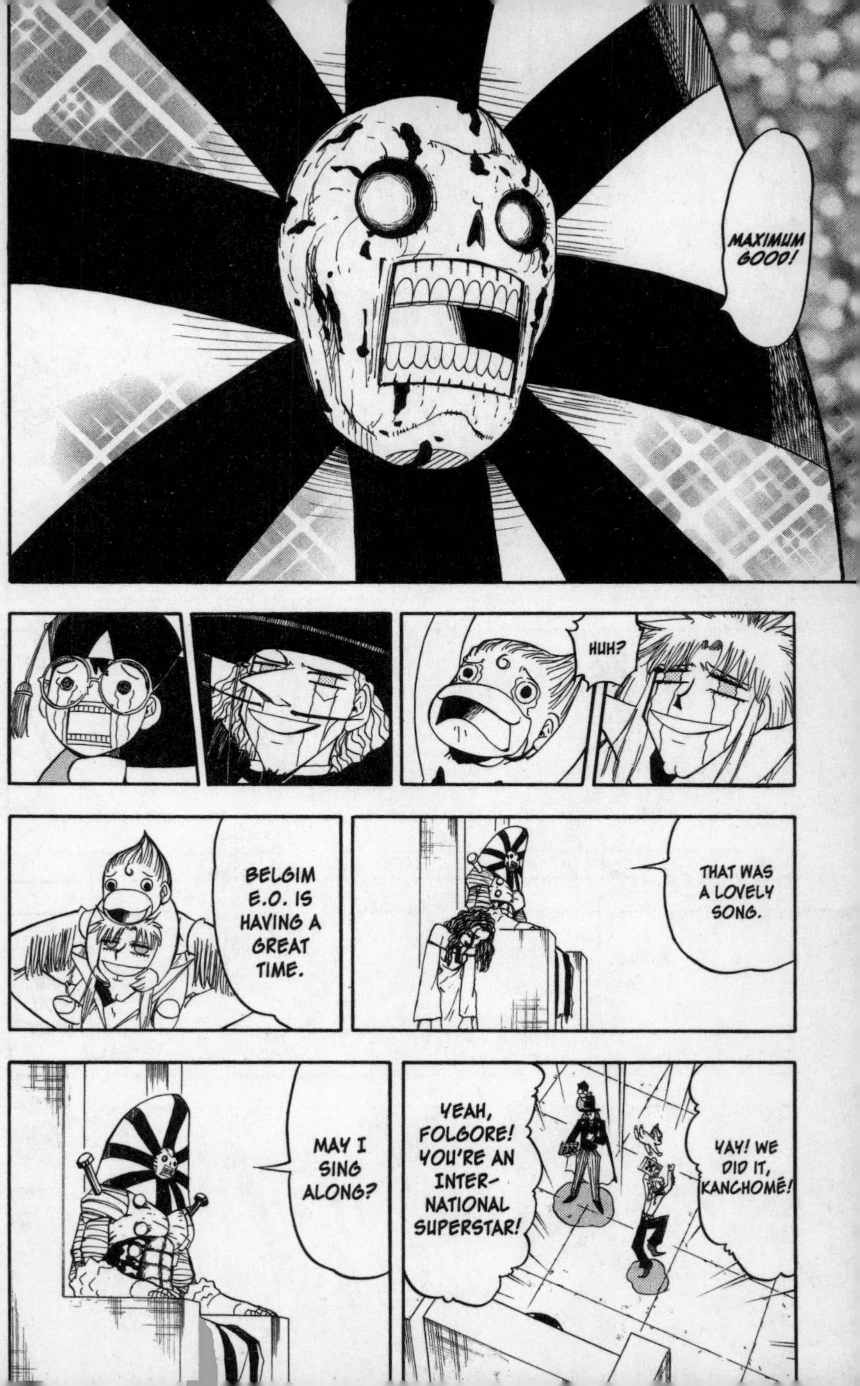
MAXIMUM GOOD!
HUH?
THAT WAS A LOVELY SONG.
BELGIM E.O. IS HAVING A GREAT TIME.
YAY! WE DID IT, KANCHOMÉ!
YEAH, FOLGORE! YOU'RE AN INTER-NATIONAL SUPERSTAR!
MAY I SING ALONG?

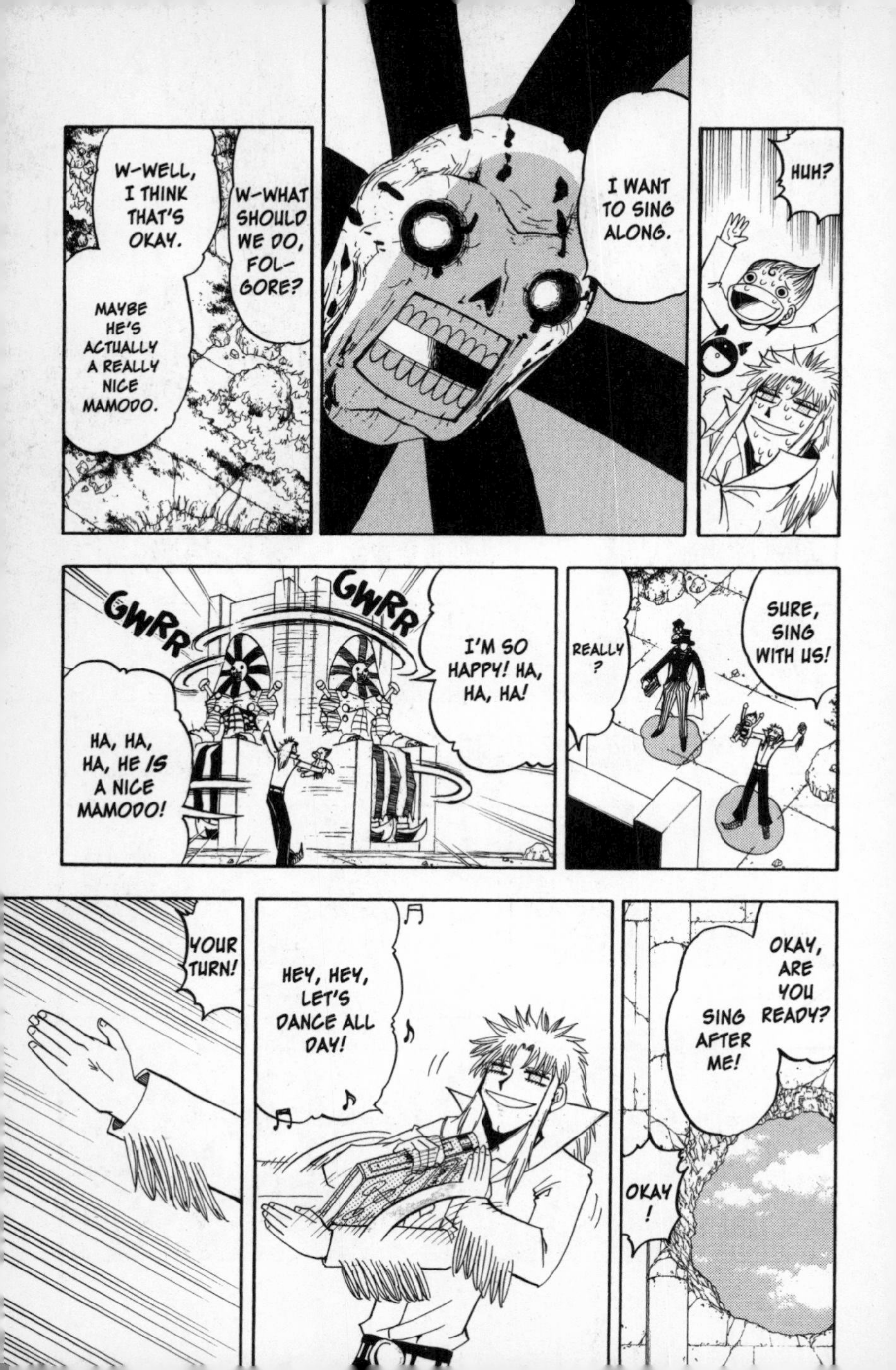
HUH?
I WANT TO SING ALONG.
W-WHAT SHOULD WE DO, FOLGORE?
W-WELL, I THINK THAT'S OKAY.
MAYBE HE'S ACTUALLY A REALLY NICE MAMODO.
SURE, SING WITH US!
REALLY?
GWRR
I'M SO HAPPY! HA, HA, HA!
GWRR
HA, HA, HA, HE IS A NICE MAMODO!
OKAY, ARE YOU READY?
SING AFTER ME!
OKAY!
HEY, HEY, LET'S DANCE ALL DAY!
YOUR TURN!

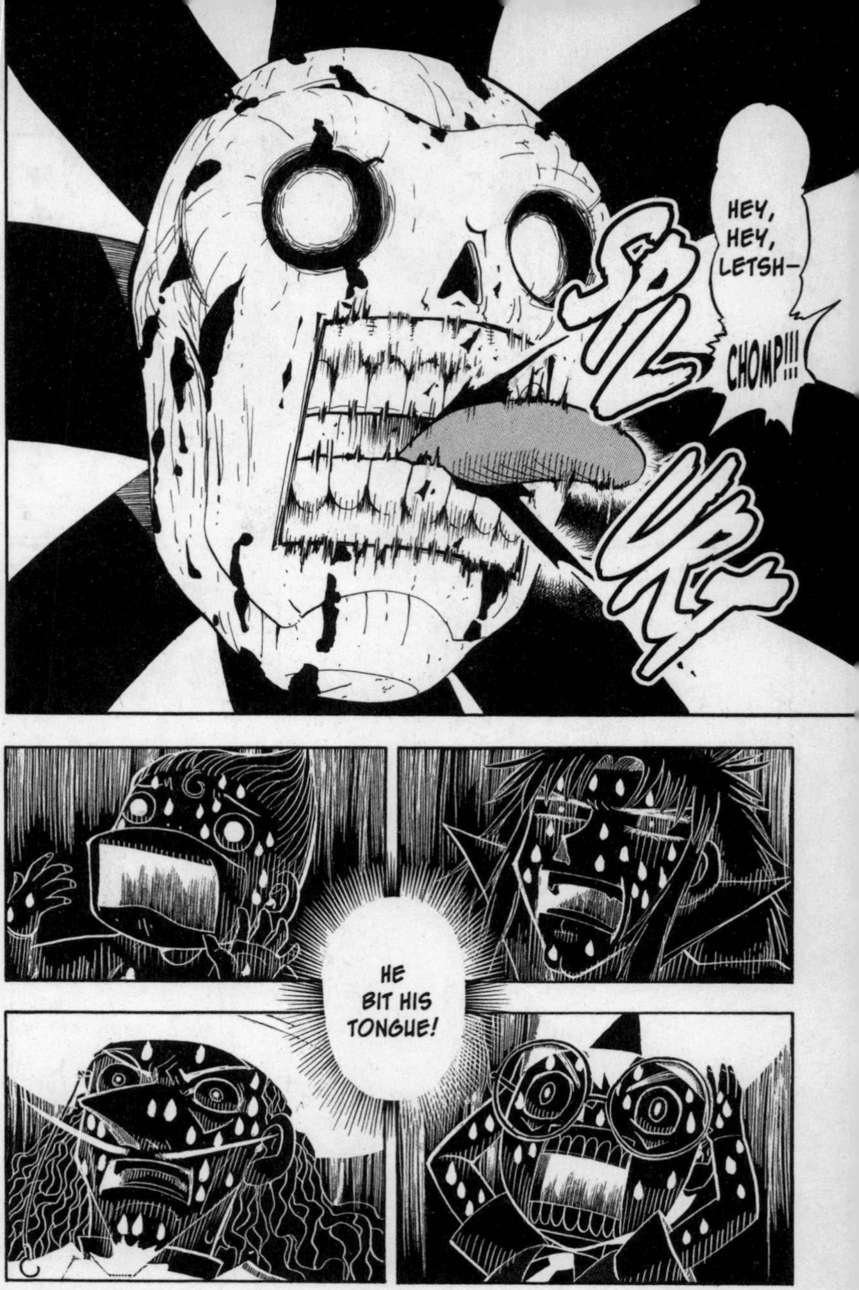
HEY, HEY, LETSH—
CHOMP!!!
SPLURT
HE BIT HIS TONGUE!

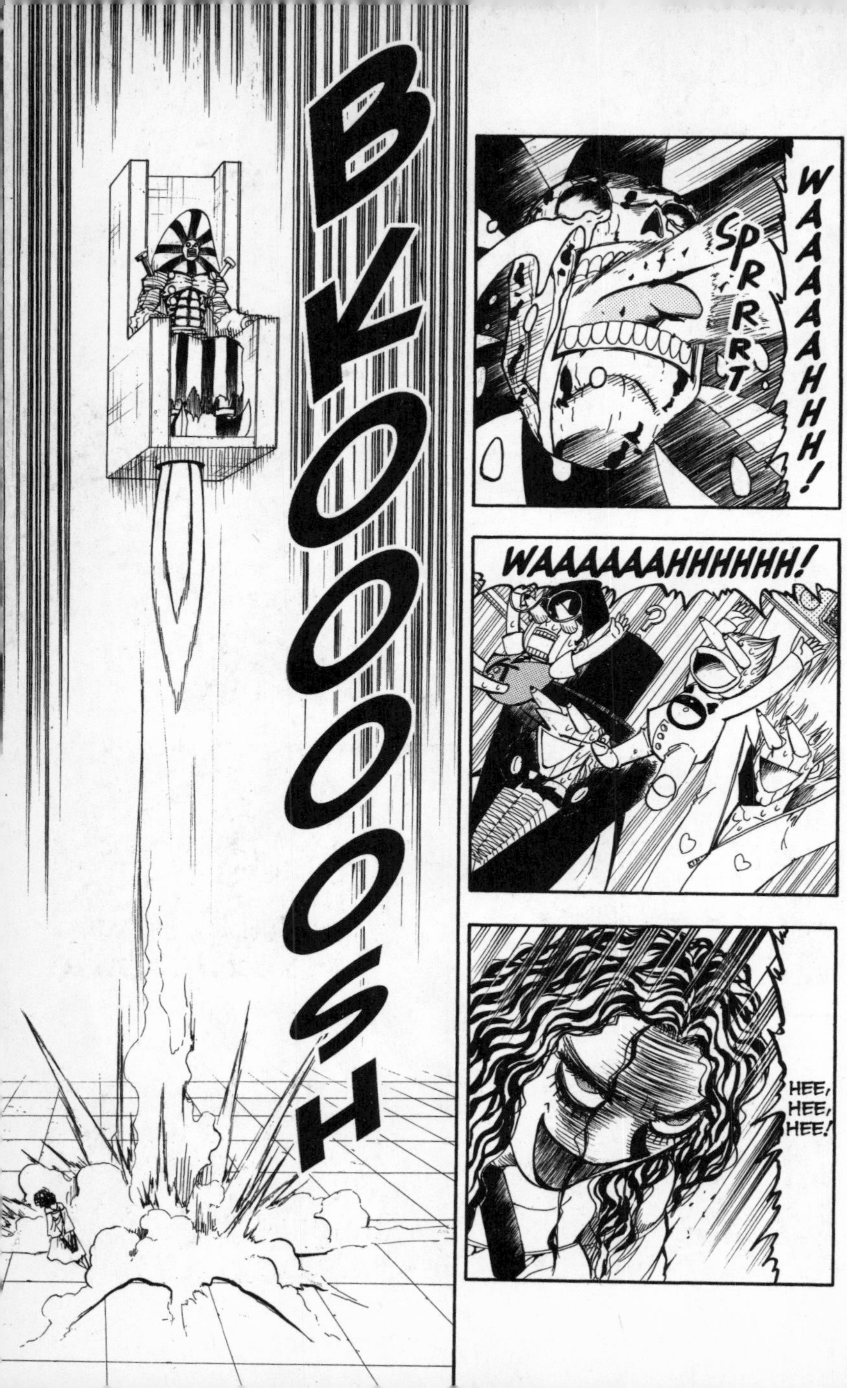
WAAAAAHHH!
SPRRRT
WAAAAAAHHHHHH!
HEE, HEE, HEE!
BWOOOOOSH

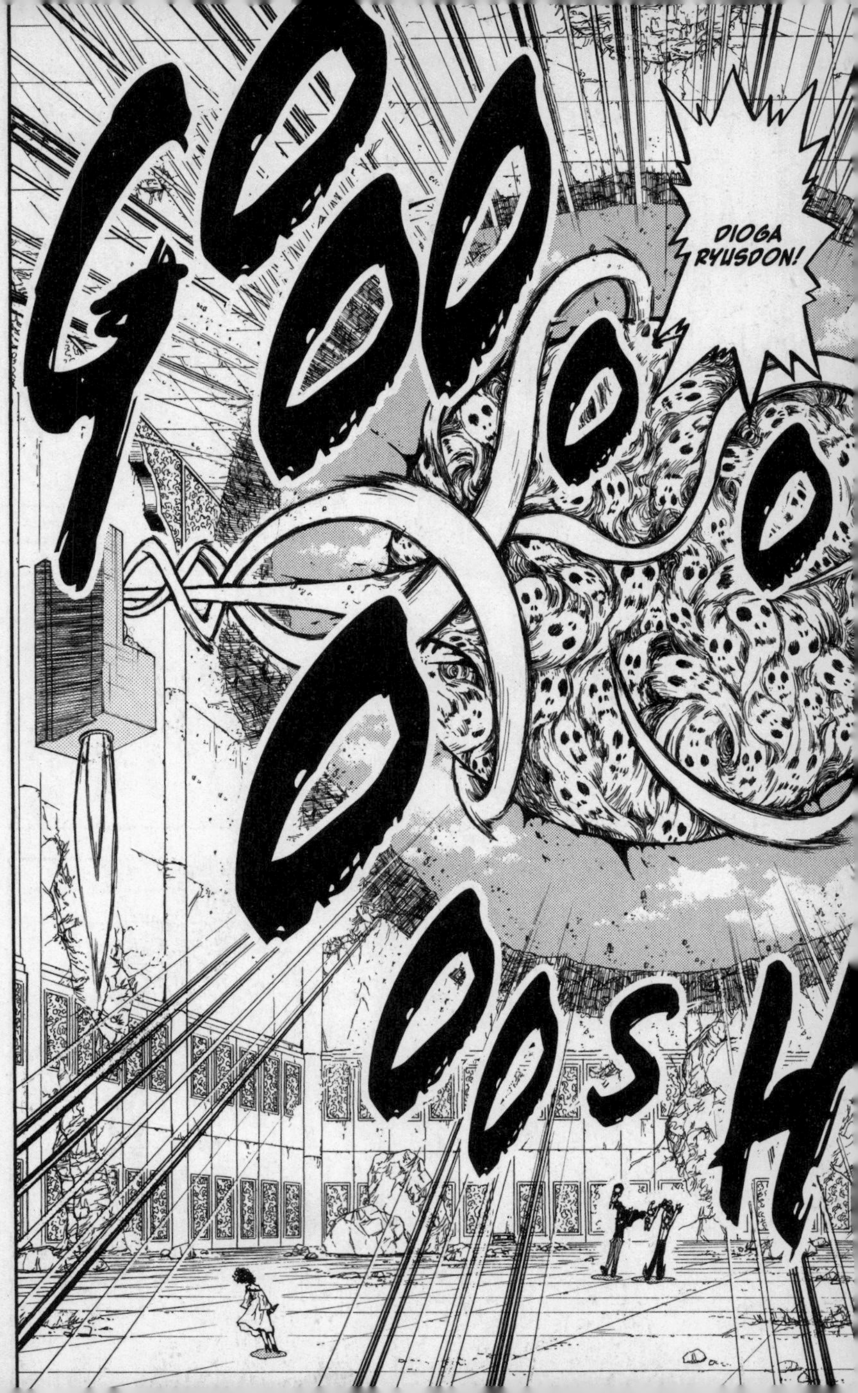
DIOGA RYUSDON!
GOOOOOOOOSH

GI-TUNK

AAAAAAHHHHH!

THE LIGHT BEAM IS BURNING MY TONGUE

AHH... I-I-I-I-IT HURTS...

WUB WUB

WAAAAAHHHHH!

IT'S YOUR OWN FAULT!

W-WE'RE SORRY, BUT IT WASN'T OUR FAULT THAT YOU BIT YOUR TONGUE!

WHAT HAVE YOU DONE TO ME?

HOW DARE YOU...

MY NAME IS BELGIM E.O. AND I'LL DESTROY YOU ALL FOR THIS INSOLENCE!

SILENCE, YOU IMPUDENT BUFFOONS!

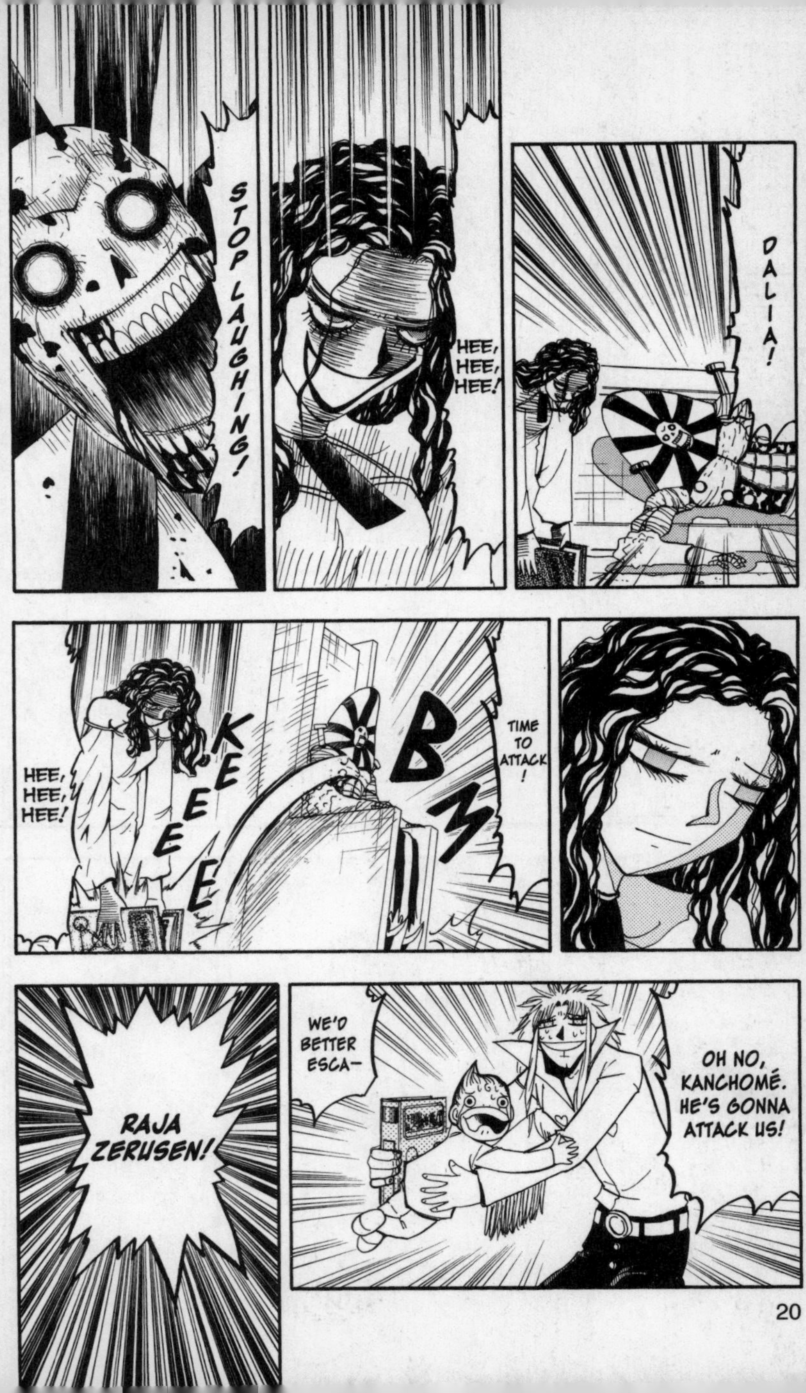
DALIA!
HEE, HEE, HEE!
STOP LAUGHING!
TIME TO ATTACK!
BM
KEEEEE
HEE, HEE, HEE!
OH NO, KANCHOMÉ. HE'S GONNA ATTACK US!
WE'D BETTER ESCA—
RAJA ZERUSEN!

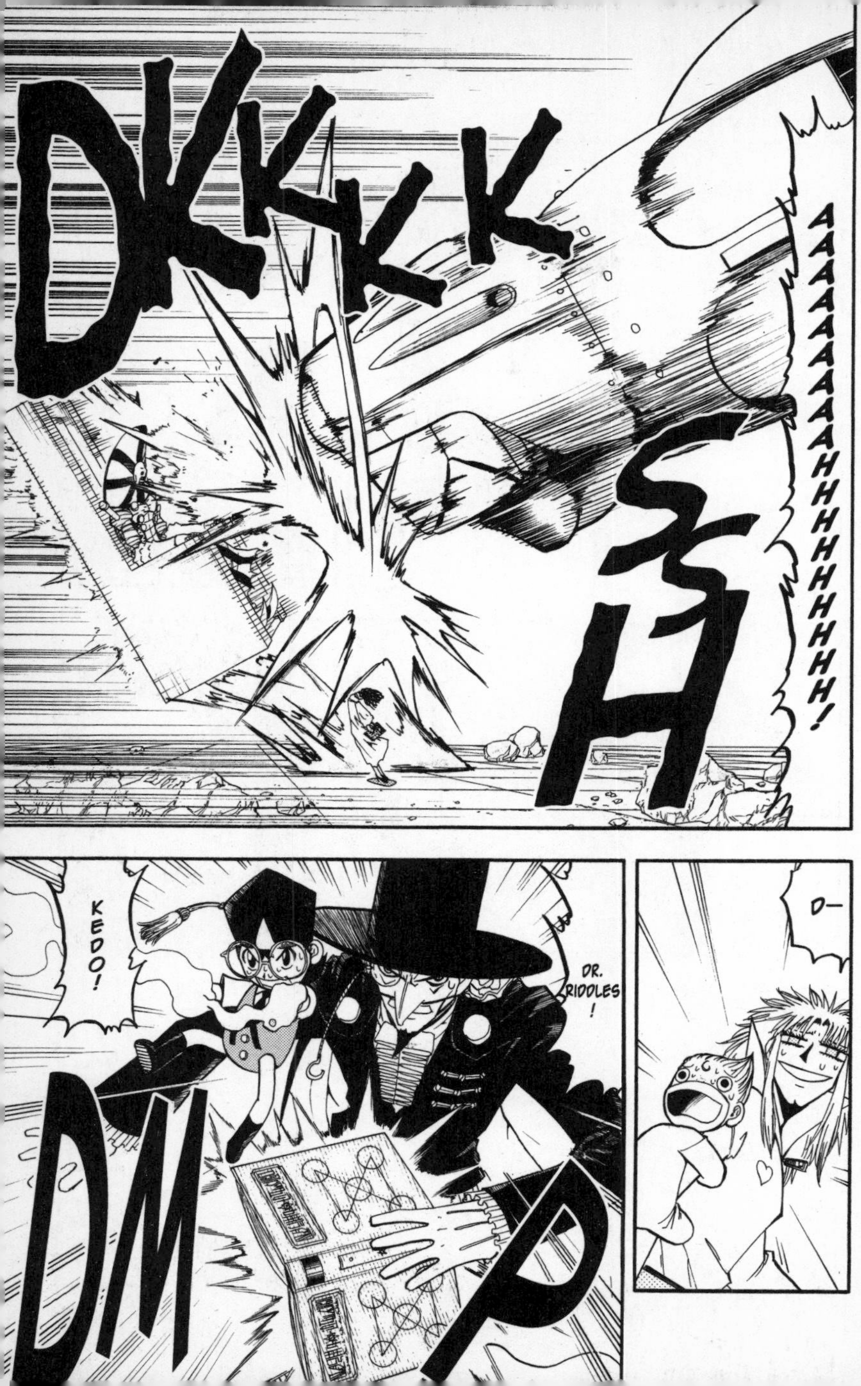
AAAAAAAAAAHHHHHHHHHH!
SH
DKKKK
D—
DR. RIDDLES!
KEDO!
DMP

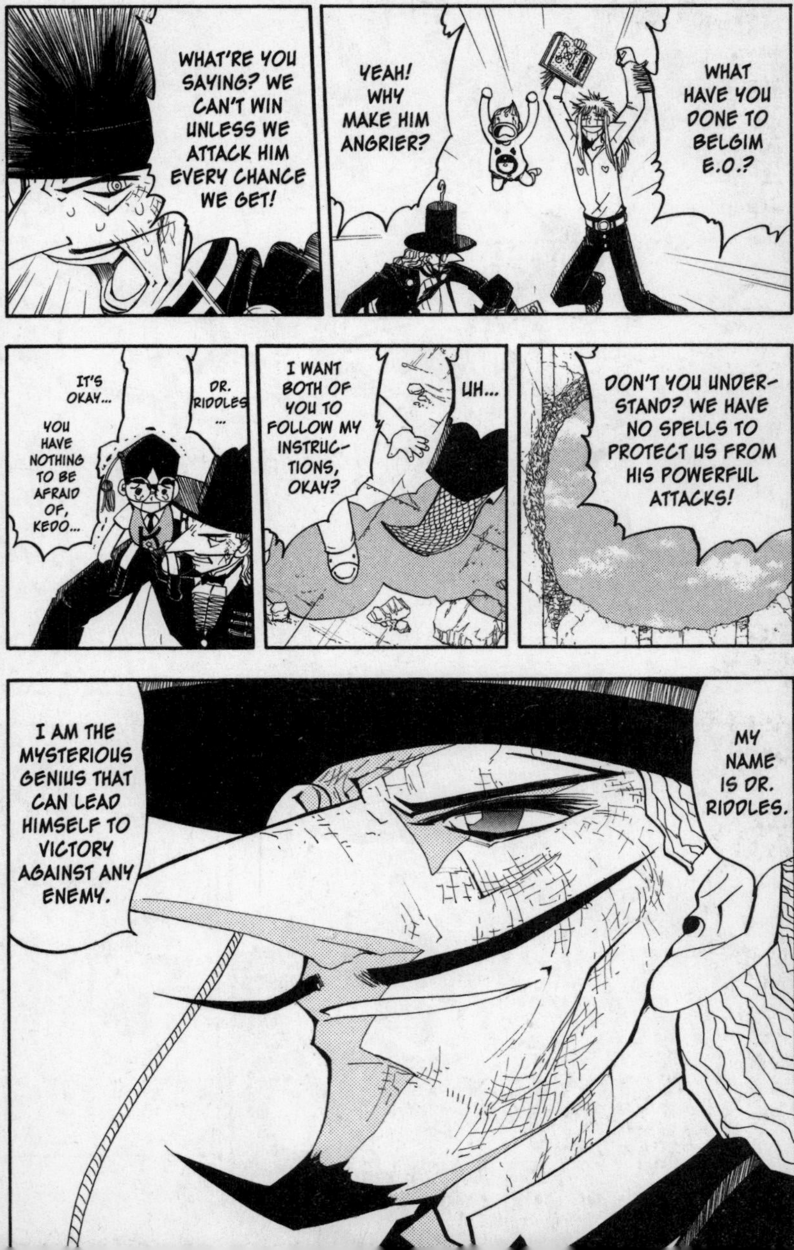
WHAT HAVE YOU DONE TO BELGIM E.O.?
YEAH! WHY MAKE HIM ANGRIER?
WHAT'RE YOU SAYING? WE CAN'T WIN UNLESS WE ATTACK HIM EVERY CHANCE WE GET!
DON'T YOU UNDER-STAND? WE HAVE NO SPELLS TO PROTECT US FROM HIS POWERFUL ATTACKS!
UH...
I WANT BOTH OF YOU TO FOLLOW MY INSTRUC-TIONS, OKAY?
DR. RIDDLES ...
IT'S OKAY...
YOU HAVE NOTHING TO BE AFRAID OF, KEDO...
MY NAME IS DR. RIDDLES.
I AM THE MYSTERIOUS GENIUS THAT CAN LEAD HIMSELF TO VICTORY AGAINST ANY ENEMY.

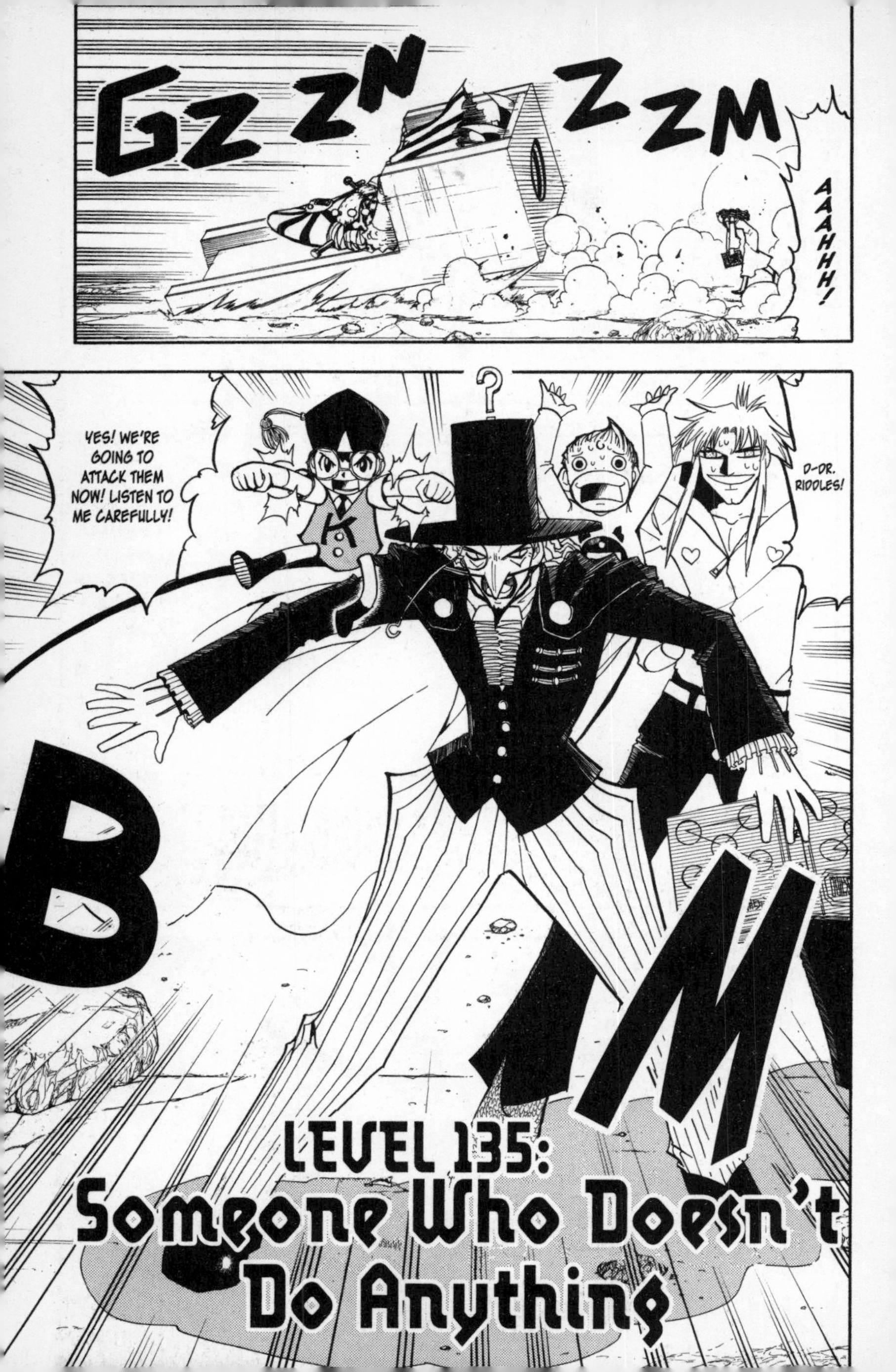
GZZN ZZZM
AAAHHH!
D-DR. RIDDLES!
YES! WE'RE GOING TO ATTACK THEM NOW! LISTEN TO ME CAREFULLY!
BM

LEVEL 135: Someone Who Doesn't Do Anything

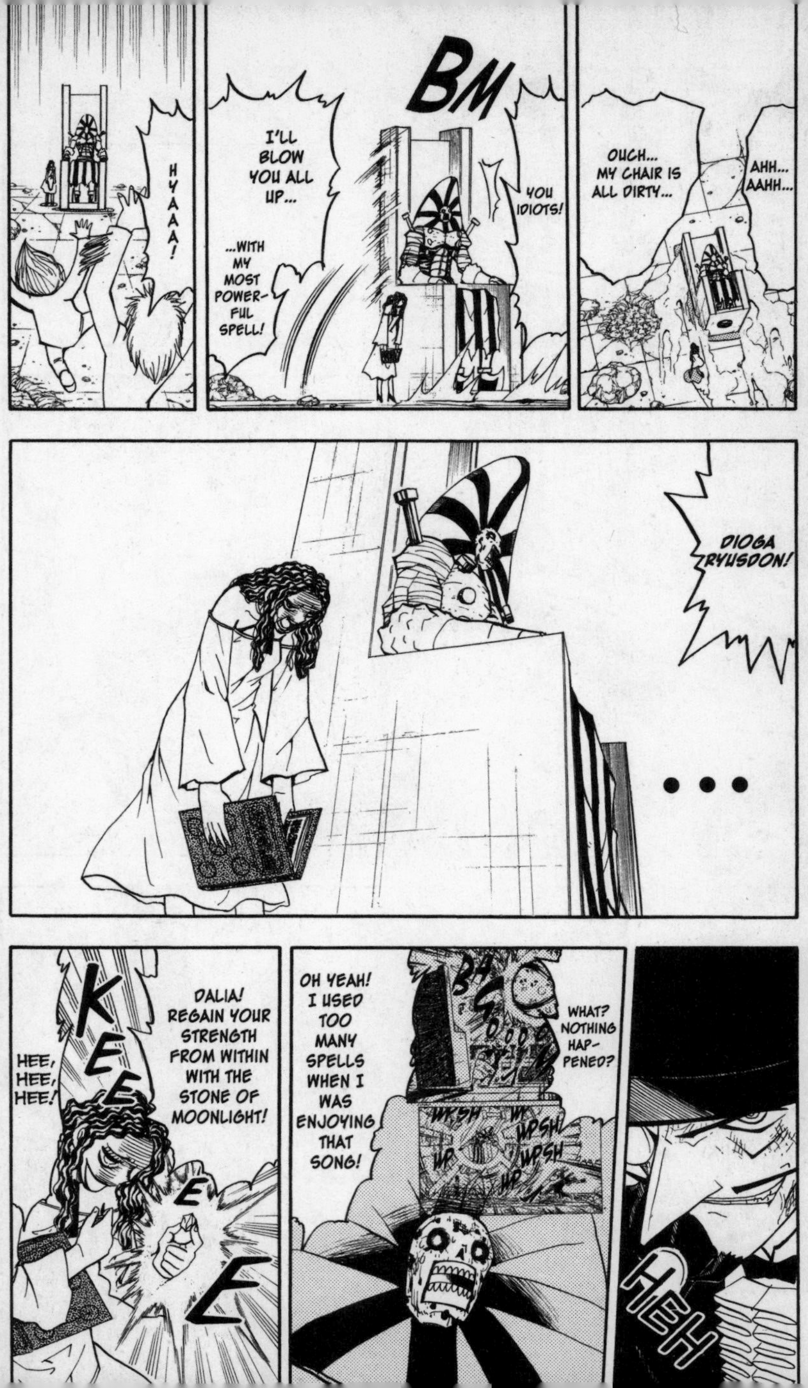
AHH... AAHH...
OUCH... MY CHAIR IS ALL DIRTY...
BM
YOU IDIOTS!
I'LL BLOW YOU ALL UP...
...WITH MY MOST POWER-FUL SPELL!
HYAAAA!
DIOGA RYUSDON!
• • •
HEH
WHAT? NOTHING HAP-PENED?
OH YEAH! I USED TOO MANY SPELLS WHEN I WAS ENJOYING THAT SONG!
WPSH
WPSH
WPSH
DALIA! REGAIN YOUR STRENGTH FROM WITHIN WITH THE STONE OF MOONLIGHT!
KEEEE
HEE, HEE, HEE!

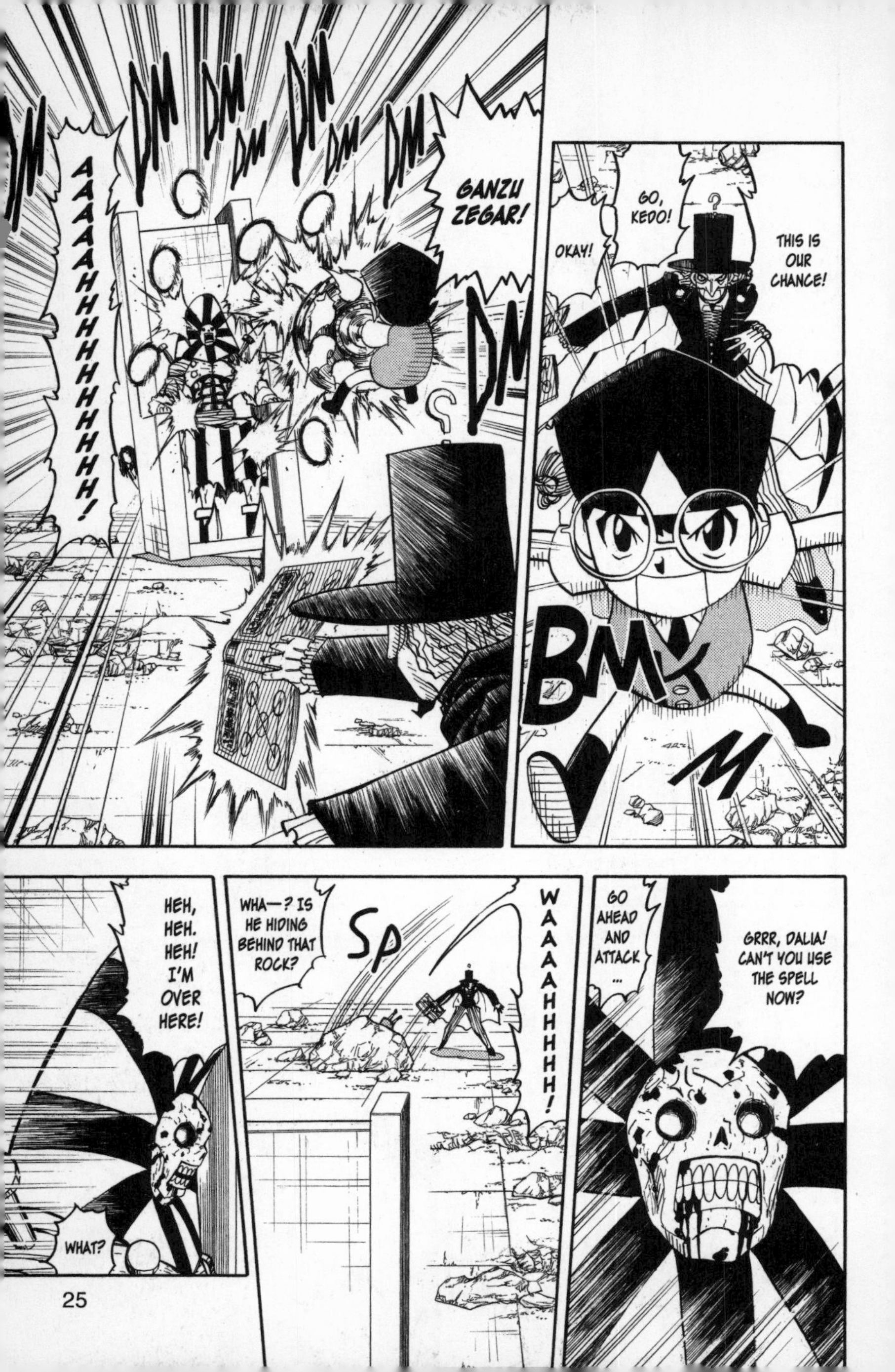
GO, KEDO!
THIS IS OUR CHANCE!
OKAY!
BMM
GANZU ZEGAR!
DM DM DM DM DM DM DM DM
AAAAAAHHHHHHHHHHHH!
GO AHEAD AND ATTACK ...
GRRR, DALIA! CAN'T YOU USE THE SPELL NOW?
WAAAAAHHHHHHH!
SP
WHA—? IS HE HIDING BEHIND THAT ROCK?
HEH, HEH. HEH! I'M OVER HERE!
WHAT?

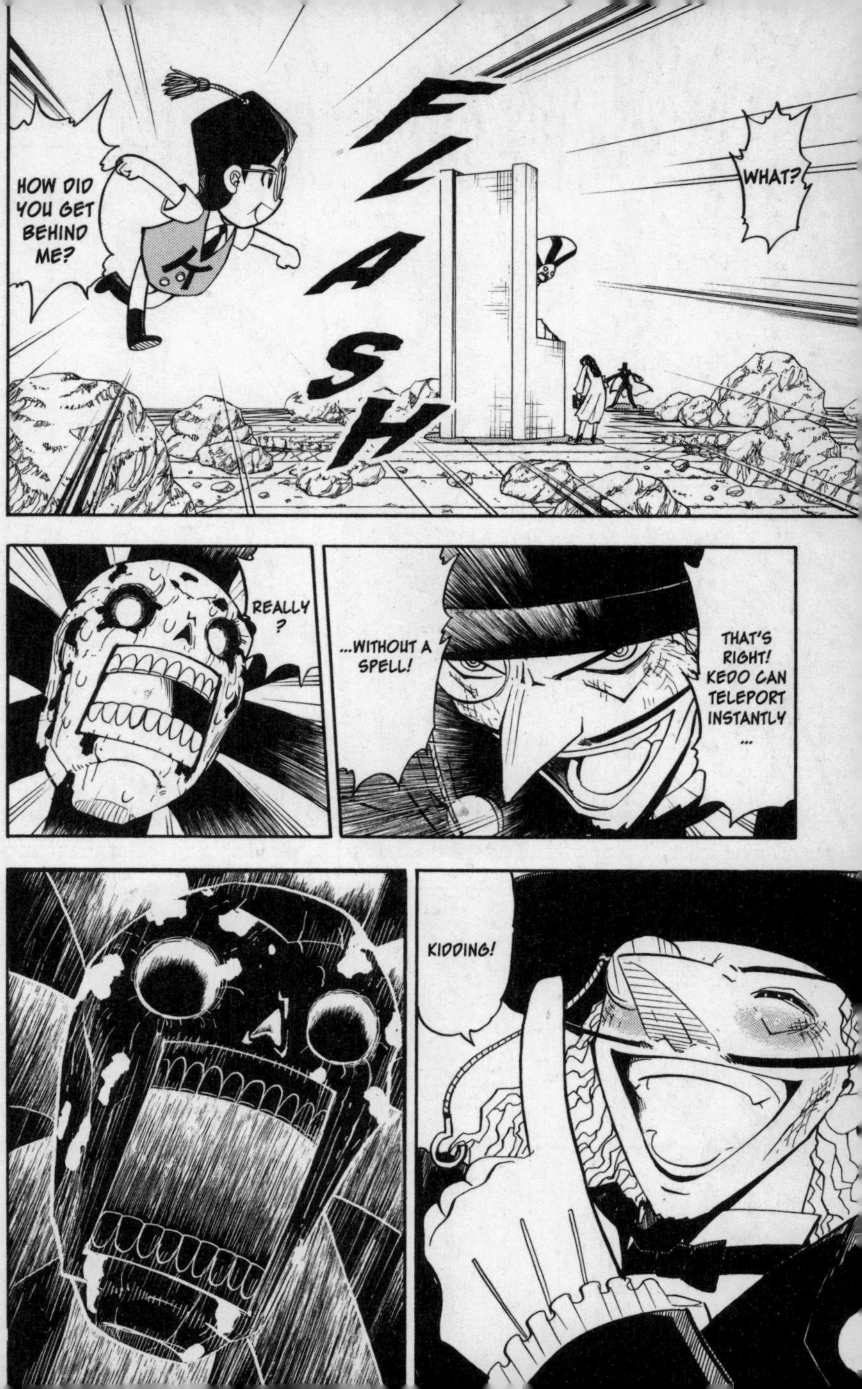
WHAT?
FLASH
HOW DID YOU GET BEHIND ME?
THAT'S RIGHT! KEDO CAN TELEPORT INSTANTLY ...
...WITHOUT A SPELL!
REALLY ?
KIDDING!

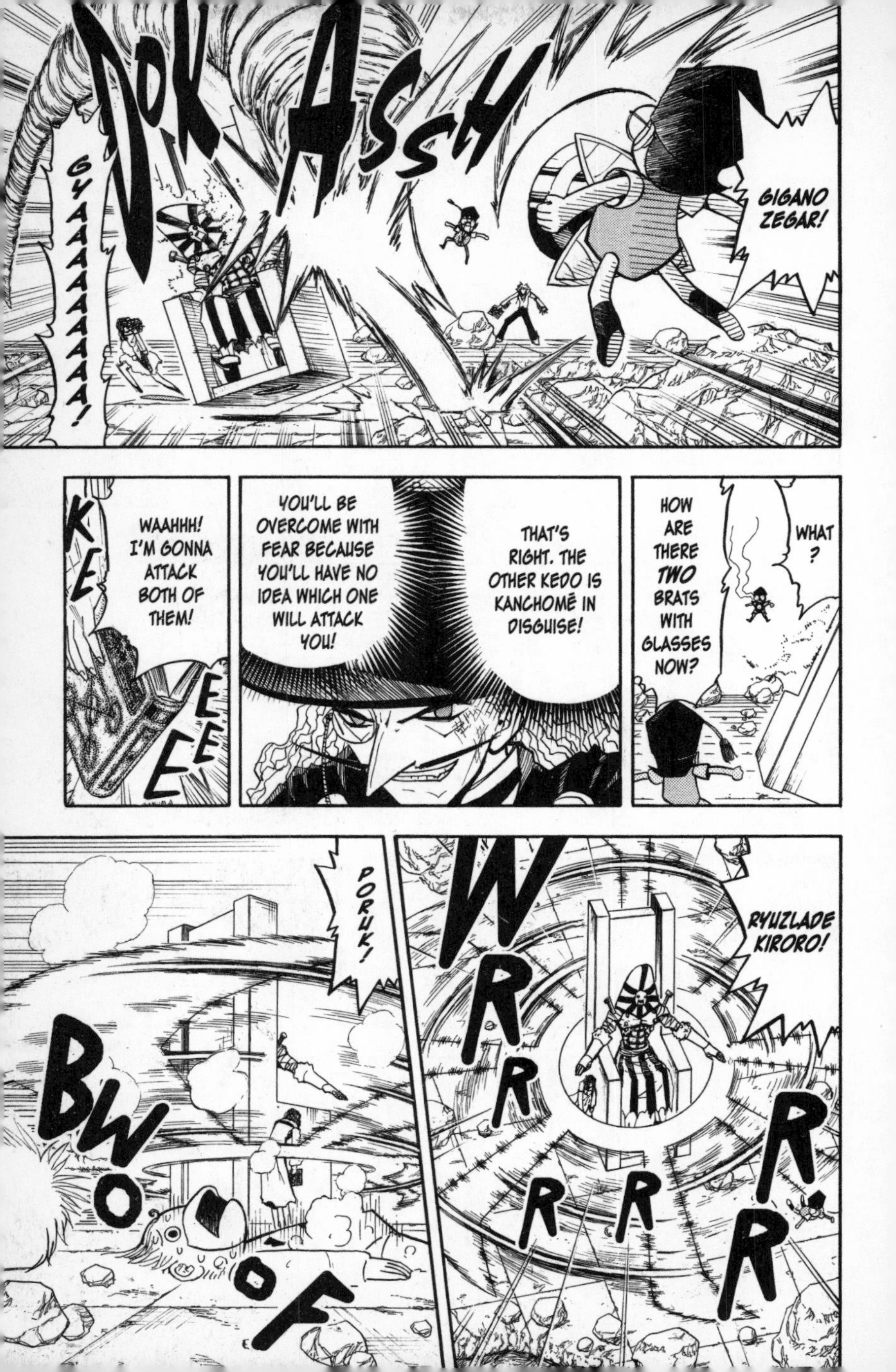
GIGANO ZEGAR!
DOKASSH
GYAAAAAAAAAA!
WHAT?
HOW ARE THERE TWO BRATS WITH GLASSES NOW?
THAT'S RIGHT. THE OTHER KEDO IS KANCHOMĒ IN DISGUISE!
YOU'LL BE OVERCOME WITH FEAR BECAUSE YOU'LL HAVE NO IDEA WHICH ONE WILL ATTACK YOU!
KEEEE
WAAHHH! I'M GONNA ATTACK BOTH OF THEM!
RYUZLADE KIRORO!
WRRRRRRR
PORUK!
BWOOF

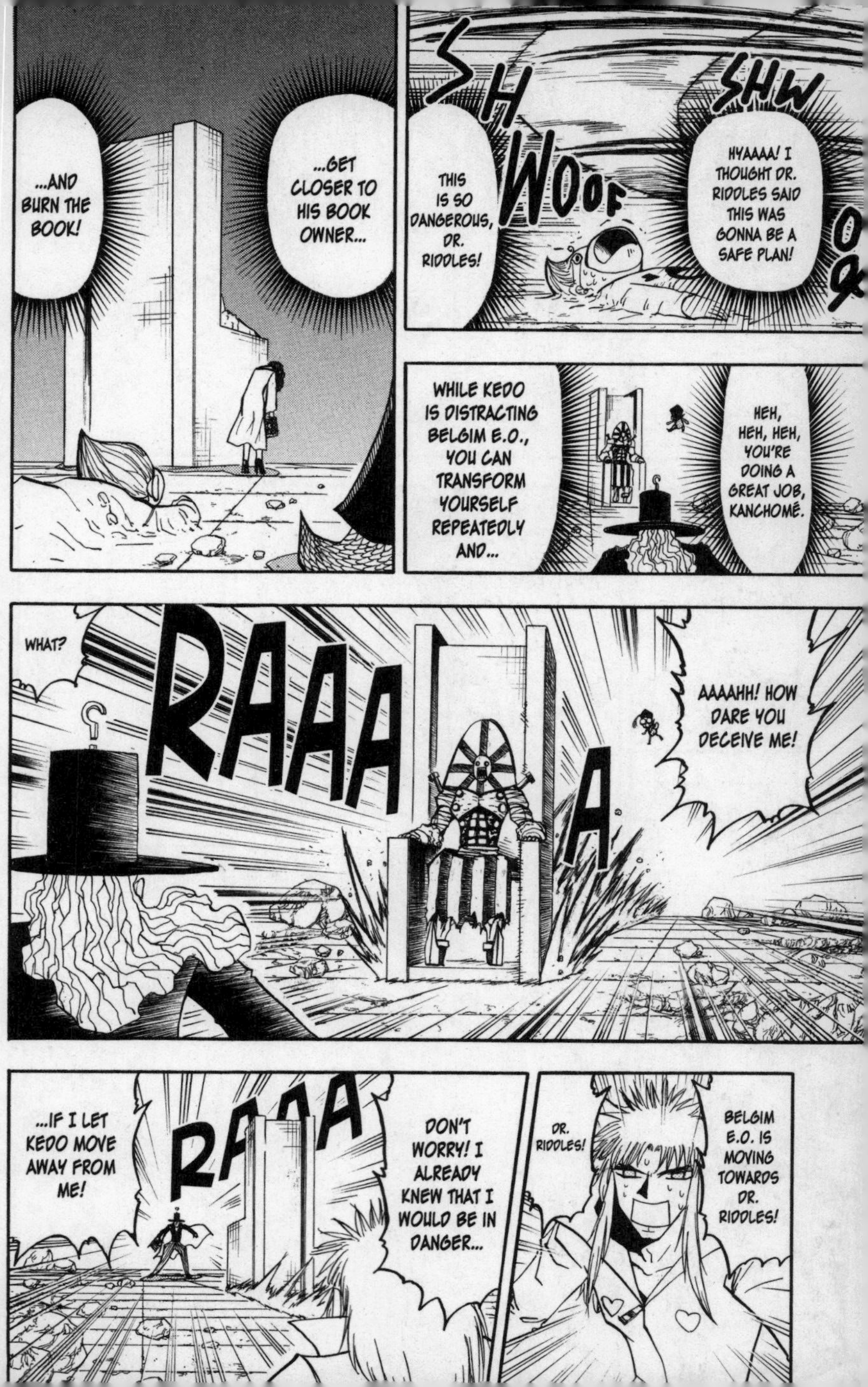
SHW
OOF
HYAAAA! I THOUGHT DR. RIDDLES SAID THIS WAS GONNA BE A SAFE PLAN!
SH
WOOF
THIS IS SO DANGEROUS, DR. RIDDLES!
HEH, HEH, HEH, YOU'RE DOING A GREAT JOB, KANCHOMÉ.
WHILE KEDO IS DISTRACTING BELGIM E.O., YOU CAN TRANSFORM YOURSELF REPEATEDLY AND...
...GET CLOSER TO HIS BOOK OWNER...
...AND BURN THE BOOK!
AAAAHH! HOW DARE YOU DECEIVE ME!
RAAAA
WHAT?
BELGIM E.O. IS MOVING TOWARDS DR. RIDDLES!
DR. RIDDLES!
DON'T WORRY! I ALREADY KNEW THAT I WOULD BE IN DANGER...
RAAA
...IF I LET KEDO MOVE AWAY FROM ME!

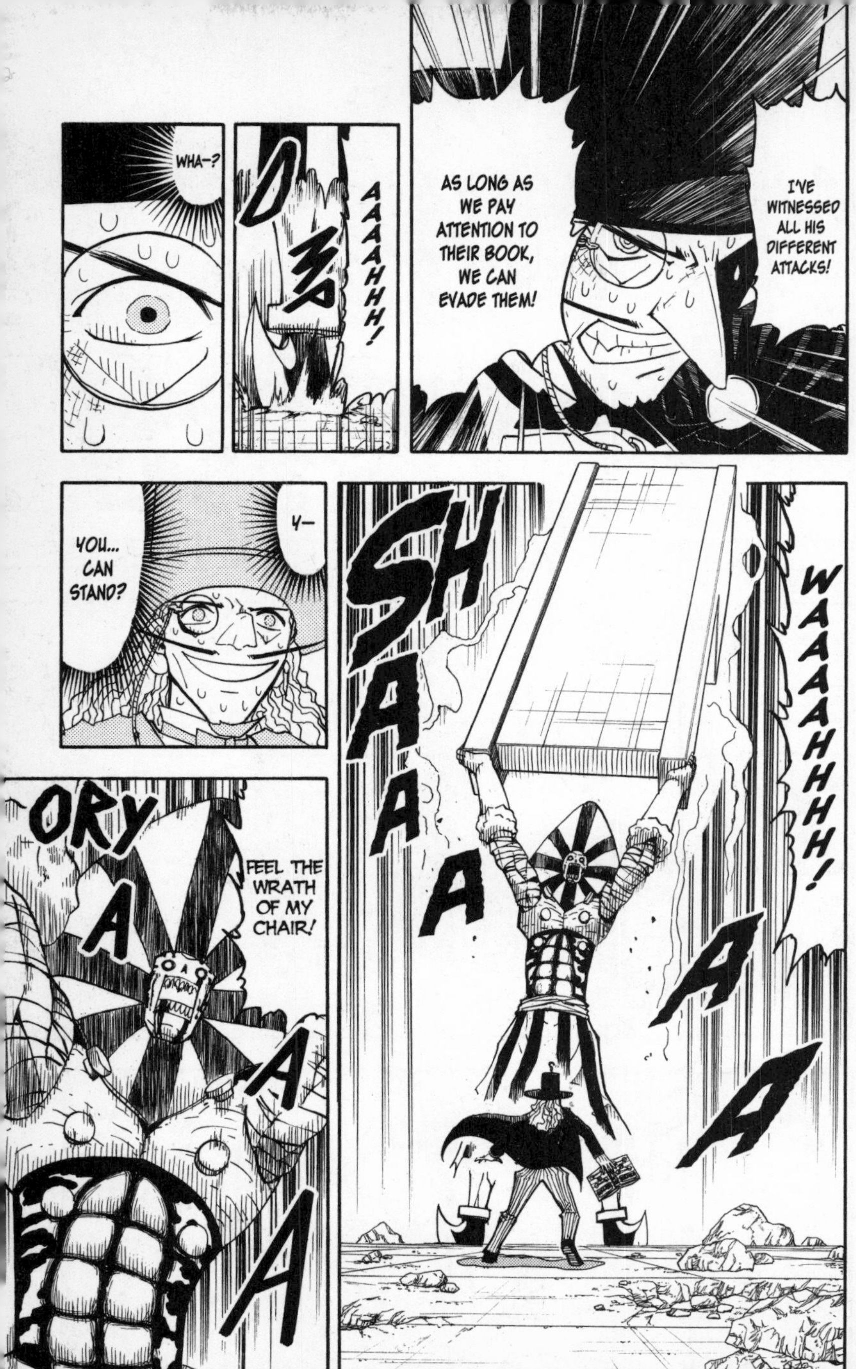
I'VE WITNESSED ALL HIS DIFFERENT ATTACKS!
AS LONG AS WE PAY ATTENTION TO THEIR BOOK, WE CAN EVADE THEM!
AAAAAHHH!
WHA-?
WAAAAAAHHHHHH!
SHAAA
AAA
Y-
YOU... CAN STAND?
ORYAAAA
FEEL THE WRATH OF MY CHAIR!

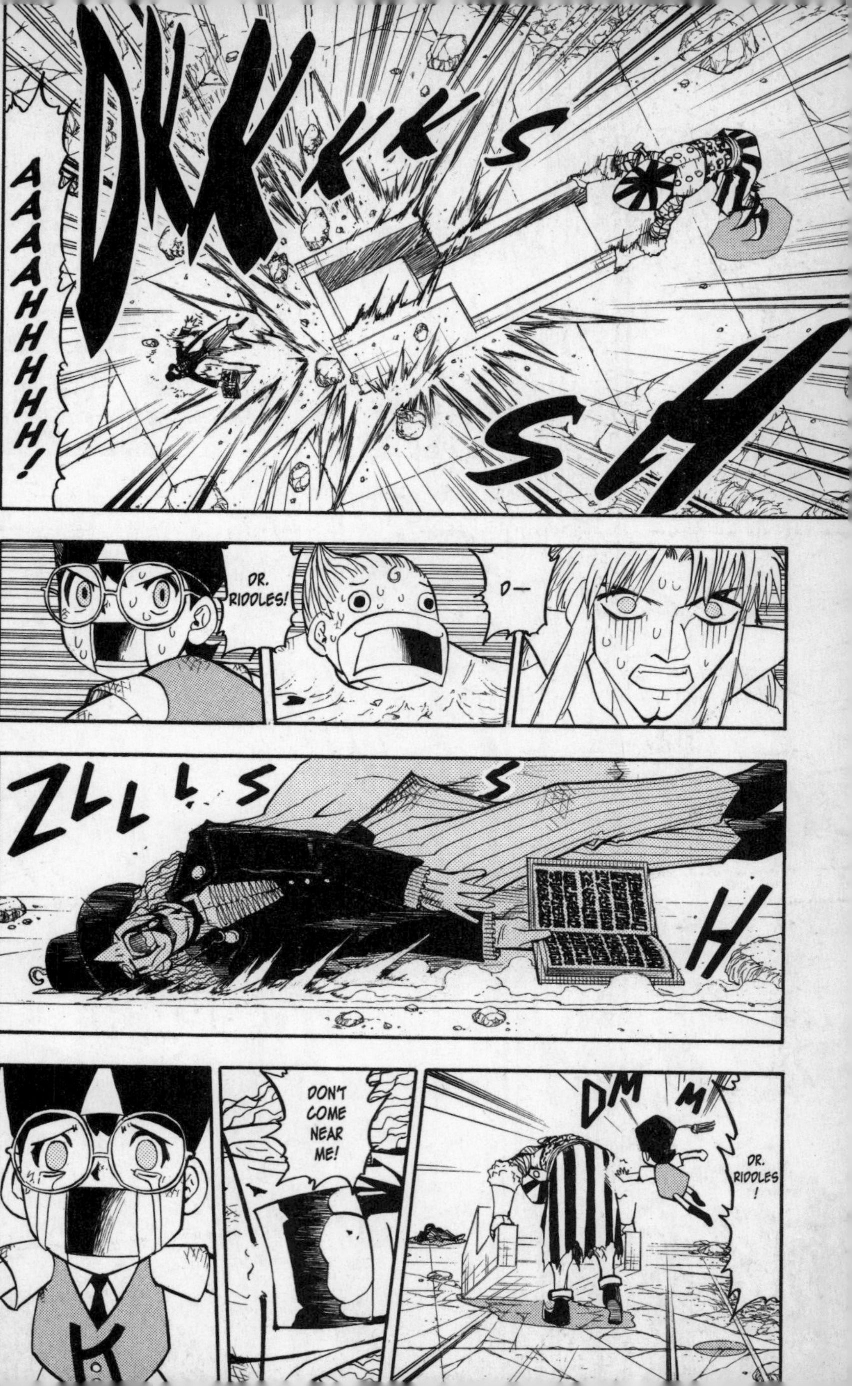
DKKKSSH
AAAAAHHHHHH!
D—
DR. RIDDLES!
ZLLLSSH
DR. RIDDLES!
DMM
DON'T COME NEAR ME!

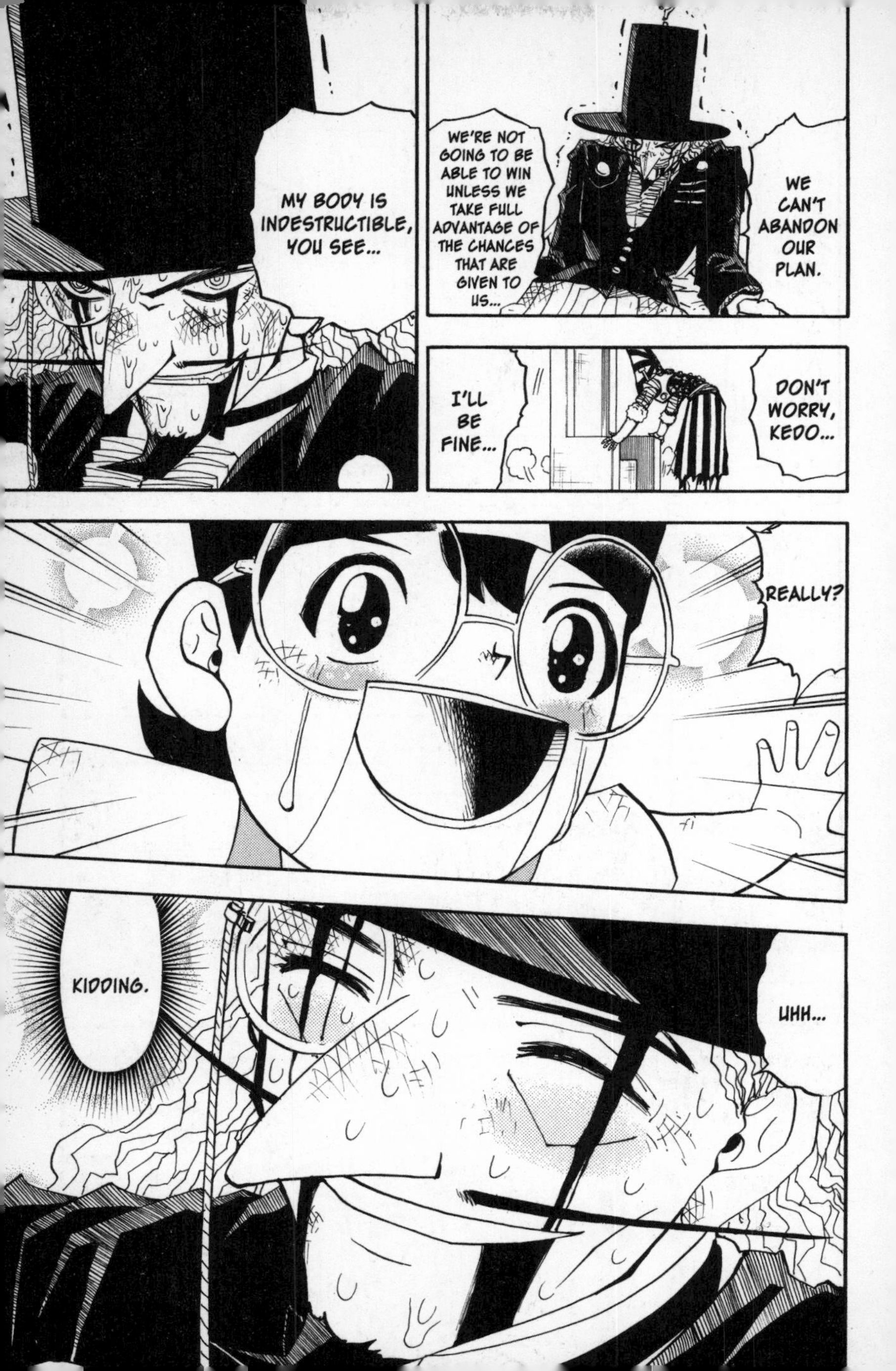
WE CAN'T ABANDON OUR PLAN.
WE'RE NOT GOING TO BE ABLE TO WIN UNLESS WE TAKE FULL ADVANTAGE OF THE CHANCES THAT ARE GIVEN TO US...
DON'T WORRY, KEDO...
I'LL BE FINE...
MY BODY IS INDESTRUCTIBLE, YOU SEE...
REALLY?
UHH...
KIDDING.

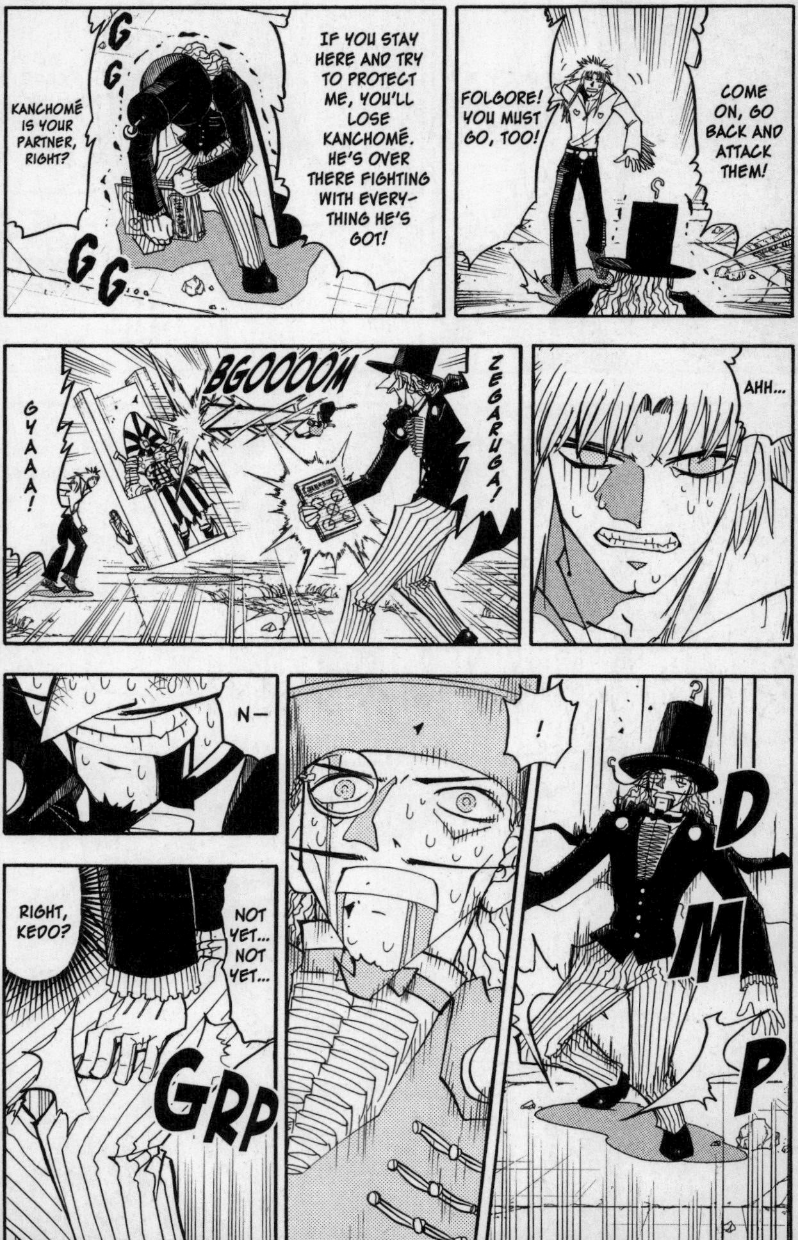
COME ON, GO BACK AND ATTACK THEM!
FOLGORE! YOU MUST GO, TOO!
GGGG...
IF YOU STAY HERE AND TRY TO PROTECT ME, YOU'LL LOSE KANCHOMÉ. HE'S OVER THERE FIGHTING WITH EVERYTHING HE'S GOT!
KANCHOMÉ IS YOUR PARTNER, RIGHT?
AHH...
ZEGARUGA!
BGOOOOM
GYAAAA!
!
DMP
N—
NOT YET... NOT YET...
RIGHT, KEDO?
GRP

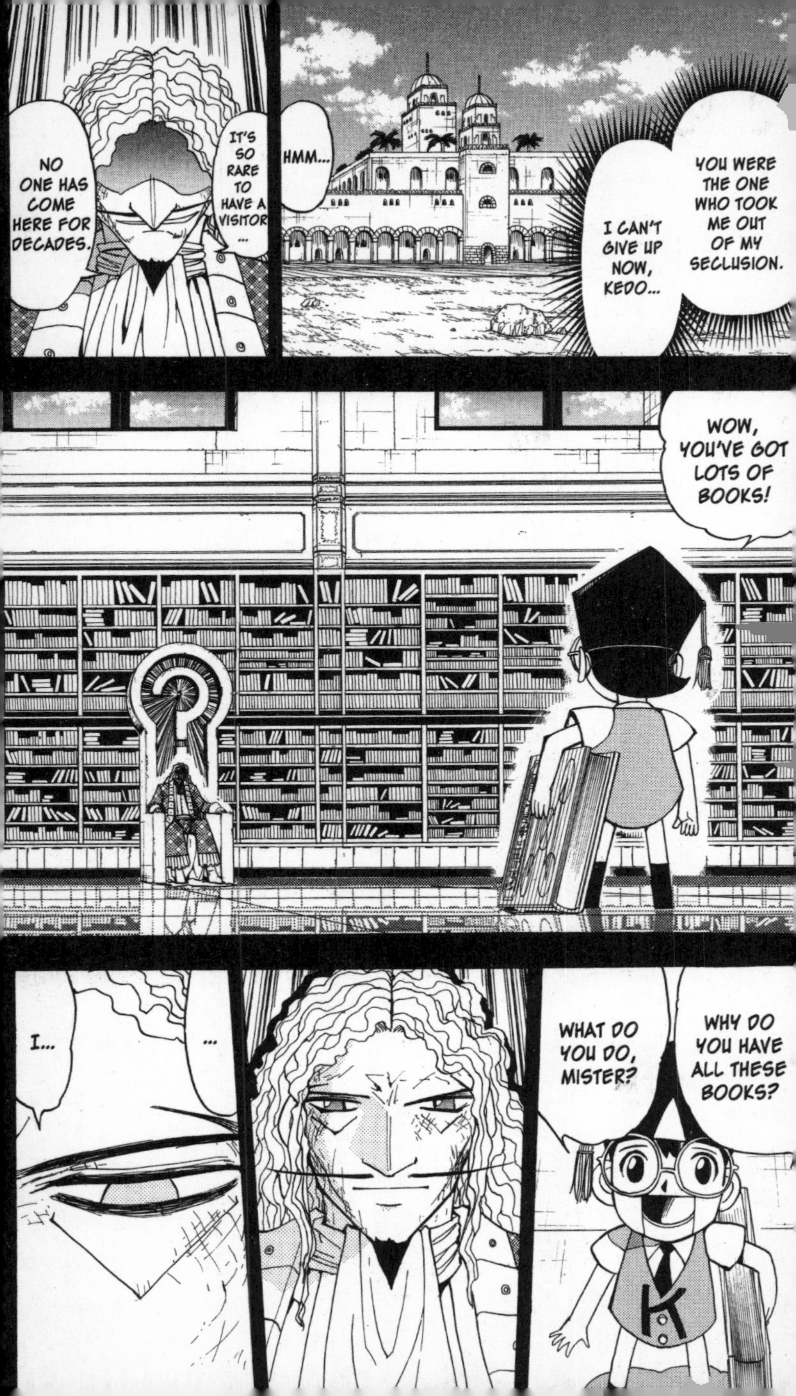

YOU WERE THE ONE WHO TOOK ME OUT OF MY SECLUSION.
I CAN'T GIVE UP NOW, KEDO...
HMM...
IT'S SO RARE TO HAVE A VISITOR...
NO ONE HAS COME HERE FOR DECADES.
WOW, YOU'VE GOT LOTS OF BOOKS!
WHY DO YOU HAVE ALL THESE BOOKS?
WHAT DO YOU DO, MISTER?
...
I...

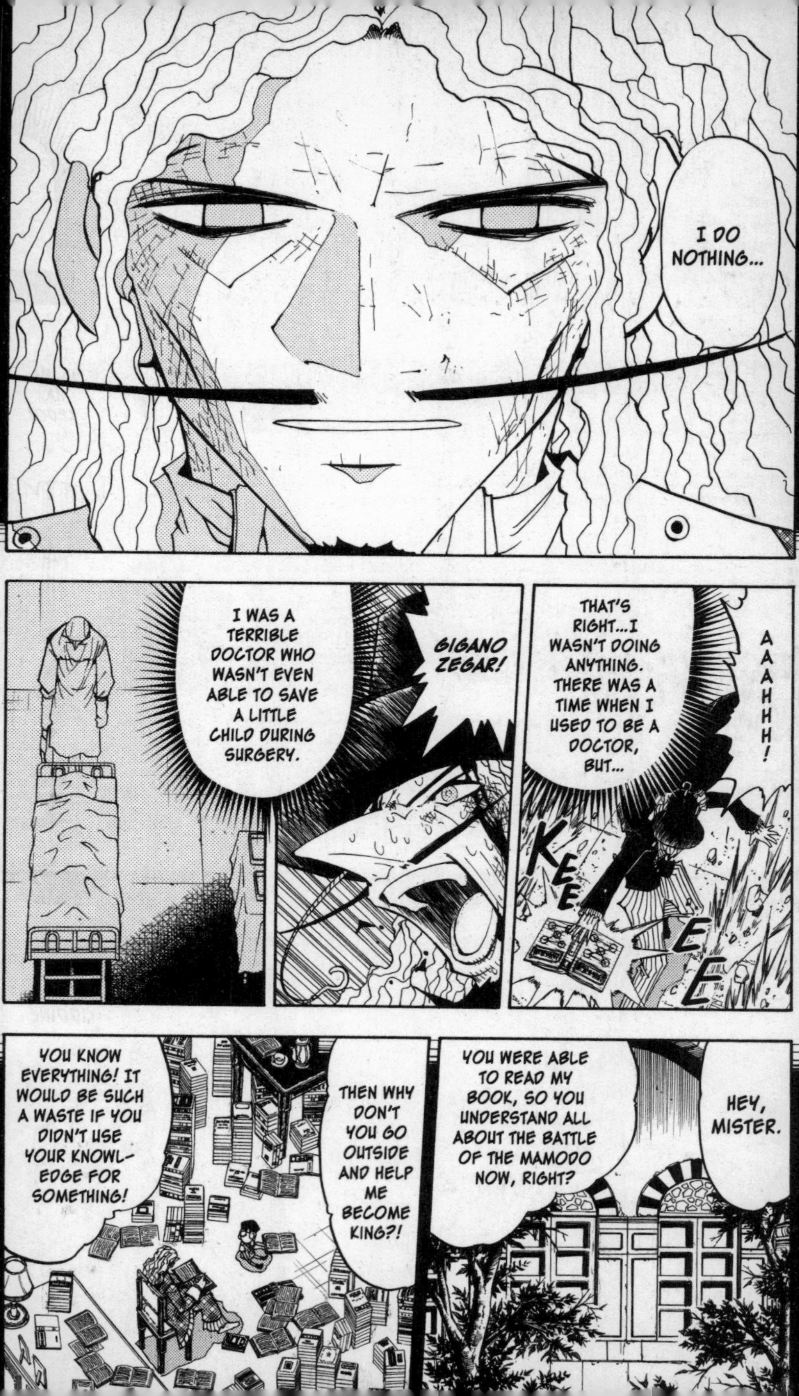
I DO NOTHING...
AAAHHH!
THAT'S RIGHT...I WASN'T DOING ANYTHING. THERE WAS A TIME WHEN I USED TO BE A DOCTOR, BUT...
KEEEE
GIGANO ZEGAR!
I WAS A TERRIBLE DOCTOR WHO WASN'T EVEN ABLE TO SAVE A LITTLE CHILD DURING SURGERY.
HEY, MISTER.
YOU WERE ABLE TO READ MY BOOK, SO YOU UNDERSTAND ALL ABOUT THE BATTLE OF THE MAMODO NOW, RIGHT?
THEN WHY DON'T YOU GO OUTSIDE AND HELP ME BECOME KING?!
YOU KNOW EVERYTHING! IT WOULD BE SUCH A WASTE IF YOU DIDN'T USE YOUR KNOWL-EDGE FOR SOMETHING!

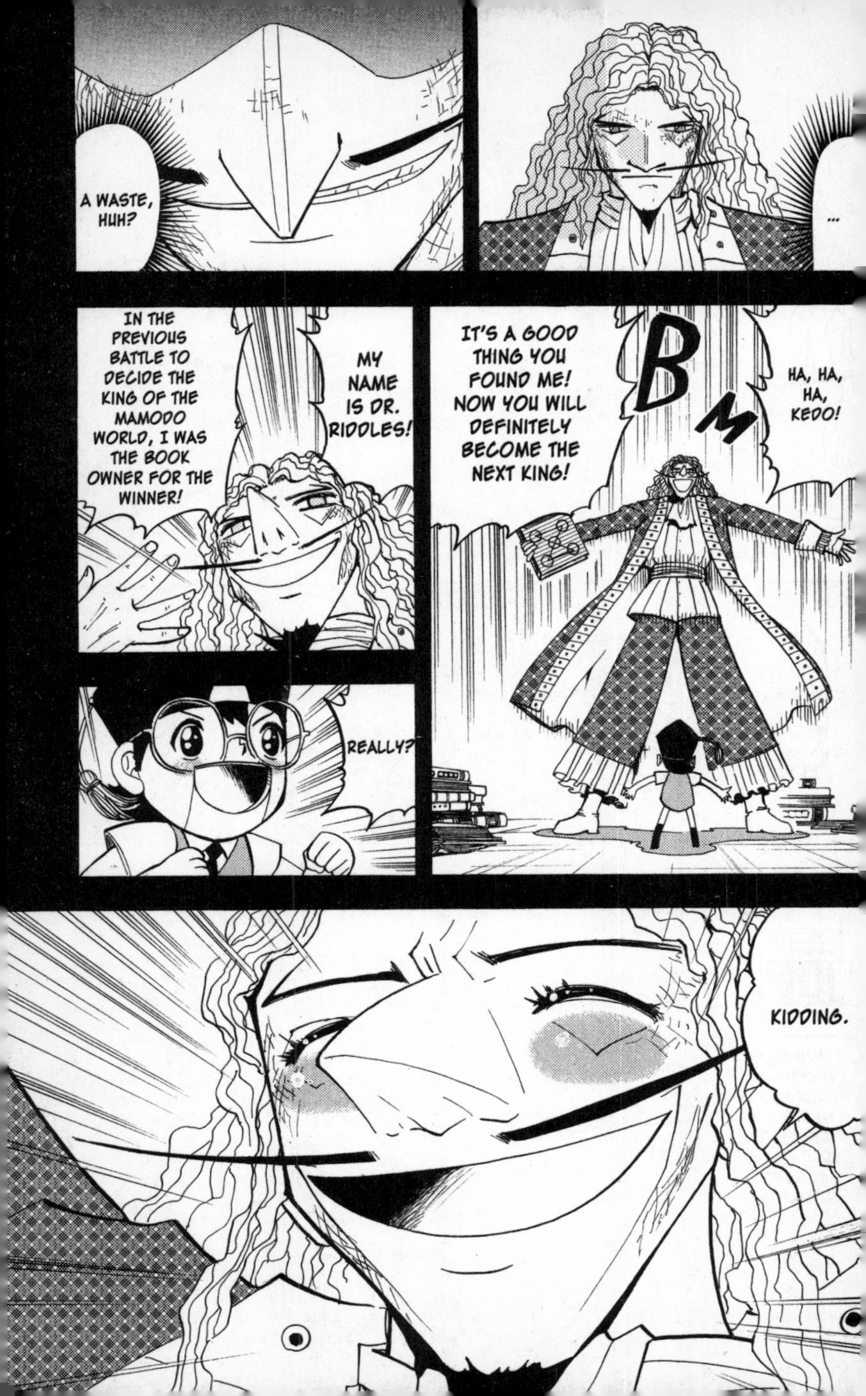
...
A WASTE, HUH?
HA, HA, HA, KEDO!
BM
IT'S A GOOD THING YOU FOUND ME! NOW YOU WILL DEFINITELY BECOME THE NEXT KING!
MY NAME IS DR. RIDDLES!
IN THE PREVIOUS BATTLE TO DECIDE THE KING OF THE MAMODO WORLD, I WAS THE BOOK OWNER FOR THE WINNER!
REALLY?
KIDDING.

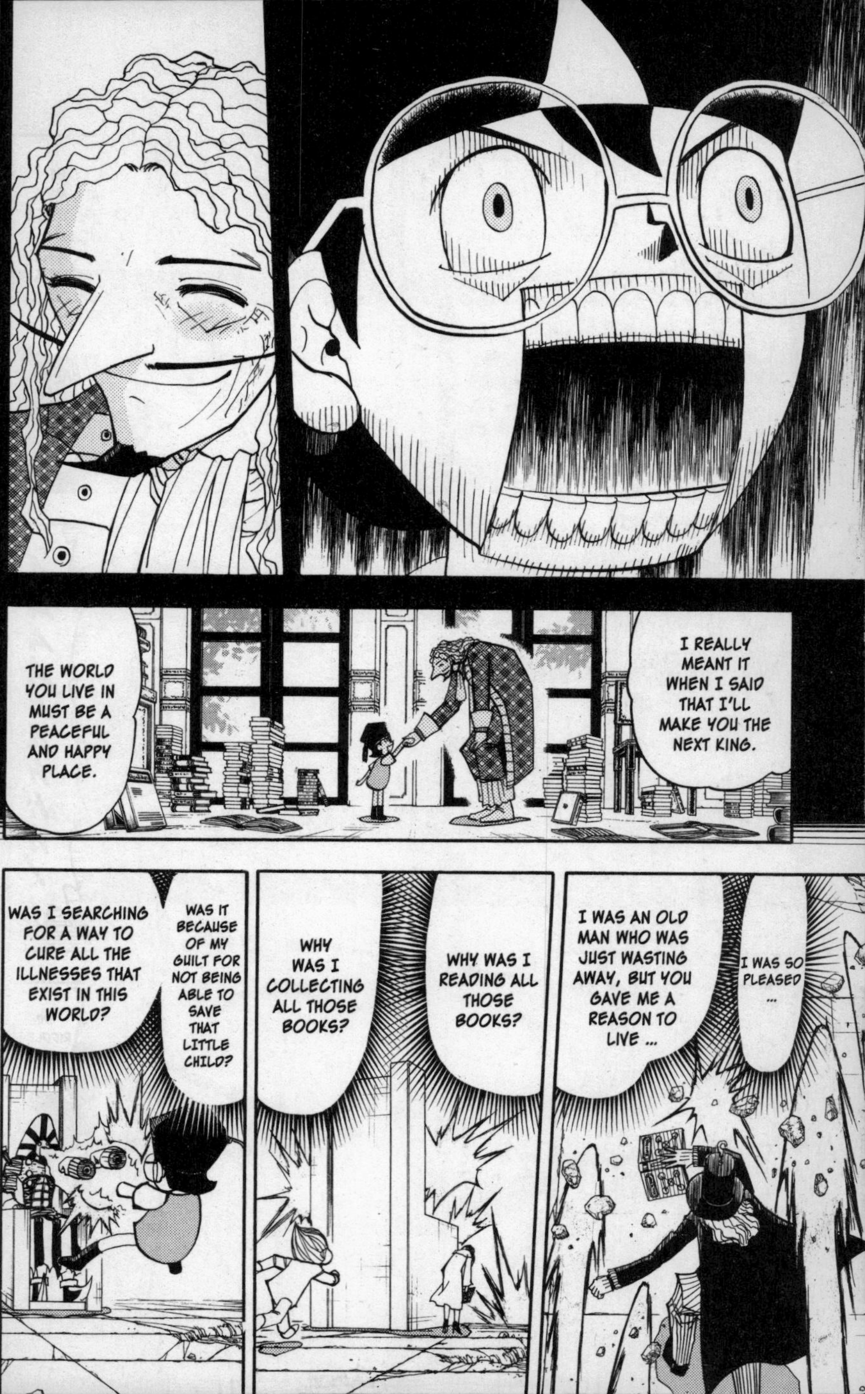
I REALLY MEANT IT WHEN I SAID THAT I'LL MAKE YOU THE NEXT KING.
THE WORLD YOU LIVE IN MUST BE A PEACEFUL AND HAPPY PLACE.
I WAS SO PLEASED ...
I WAS AN OLD MAN WHO WAS JUST WASTING AWAY, BUT YOU GAVE ME A REASON TO LIVE ...
WHY WAS I READING ALL THOSE BOOKS?
WHY WAS I COLLECTING ALL THOSE BOOKS?
WAS IT BECAUSE OF MY GUILT FOR NOT BEING ABLE TO SAVE THAT LITTLE CHILD?
WAS I SEARCHING FOR A WAY TO CURE ALL THE ILLNESSES THAT EXIST IN THIS WORLD?

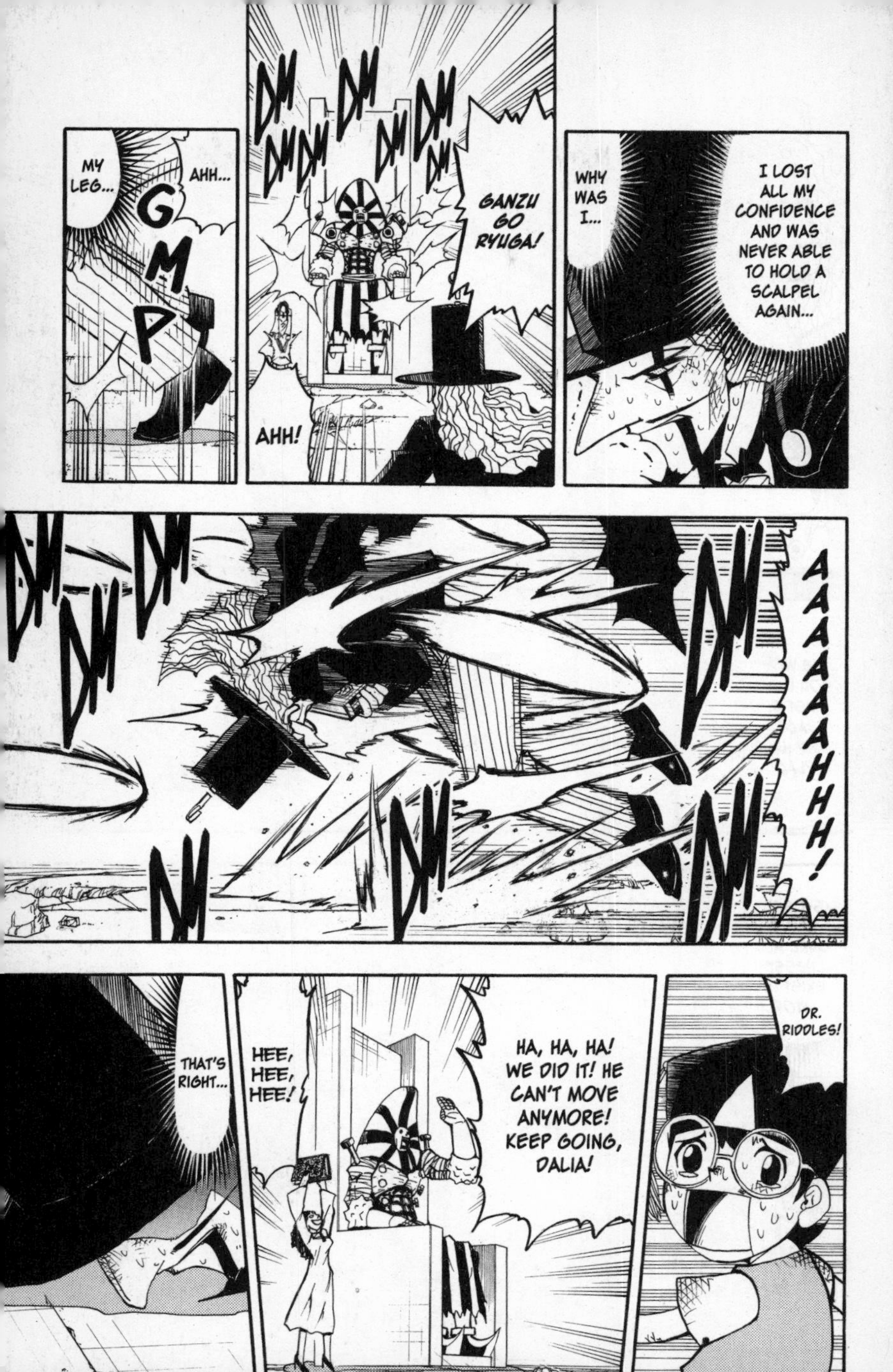
I LOST ALL MY CONFIDENCE AND WAS NEVER ABLE TO HOLD A SCALPEL AGAIN...
WHY WAS I...
DM DM DM DM DM DM DM DM DM
GANZU GO RYUGA!
AHH!
AHH...
MY LEG...
GMP
AAAAAAAHHH!
DM DM DM DM DM DM DM DM
DR. RIDDLES!
HA, HA, HA! WE DID IT! HE CAN'T MOVE ANYMORE! KEEP GOING, DALIA!
HEE, HEE, HEE!
THAT'S RIGHT...

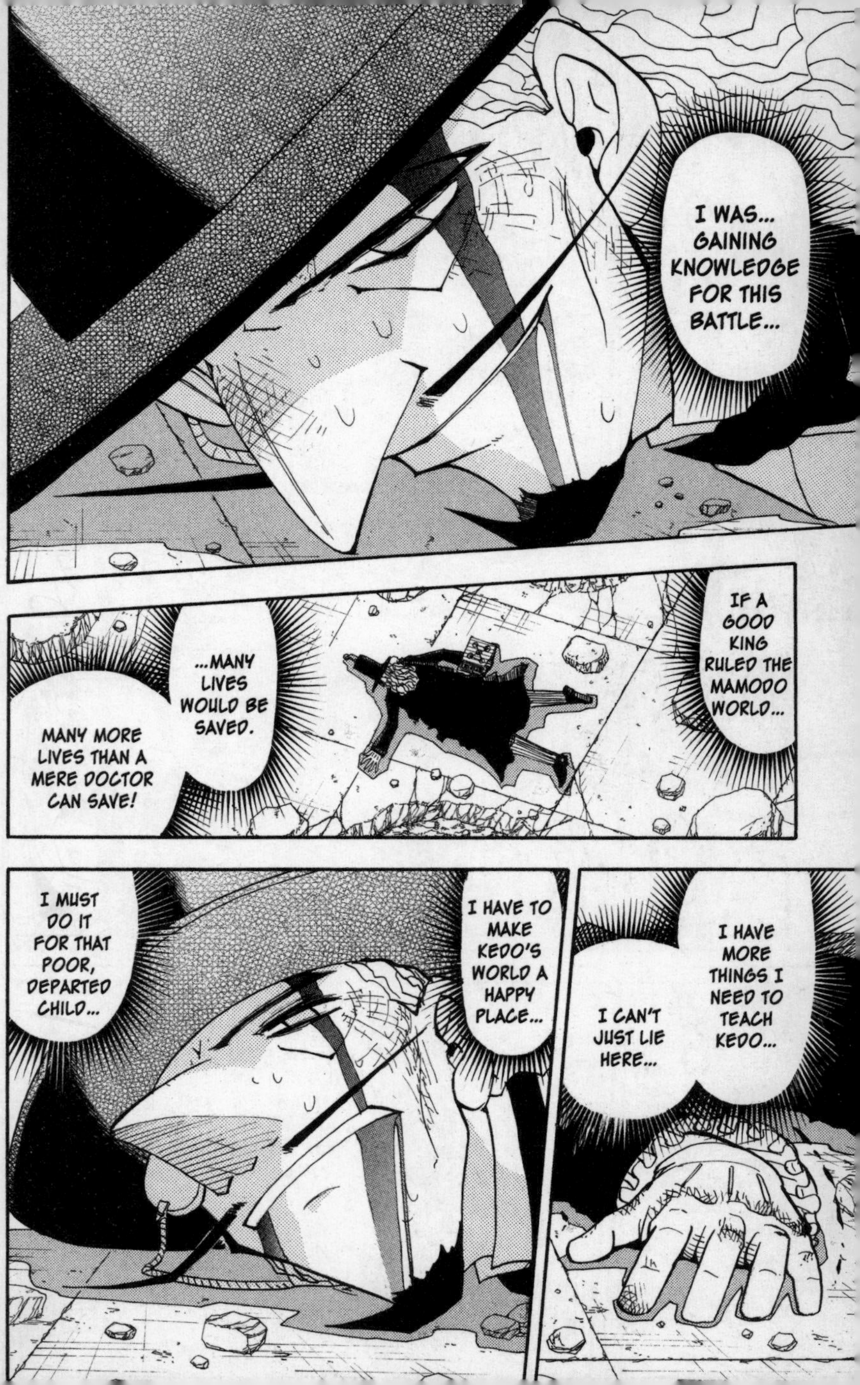
I WAS... GAINING KNOWLEDGE FOR THIS BATTLE...
IF A GOOD KING RULED THE MAMODO WORLD...
...MANY LIVES WOULD BE SAVED.
MANY MORE LIVES THAN A MERE DOCTOR CAN SAVE!
I HAVE MORE THINGS I NEED TO TEACH KEDO...
I CAN'T JUST LIE HERE...
I HAVE TO MAKE KEDO'S WORLD A HAPPY PLACE...
I MUST DO IT FOR THAT POOR, DEPARTED CHILD...

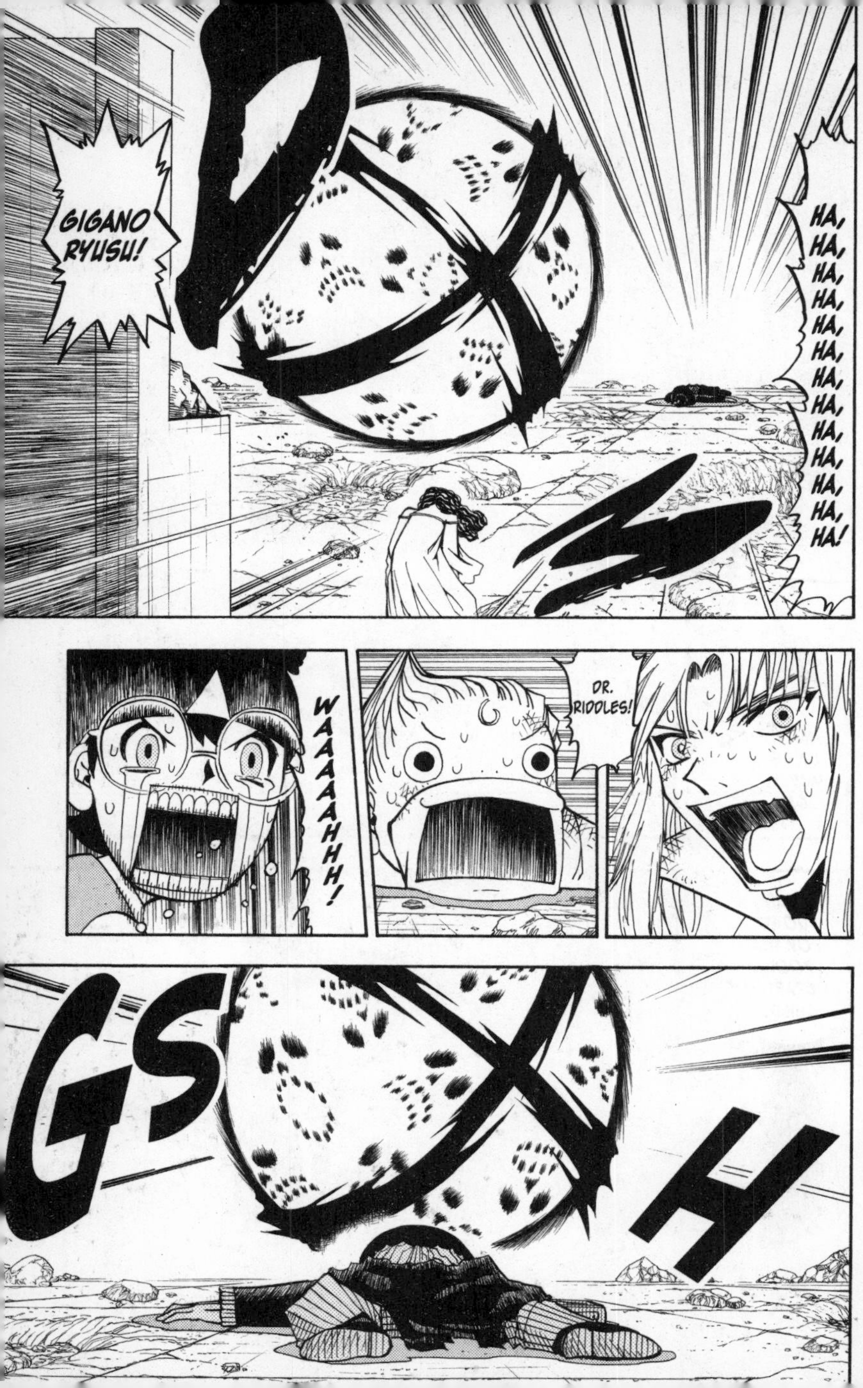
HA, HA, HA, HA, HA, HA, HA, HA, HA, HA, HA, HA, HA!
GIGANO RYUSU!
DR. RIDDLES!
WAAAAAAHHH!
GSH

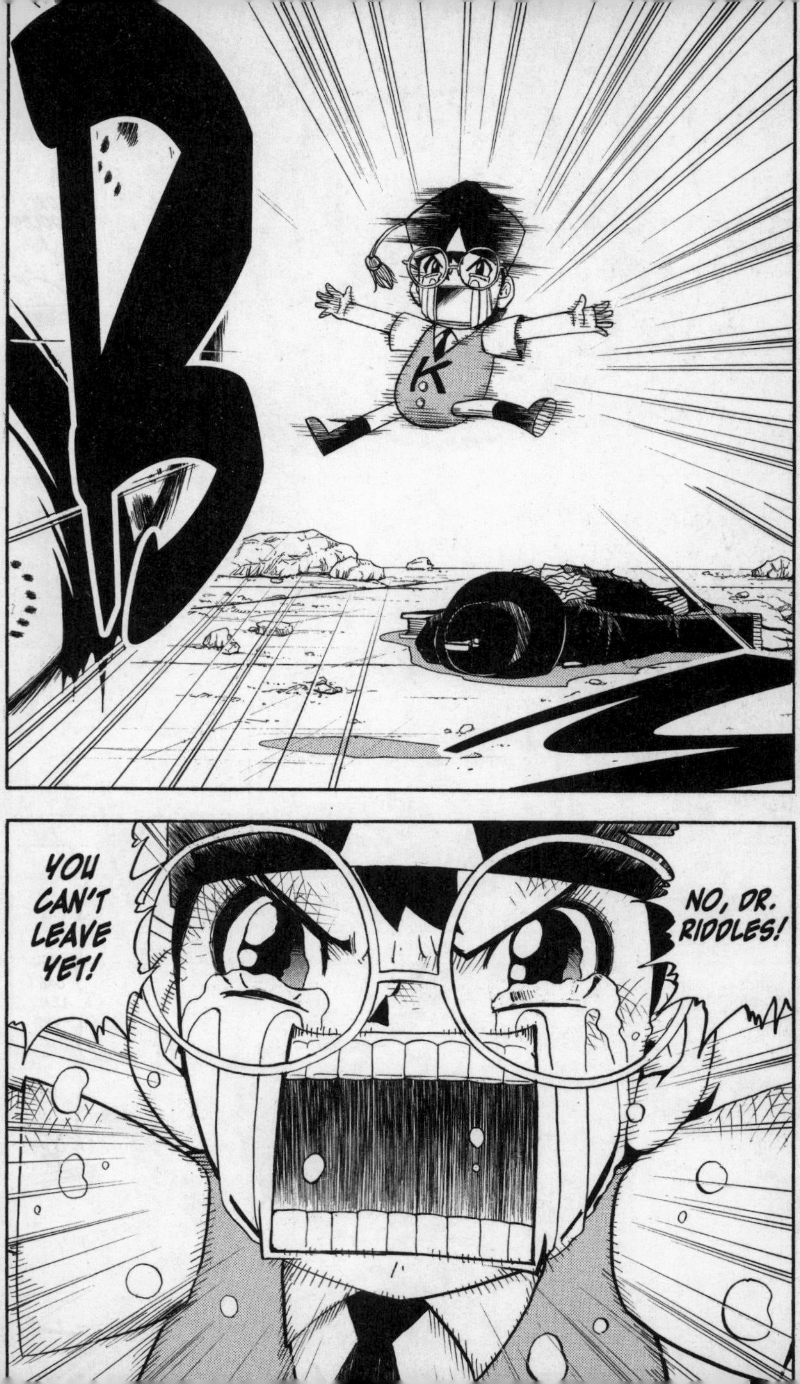
NO, DR. RIDDLES!
YOU CAN'T LEAVE YET!

LEVEL 136: My King

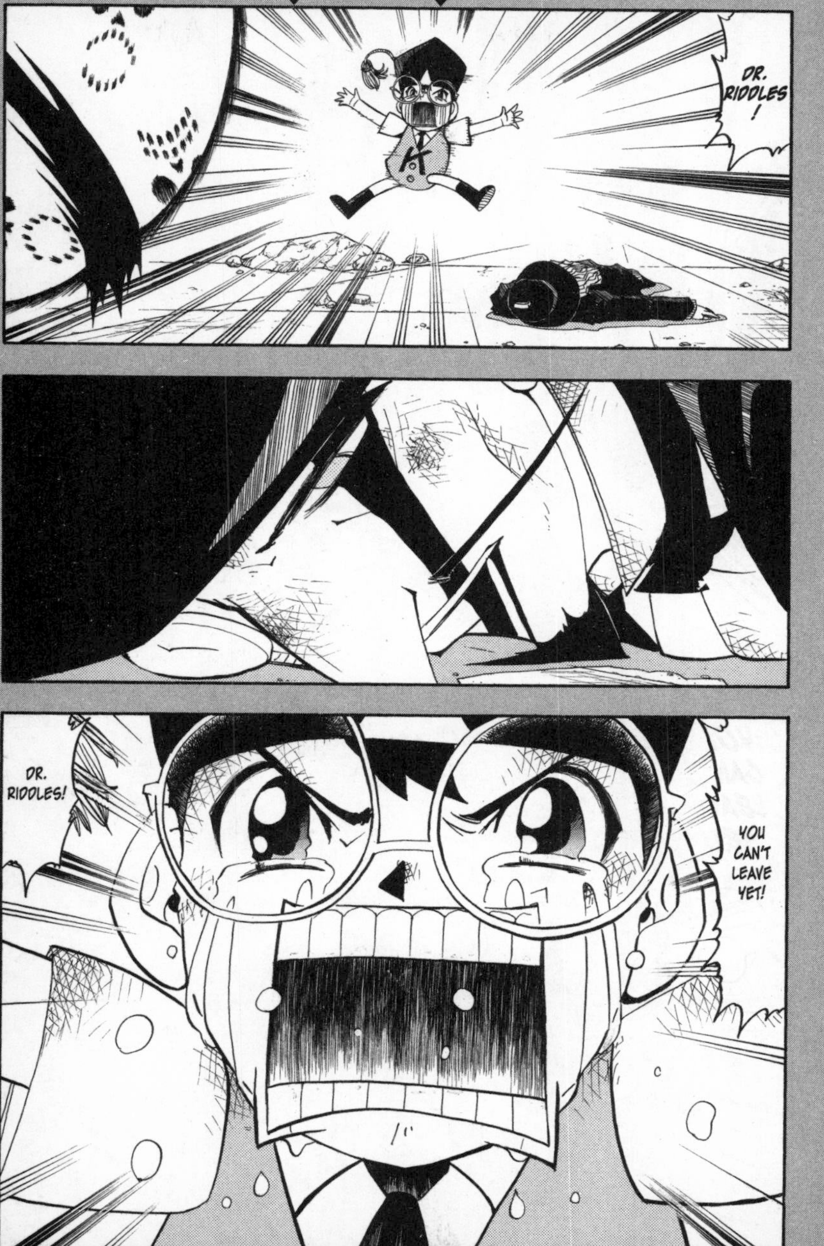
DR. RIDDLES!
DR. RIDDLES!
YOU CAN'T LEAVE YET!

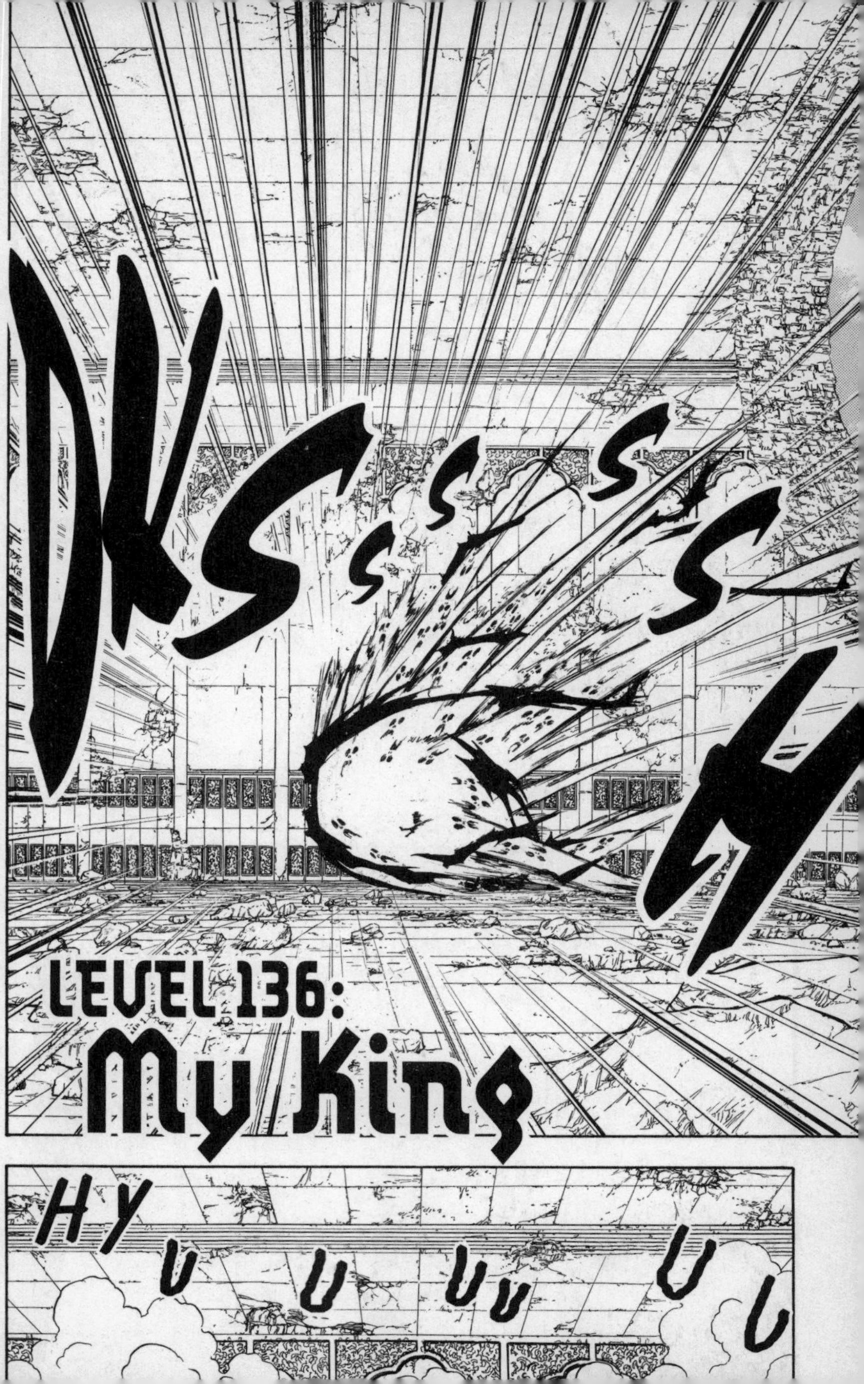
LEVEL 136:
My King

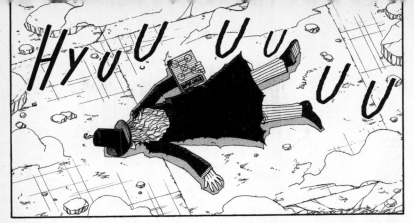

HYUUUUUUUU
WHAT HAPPENED?
AM I ALIVE?
WHAT'S GOING ON?
WHERE'S KEDO?
I MUST PROTECT KEDO...
I'M FADING AWAY...
WHERE IS...
...EVERY-BODY?
...!
A VOICE?
I HEAR A VOICE...
WHOSE VOICE IS IT?
WHOSE ...
...!

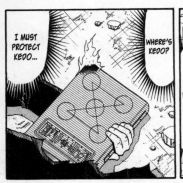

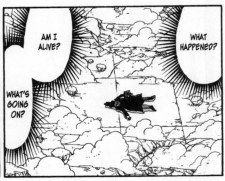

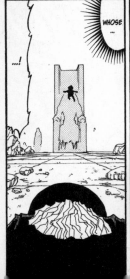

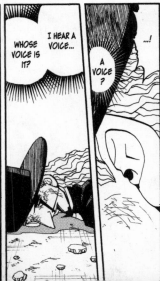

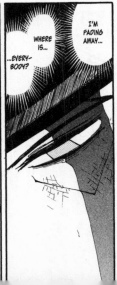

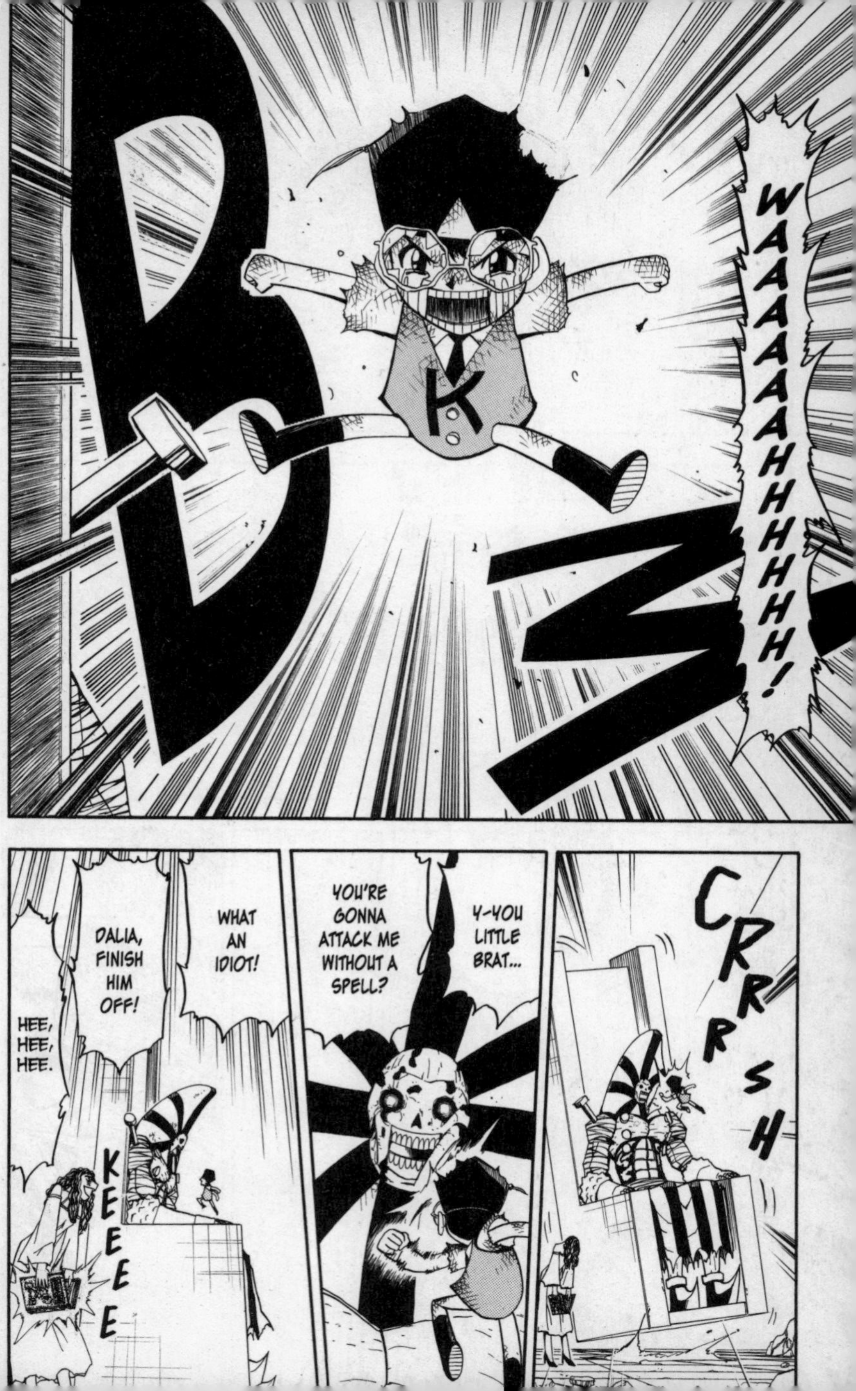
WAAAAAHHHHHH!
CRRRRSH
Y-YOU LITTLE BRAT...
YOU'RE GONNA ATTACK ME WITHOUT A SPELL?
WHAT AN IDIOT!
DALIA, FINISH HIM OFF!
HEE, HEE, HEE.
KEEEEE

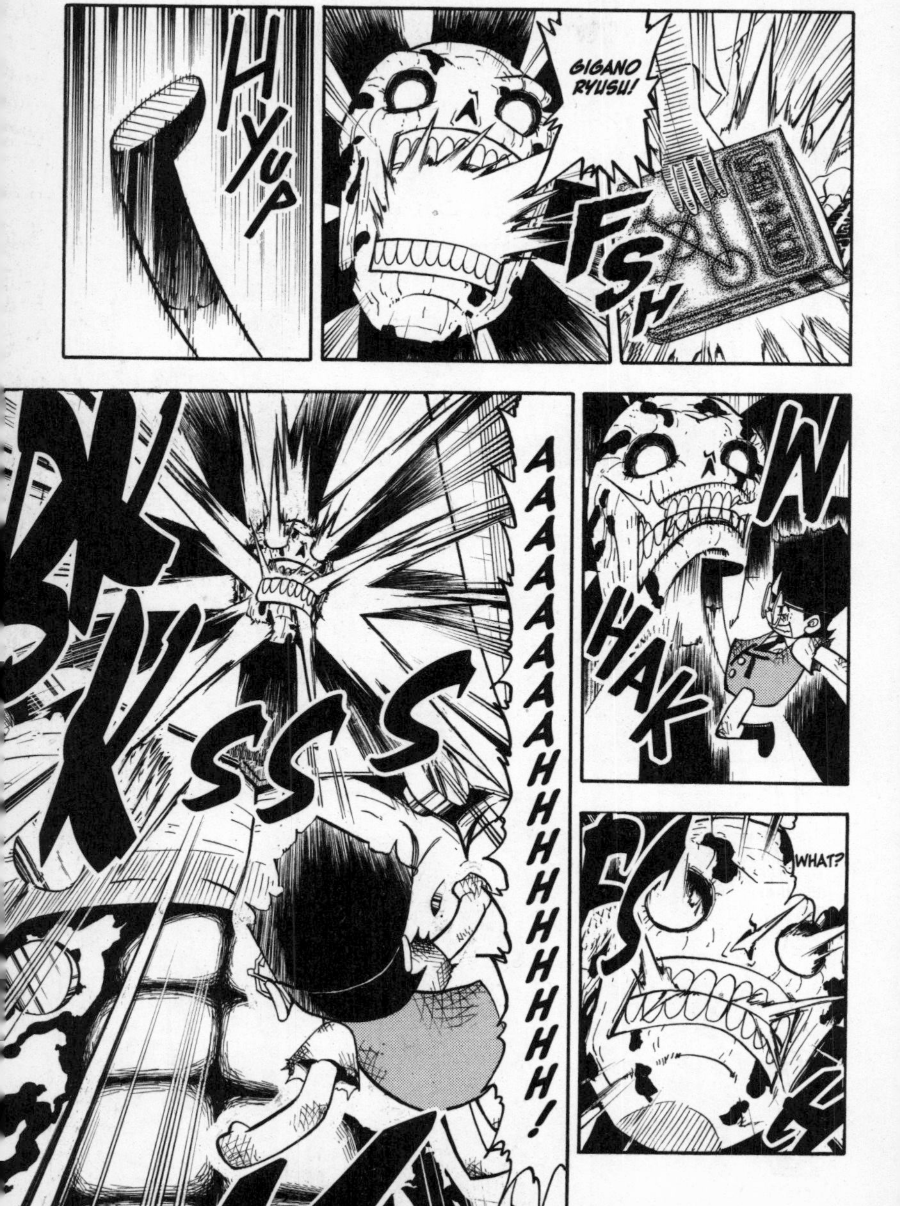
GIGANO RYUSU!
FSH
HYUP
WHAK
WHAT?
SSS
AAAAAAAAAAAAHHHHHHHHHHH!

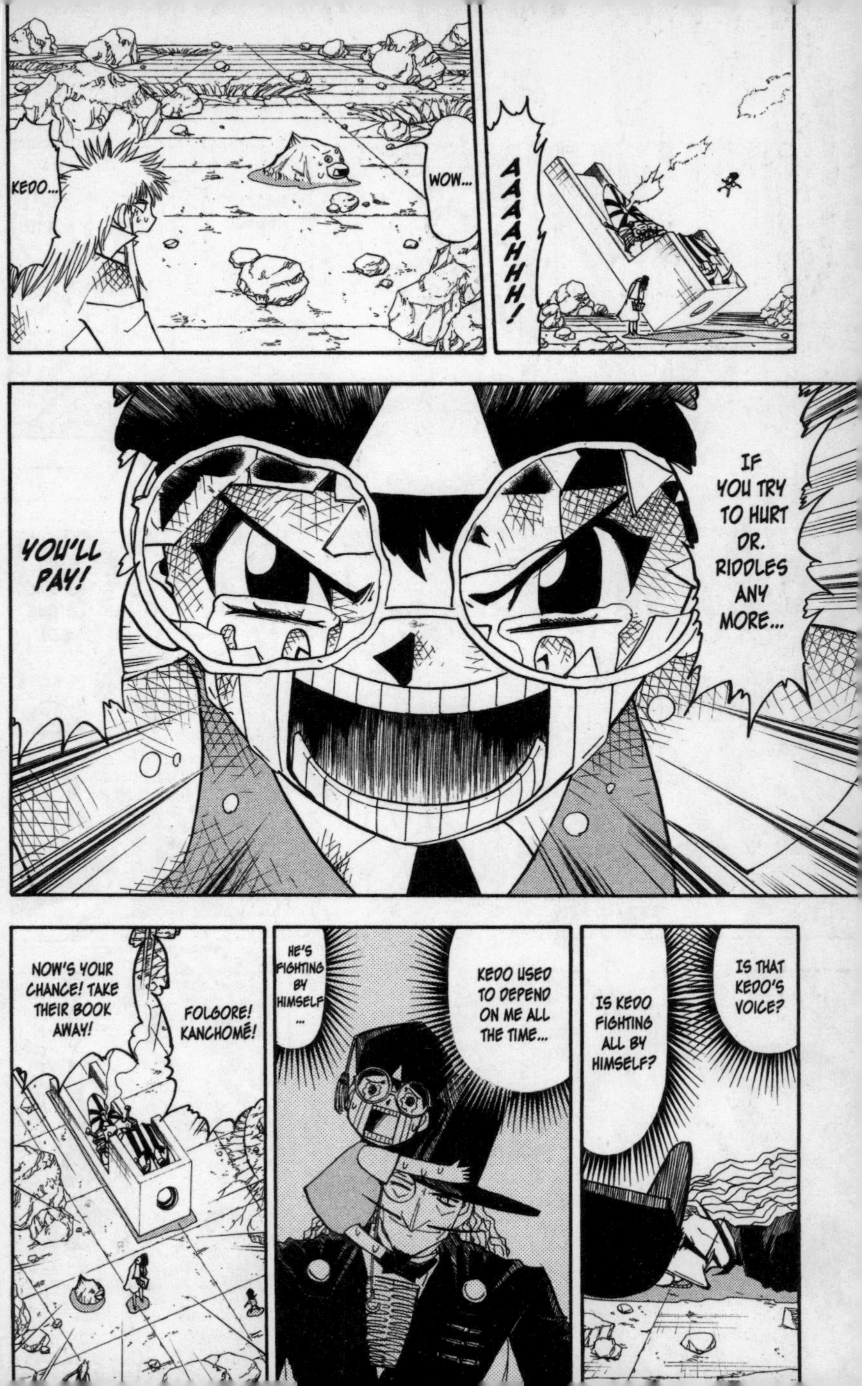
AAAAAHHH!
WOW...
KEDO...
IF YOU TRY TO HURT DR. RIDDLES ANY MORE...
YOU'LL PAY!
IS THAT KEDO'S VOICE?
IS KEDO FIGHTING ALL BY HIMSELF?
KEDO USED TO DEPEND ON ME ALL THE TIME...
HE'S FIGHTING BY HIMSELF...
FOLGORE! KANCHOMÉ!
NOW'S YOUR CHANCE! TAKE THEIR BOOK AWAY!

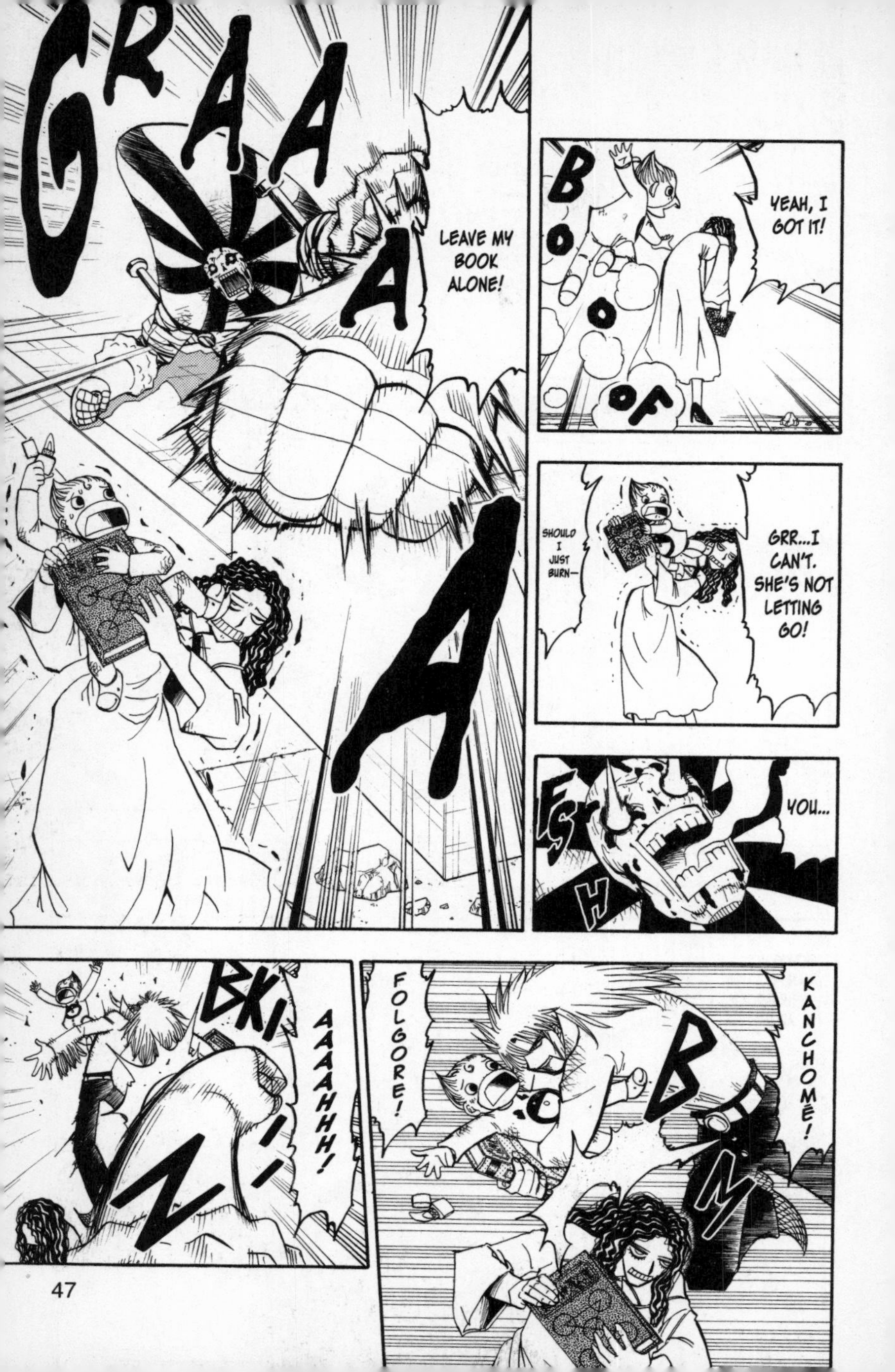
BOOF
YEAH, I GOT IT!
GRR...I CAN'T. SHE'S NOT LETTING GO!
SHOULD I JUST BURN—
FSSH
YOU...
GRAAAAA
LEAVE MY BOOK ALONE!
KANCHOMÉ!
BOM
FOLGORE!
AAAAAHHH!
BKIIN

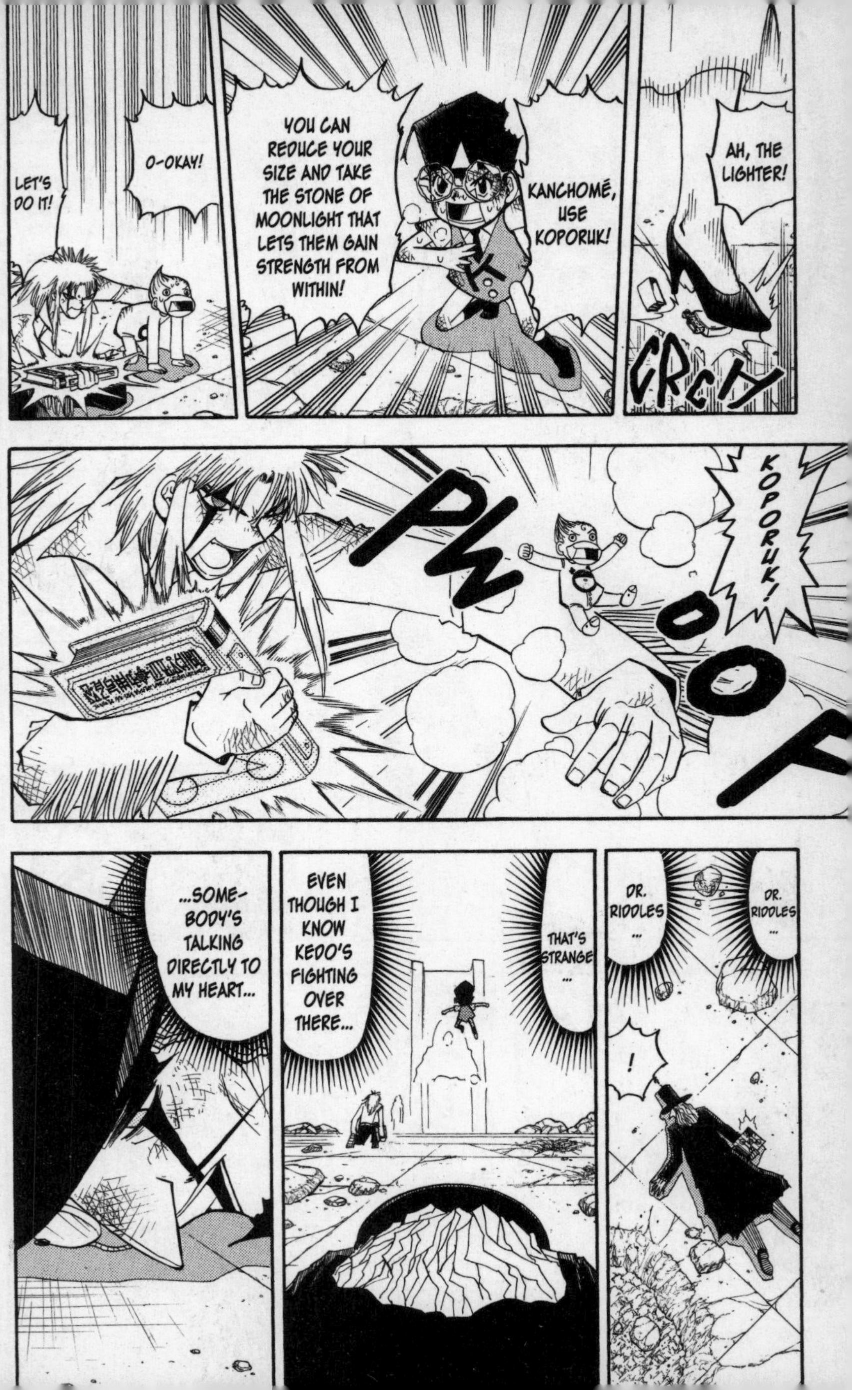
AH, THE LIGHTER!
KANCHOMÉ, USE KOPORUK!
YOU CAN REDUCE YOUR SIZE AND TAKE THE STONE OF MOONLIGHT THAT LETS THEM GAIN STRENGTH FROM WITHIN!
O-OKAY!
LET'S DO IT!
KOPORUK!
PWOOOF
DR. RIDDLES...
DR. RIDDLES...
!
THAT'S STRANGE...
EVEN THOUGH I KNOW KEDO'S FIGHTING OVER THERE...
...SOMEBODY'S TALKING DIRECTLY TO MY HEART...

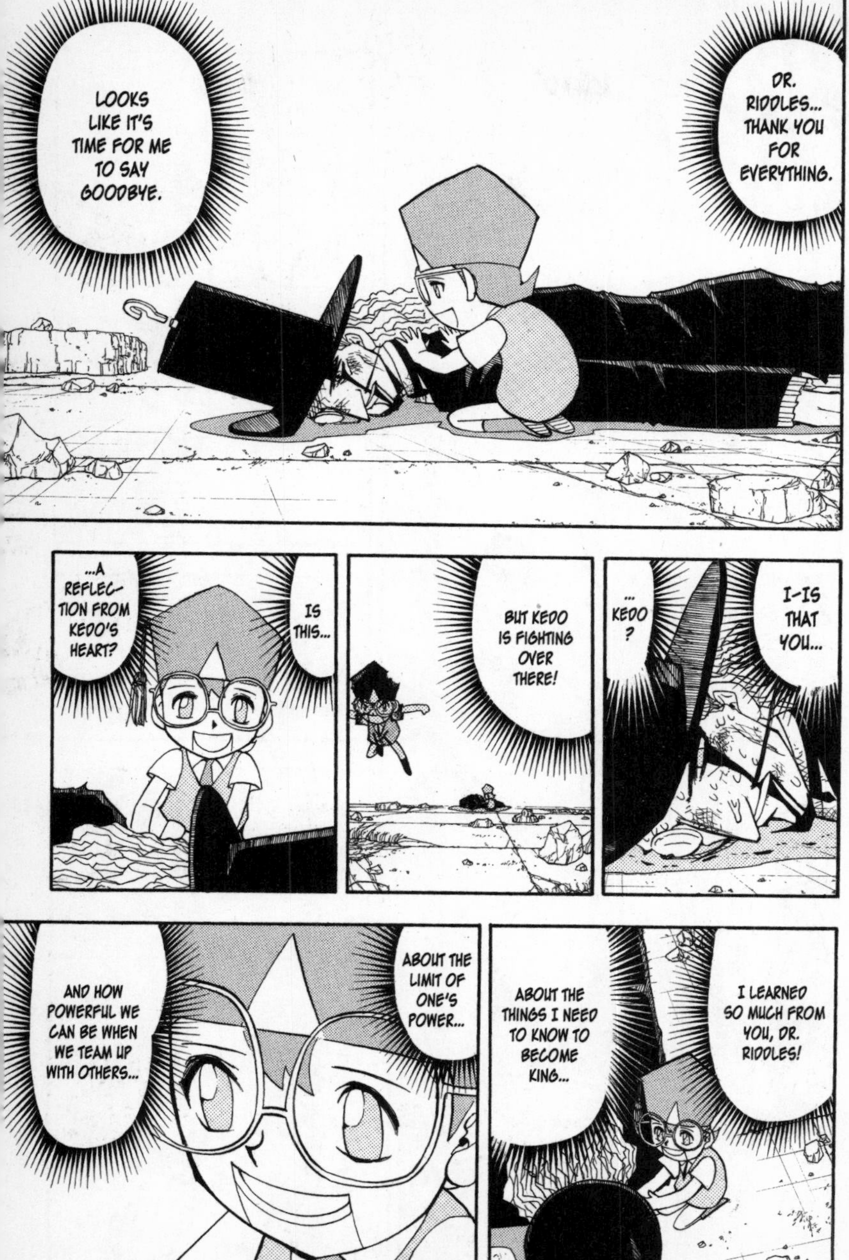
DR. RIDDLES... THANK YOU FOR EVERYTHING.
LOOKS LIKE IT'S TIME FOR ME TO SAY GOODBYE.
I-IS THAT YOU...
...KEDO?
BUT KEDO IS FIGHTING OVER THERE!
IS THIS...
...A REFLECTION FROM KEDO'S HEART?
I LEARNED SO MUCH FROM YOU, DR. RIDDLES!
ABOUT THE THINGS I NEED TO KNOW TO BECOME KING...
ABOUT THE LIMIT OF ONE'S POWER...
AND HOW POWERFUL WE CAN BE WHEN WE TEAM UP WITH OTHERS...

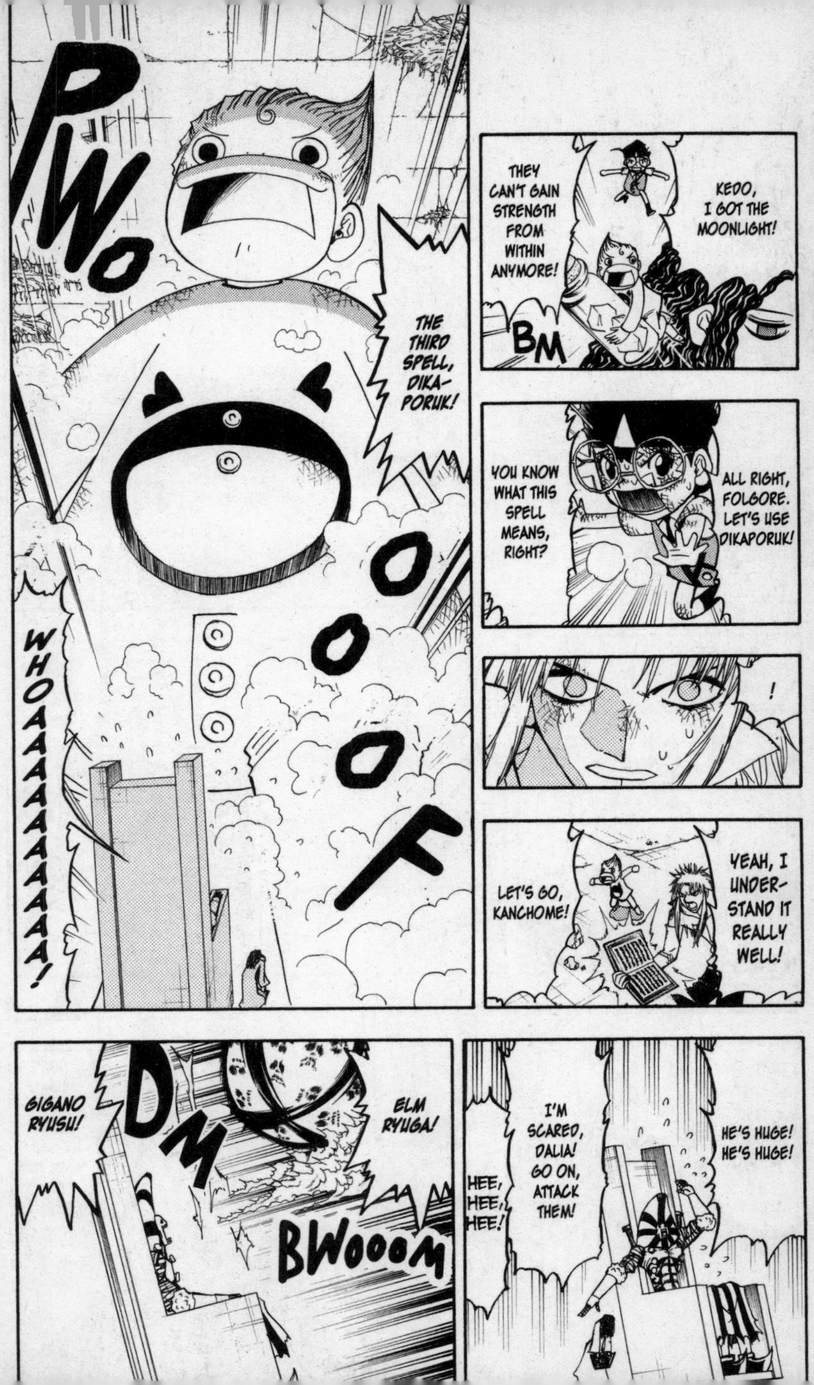
KEDO, I GOT THE MOONLIGHT!
THEY CAN'T GAIN STRENGTH FROM WITHIN ANYMORE!
BM
ALL RIGHT, FOLGORE. LET'S USE DIKAPORUK!
YOU KNOW WHAT THIS SPELL MEANS, RIGHT?
!
YEAH, I UNDER-STAND IT REALLY WELL!
LET'S GO, KANCHOME!
THE THIRD SPELL, DIKA-PORUK!
PWOOOOF
WHOAAAAAAAAAAAA!
HE'S HUGE! HE'S HUGE!
I'M SCARED, DALIA! GO ON, ATTACK THEM!
HEE, HEE, HEE!
ELM RYUGA!
GIGANO RYUSU!
DM
BWoooM

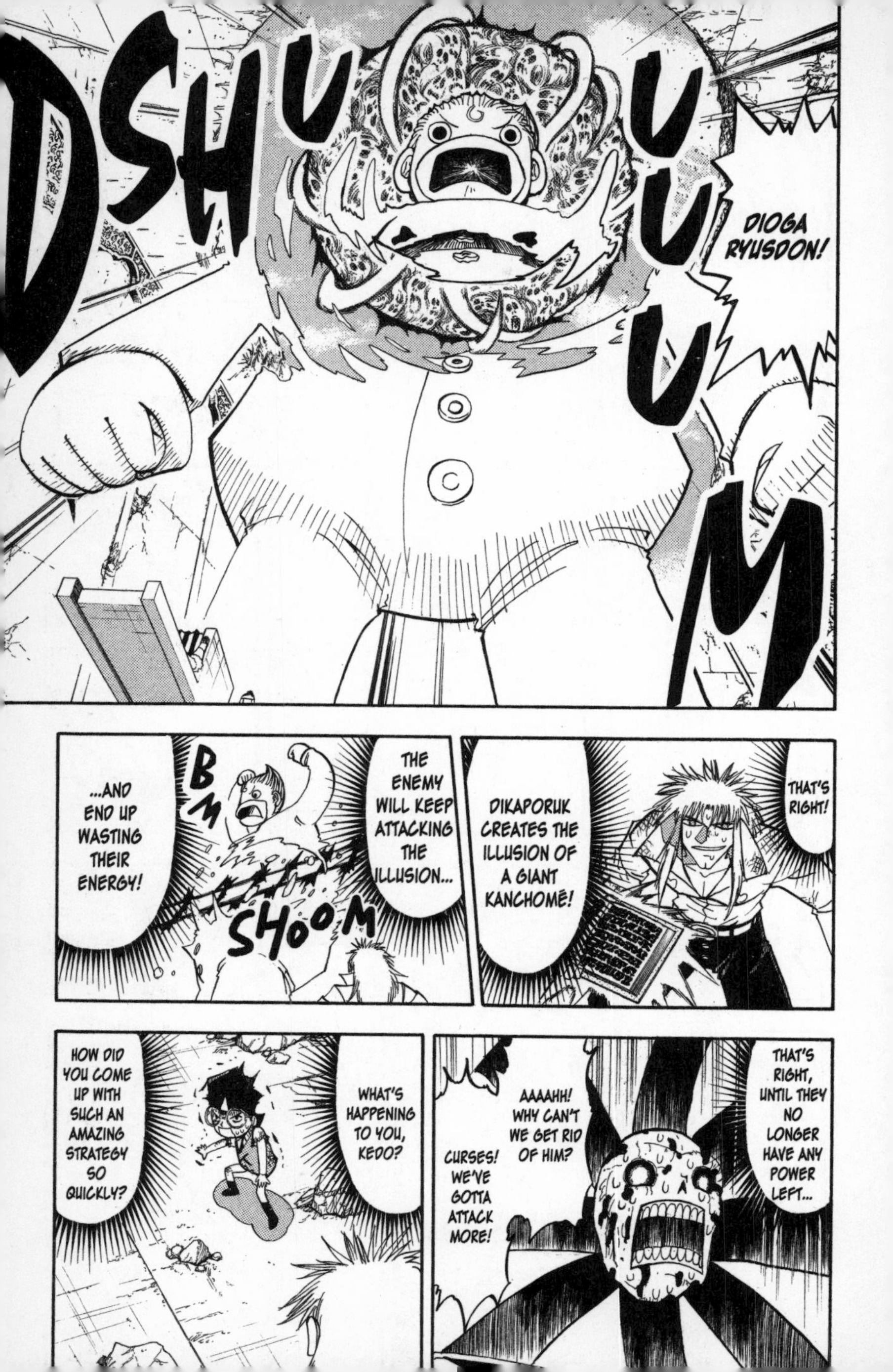
DIOGA RYUSDON!
DSHUUUUUM
THAT'S RIGHT!
DIKAPORUK CREATES THE ILLUSION OF A GIANT KANCHOMÉ!
THE ENEMY WILL KEEP ATTACKING THE ILLUSION...
BM
SHOOM
...AND END UP WASTING THEIR ENERGY!
THAT'S RIGHT, UNTIL THEY NO LONGER HAVE ANY POWER LEFT...
AAAAHH! WHY CAN'T WE GET RID OF HIM?
CURSES! WE'VE GOTTA ATTACK MORE!
WHAT'S HAPPENING TO YOU, KEDO?
HOW DID YOU COME UP WITH SUCH AN AMAZING STRATEGY SO QUICKLY?

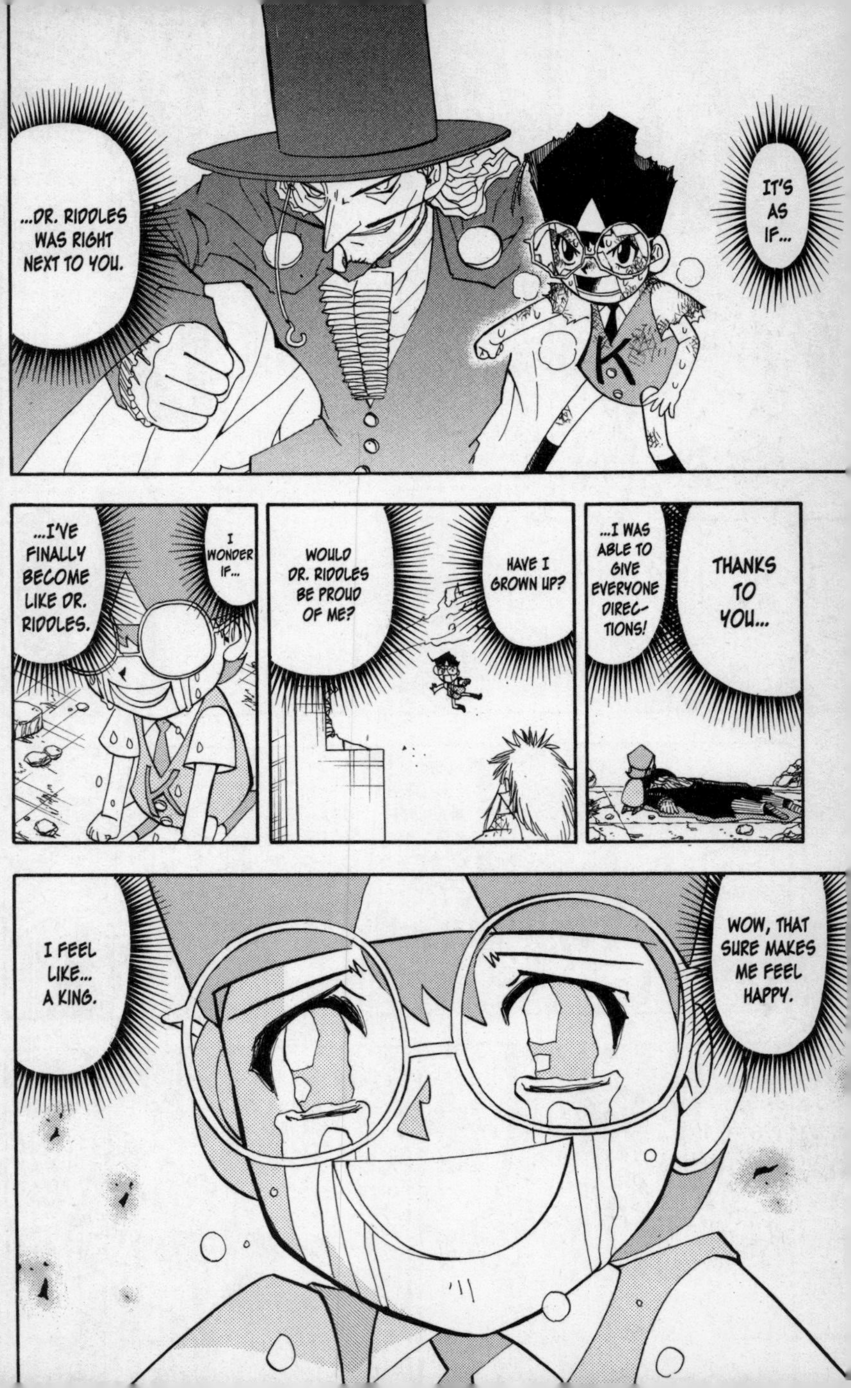
IT'S AS IF...
...DR. RIDDLES WAS RIGHT NEXT TO YOU.
THANKS TO YOU...
...I WAS ABLE TO GIVE EVERYONE DIRECTIONS!
HAVE I GROWN UP?
WOULD DR. RIDDLES BE PROUD OF ME?
I WONDER IF...
...I'VE FINALLY BECOME LIKE DR. RIDDLES.
WOW, THAT SURE MAKES ME FEEL HAPPY.
I FEEL LIKE... A KING.

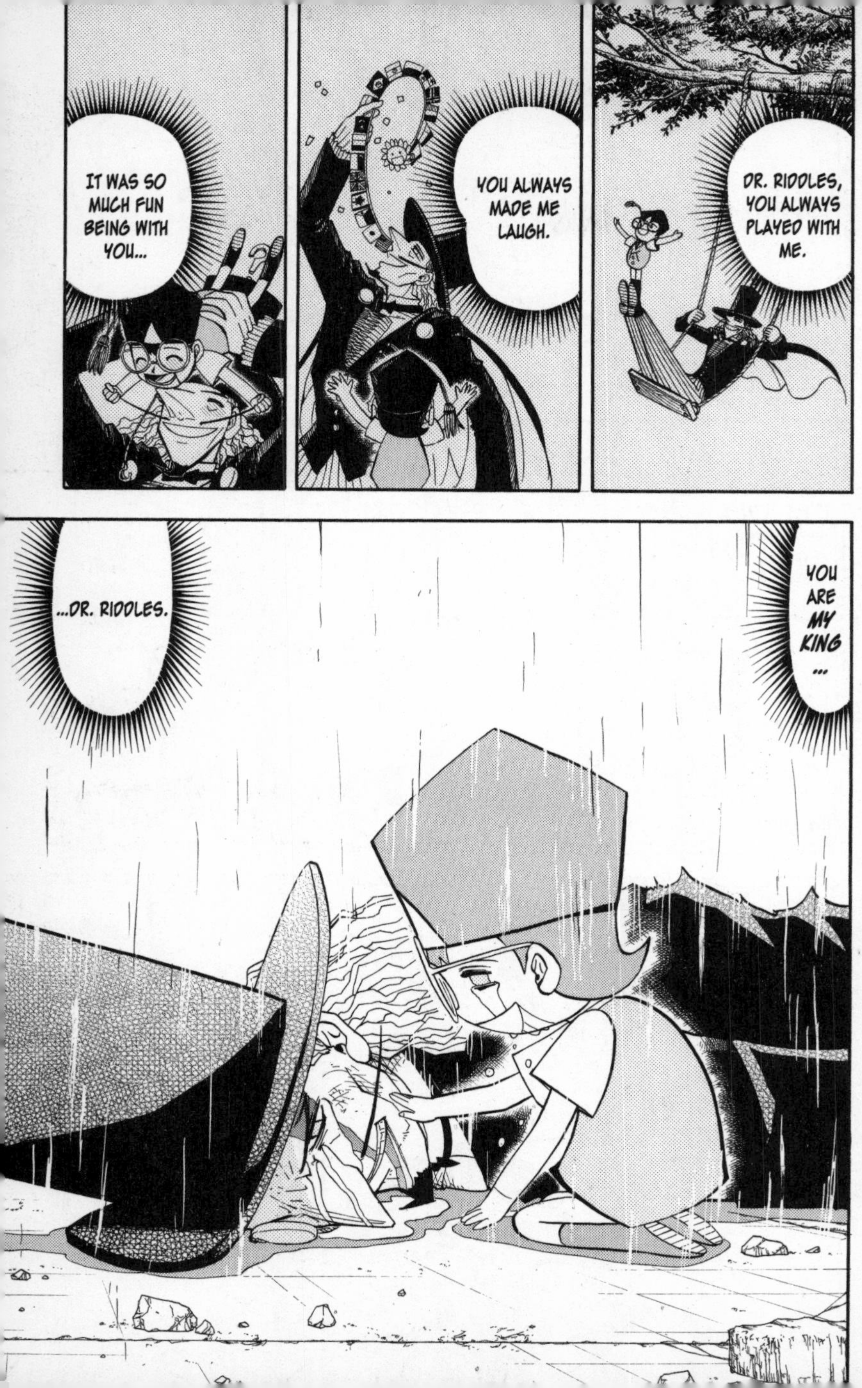
DR. RIDDLES, YOU ALWAYS PLAYED WITH ME.
YOU ALWAYS MADE ME LAUGH.
IT WAS SO MUCH FUN BEING WITH YOU...
YOU ARE *MY KING* ...
...DR. RIDDLES.

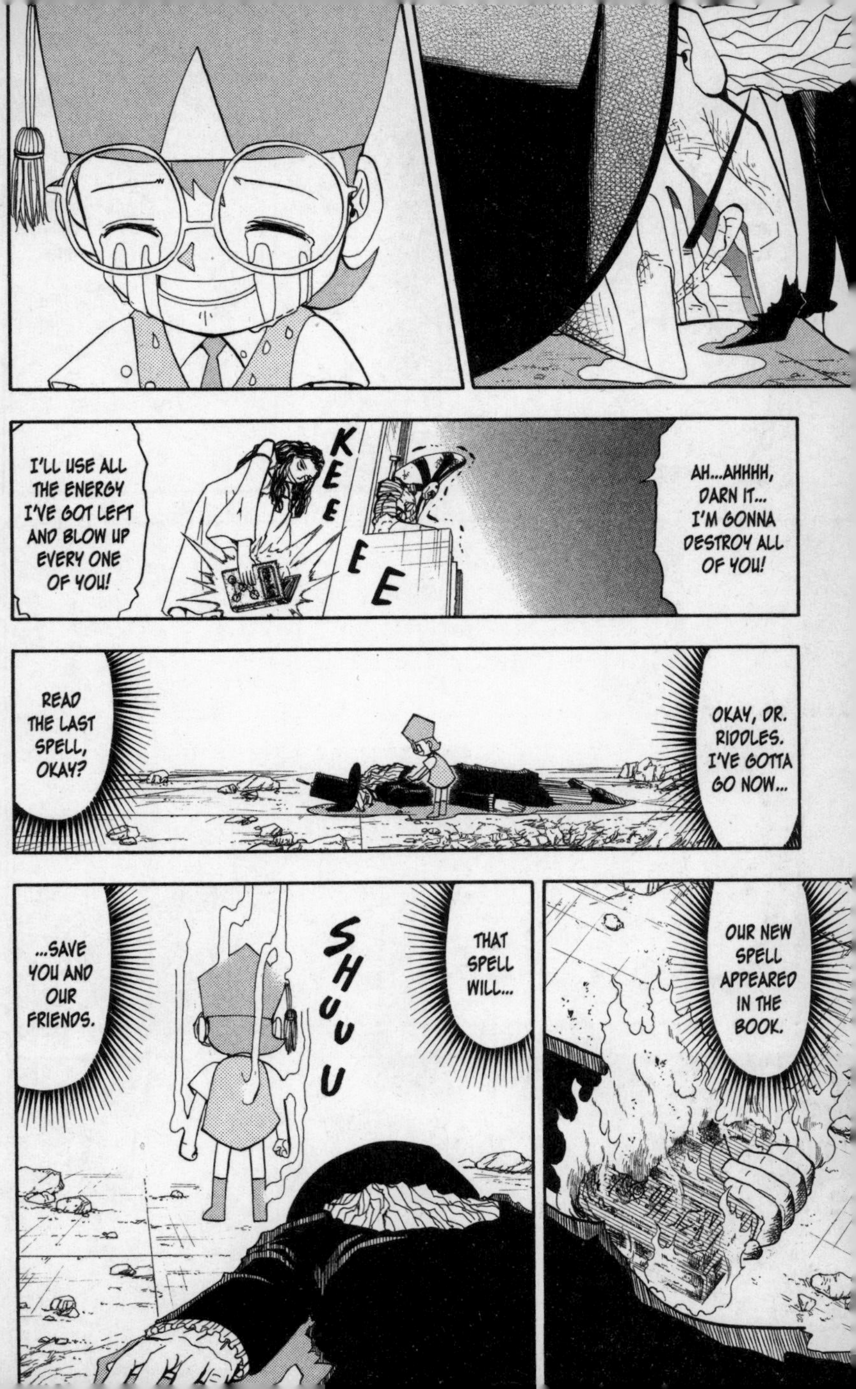
AH...AHHHH, DARN IT... I'M GONNA DESTROY ALL OF YOU!
KEEEEE
I'LL USE ALL THE ENERGY I'VE GOT LEFT AND BLOW UP EVERY ONE OF YOU!
OKAY, DR. RIDDLES. I'VE GOTTA GO NOW...
READ THE LAST SPELL, OKAY?
OUR NEW SPELL APPEARED IN THE BOOK.
THAT SPELL WILL...
SHUUUU
...SAVE YOU AND OUR FRIENDS.

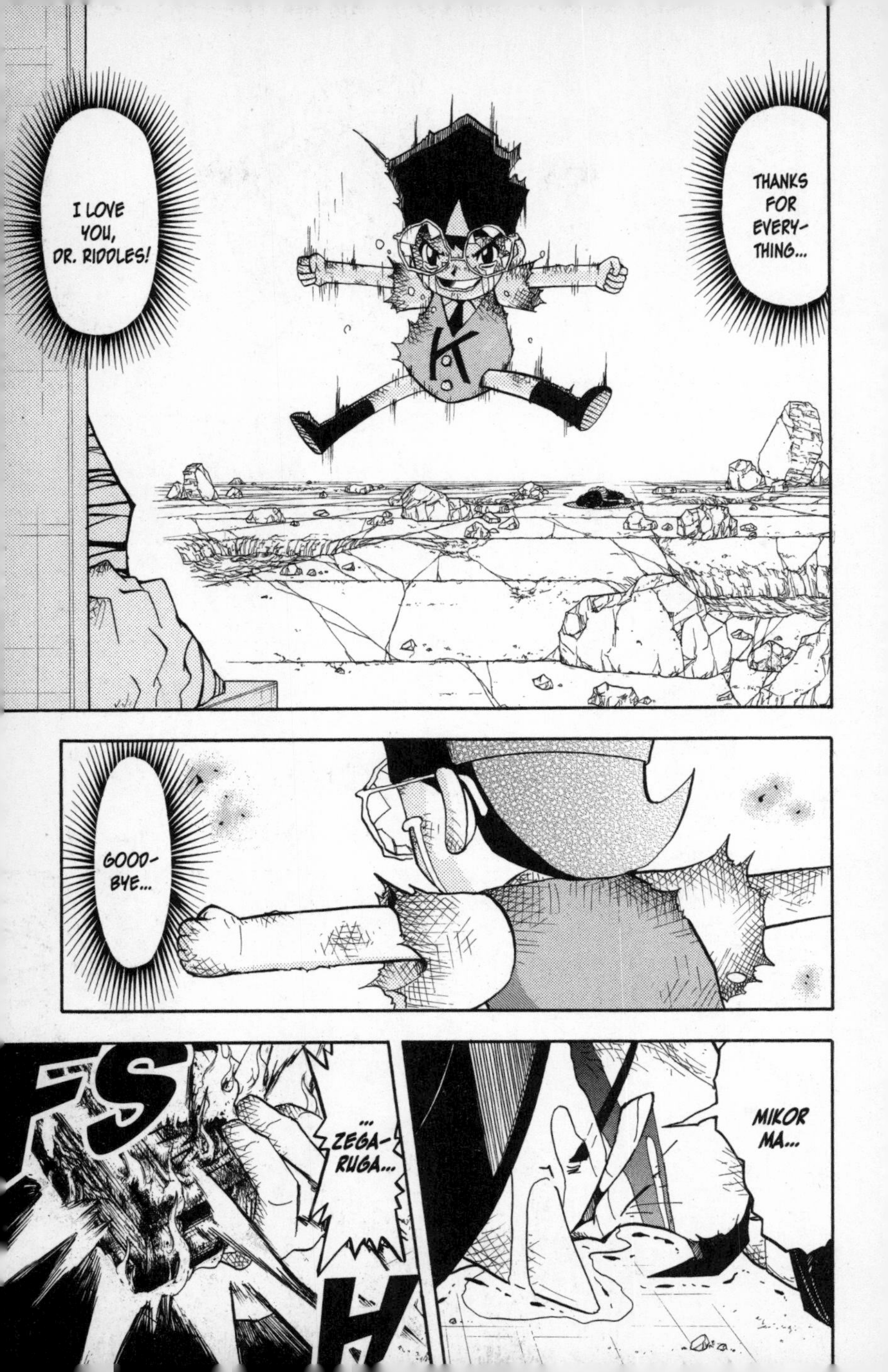
THANKS FOR EVERY-THING...
I LOVE YOU, DR. RIDDLES!
GOOD-BYE...
MIKOR MA...
... ZEGA-RUGA...

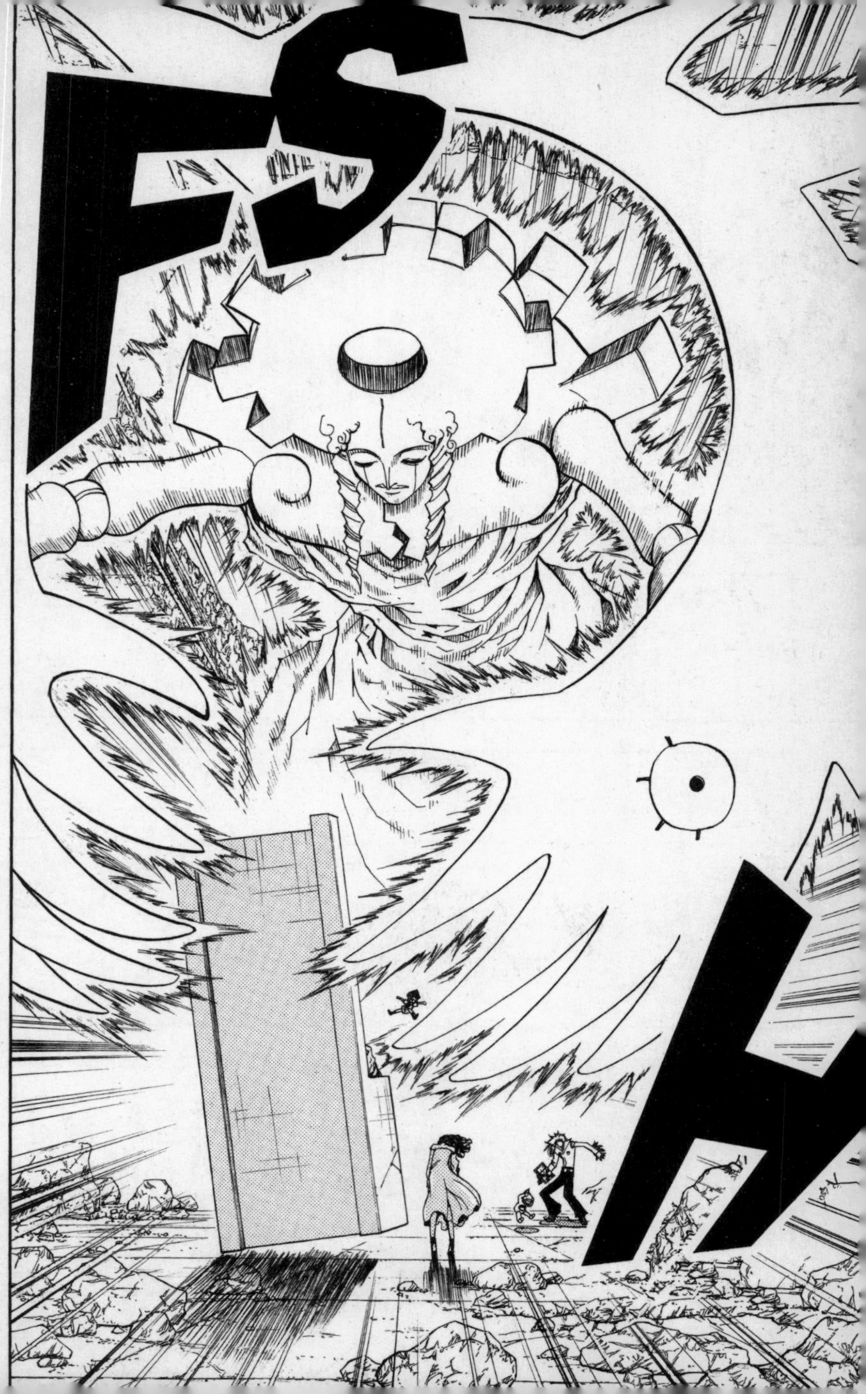
FSH

...DR. RIDDLES...

I'M SORRY...

DR. RIDDLES ...

DR. RIDDLES ...

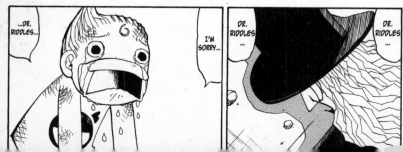

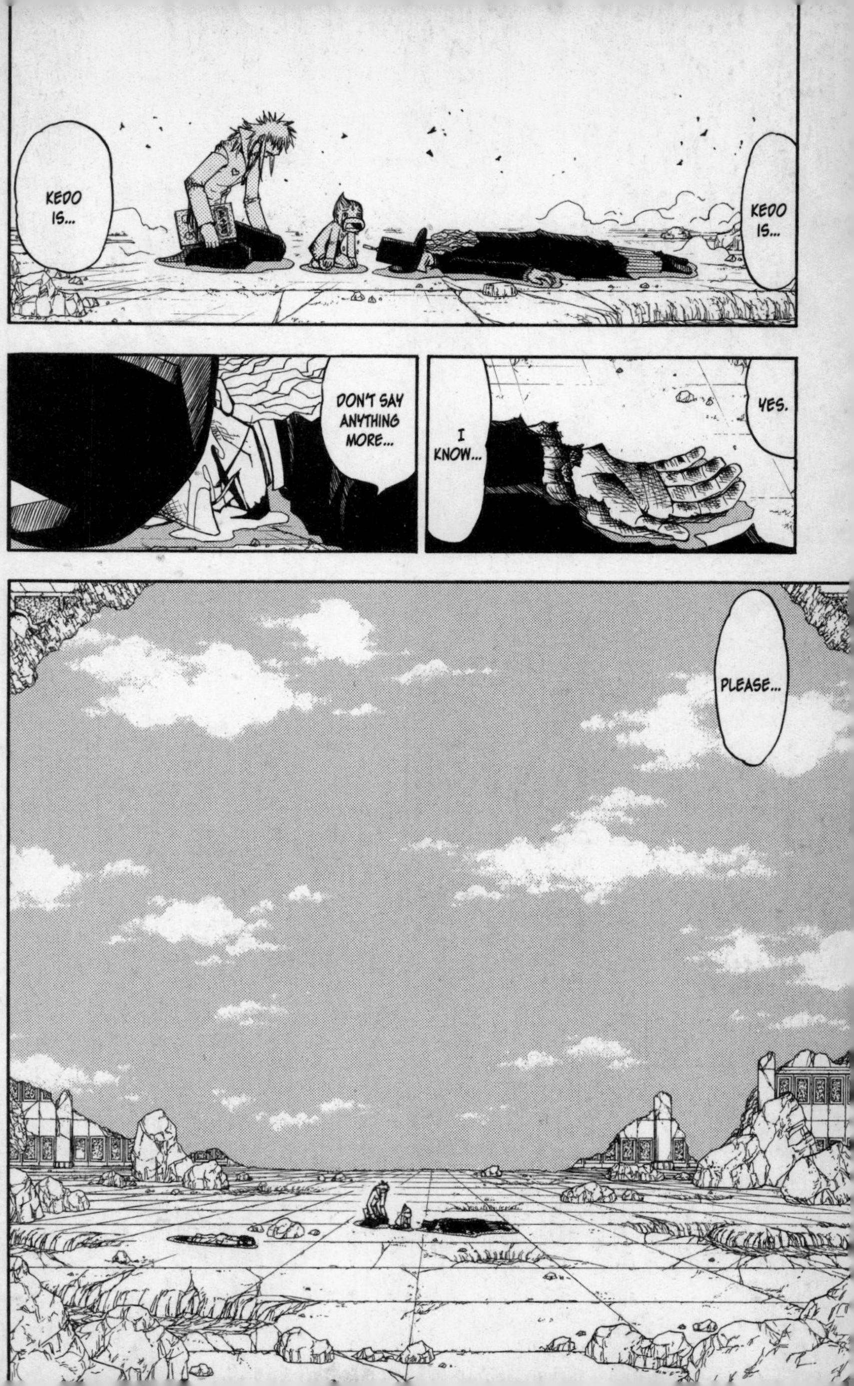
KEDO IS...
KEDO IS...
YES.
I KNOW...
DON'T SAY ANYTHING MORE...
PLEASE...

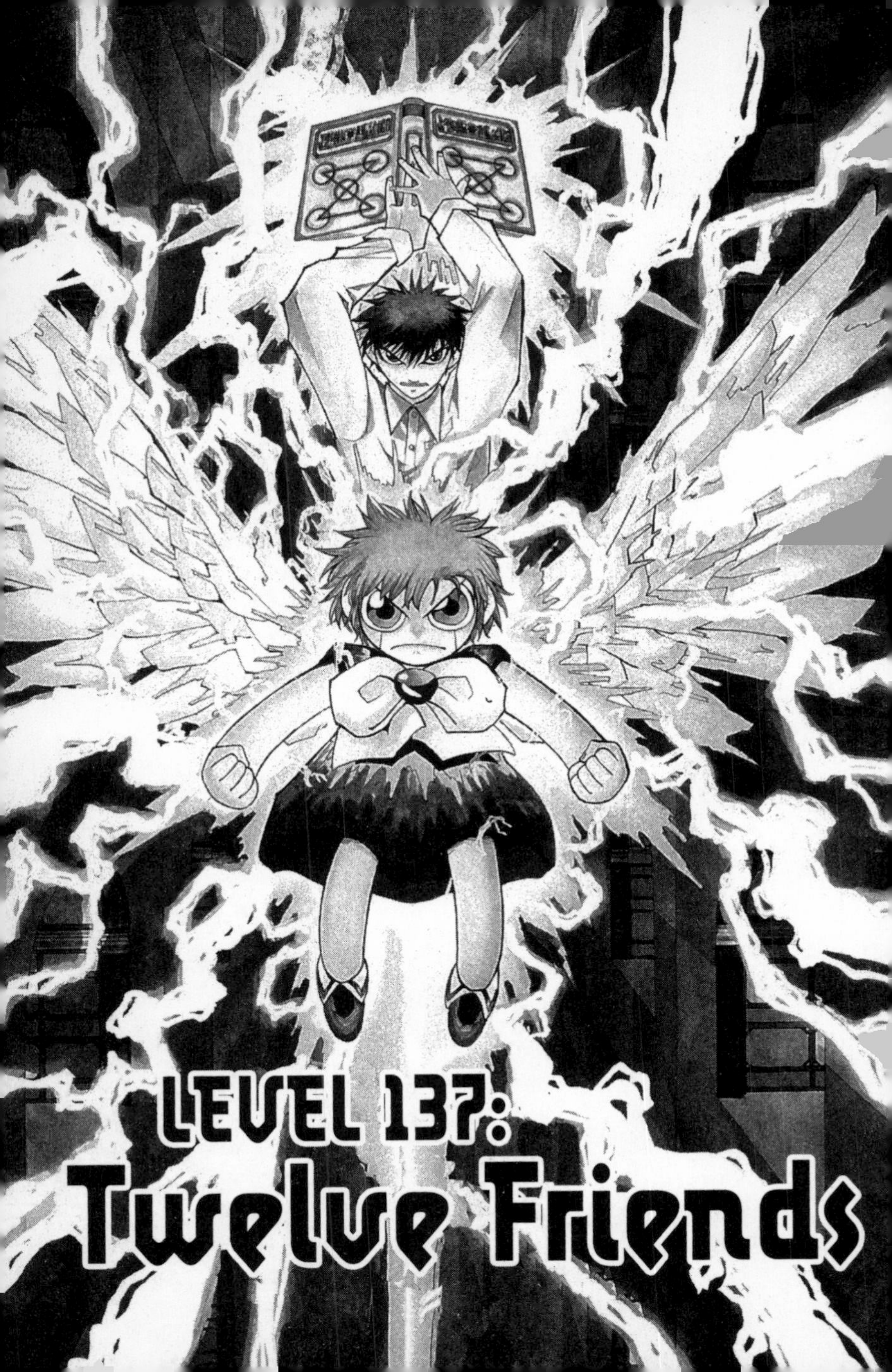
LEVEL 137:
Twelve Friends

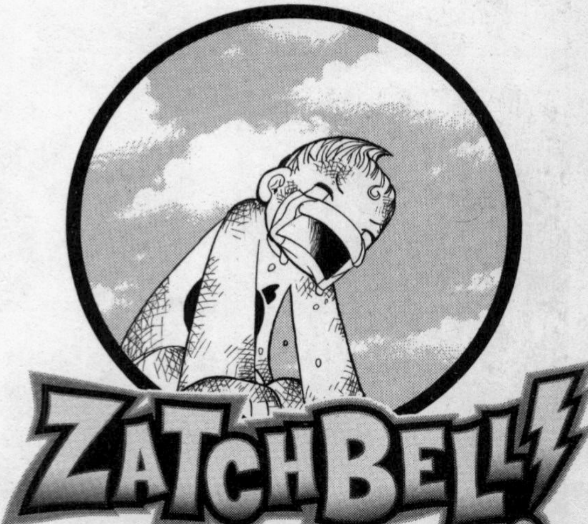
ZATCHBELL!

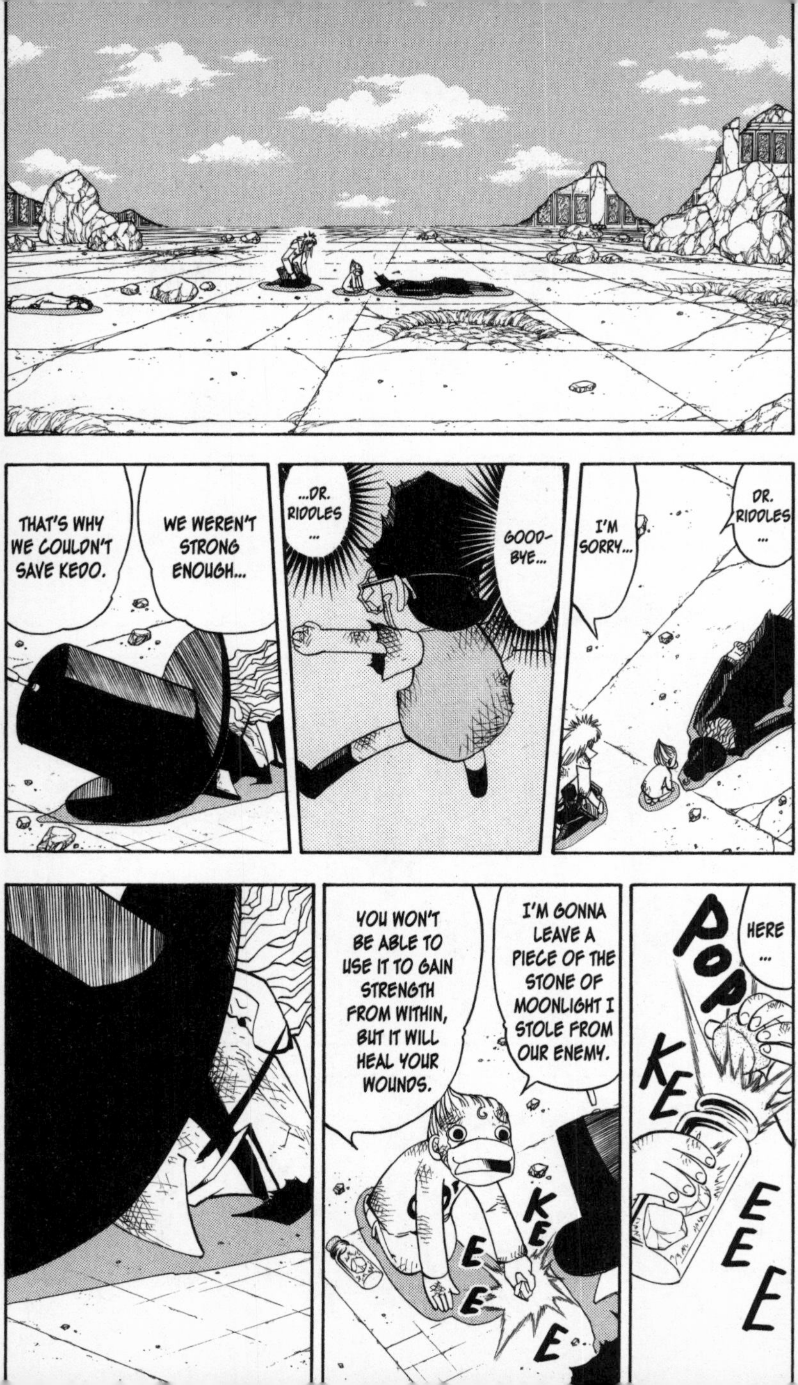
DR. RIDDLES ...
I'M SORRY...
...DR. RIDDLES ...
GOOD-BYE...
WE WEREN'T STRONG ENOUGH...
THAT'S WHY WE COULDN'T SAVE KEDO.
HERE ...
POP
KEEEE
I'M GONNA LEAVE A PIECE OF THE STONE OF MOONLIGHT I STOLE FROM OUR ENEMY.
YOU WON'T BE ABLE TO USE IT TO GAIN STRENGTH FROM WITHIN, BUT IT WILL HEAL YOUR WOUNDS.
KEEEE

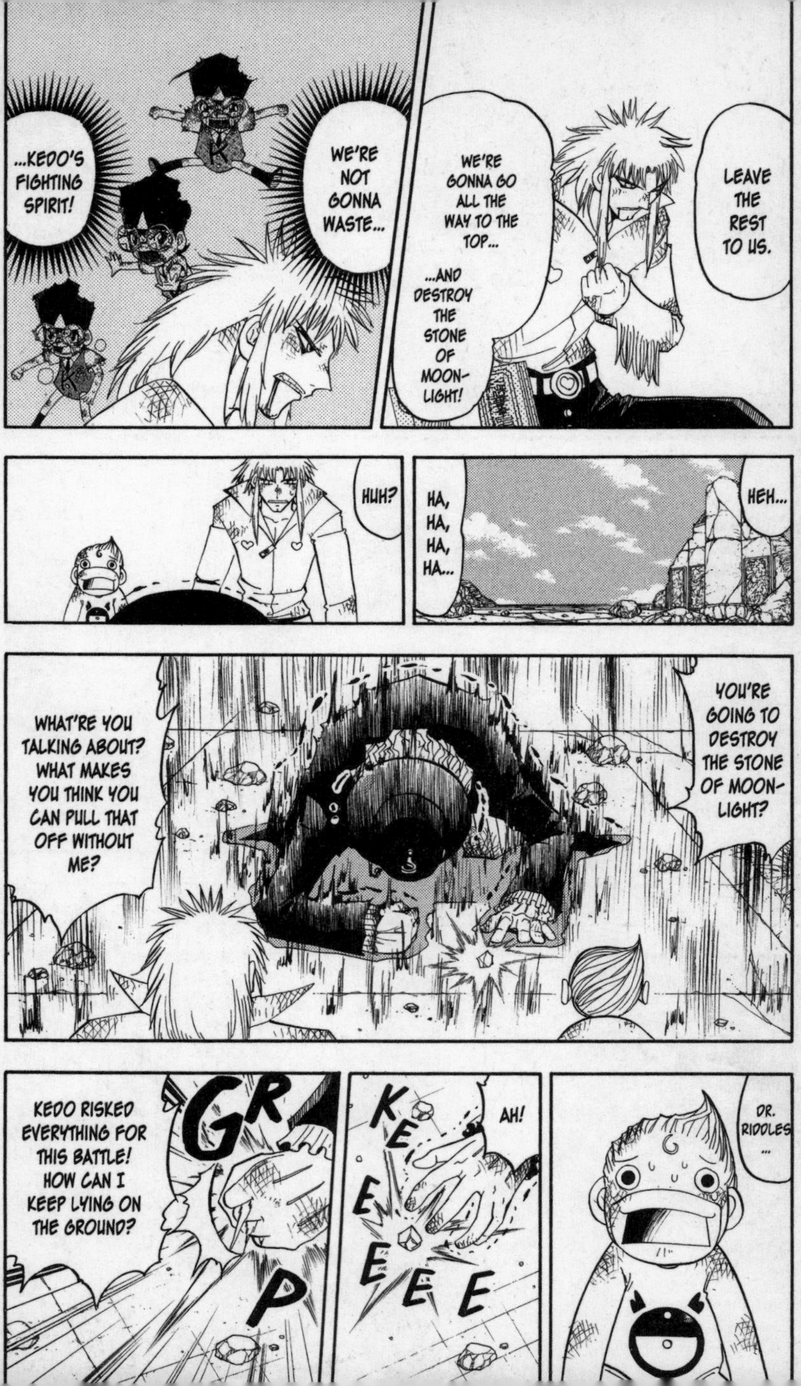
LEAVE THE REST TO US.
WE'RE GONNA GO ALL THE WAY TO THE TOP...
...AND DESTROY THE STONE OF MOONLIGHT!
WE'RE NOT GONNA WASTE...
...KEDO'S FIGHTING SPIRIT!
HEH...
HA, HA, HA, HA...
HUH?
YOU'RE GOING TO DESTROY THE STONE OF MOONLIGHT?
WHAT'RE YOU TALKING ABOUT? WHAT MAKES YOU THINK YOU CAN PULL THAT OFF WITHOUT ME?
DR. RIDDLES...
AH!
KEEEEEE
GR
P
KEDO RISKED EVERYTHING FOR THIS BATTLE! HOW CAN I KEEP LYING ON THE GROUND?

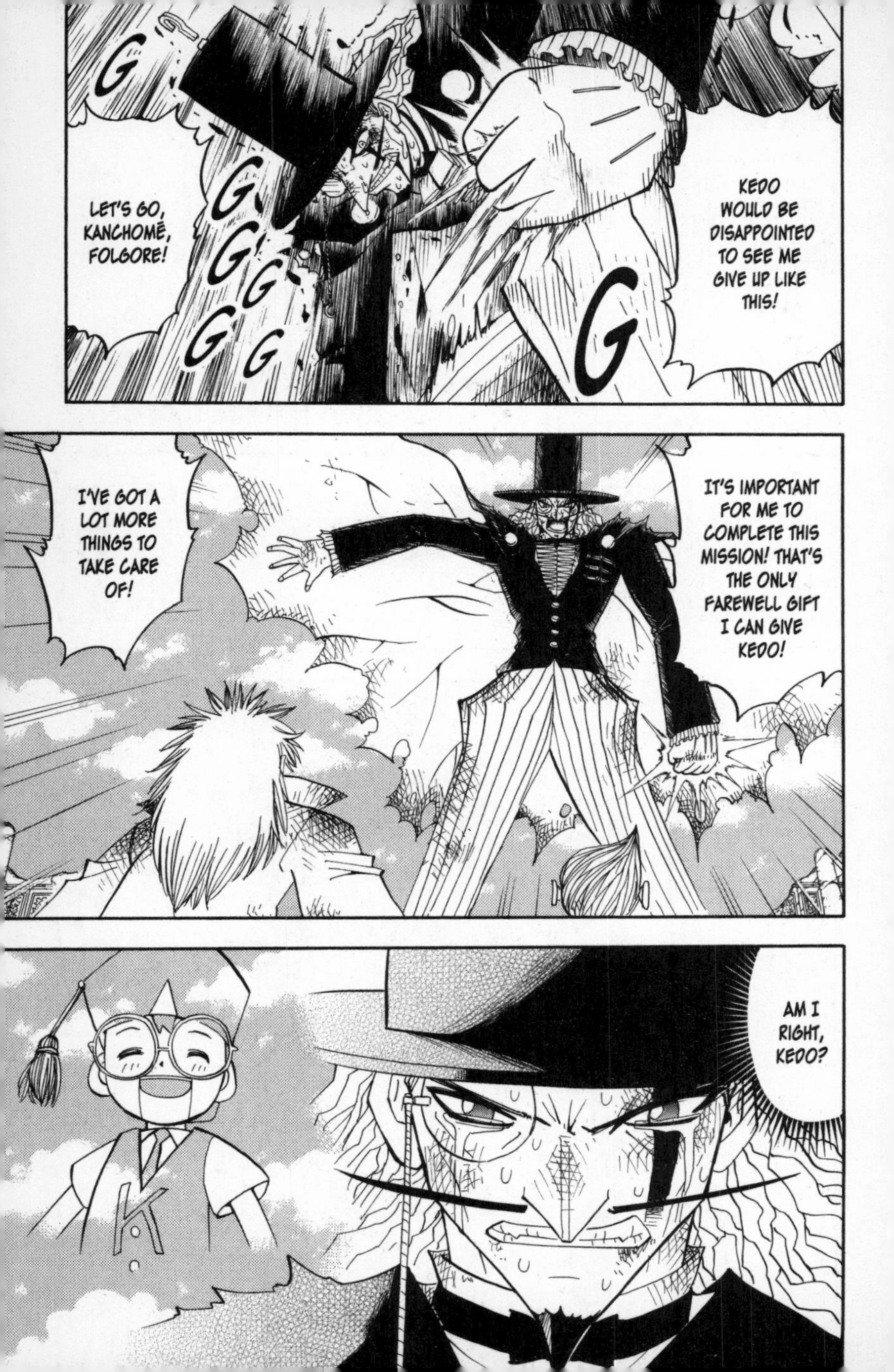
KEDO WOULD BE DISAPPOINTED TO SEE ME GIVE UP LIKE THIS!
LET'S GO, KANCHOMÉ, FOLGORE!
G
GGGGGG
G
IT'S IMPORTANT FOR ME TO COMPLETE THIS MISSION! THAT'S THE ONLY FAREWELL GIFT I CAN GIVE KEDO!
I'VE GOT A LOT MORE THINGS TO TAKE CARE OF!
AM I RIGHT, KEDO?

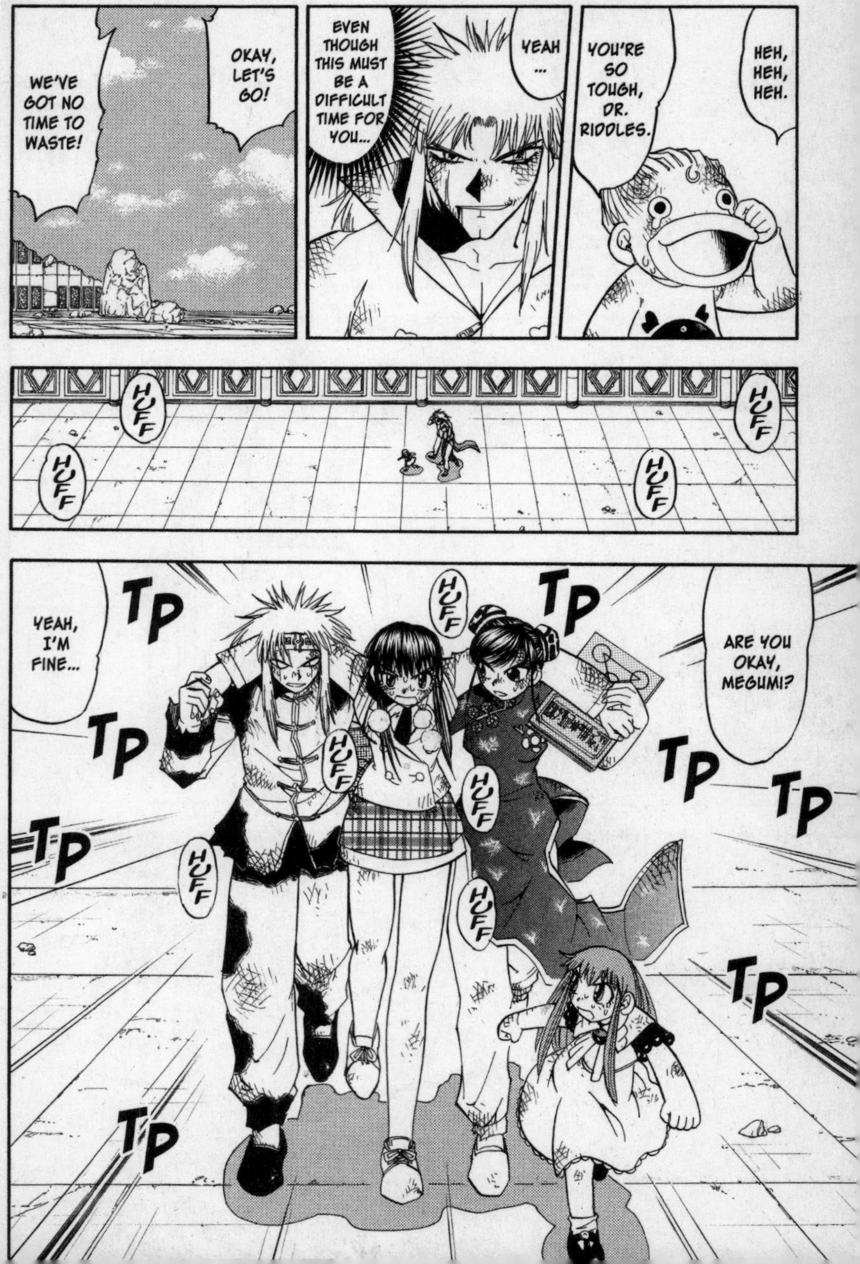
HEH, HEH, HEH.
YOU'RE SO TOUGH, DR. RIDDLES.
YEAH ...
EVEN THOUGH THIS MUST BE A DIFFICULT TIME FOR YOU...
OKAY, LET'S GO!
WE'VE GOT NO TIME TO WASTE!
HUFF
HUFF
HUFF
HUFF
ARE YOU OKAY, MEGUMI?
TP
TP
TP
HUFF
TP
HUFF
HUFF
HUFF
HUFF
YEAH, I'M FINE...
TP
TP
TP
TP

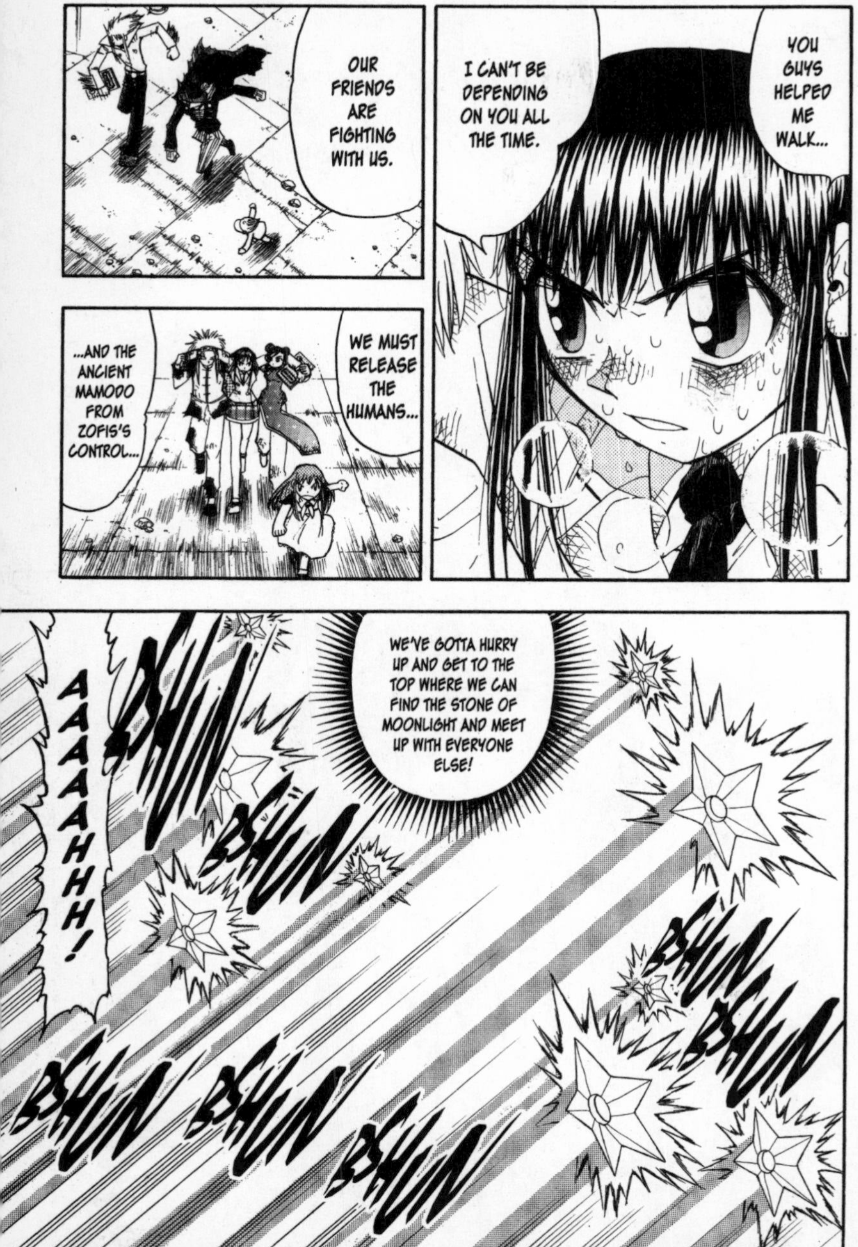
YOU GUYS HELPED ME WALK...
I CAN'T BE DEPENDING ON YOU ALL THE TIME.
OUR FRIENDS ARE FIGHTING WITH US.
WE MUST RELEASE THE HUMANS...
...AND THE ANCIENT MAMODO FROM ZOFIS'S CONTROL...
WE'VE GOTTA HURRY UP AND GET TO THE TOP WHERE WE CAN FIND THE STONE OF MOONLIGHT AND MEET UP WITH EVERYONE ELSE!
BHUN BHUN
BHUN BHUN
AAAAAHHH!
BHUN
BHUN BHUN BHUN

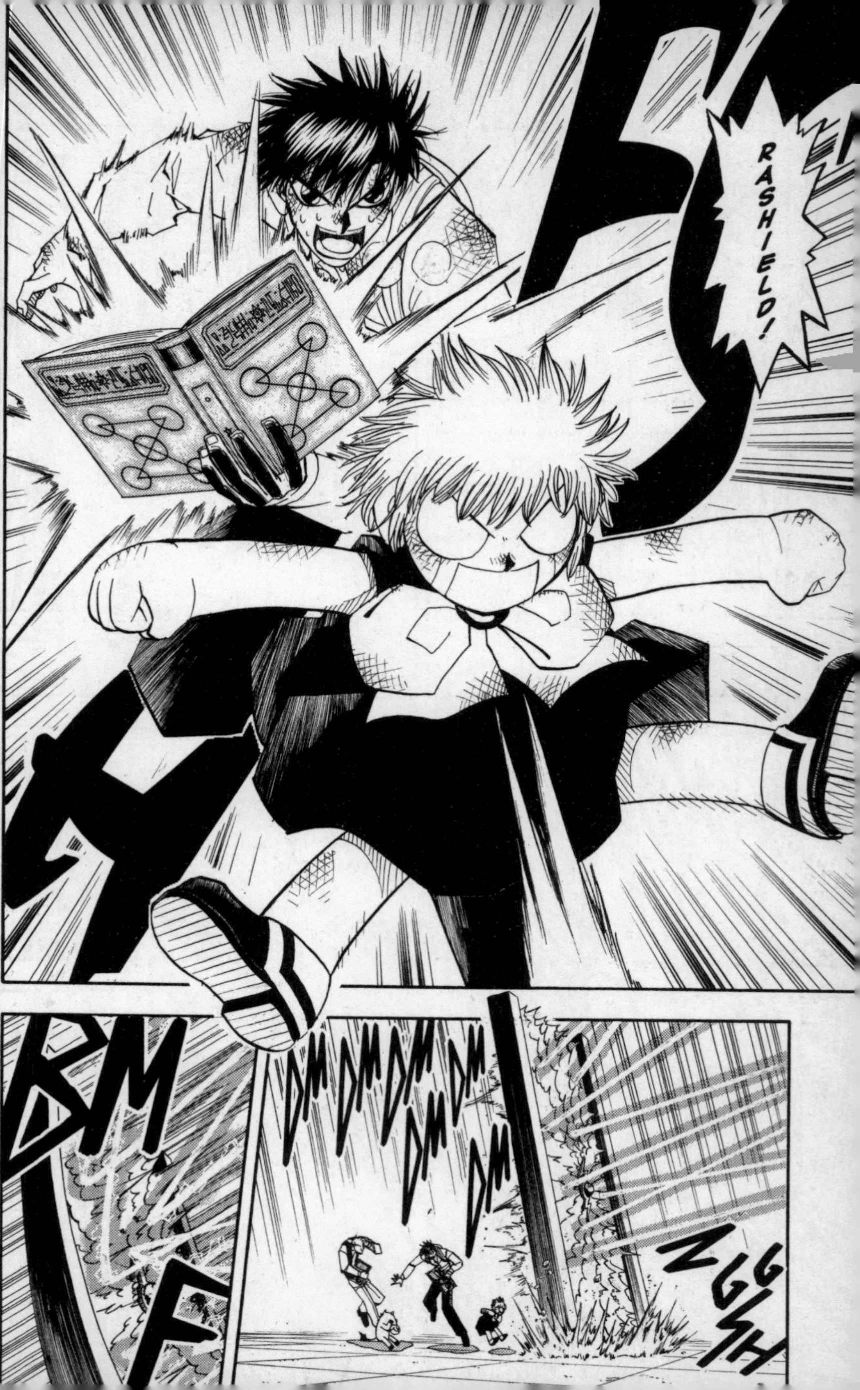
RASHIELD!
DM DM DM DM DM DM DM DM
ZGGSH
BMF

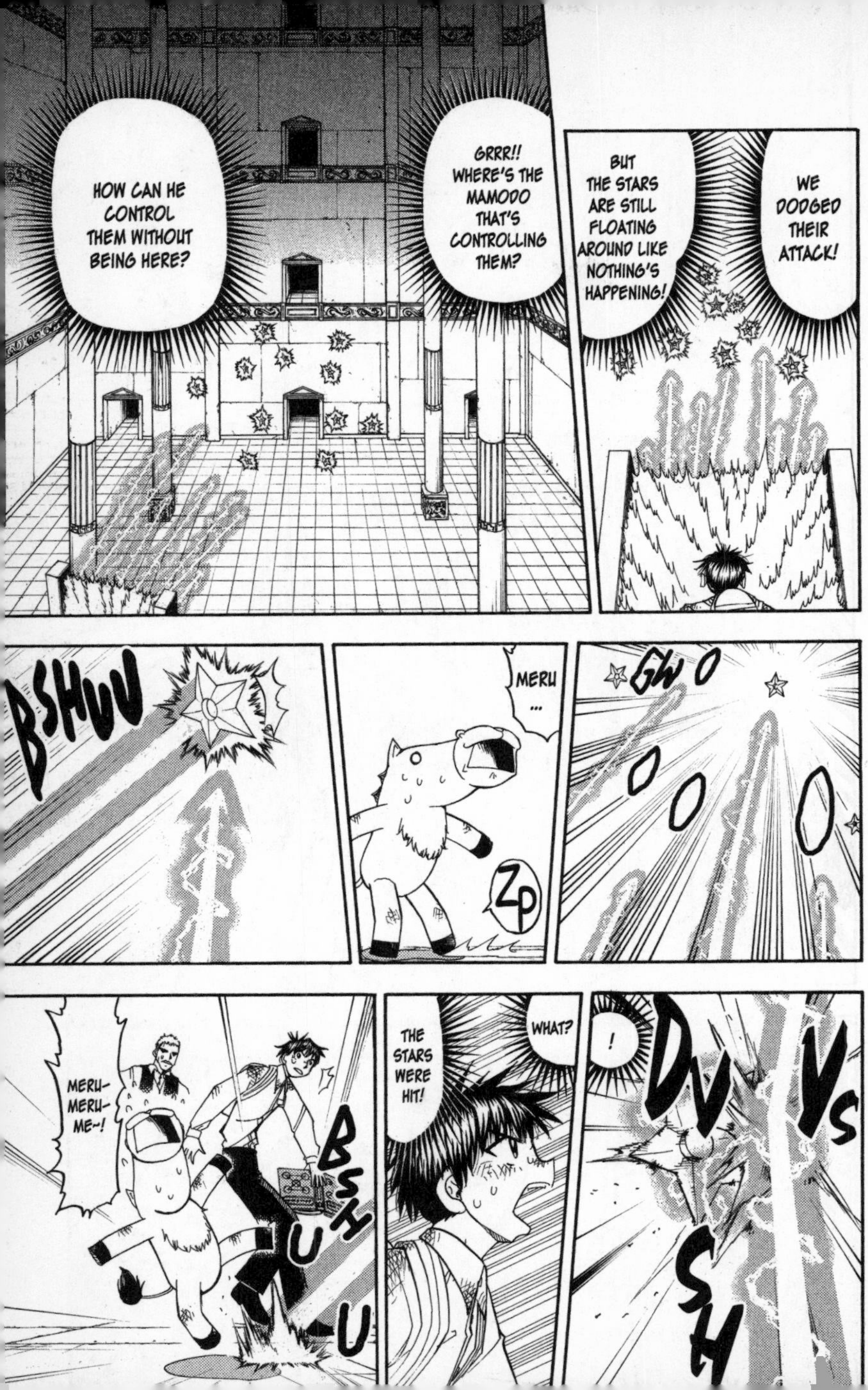
WE DODGED THEIR ATTACK!
BUT THE STARS ARE STILL FLOATING AROUND LIKE NOTHING'S HAPPENING!
GRRR!! WHERE'S THE MAMODO THAT'S CONTROLLING THEM?
HOW CAN HE CONTROL THEM WITHOUT BEING HERE?
GWOOOO
MERU...
ZP
BSHUU
!
DVVS
SH
WHAT?
THE STARS WERE HIT!
MERU-MERU-ME~!
BSHUU

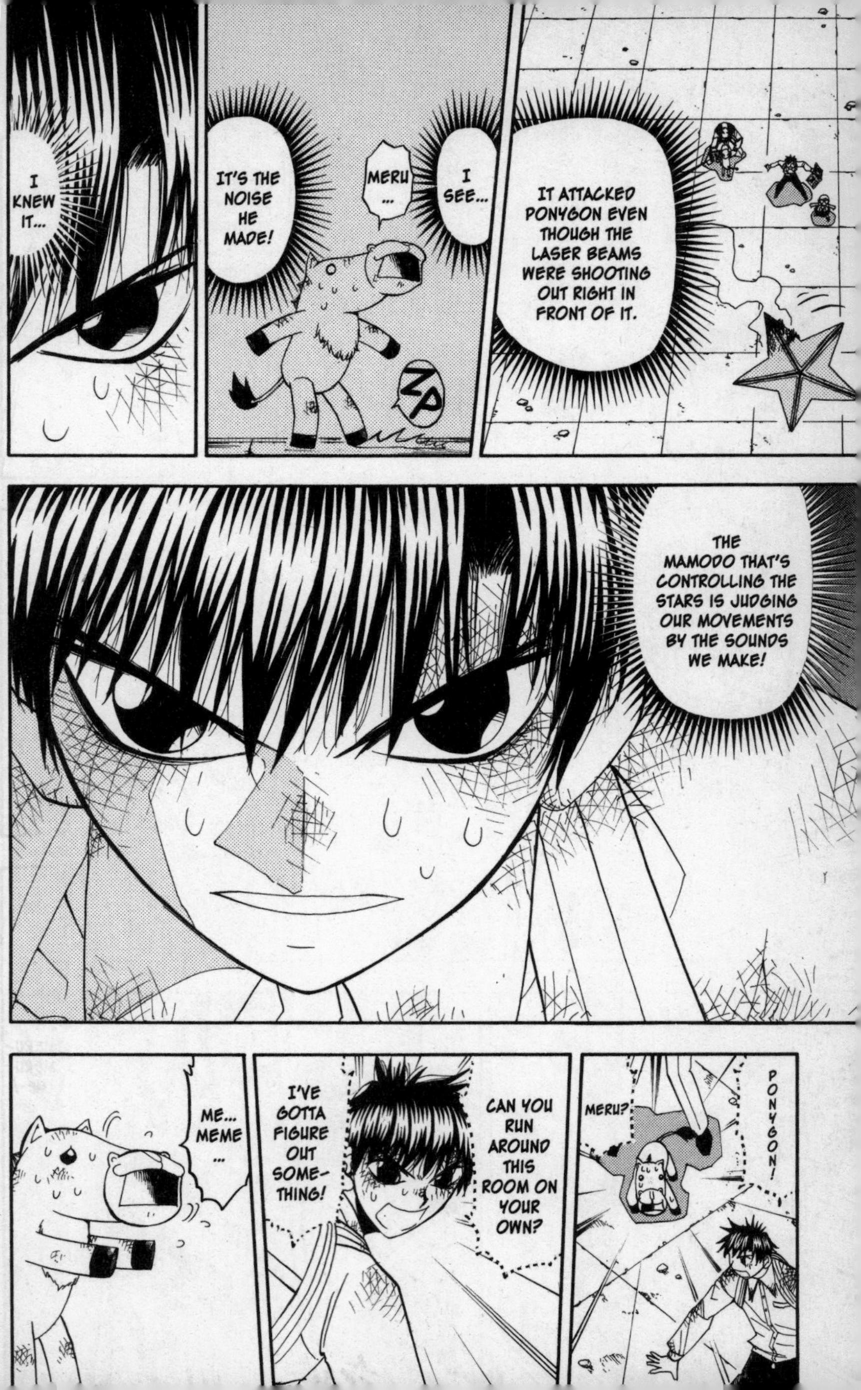
IT ATTACKED PONYGON EVEN THOUGH THE LASER BEAMS WERE SHOOTING OUT RIGHT IN FRONT OF IT.
I SEE...
MERU ...
ZP
IT'S THE NOISE HE MADE!
I KNEW IT...
THE MAMODO THAT'S CONTROLLING THE STARS IS JUDGING OUR MOVEMENTS BY THE SOUNDS WE MAKE!
PONYGON!
MERU?
CAN YOU RUN AROUND THIS ROOM ON YOUR OWN?
I'VE GOTTA FIGURE OUT SOME-THING!
ME... MEME ...

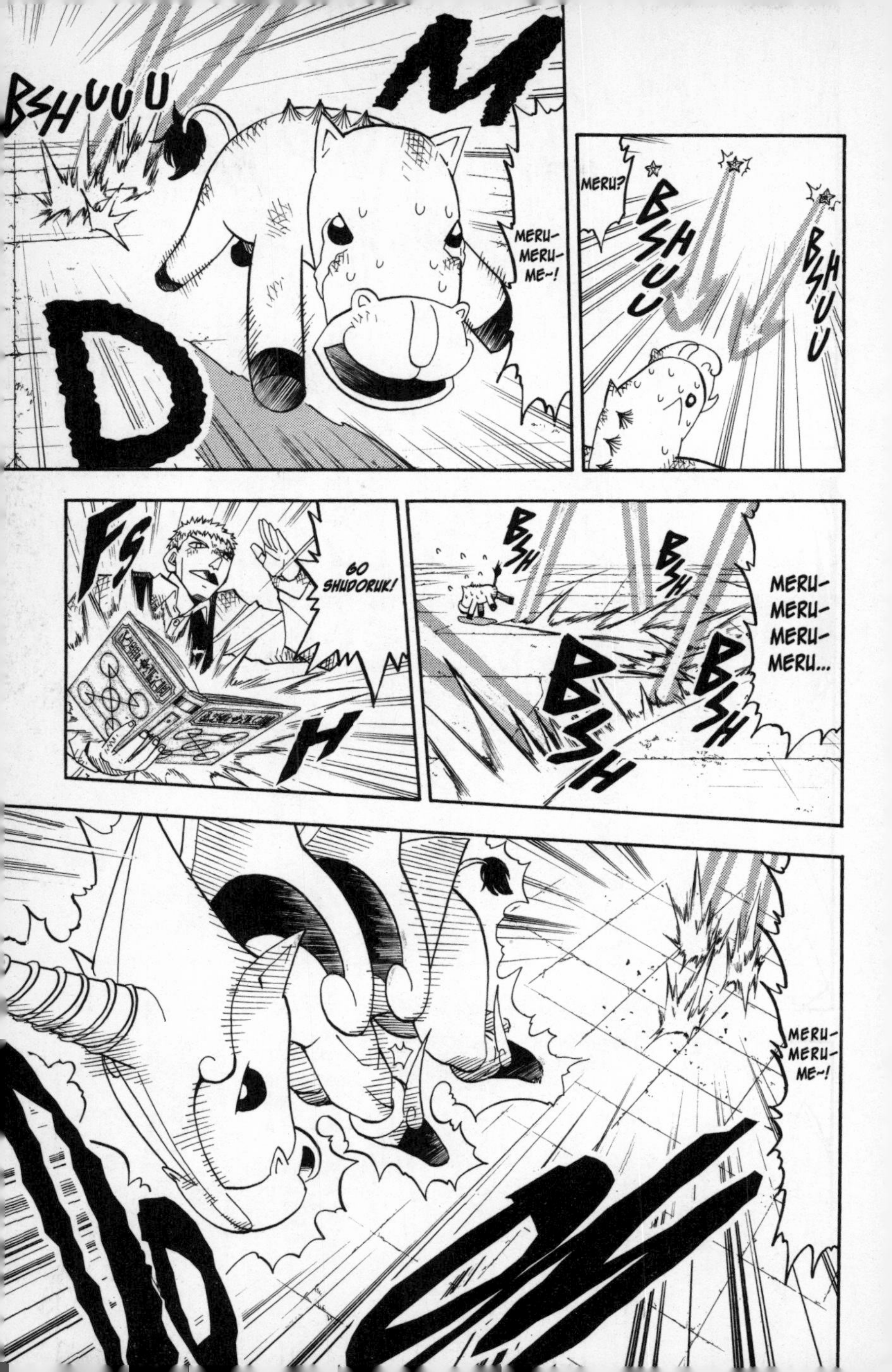
MERU?
BSHUUU
BSHUUU
M
MERU-MERU-ME~!
BSHUUU
D
BSH
BSH
MERU-MERU-MERU-MERU...
BSH
BSH
FS
GO SHUDORUK!
H
MERU-MERU-ME~!

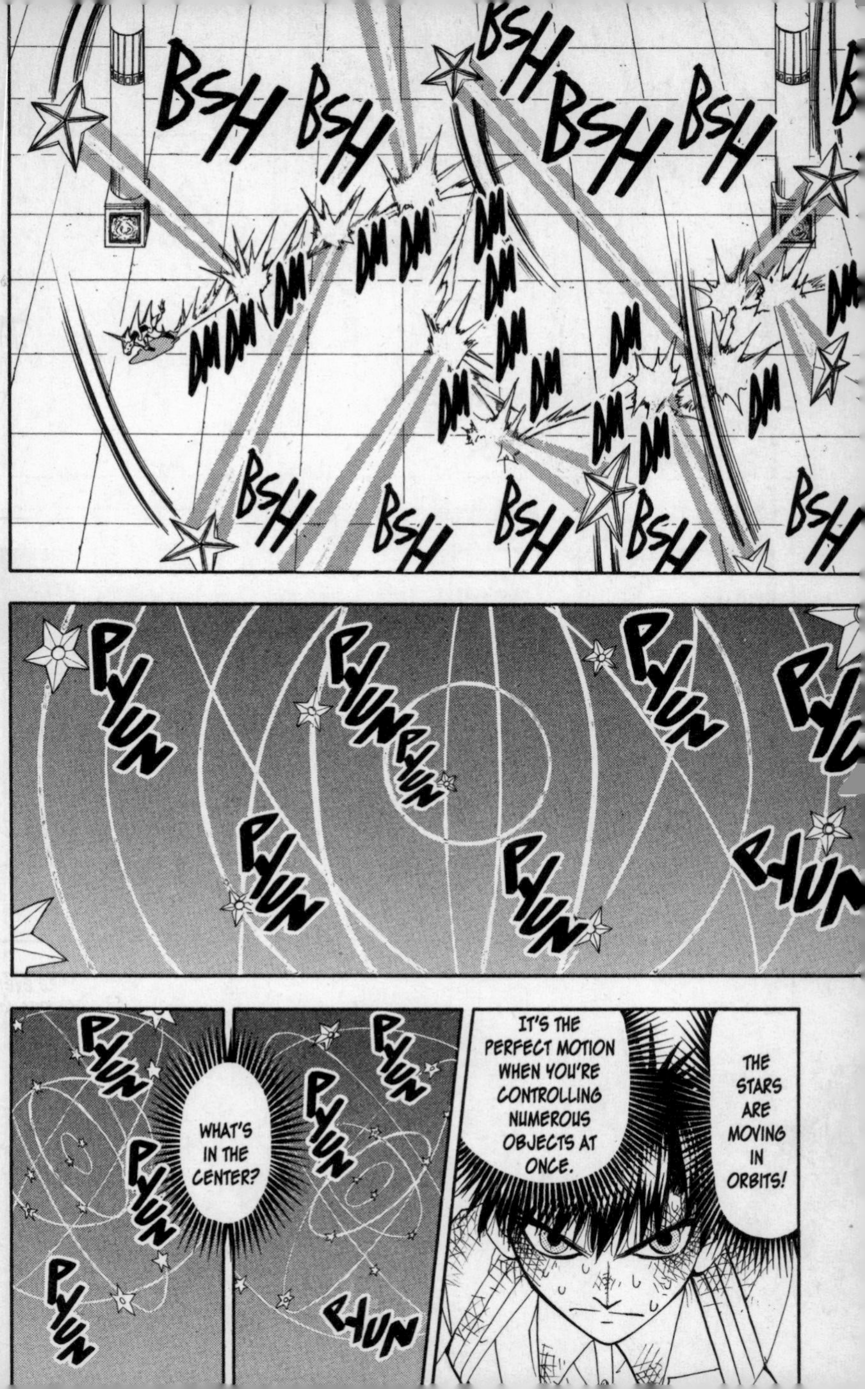
BSH
BSH
BSH
BSH
BSH
DM DM DM DM DM DM DM DM DM DM DM DM DM
BSH
BSH
BSH
BSH
BSH
PYUN
PYUN
PYUN
PYUN PYUN
PYUN
PYUN
PYUN
THE STARS ARE MOVING IN ORBITS!
IT'S THE PERFECT MOTION WHEN YOU'RE CONTROLLING NUMEROUS OBJECTS AT ONCE.
PYUN
PYUN
PYUN
WHAT'S IN THE CENTER?
PYUN
PYUN
PYUN

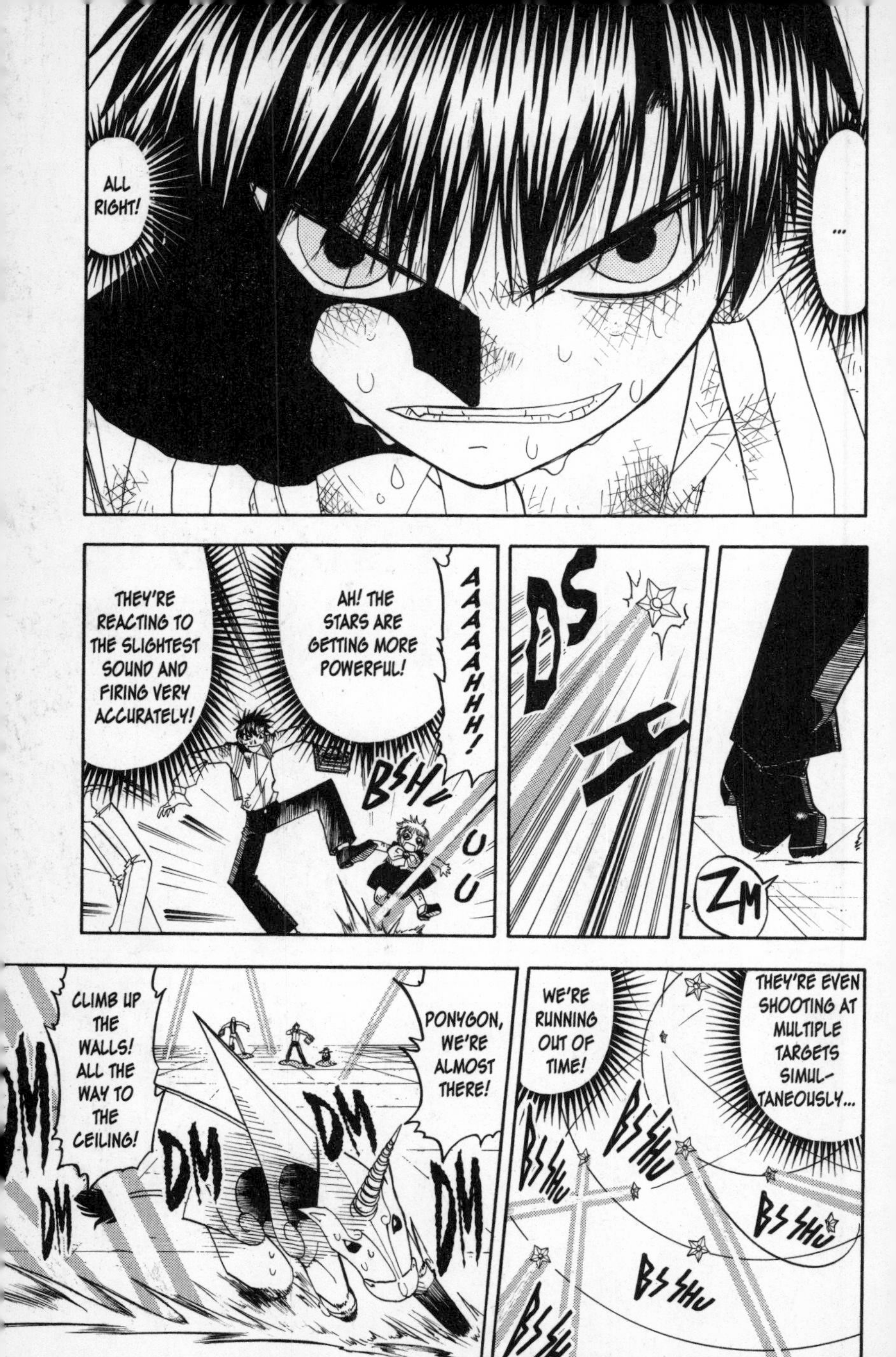
...
ALL RIGHT!
ZM
DSH
AAAAAHHH!
AH! THE STARS ARE GETTING MORE POWERFUL!
THEY'RE REACTING TO THE SLIGHTEST SOUND AND FIRING VERY ACCURATELY!
BSHU
UU
THEY'RE EVEN SHOOTING AT MULTIPLE TARGETS SIMUL-TANEOUSLY...
WE'RE RUNNING OUT OF TIME!
BSSHU
BSSHU
BSSHU
BSSHU
BSSHU
PONYGON, WE'RE ALMOST THERE!
CLIMB UP THE WALLS! ALL THE WAY TO THE CEILING!
DM
DM
DM
DM
DM

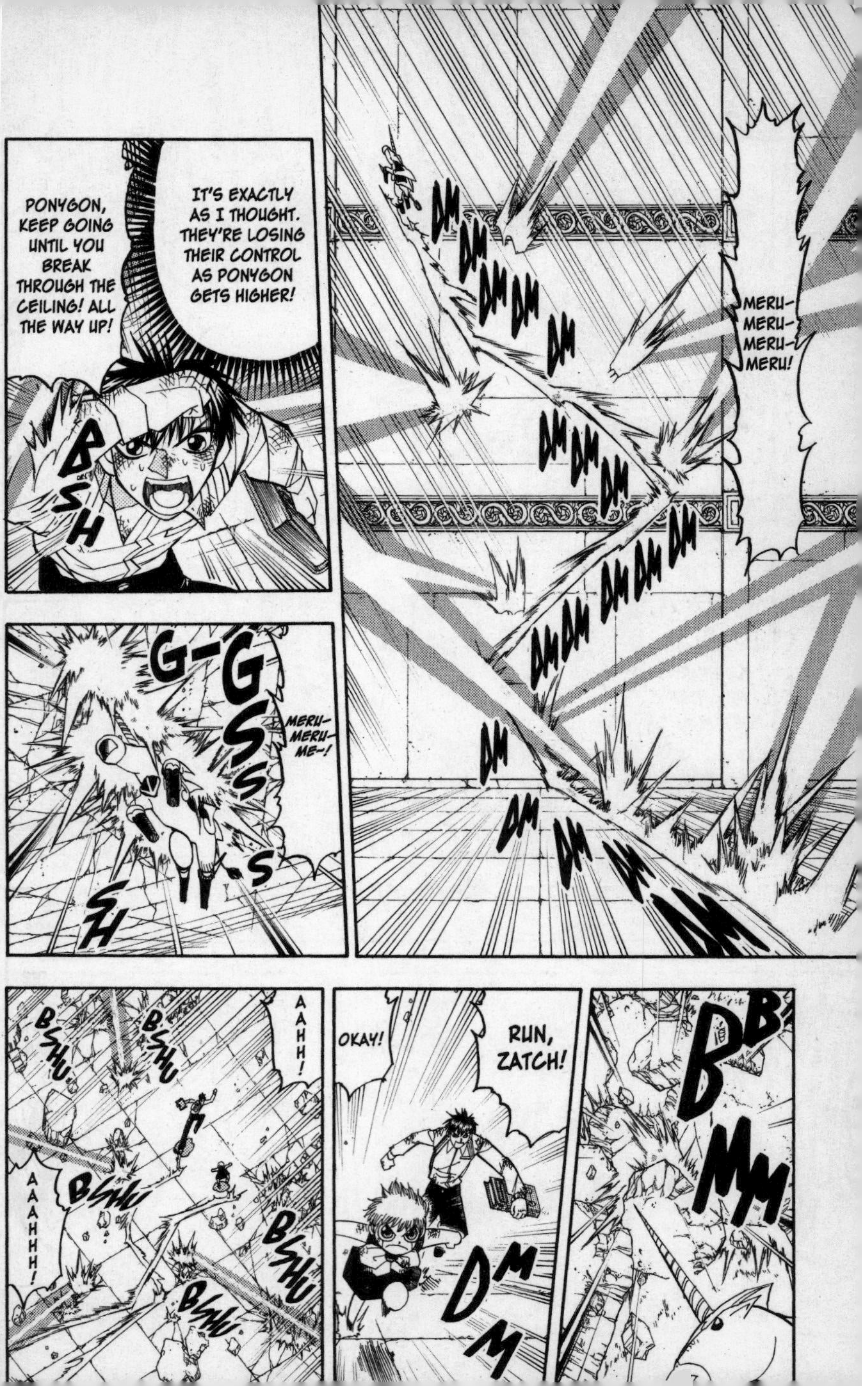

MERU-MERU-MERU-MERU!
DM DM DM DM DM DM DM DM DM DM DM DM DM DM DM DM DM DM DM
IT'S EXACTLY AS I THOUGHT. THEY'RE LOSING THEIR CONTROL AS PONYGON GETS HIGHER!
PONYGON, KEEP GOING UNTIL YOU BREAK THROUGH THE CEILING! ALL THE WAY UP!
BASH
G-G
MERU-MERU ME-!
SSSSH
BBMMM
RUN, ZATCH!
OKAY!
DMM
AAHH!
BSHU BSHU
AAAHHH!
BSHU BSHU BSHU

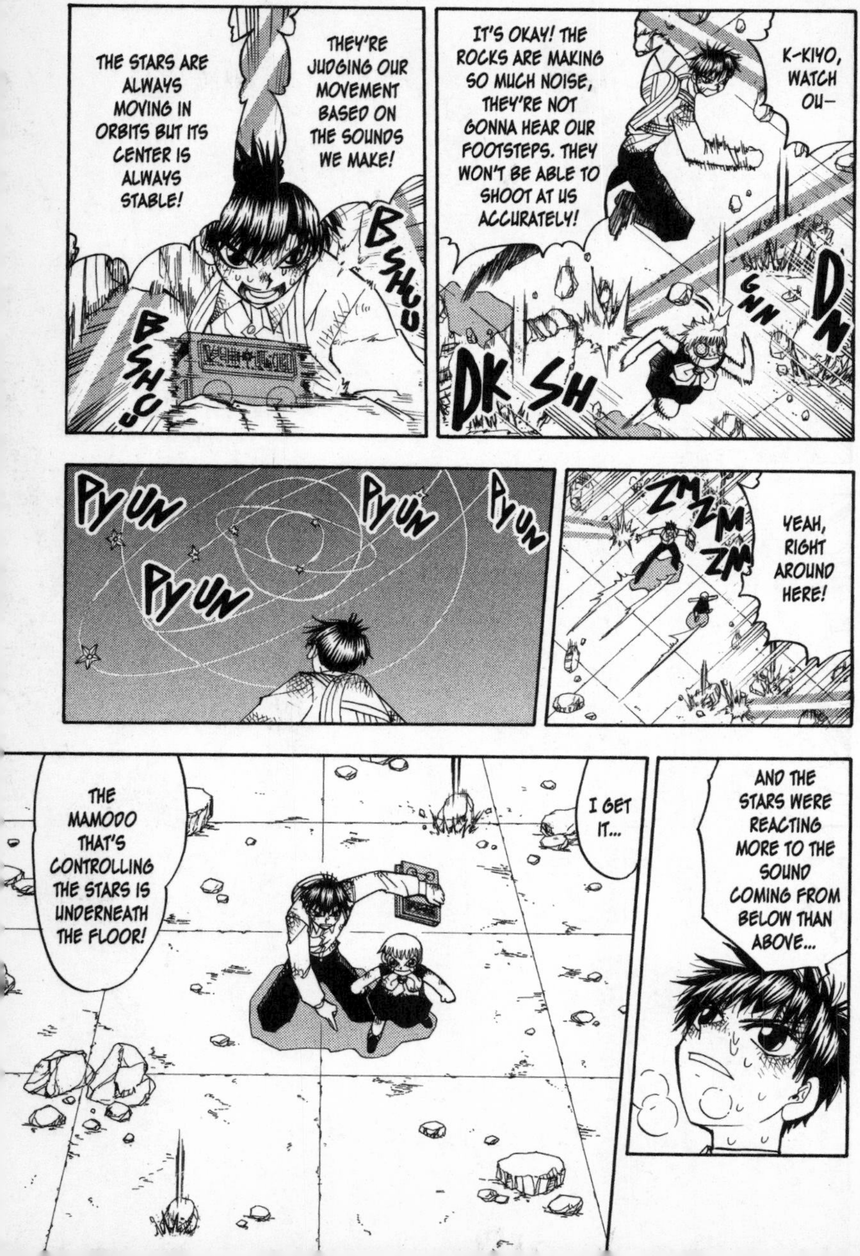
K-KIYO, WATCH OU—
IT'S OKAY! THE ROCKS ARE MAKING SO MUCH NOISE, THEY'RE NOT GONNA HEAR OUR FOOTSTEPS. THEY WON'T BE ABLE TO SHOOT AT US ACCURATELY!
DN
GNN
SH
DK
THEY'RE JUDGING OUR MOVEMENT BASED ON THE SOUNDS WE MAKE!
THE STARS ARE ALWAYS MOVING IN ORBITS BUT ITS CENTER IS ALWAYS STABLE!
BSHUU
BSHUU
ZMZMZM
YEAH, RIGHT AROUND HERE!
PYUN
PYUN
PYUN
PYUN
AND THE STARS WERE REACTING MORE TO THE SOUND COMING FROM BELOW THAN ABOVE...
I GET IT...
THE MAMODO THAT'S CONTROLLING THE STARS IS UNDERNEATH THE FLOOR!

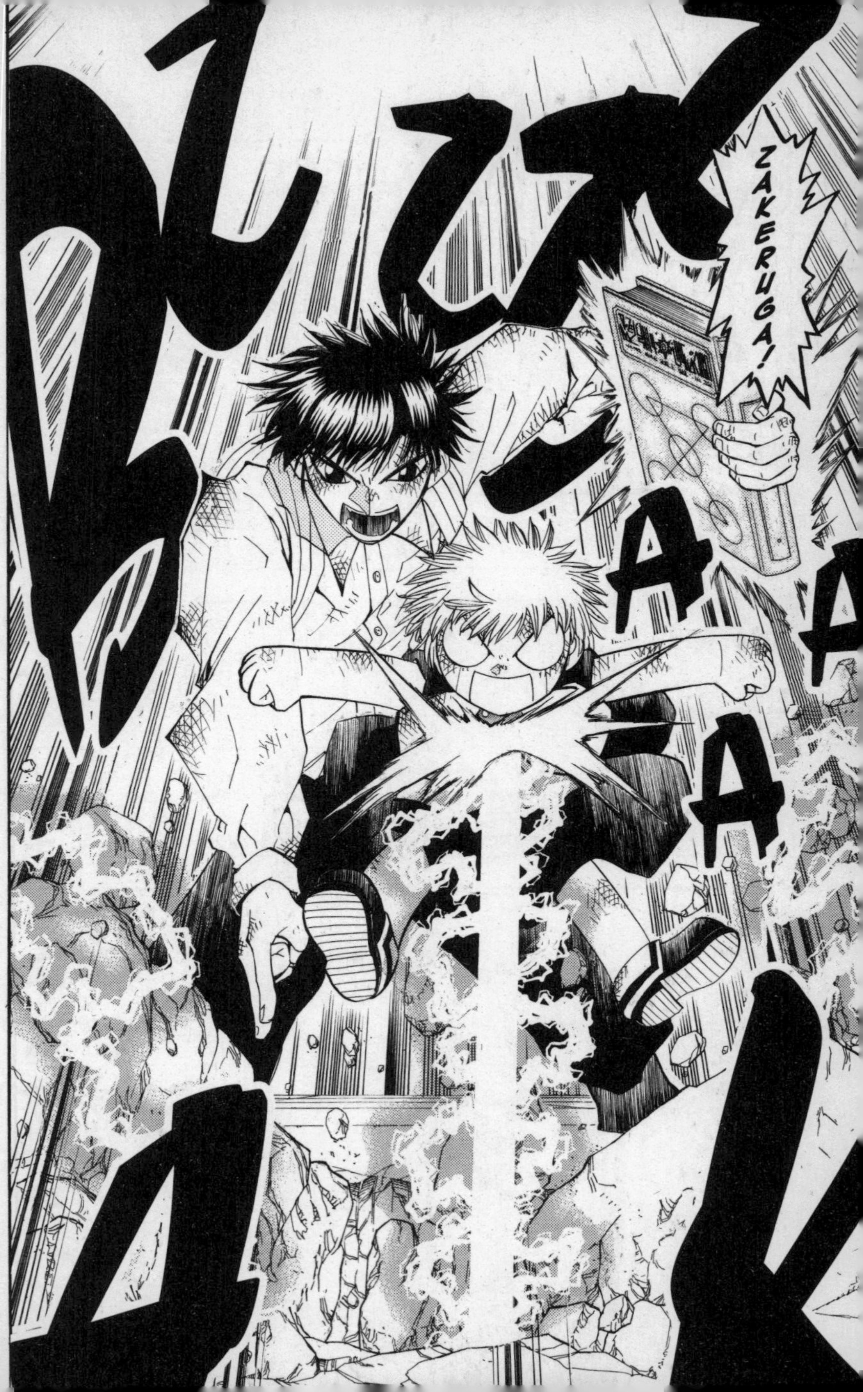
ZAKERUGA!
AAAA

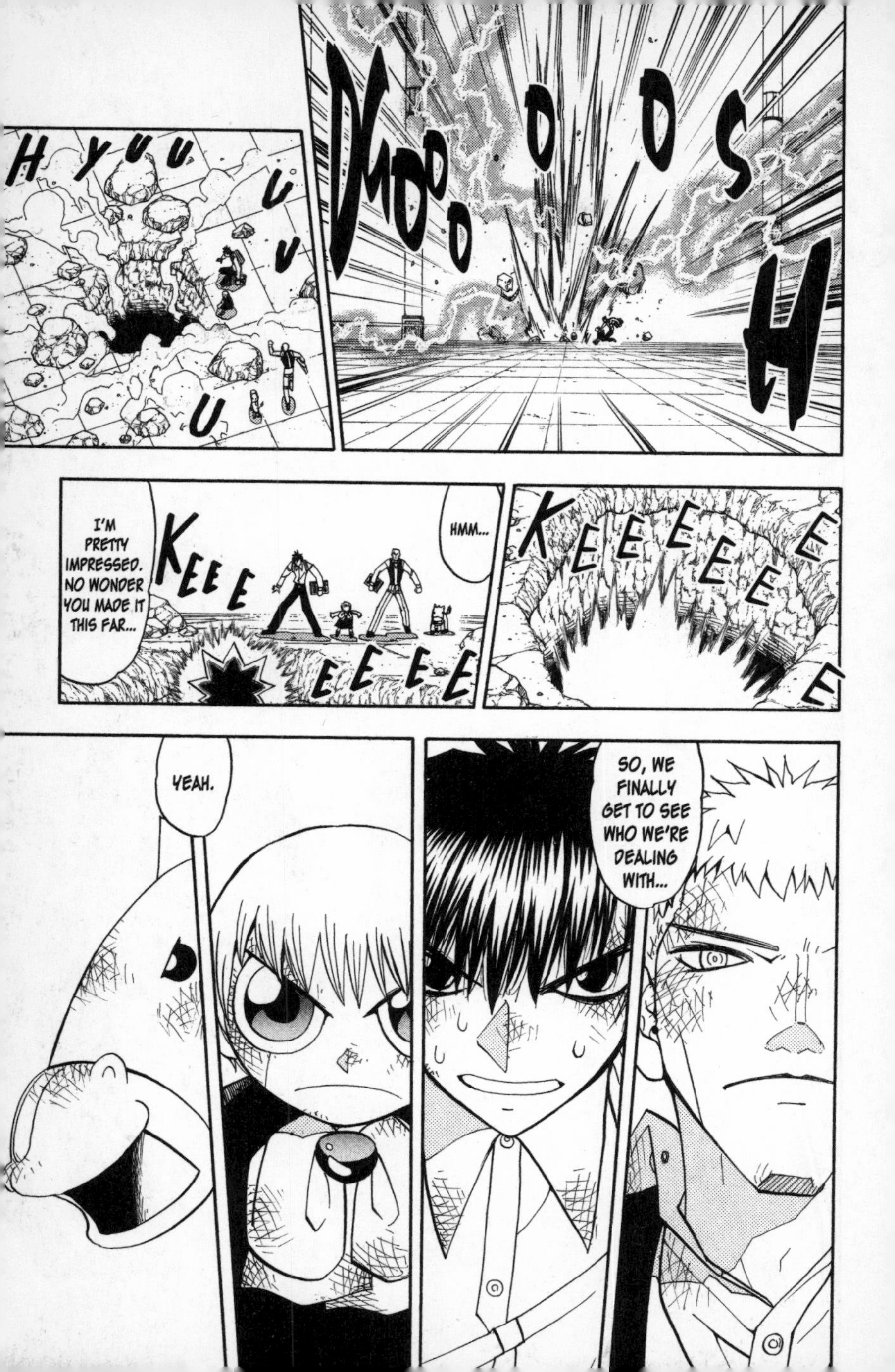
DOOOOOSH
HYUUUUUU
KEEEEEEEE
HMM...
I'M PRETTY IMPRESSED. NO WONDER YOU MADE IT THIS FAR...
KEEEEEEE
SO, WE FINALLY GET TO SEE WHO WE'RE DEALING WITH...
YEAH.

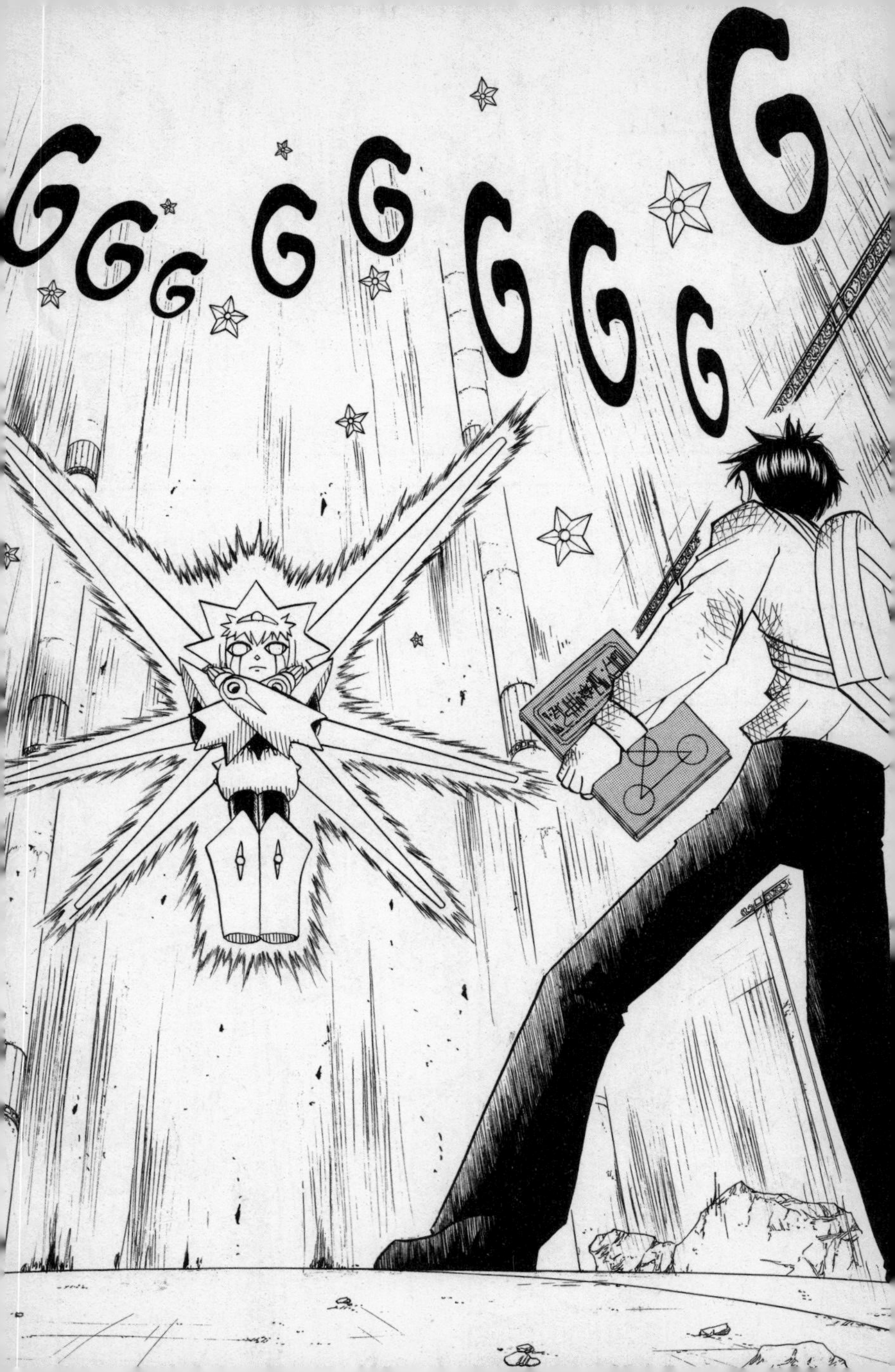
GGGGGGGGGG

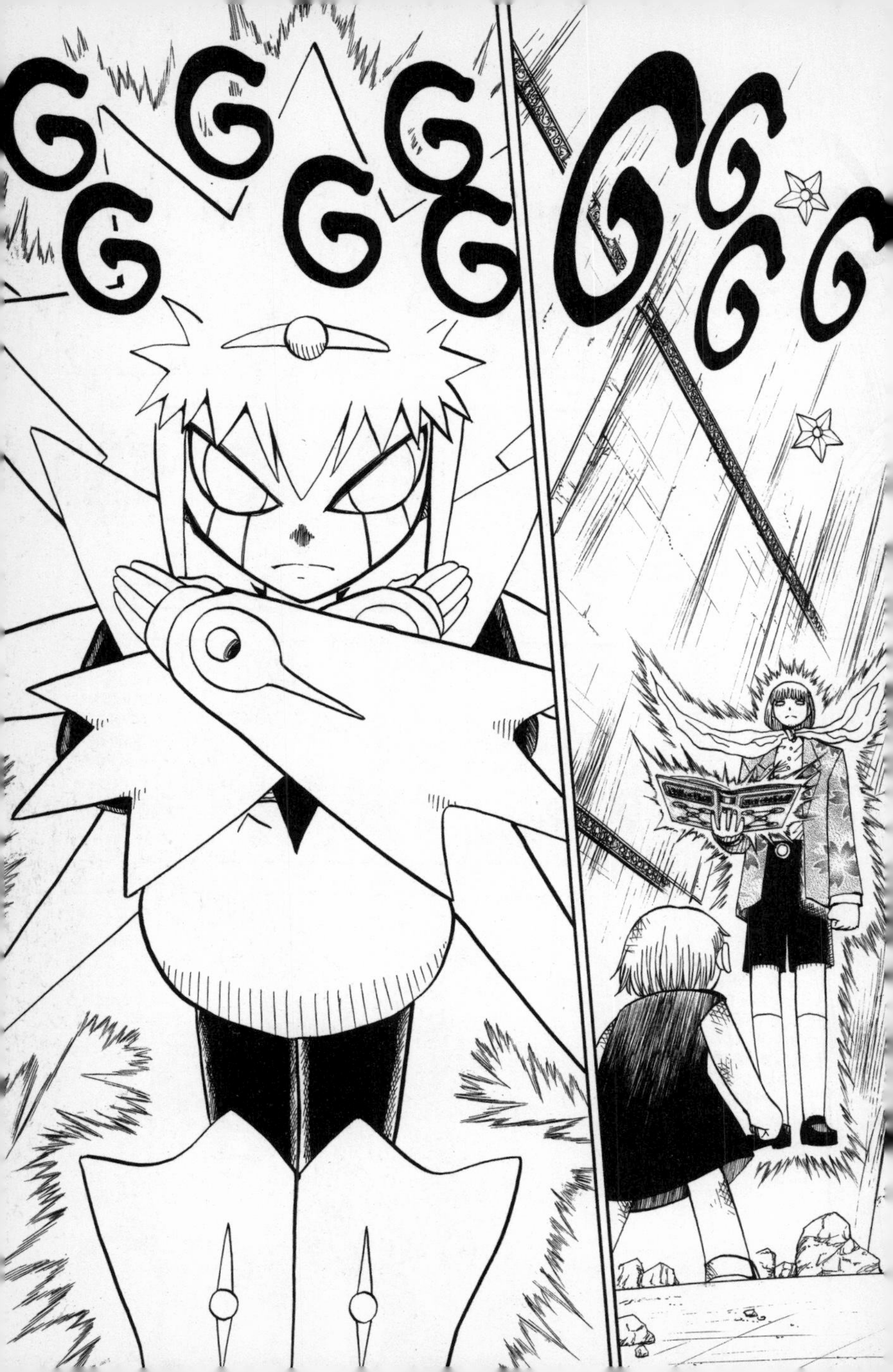
GGGGGGGGGGG

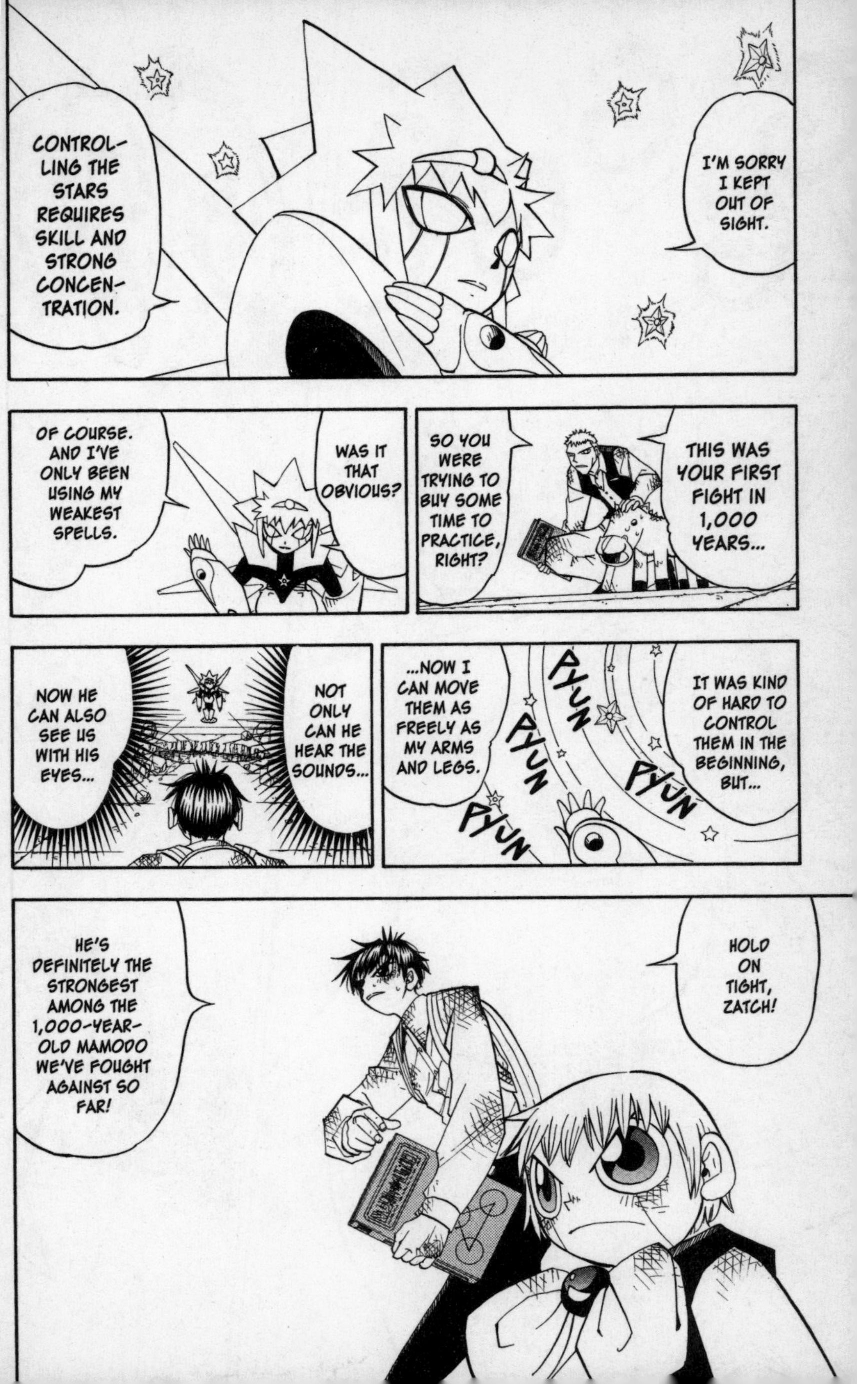
I'M SORRY I KEPT OUT OF SIGHT.
CONTROLLING THE STARS REQUIRES SKILL AND STRONG CONCENTRATION.
THIS WAS YOUR FIRST FIGHT IN 1,000 YEARS...
SO YOU WERE TRYING TO BUY SOME TIME TO PRACTICE, RIGHT?
WAS IT THAT OBVIOUS?
OF COURSE. AND I'VE ONLY BEEN USING MY WEAKEST SPELLS.
IT WAS KIND OF HARD TO CONTROL THEM IN THE BEGINNING, BUT...
PYUN
PYUN
PYUN
PYUN
...NOW I CAN MOVE THEM AS FREELY AS MY ARMS AND LEGS.
NOT ONLY CAN HE HEAR THE SOUNDS...
NOW HE CAN ALSO SEE US WITH HIS EYES...
HOLD ON TIGHT, ZATCH!
HE'S DEFINITELY THE STRONGEST AMONG THE 1,000-YEAR-OLD MAMODO WE'VE FOUGHT AGAINST SO FAR!

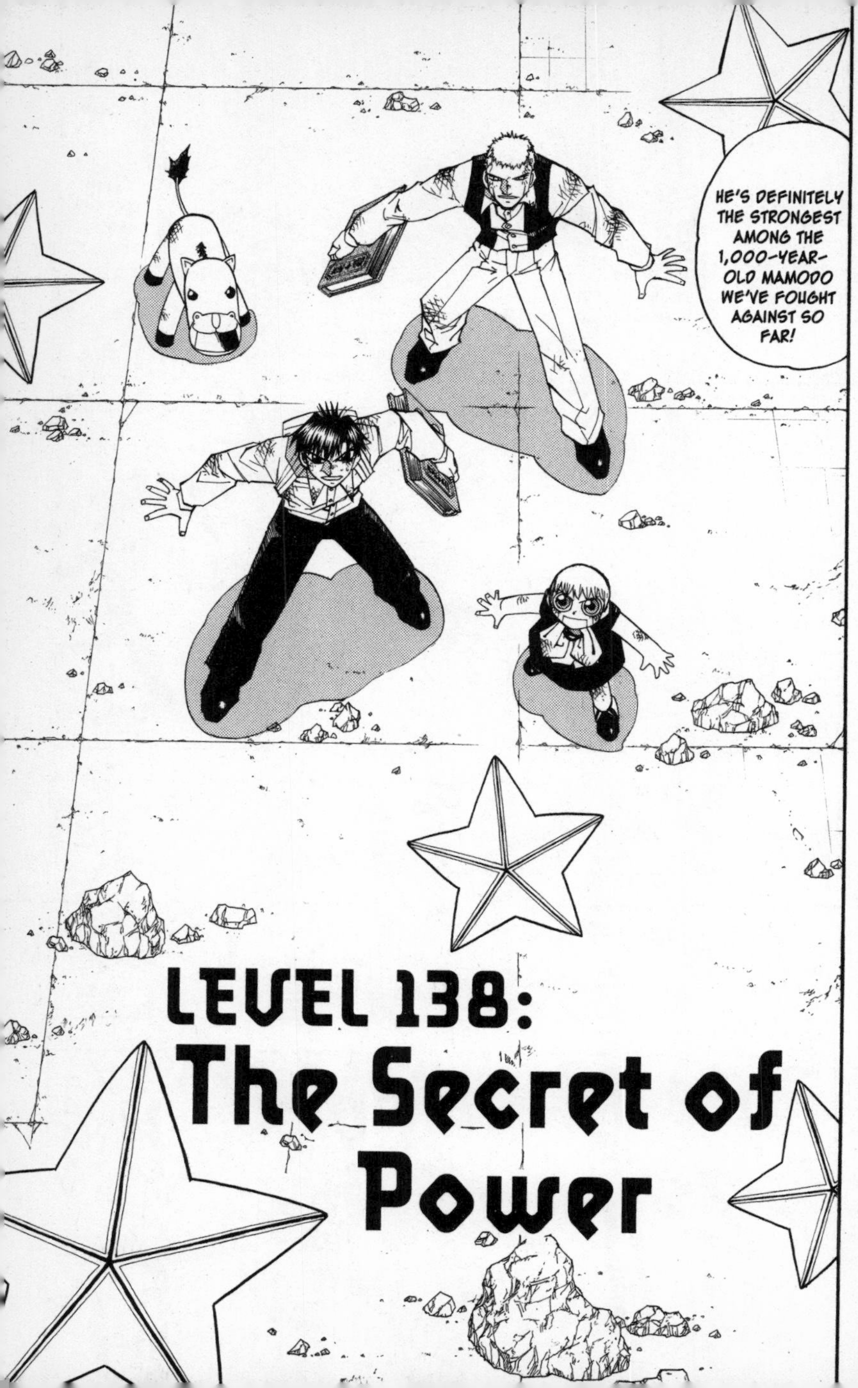
HE'S DEFINITELY THE STRONGEST AMONG THE 1,000-YEAR-OLD MAMODO WE'VE FOUGHT AGAINST SO FAR!
LEVEL 138:
The Secret of Power

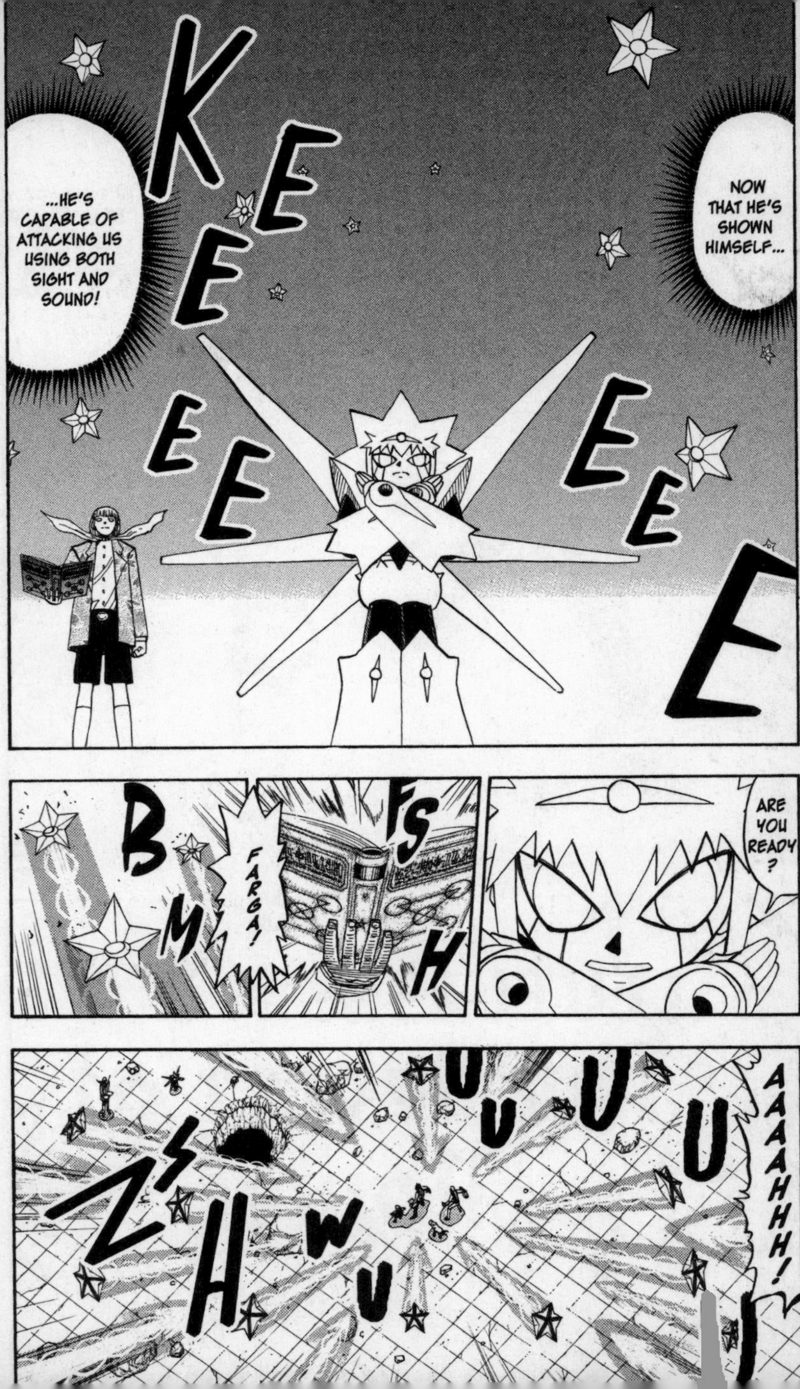
NOW THAT HE'S SHOWN HIMSELF...
...HE'S CAPABLE OF ATTACKING US USING BOTH SIGHT AND SOUND!
KEEEEEEEE
ARE YOU READY?
FARGA!
FSH
BM
AAAAAHHH!
UUUUU
ZSHWU

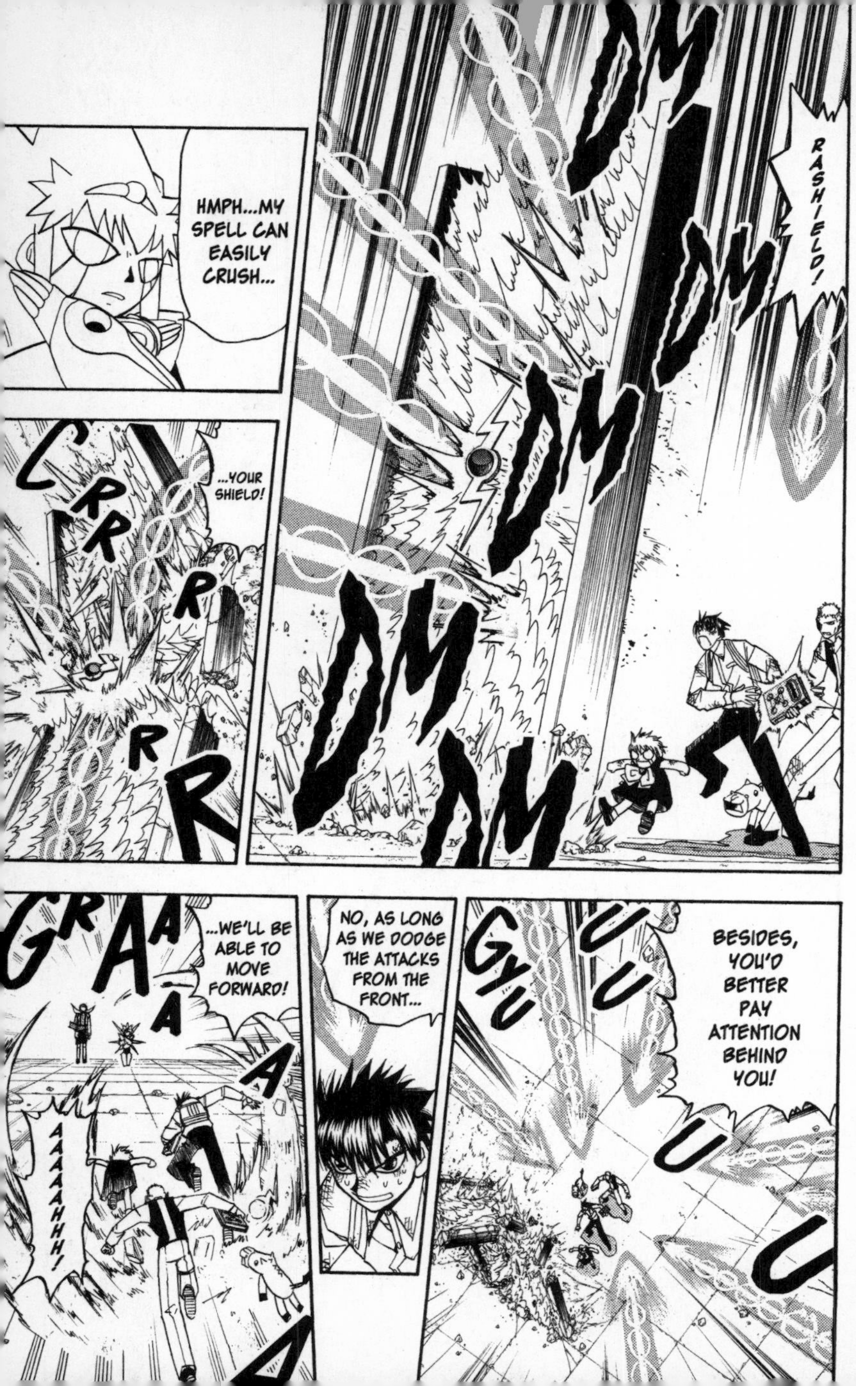
RASHIELD!
DM DM DM DM DM
HMPH...MY SPELL CAN EASILY CRUSH...
CRRRRR
...YOUR SHIELD!
GYUUUUUU
BESIDES, YOU'D BETTER PAY ATTENTION BEHIND YOU!
NO, AS LONG AS WE DODGE THE ATTACKS FROM THE FRONT...
GRAAAAA
...WE'LL BE ABLE TO MOVE FORWARD!
AAAAAAHHH!

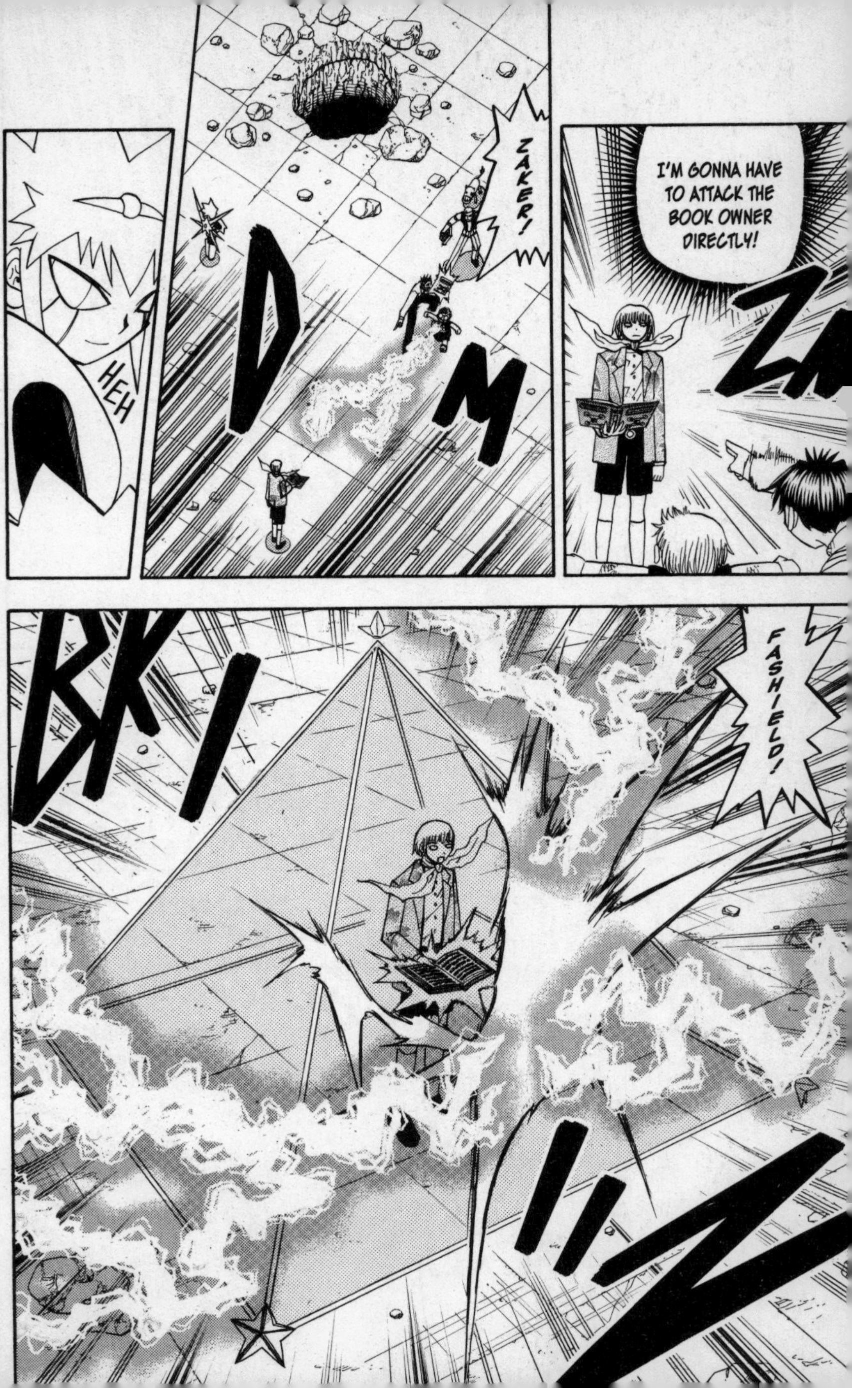
I'M GONNA HAVE TO ATTACK THE BOOK OWNER DIRECTLY!
ZA
ZAKER!
D
M
HEH
FASHIELD!
BK
I
IN

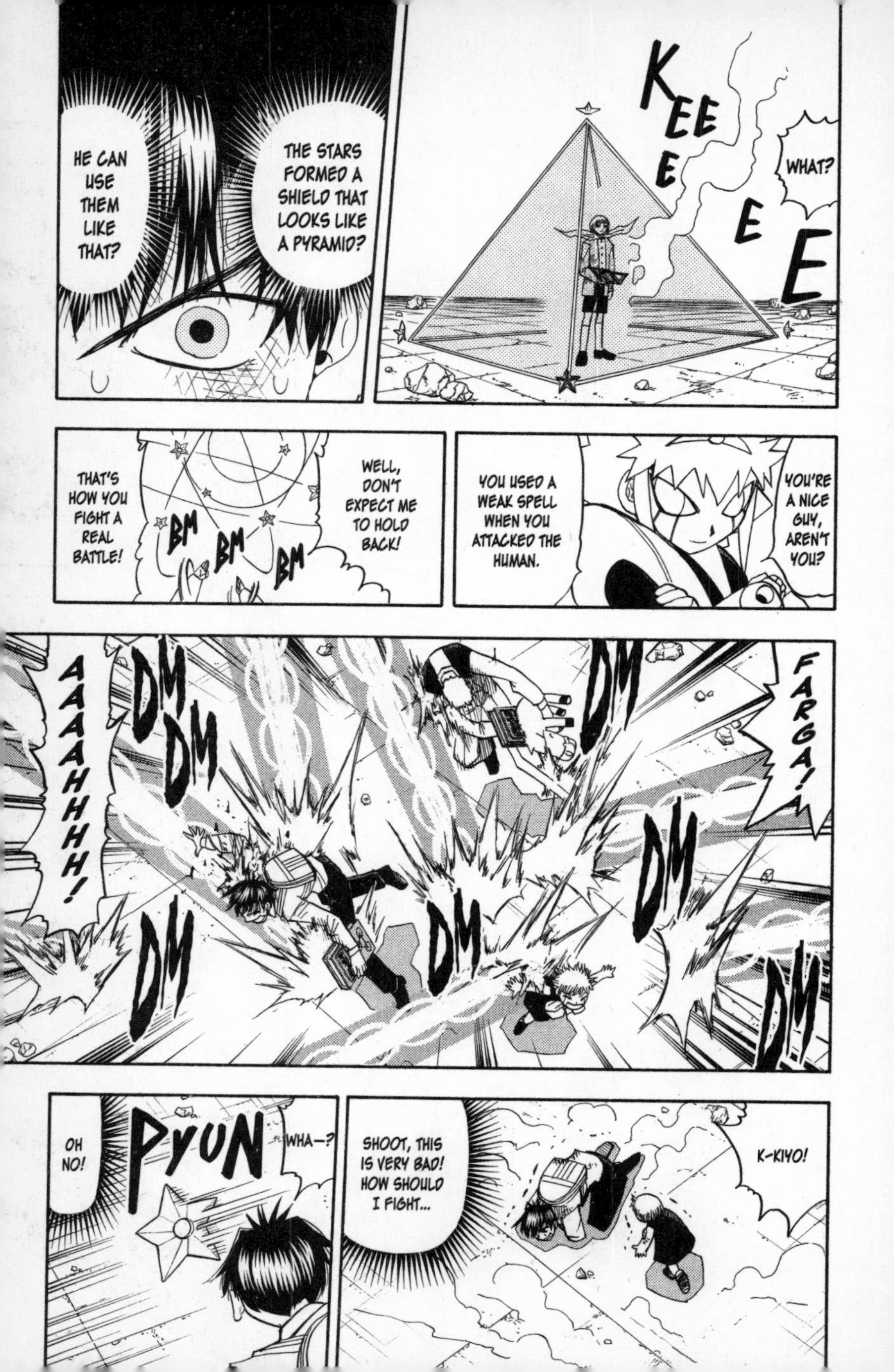
KEEEEEE
WHAT?
THE STARS FORMED A SHIELD THAT LOOKS LIKE A PYRAMID?
HE CAN USE THEM LIKE THAT?
YOU'RE A NICE GUY, AREN'T YOU?
YOU USED A WEAK SPELL WHEN YOU ATTACKED THE HUMAN.
WELL, DON'T EXPECT ME TO HOLD BACK!
THAT'S HOW YOU FIGHT A REAL BATTLE!
BM BM BM
FARGA!
DM DM DM DM DM DM DM
AAAAHHHH!
K-KIYO!
SHOOT, THIS IS VERY BAD! HOW SHOULD I FIGHT...
WHA—?
PYUN
OH NO!

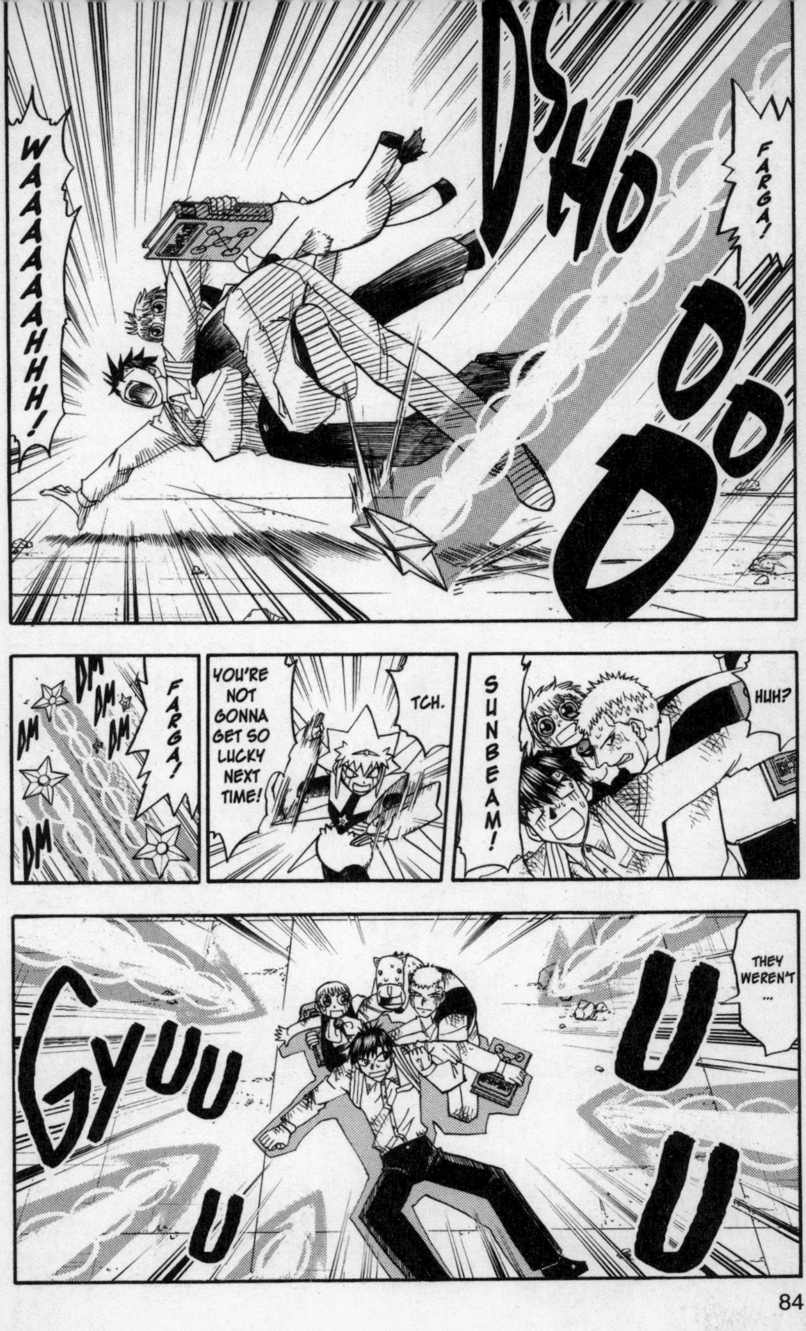
FARGA!
DSHOOOD
WAAAAAAAHHHH!
HUH?
SUNBEAM!
TCH.
YOU'RE NOT GONNA GET SO LUCKY NEXT TIME!
FARGA!
DM DM DM DM DM
THEY WEREN'T ...
UUU
GYUUU

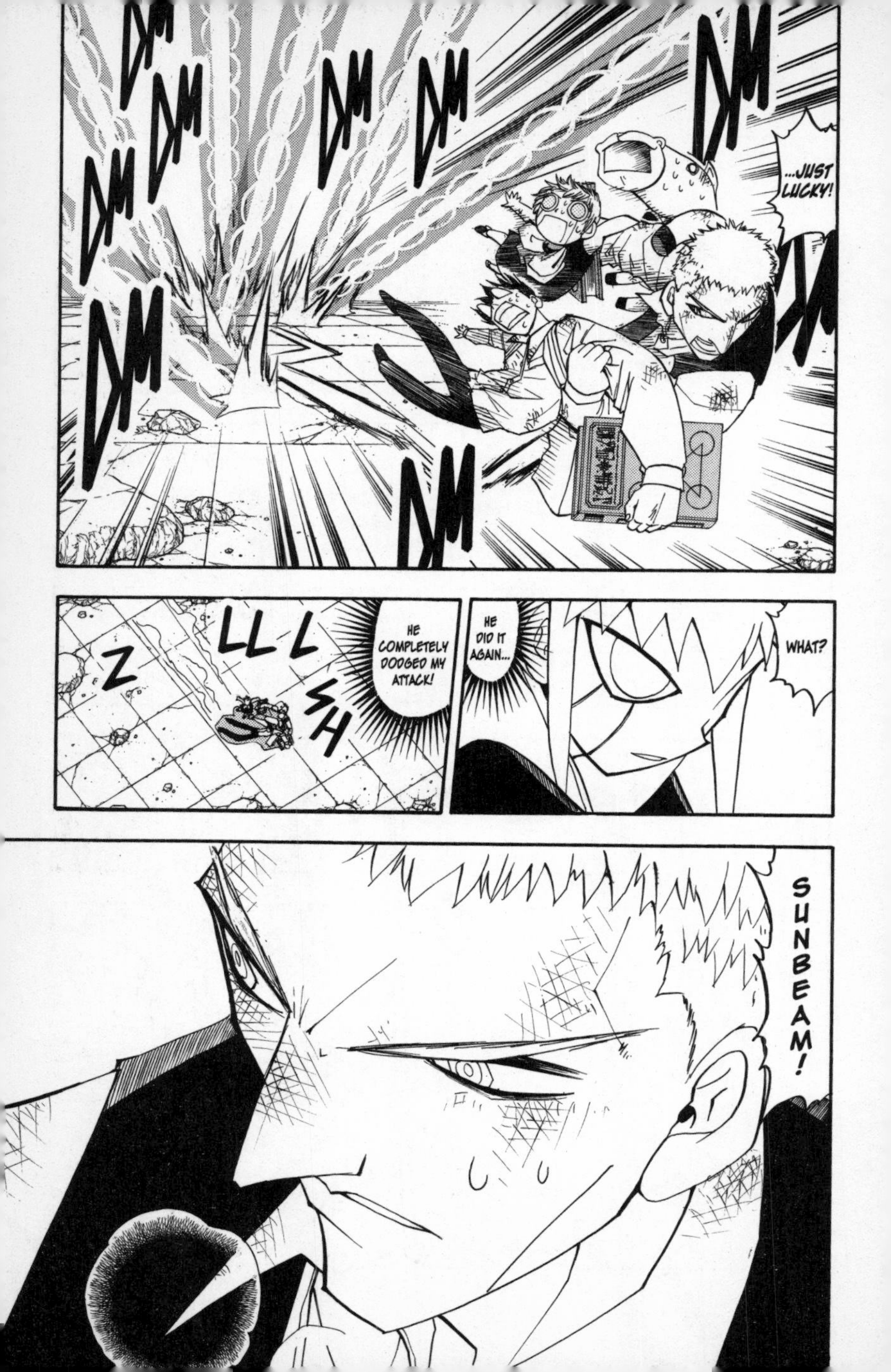

DM DM DM DM DM DM DM DM DM
...JUST LUCKY!
WHAT?
HE DID IT AGAIN...
HE COMPLETELY DODGED MY ATTACK!
ZLLLSH
SUNBEAM!

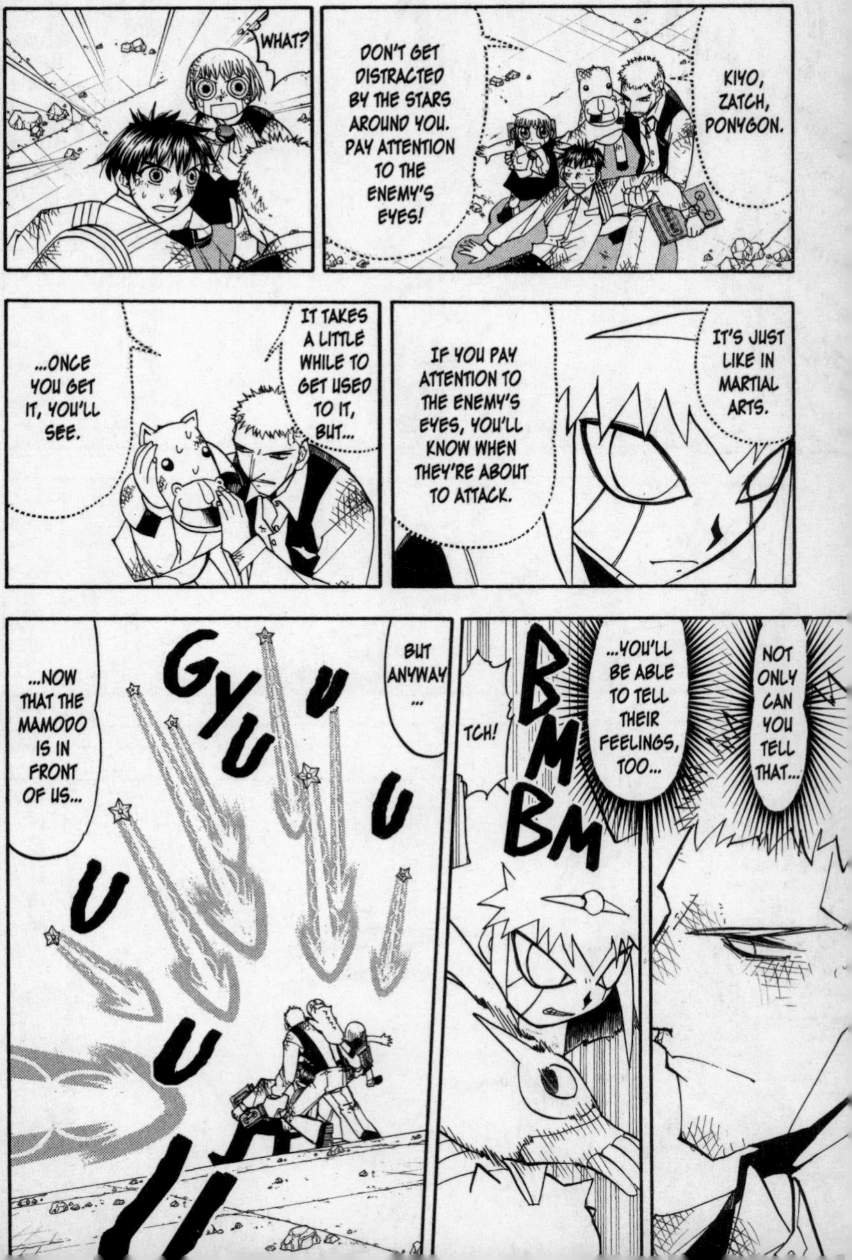
KIYO, ZATCH, PONYGON.
DON'T GET DISTRACTED BY THE STARS AROUND YOU. PAY ATTENTION TO THE ENEMY'S EYES!
WHAT?
IT'S JUST LIKE IN MARTIAL ARTS.
IF YOU PAY ATTENTION TO THE ENEMY'S EYES, YOU'LL KNOW WHEN THEY'RE ABOUT TO ATTACK.
IT TAKES A LITTLE WHILE TO GET USED TO IT, BUT...
...ONCE YOU GET IT, YOU'LL SEE.
NOT ONLY CAN YOU TELL THAT...
...YOU'LL BE ABLE TO TELL THEIR FEELINGS, TOO...
BMBM
TCH!
BUT ANYWAY...
...NOW THAT THE MAMODO IS IN FRONT OF US...
GYUUUUU!!

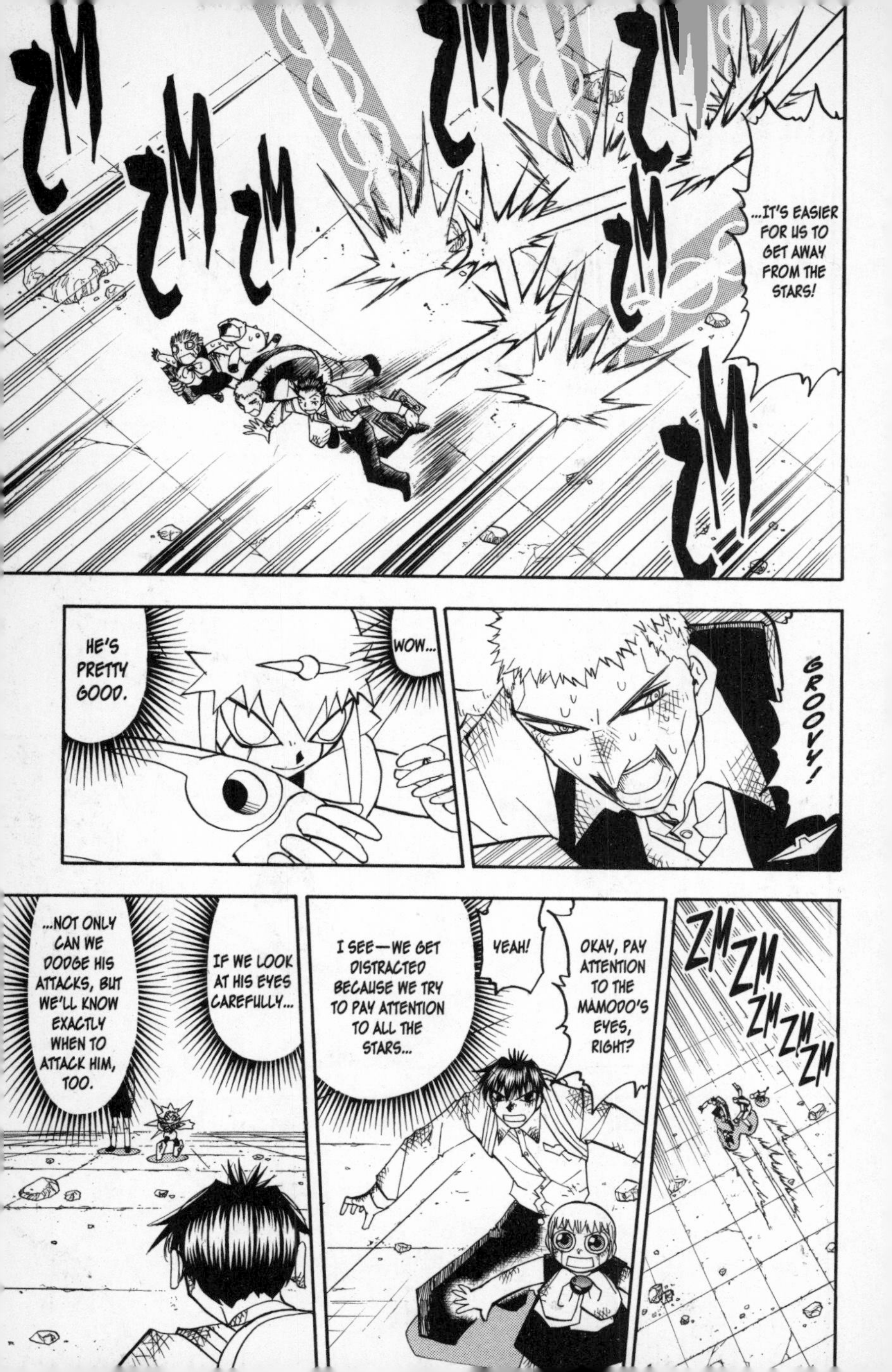
ZM ZM ZM ZM ZM ZM ZM ZM
...IT'S EASIER FOR US TO GET AWAY FROM THE STARS!
GROOVY!
WOW...
HE'S PRETTY GOOD.
ZM ZM ZM ZM ZM ZM ZM
OKAY, PAY ATTENTION TO THE MAMODO'S EYES, RIGHT?
YEAH!
I SEE—WE GET DISTRACTED BECAUSE WE TRY TO PAY ATTENTION TO ALL THE STARS...
IF WE LOOK AT HIS EYES CAREFULLY...
...NOT ONLY CAN WE DODGE HIS ATTACKS, BUT WE'LL KNOW EXACTLY WHEN TO ATTACK HIM, TOO.

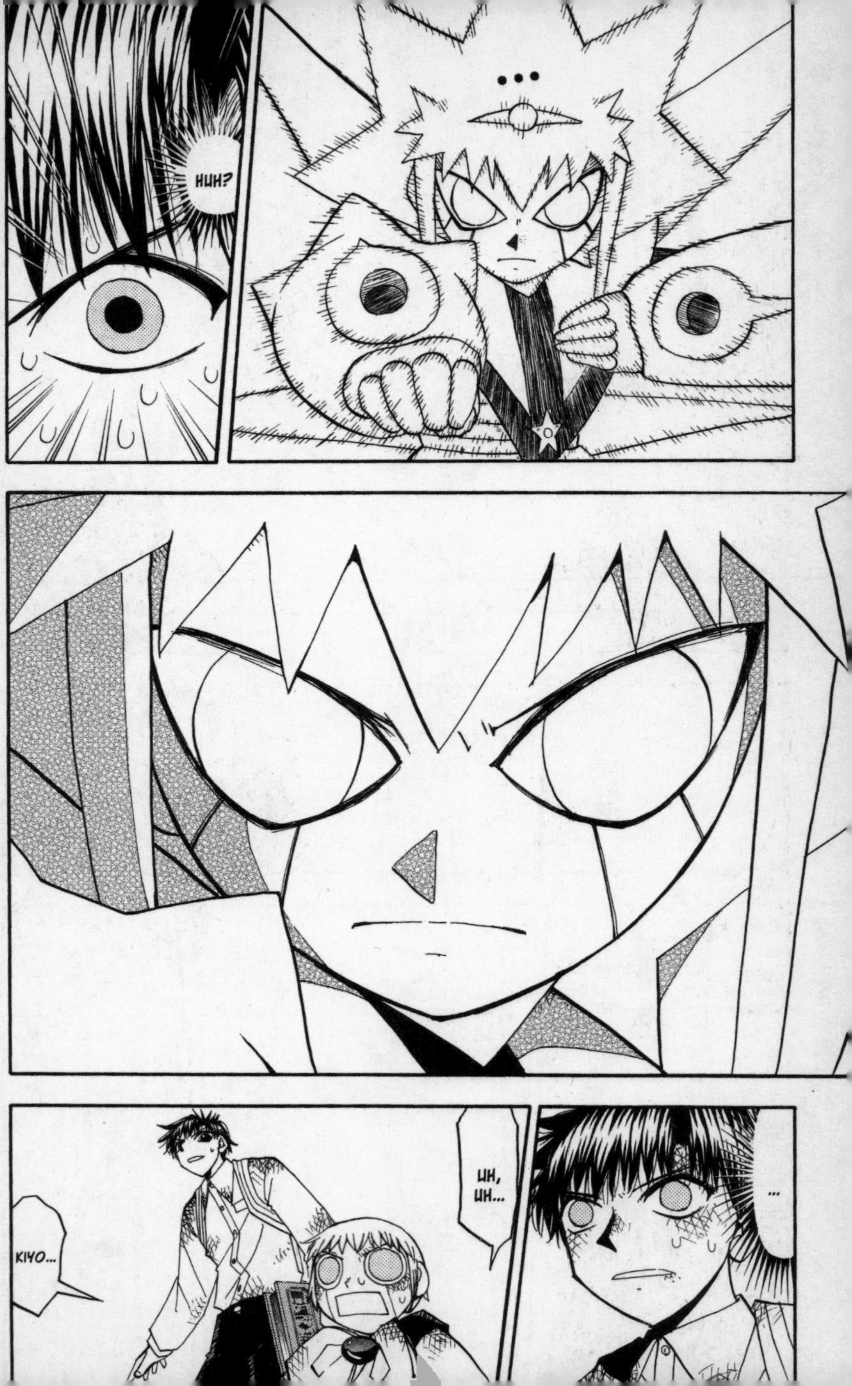

...
HUH?
...
UH, UH...
KIYO...

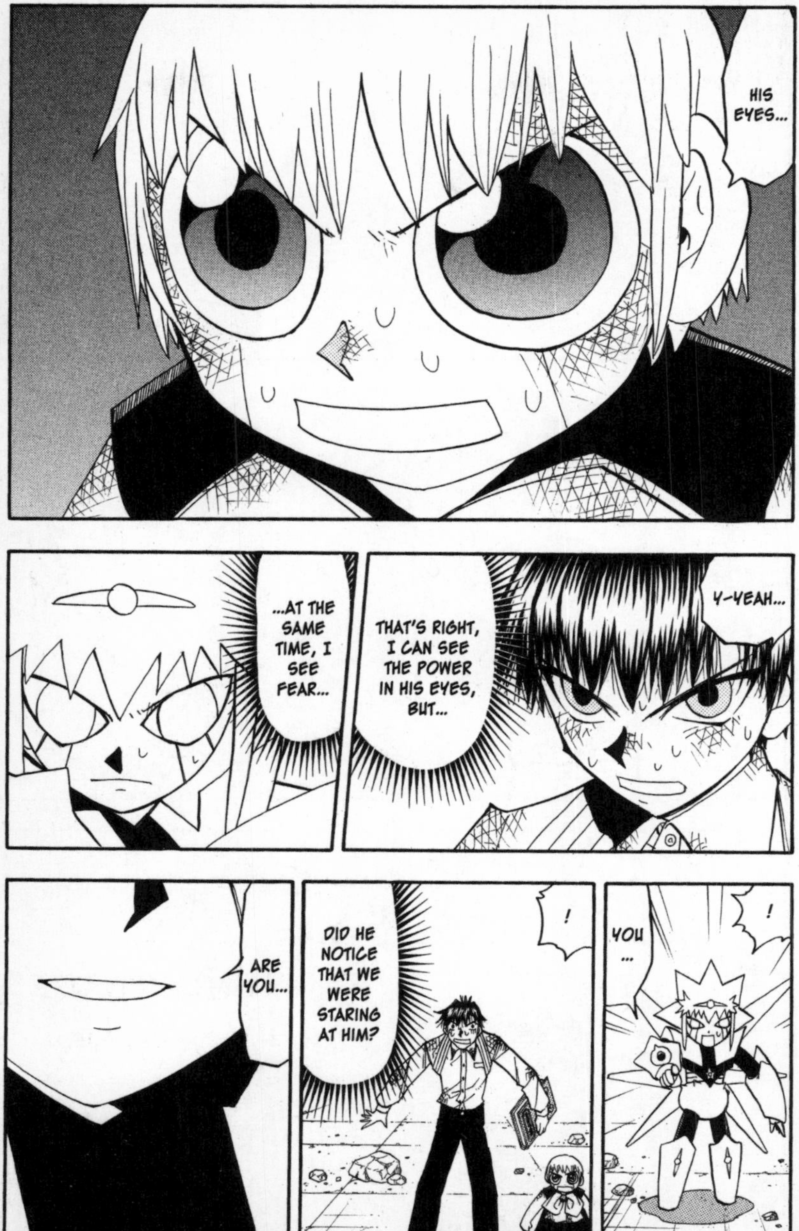
HIS EYES...
Y-YEAH...
THAT'S RIGHT, I CAN SEE THE POWER IN HIS EYES, BUT...
...AT THE SAME TIME, I SEE FEAR...
!
YOU ...
!
DID HE NOTICE THAT WE WERE STARING AT HIM?
ARE YOU...

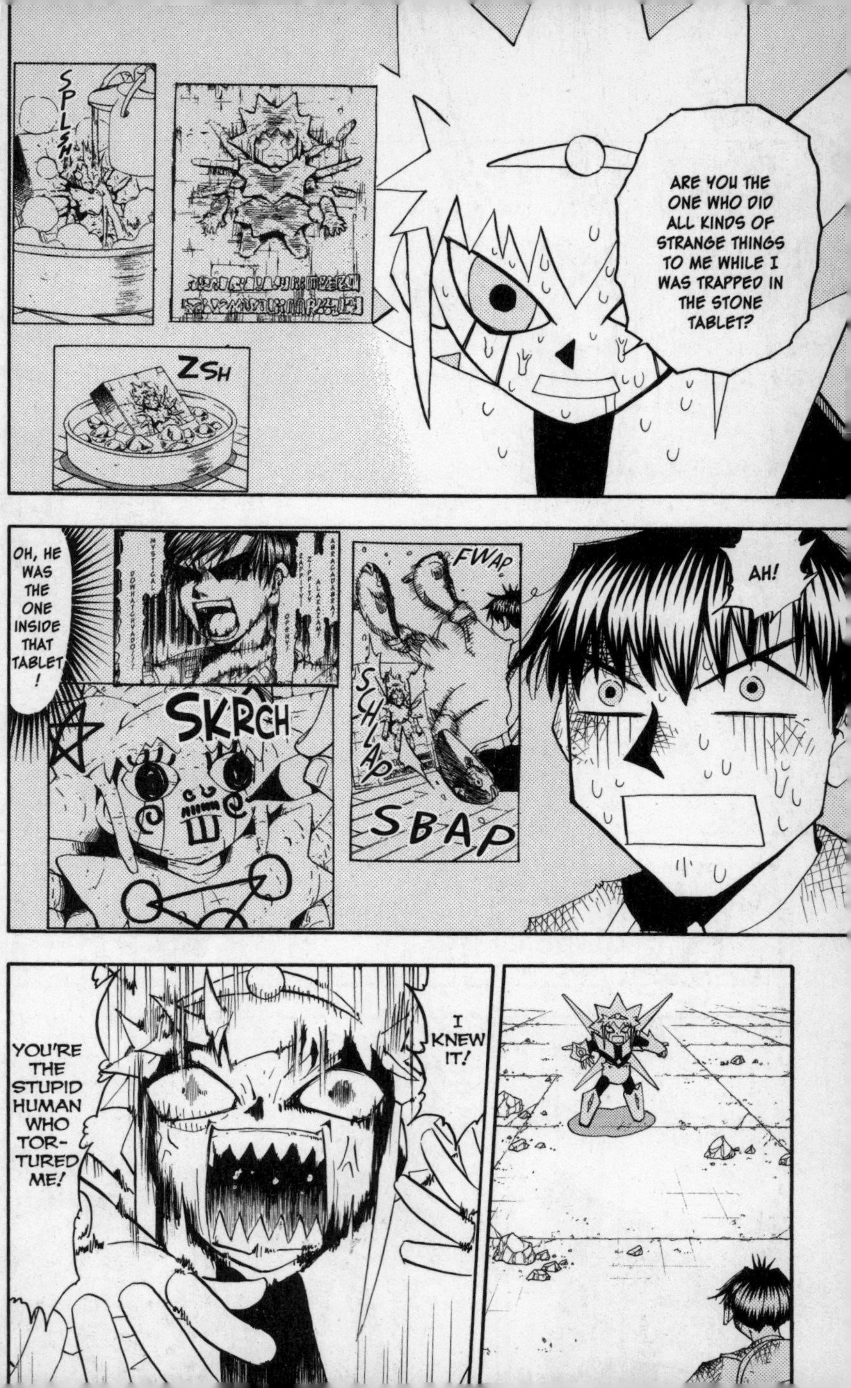
ARE YOU THE ONE WHO DID ALL KINDS OF STRANGE THINGS TO ME WHILE I WAS TRAPPED IN THE STONE TABLET?
SPLSH
ZSH
AH!
FWAP
SCHLAP
SBAP
ABRACADABRA! ALAKAZAM! ZIPPITY ZAPPITY OPEN! MYSTICAL DOWHATCHYADOO!!
OH, HE WAS THE ONE INSIDE THAT TABLET!
SKRCH
I KNEW IT!
YOU'RE THE STUPID HUMAN WHO TOR-TURED ME!

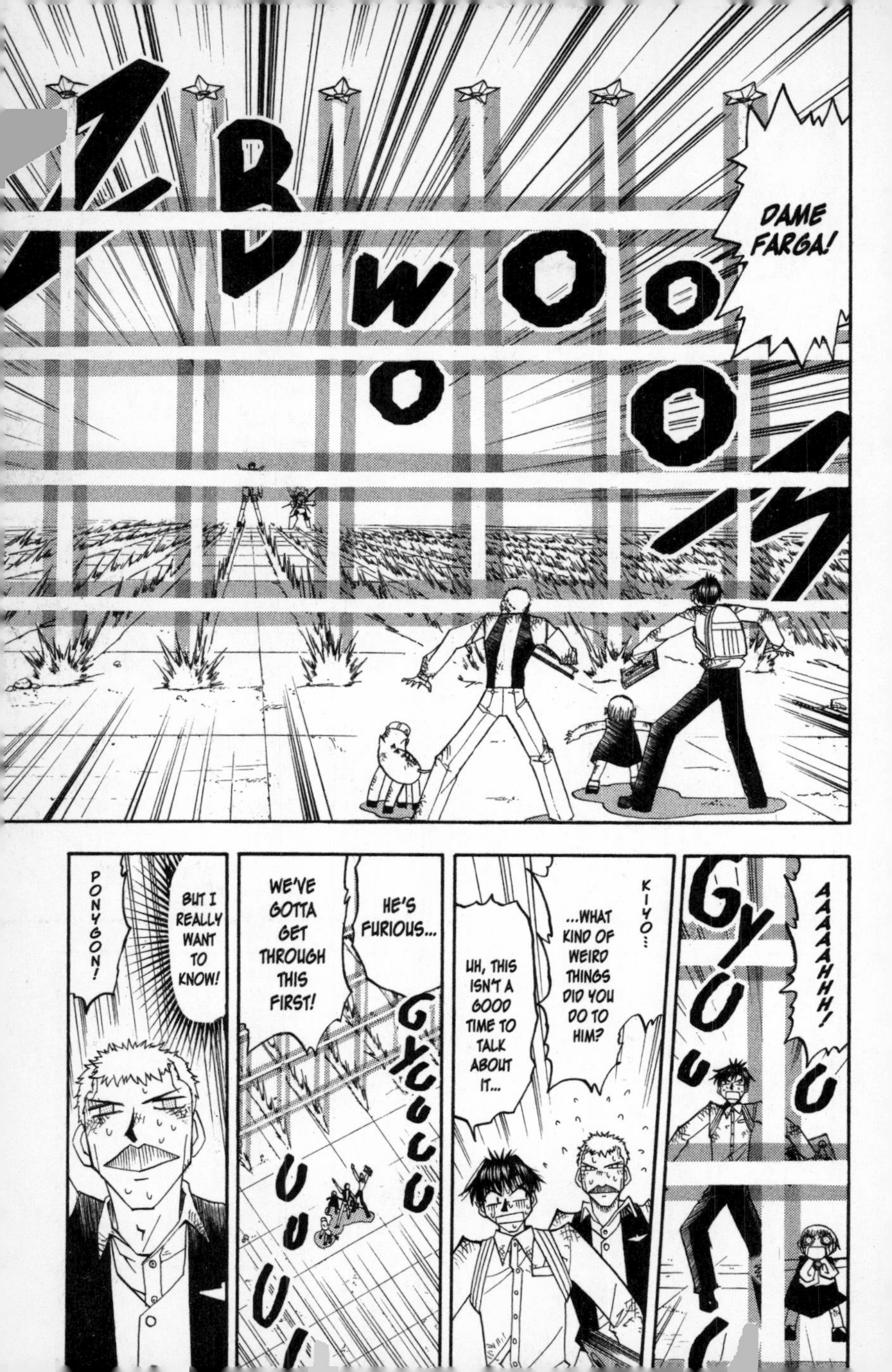

DAME FARGA!
BWOOOOM
AAAAAAHHH!
GYUUUU
KIYO...
...WHAT KIND OF WEIRD THINGS DID YOU DO TO HIM?
UH, THIS ISN'T A GOOD TIME TO TALK ABOUT IT...
HE'S FURIOUS...
WE'VE GOTTA GET THROUGH THIS FIRST!
GYUUUUUUU
BUT I REALLY WANT TO KNOW!
PONYGON!

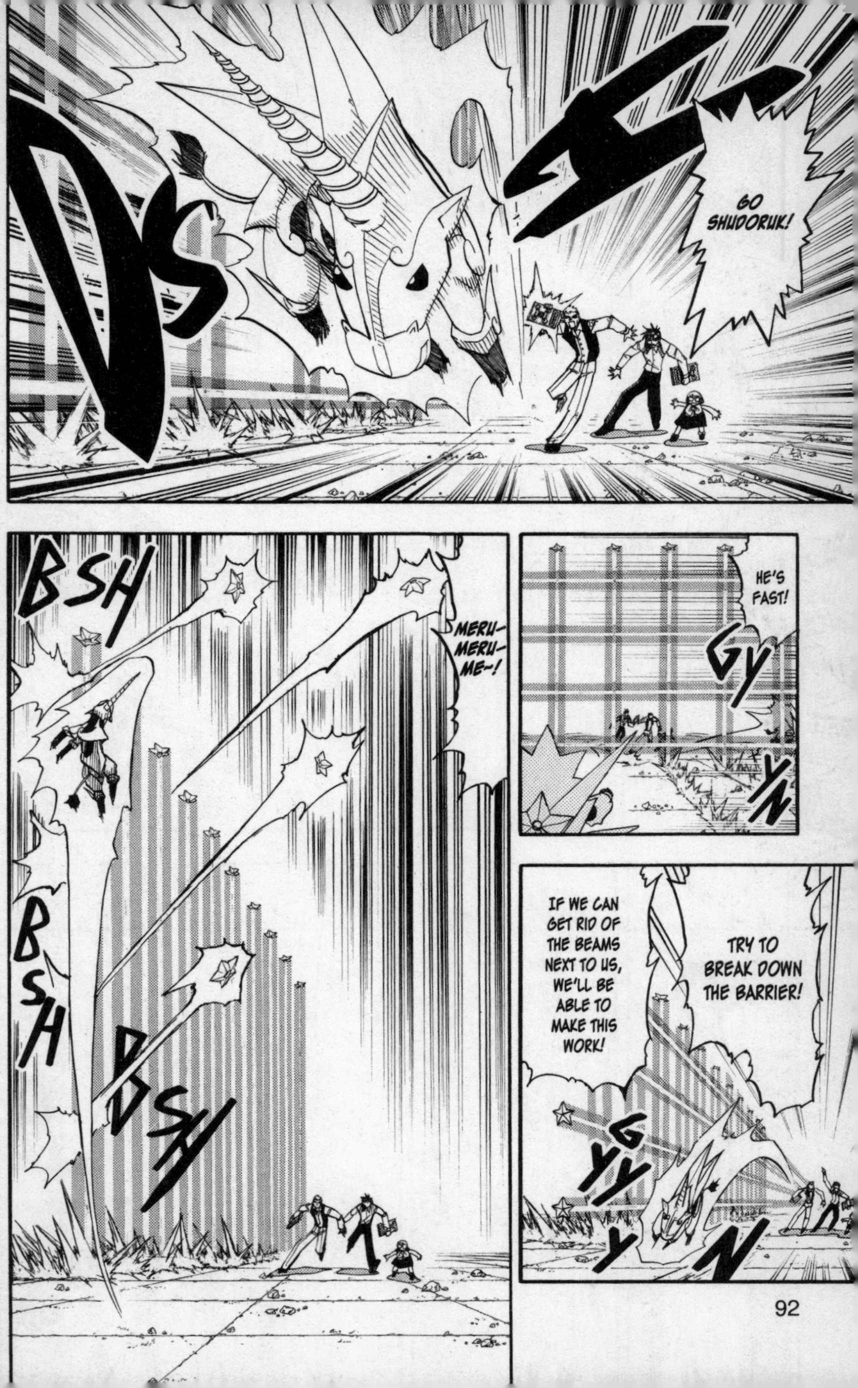
GO SHUDORUK!
DS
HE'S FAST!
GYYN
TRY TO BREAK DOWN THE BARRIER!
IF WE CAN GET RID OF THE BEAMS NEXT TO US, WE'LL BE ABLE TO MAKE THIS WORK!
GYYYN
MERU-MERU-ME~!
BSH
BSH
BSH

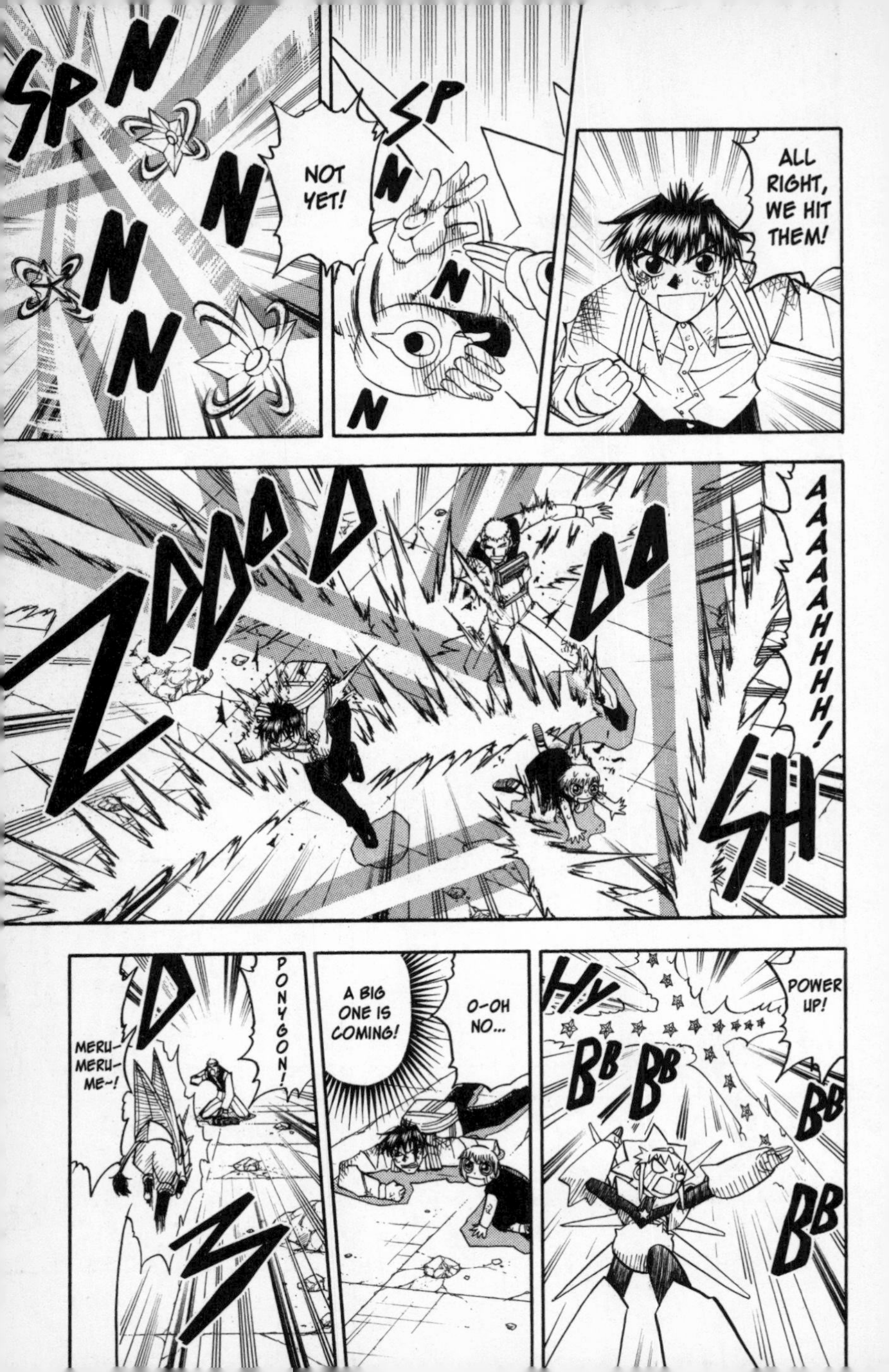
ALL RIGHT, WE HIT THEM!
NOT YET!
SPNNN
SPNNNNN
AAAAAHHHHH!
SH
DD
ZDDDDD
POWER UP!
HY
BB
BB
BB
BB
O-OH NO...
A BIG ONE IS COMING!
PONYGON!
D
MERU-MERU-ME~!
ZN

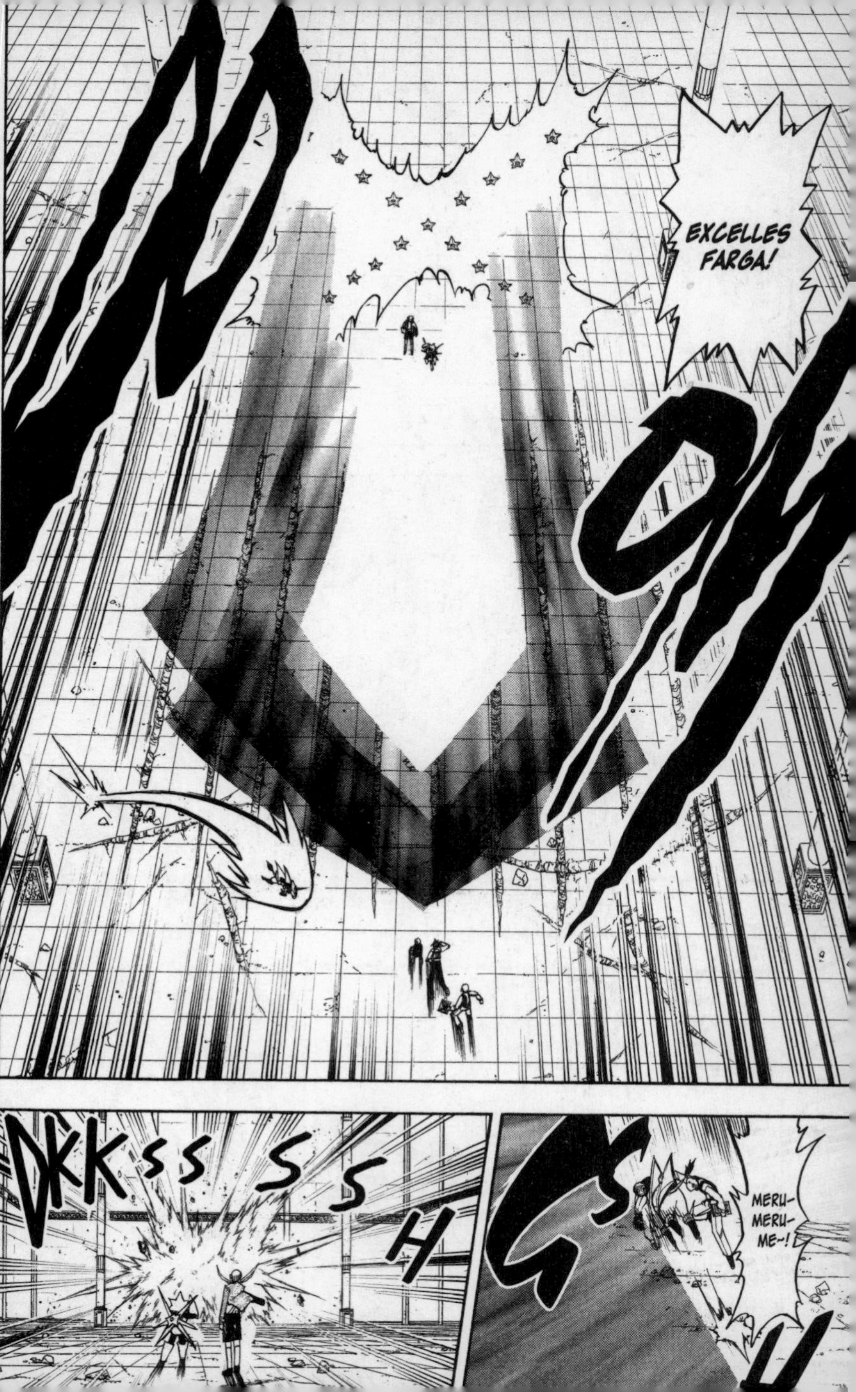
EXCELLES FARGA!
MERU-MERU-ME~!
DKKSSSSH

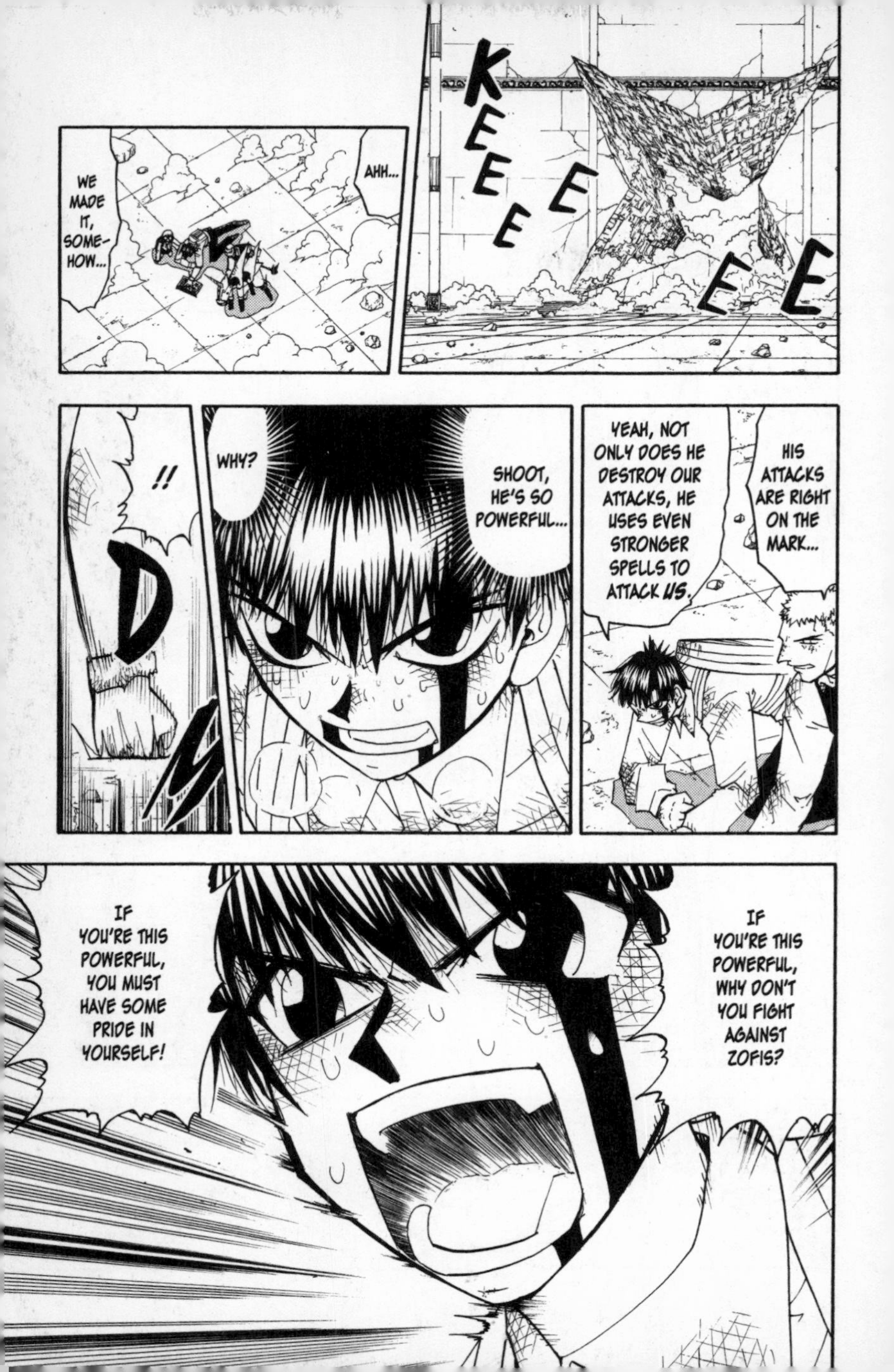
KEEEEEE
AHH...
WE MADE IT, SOME-HOW...
HIS ATTACKS ARE RIGHT ON THE MARK...
YEAH, NOT ONLY DOES HE DESTROY OUR ATTACKS, HE USES EVEN STRONGER SPELLS TO ATTACK US.
SHOOT, HE'S SO POWERFUL...
WHY?
!!
IF YOU'RE THIS POWERFUL, WHY DON'T YOU FIGHT AGAINST ZOFIS?
IF YOU'RE THIS POWERFUL, YOU MUST HAVE SOME PRIDE IN YOURSELF!

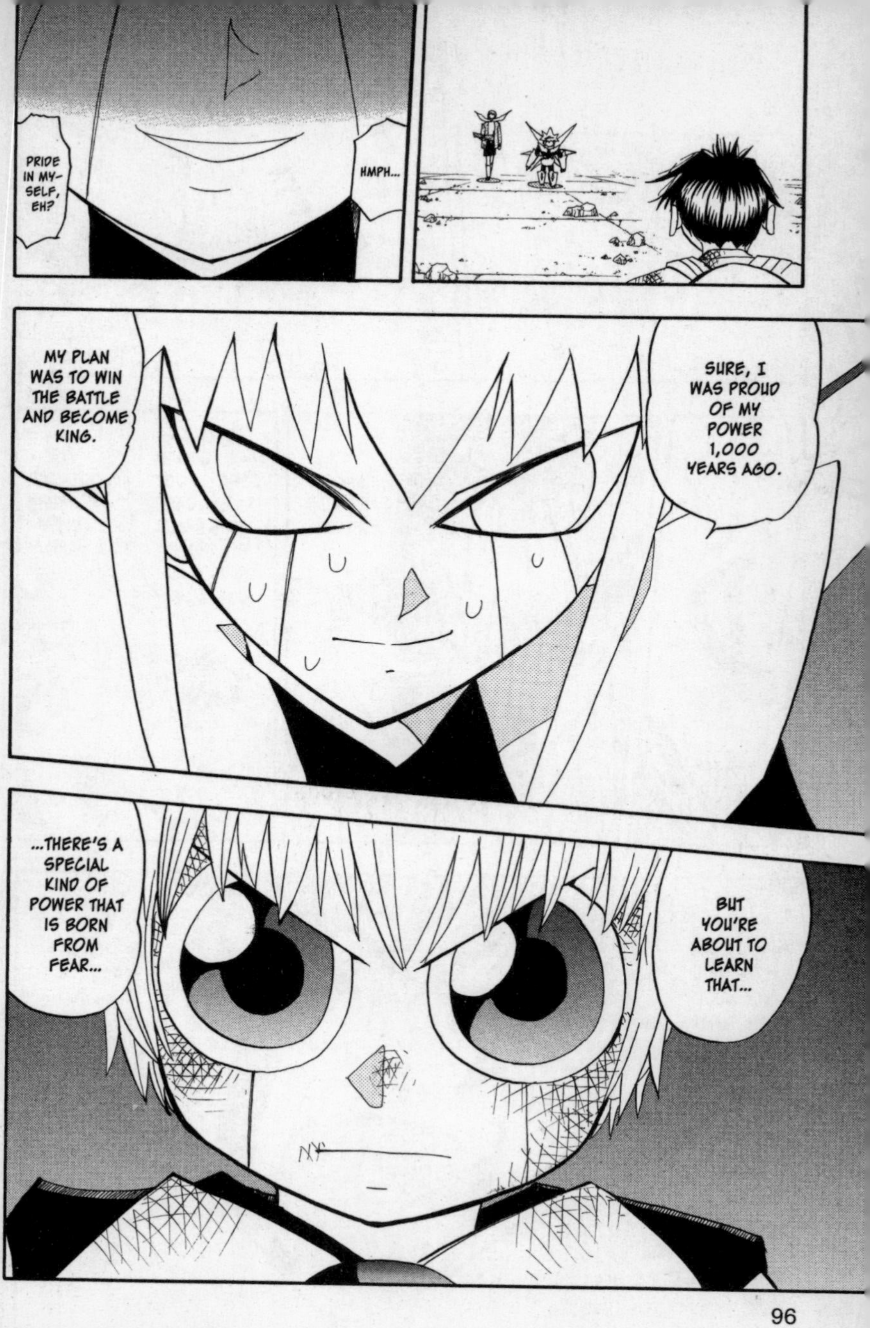
HMPH...
PRIDE IN MY-SELF, EH?
SURE, I WAS PROUD OF MY POWER 1,000 YEARS AGO.
MY PLAN WAS TO WIN THE BATTLE AND BECOME KING.
BUT YOU'RE ABOUT TO LEARN THAT...
...THERE'S A SPECIAL KIND OF POWER THAT IS BORN FROM FEAR...

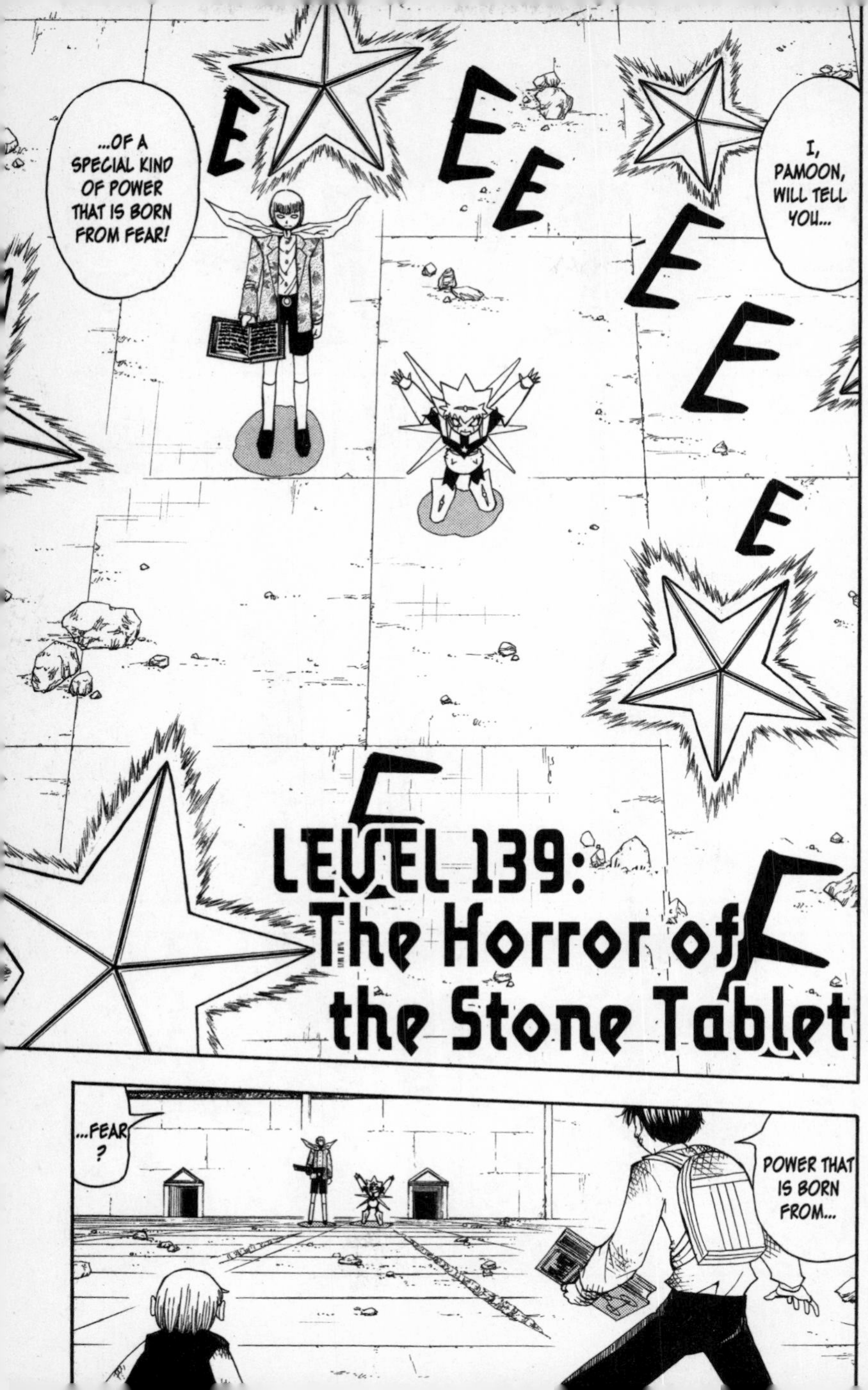
I, PAMOON, WILL TELL YOU...
...OF A SPECIAL KIND OF POWER THAT IS BORN FROM FEAR!
LEVEL 139: The Horror of the Stone Tablet
POWER THAT IS BORN FROM...
...FEAR ?

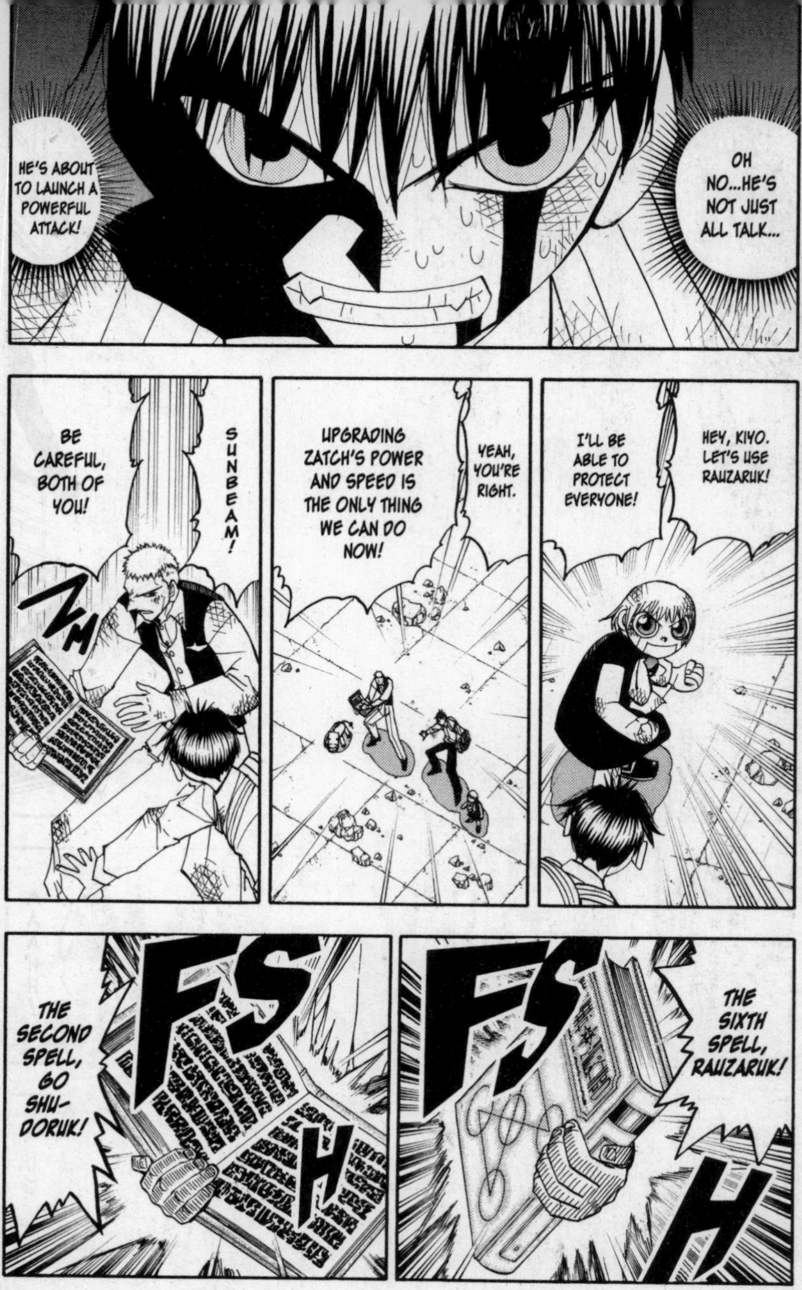
OH NO...HE'S NOT JUST ALL TALK...
HE'S ABOUT TO LAUNCH A POWERFUL ATTACK!
HEY, KIYO. LET'S USE RAUZARUK!
I'LL BE ABLE TO PROTECT EVERYONE!
YEAH, YOU'RE RIGHT.
UPGRADING ZATCH'S POWER AND SPEED IS THE ONLY THING WE CAN DO NOW!
SUNBEAM!
BE CAREFUL, BOTH OF YOU!
THE SIXTH SPELL, RAUZARUK!
FSH
THE SECOND SPELL, GO SHUDORUK!
FSH

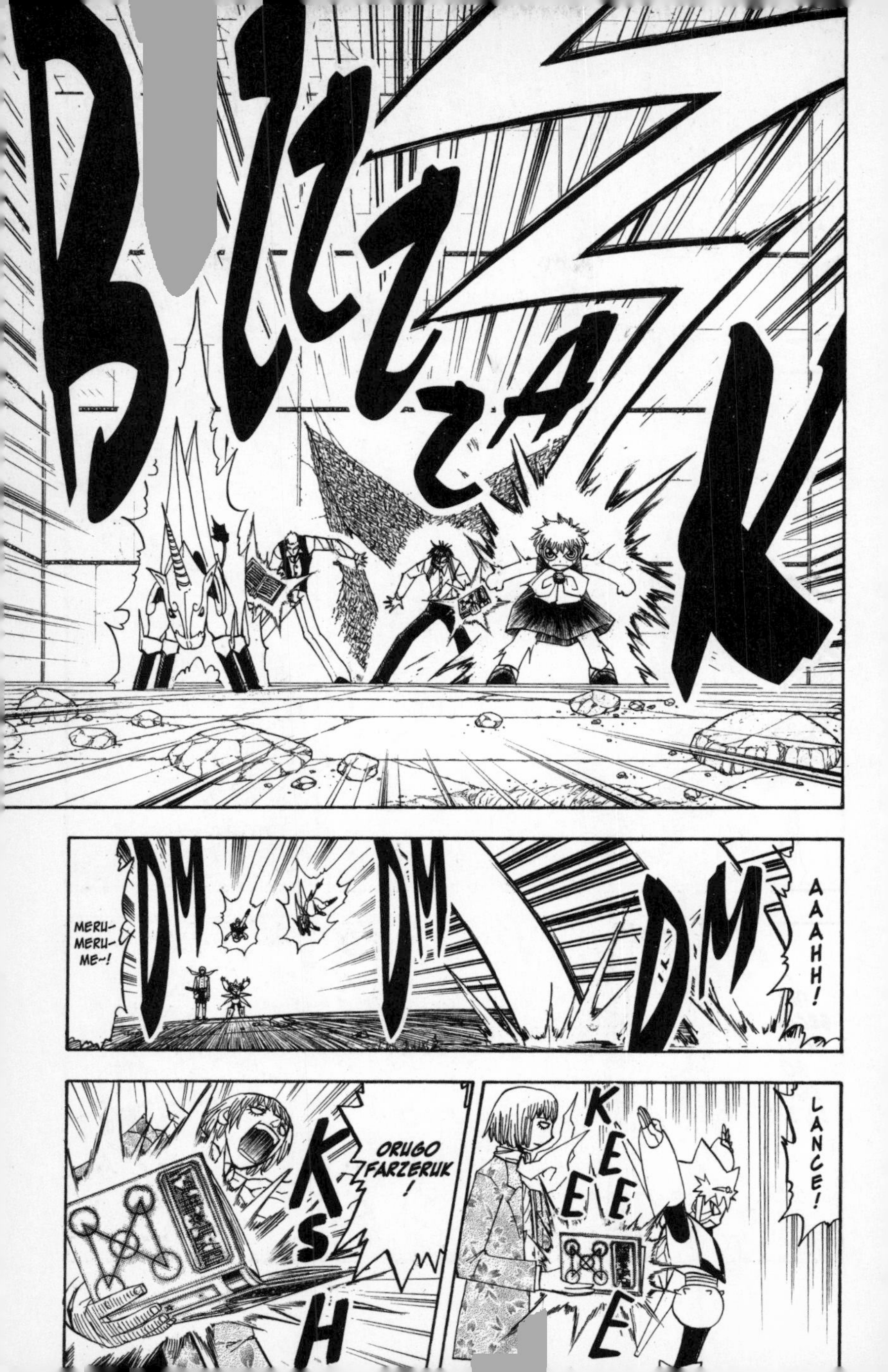
AAAAHH!
MERU-MERU-ME~!
LANCE!
ORUGO FARZERUK!

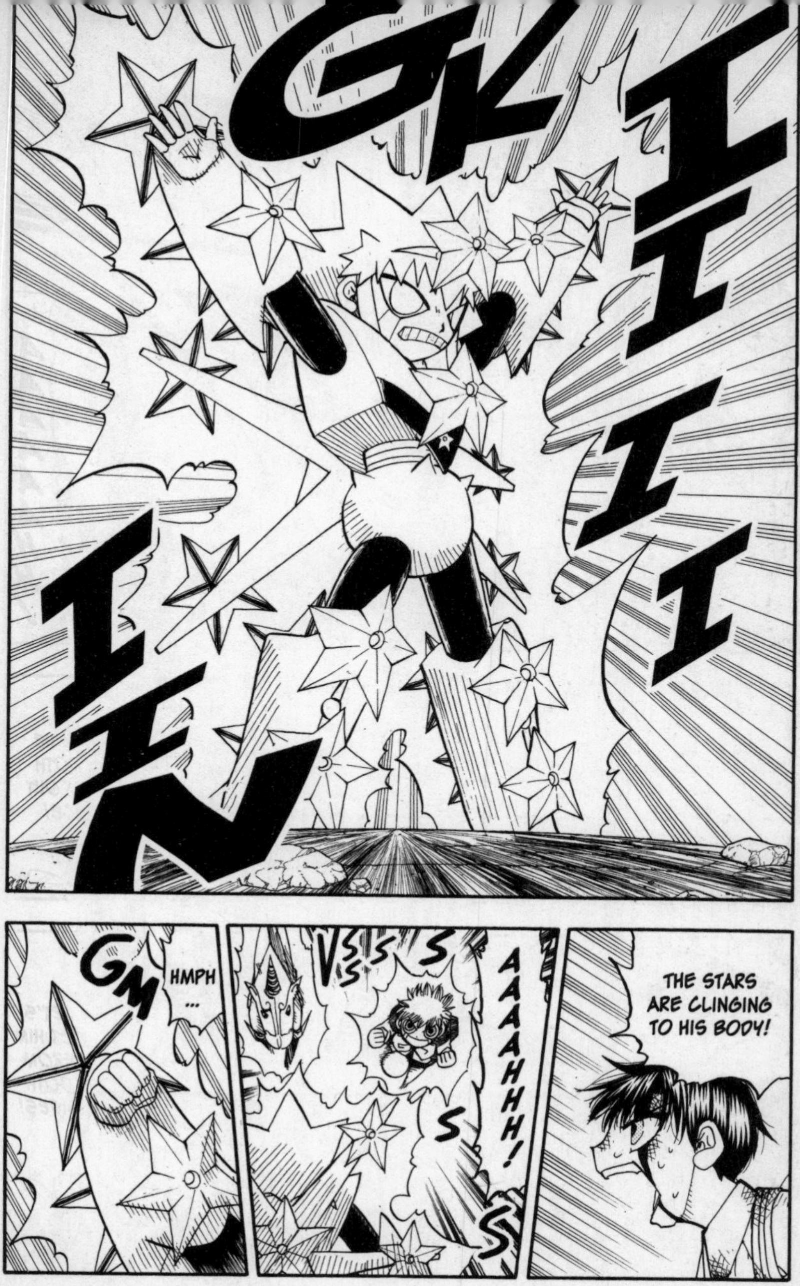
GKIIIIIIN
THE STARS ARE CLINGING TO HIS BODY!
AAAAAHHH!
VSSSS
S
S
HMPH ...
GM

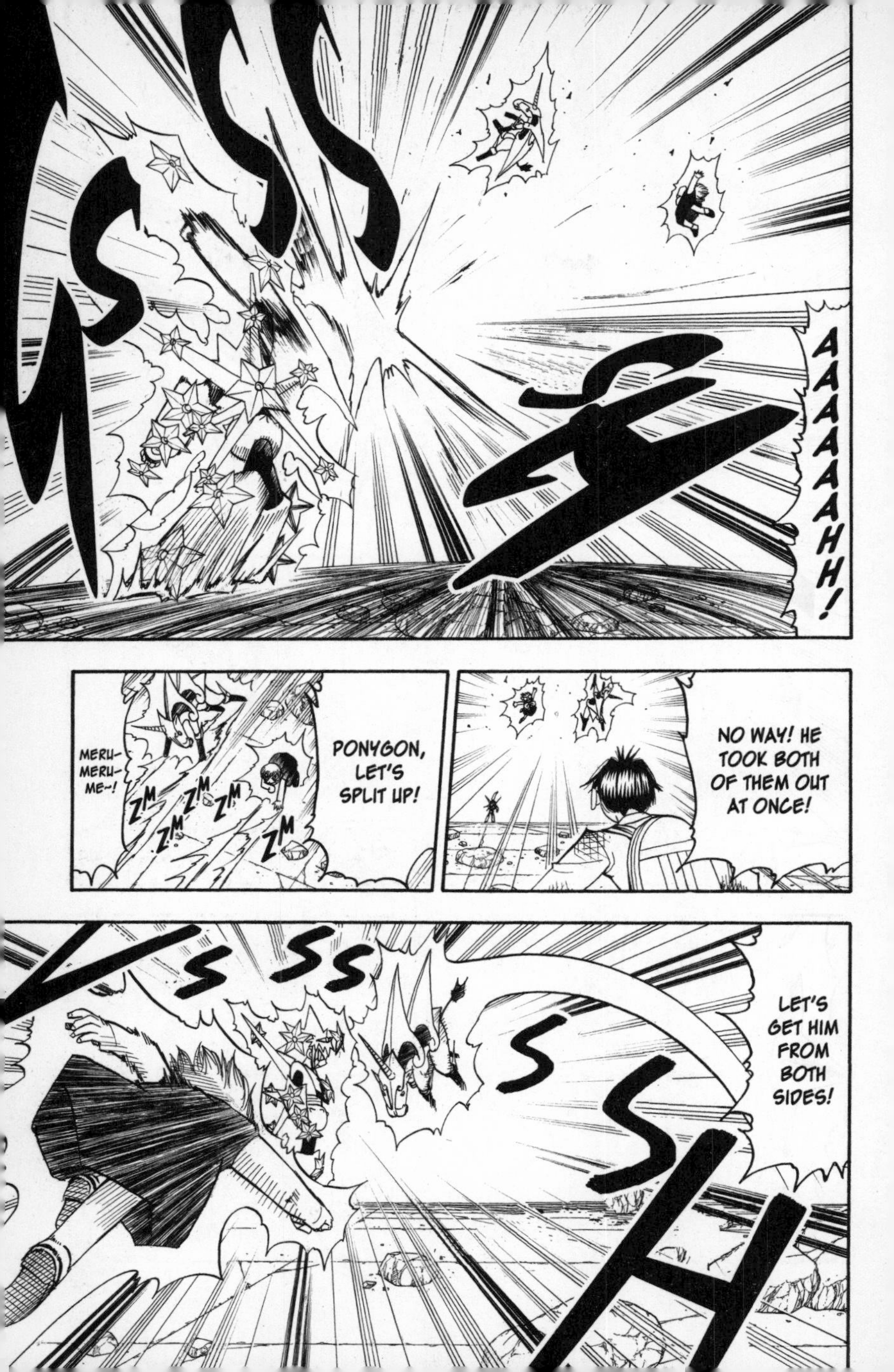
AAAAAAHH!
NO WAY! HE TOOK BOTH OF THEM OUT AT ONCE!
PONYGON, LET'S SPLIT UP!
MERU-MERU-ME~!
LET'S GET HIM FROM BOTH SIDES!

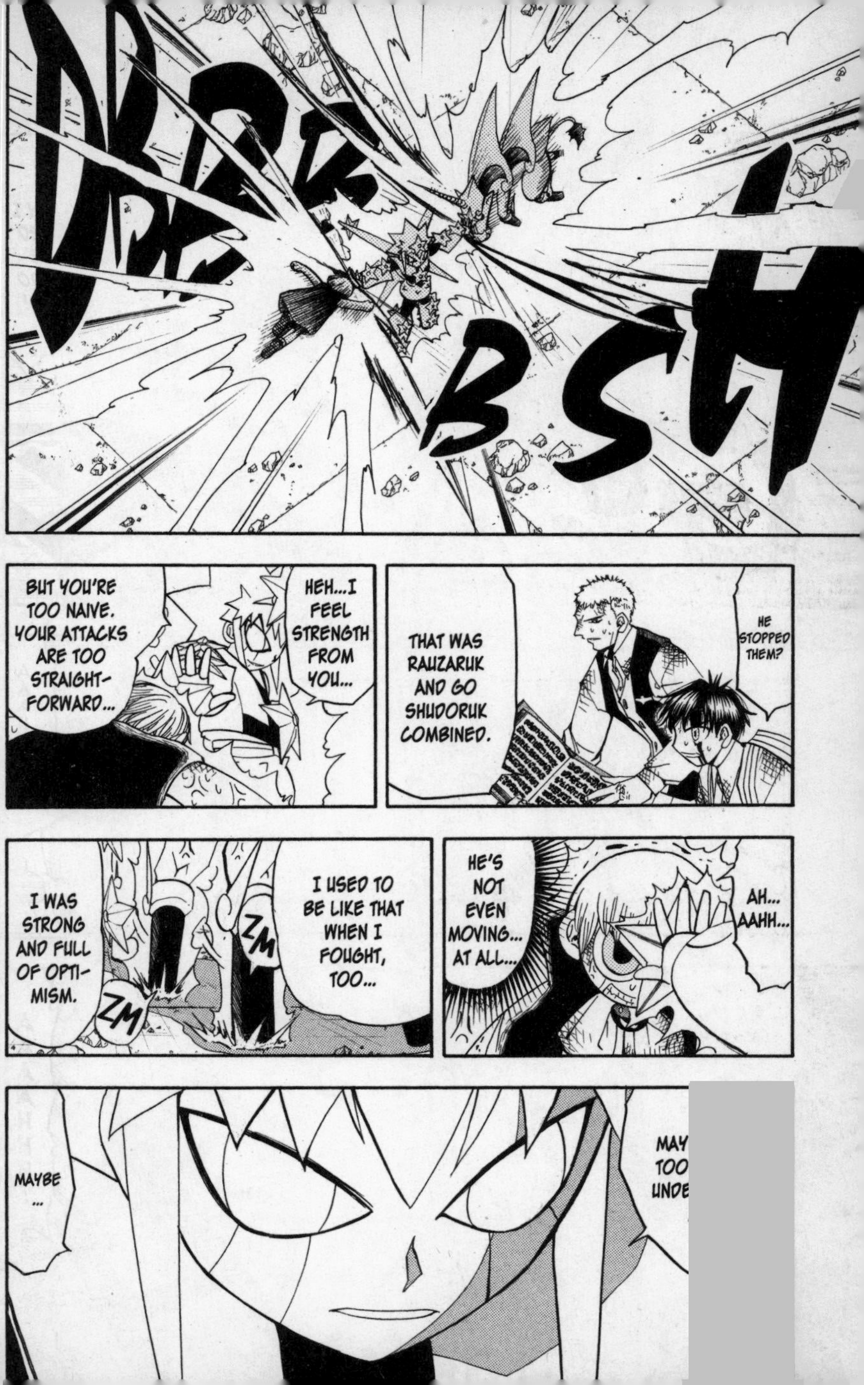
BSCH
DRRK
HE STOPPED THEM?
THAT WAS RAUZARUK AND GO SHUDORUK COMBINED.
HEH...I FEEL STRENGTH FROM YOU...
BUT YOU'RE TOO NAIVE. YOUR ATTACKS ARE TOO STRAIGHT-FORWARD...
AH... AAHH...
HE'S NOT EVEN MOVING... AT ALL...
I USED TO BE LIKE THAT WHEN I FOUGHT, TOO...
ZM
I WAS STRONG AND FULL OF OPTI-MISM.
ZM
MAY TOO UNDE
MAYBE ...

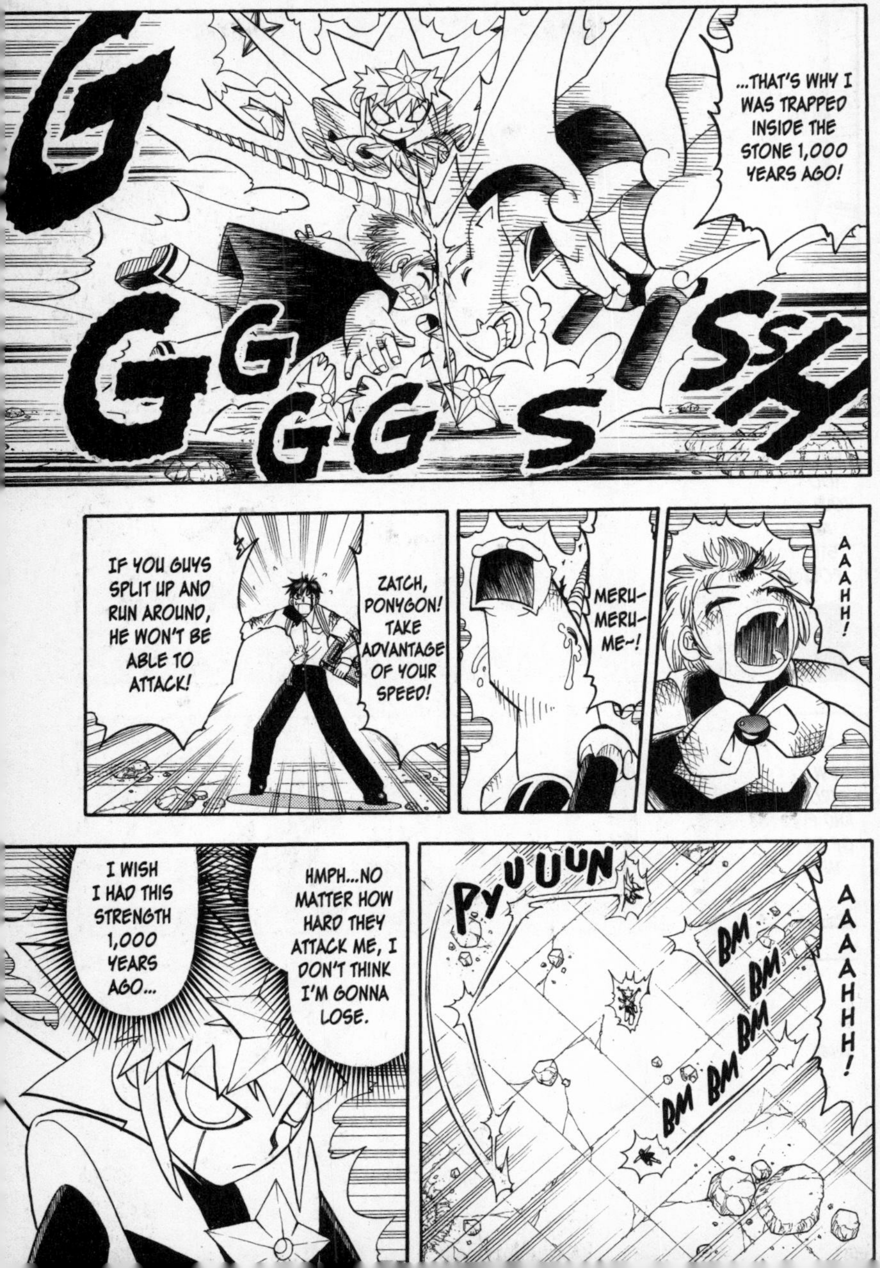
...THAT'S WHY I WAS TRAPPED INSIDE THE STONE 1,000 YEARS AGO!
GGGGG SSSH
AAAAHH!
MERU-MERU-ME~!
ZATCH, PONYGON! TAKE ADVANTAGE OF YOUR SPEED!
IF YOU GUYS SPLIT UP AND RUN AROUND, HE WON'T BE ABLE TO ATTACK!
AAAAAHHH!
PYUUUN
BM BM BM
BM BM BM
HMPH...NO MATTER HOW HARD THEY ATTACK ME, I DON'T THINK I'M GONNA LOSE.
I WISH I HAD THIS STRENGTH 1,000 YEARS AGO...

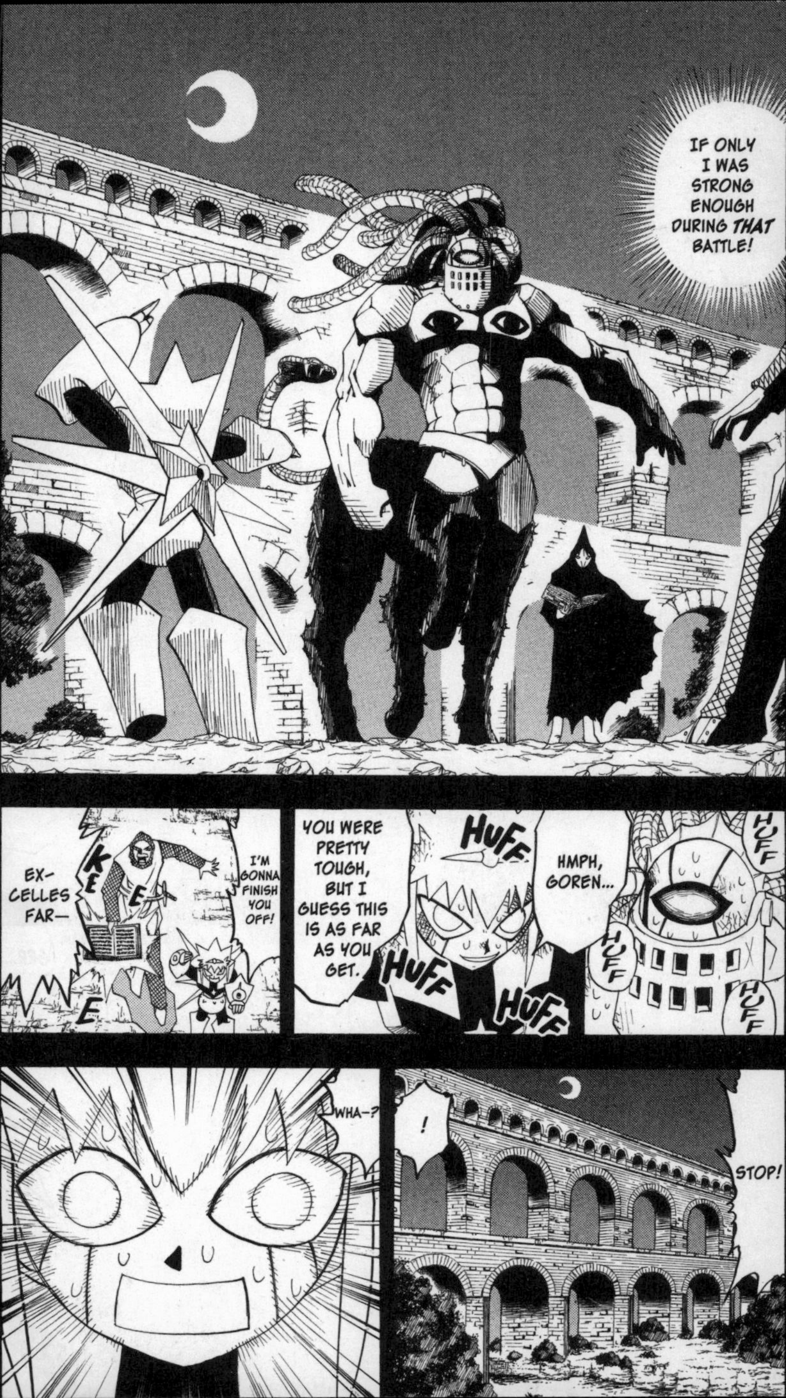
IF ONLY I WAS STRONG ENOUGH DURING THAT BATTLE!
EX-CELLES FAR—
KEEEE
I'M GONNA FINISH YOU OFF!
YOU WERE PRETTY TOUGH, BUT I GUESS THIS IS AS FAR AS YOU GET.
HUFF
HUFF
HUFF
HMPH, GOREN...
HUFF
HUFF
HUFF
WHA-?
!
STOP!

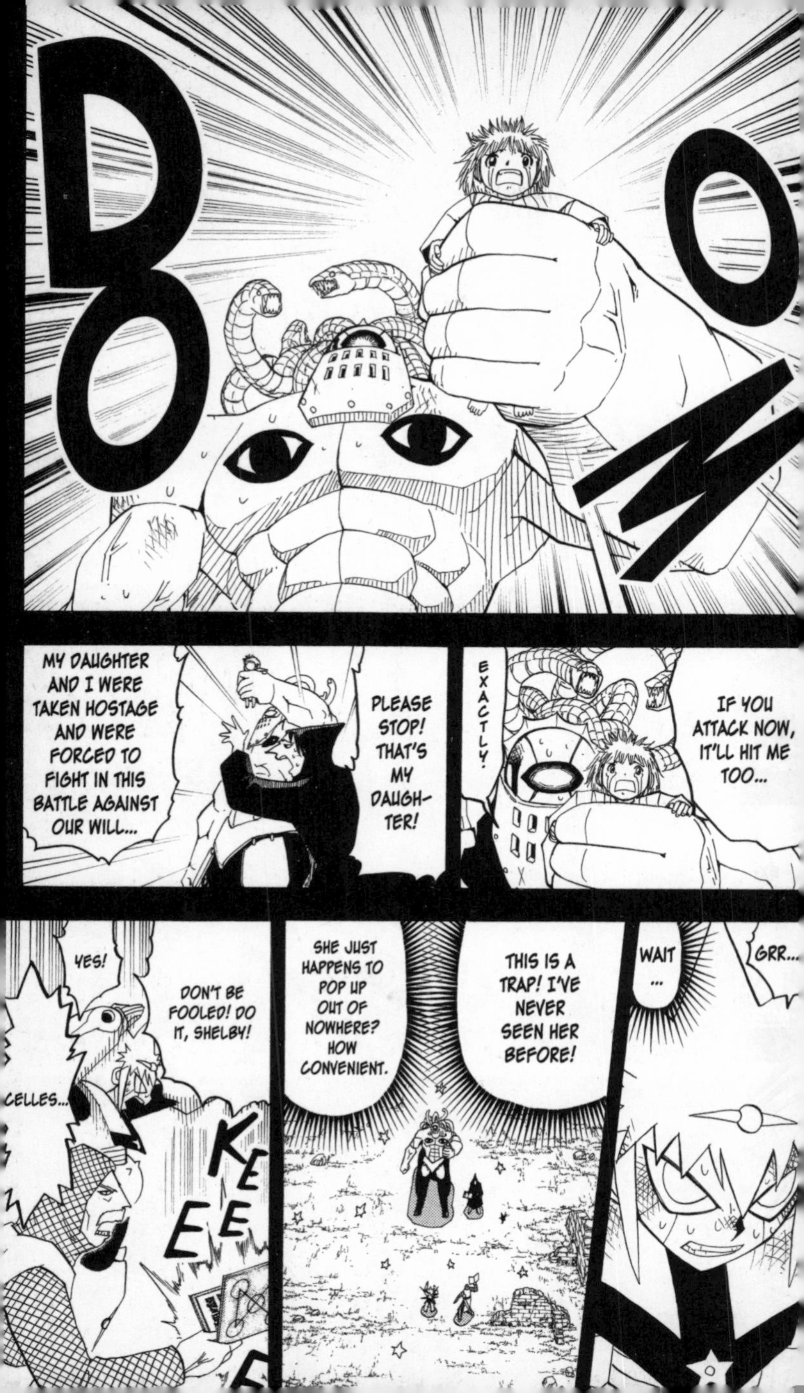
DOON
IF YOU ATTACK NOW, IT'LL HIT ME TOO...
EXACTLY.
PLEASE STOP! THAT'S MY DAUGH-TER!
MY DAUGHTER AND I WERE TAKEN HOSTAGE AND WERE FORCED TO FIGHT IN THIS BATTLE AGAINST OUR WILL...
GRR...
WAIT...
THIS IS A TRAP! I'VE NEVER SEEN HER BEFORE!
SHE JUST HAPPENS TO POP UP OUT OF NOWHERE? HOW CONVENIENT.
DON'T BE FOOLED! DO IT, SHELBY!
YES!
CELLES...
KEEEE

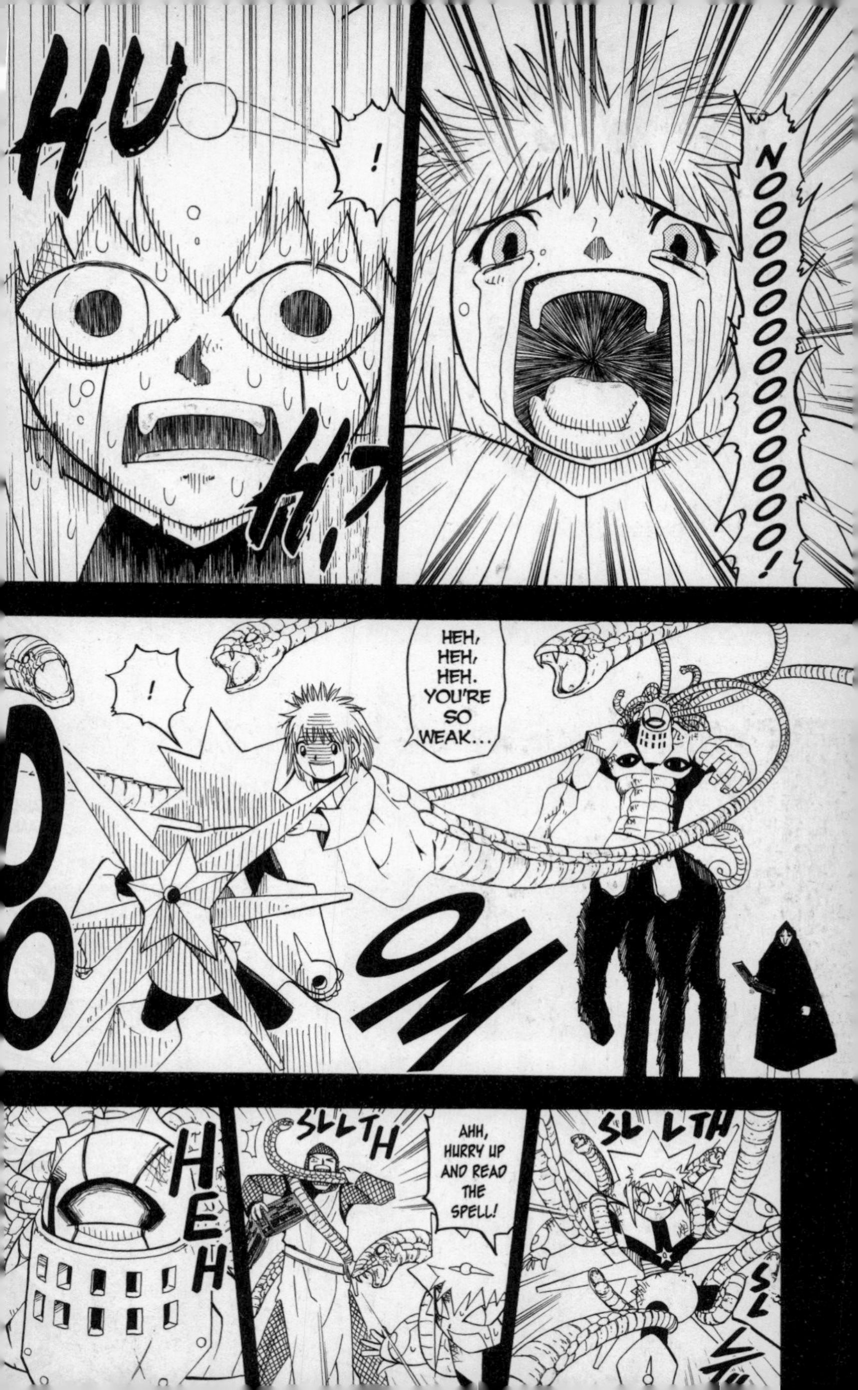
NOOOOOOOOOOOOOO!
!
HU
H?!
HEH, HEH, HEH. YOU'RE SO WEAK...
!
DOOM
SL LTH
SL
AHH, HURRY UP AND READ THE SPELL!
SLLTH
HEH HEH

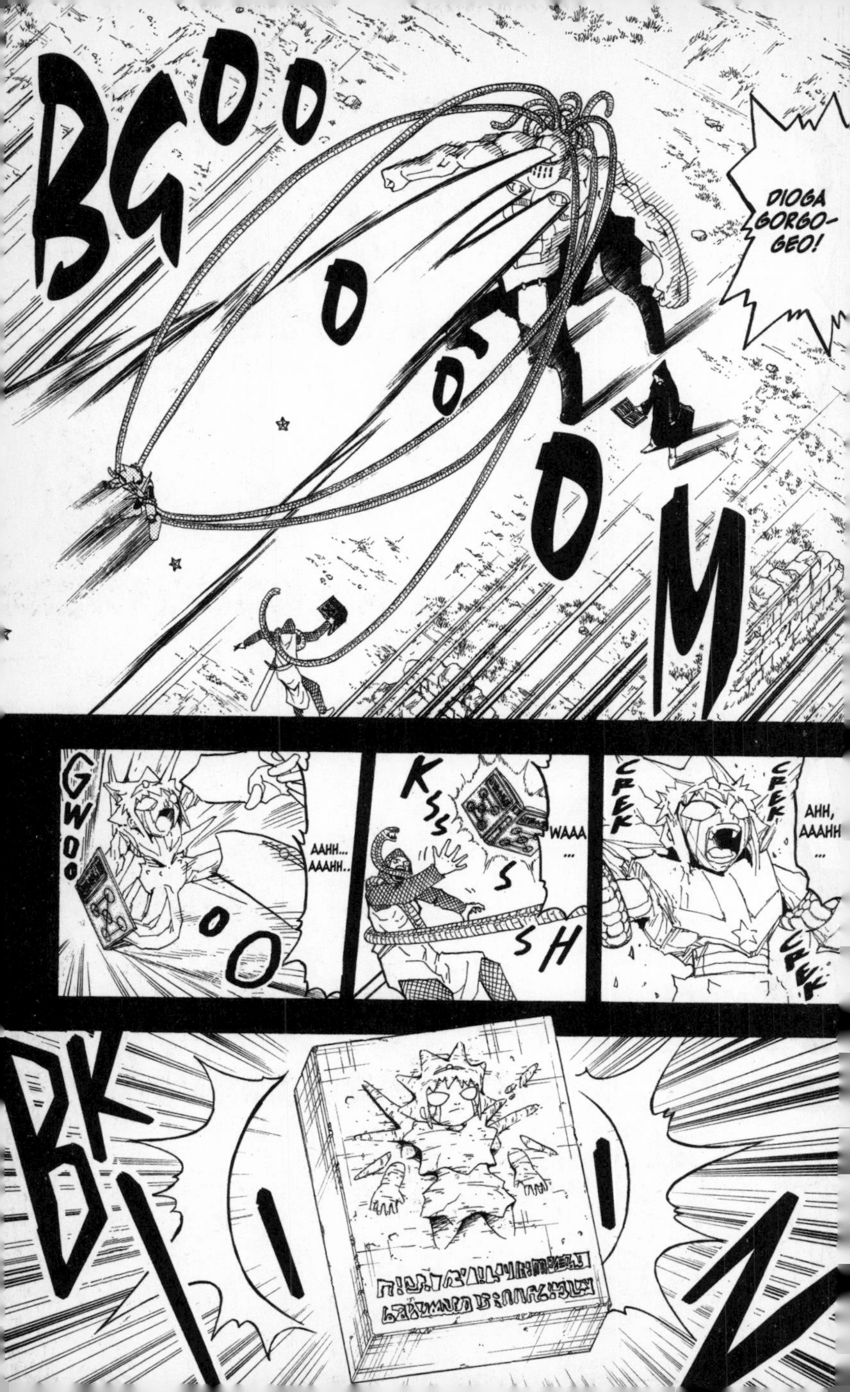
DIOGA GORGO-GEO!
BGOOOOOM
CREK
CREK
AHH, AAAHH ...
CREK
WAAA ...
KSSSSH
AAHH... AAAHH..
GWOOOO
BKIIN

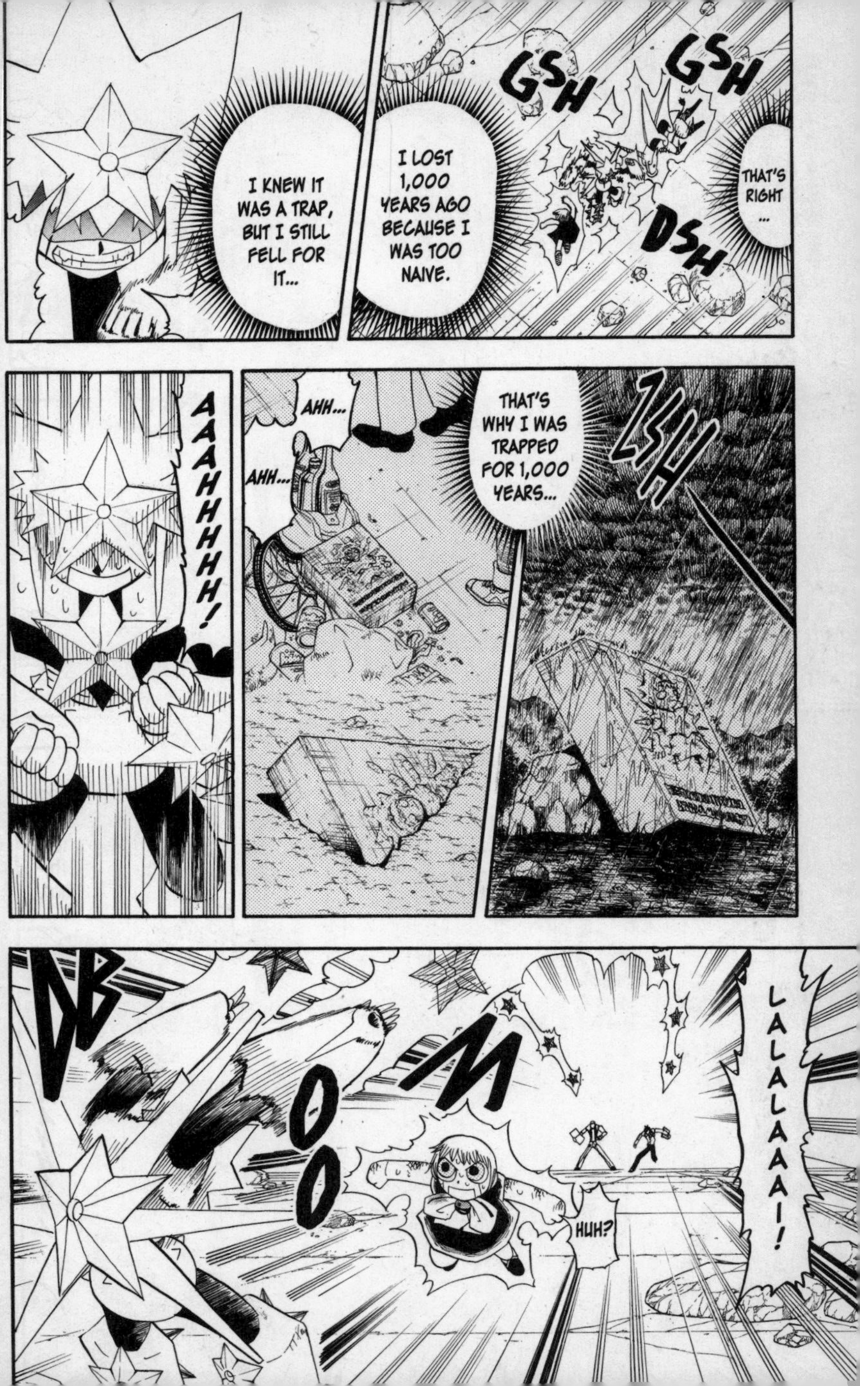
GSH GSH
THAT'S RIGHT ...
DSH
I LOST 1,000 YEARS AGO BECAUSE I WAS TOO NAIVE.
I KNEW IT WAS A TRAP, BUT I STILL FELL FOR IT...
ZSH
THAT'S WHY I WAS TRAPPED FOR 1,000 YEARS...
AHH...
AHH...
AAAHHHHHHH!
LALALAAAI!
HUH?
DBOOM

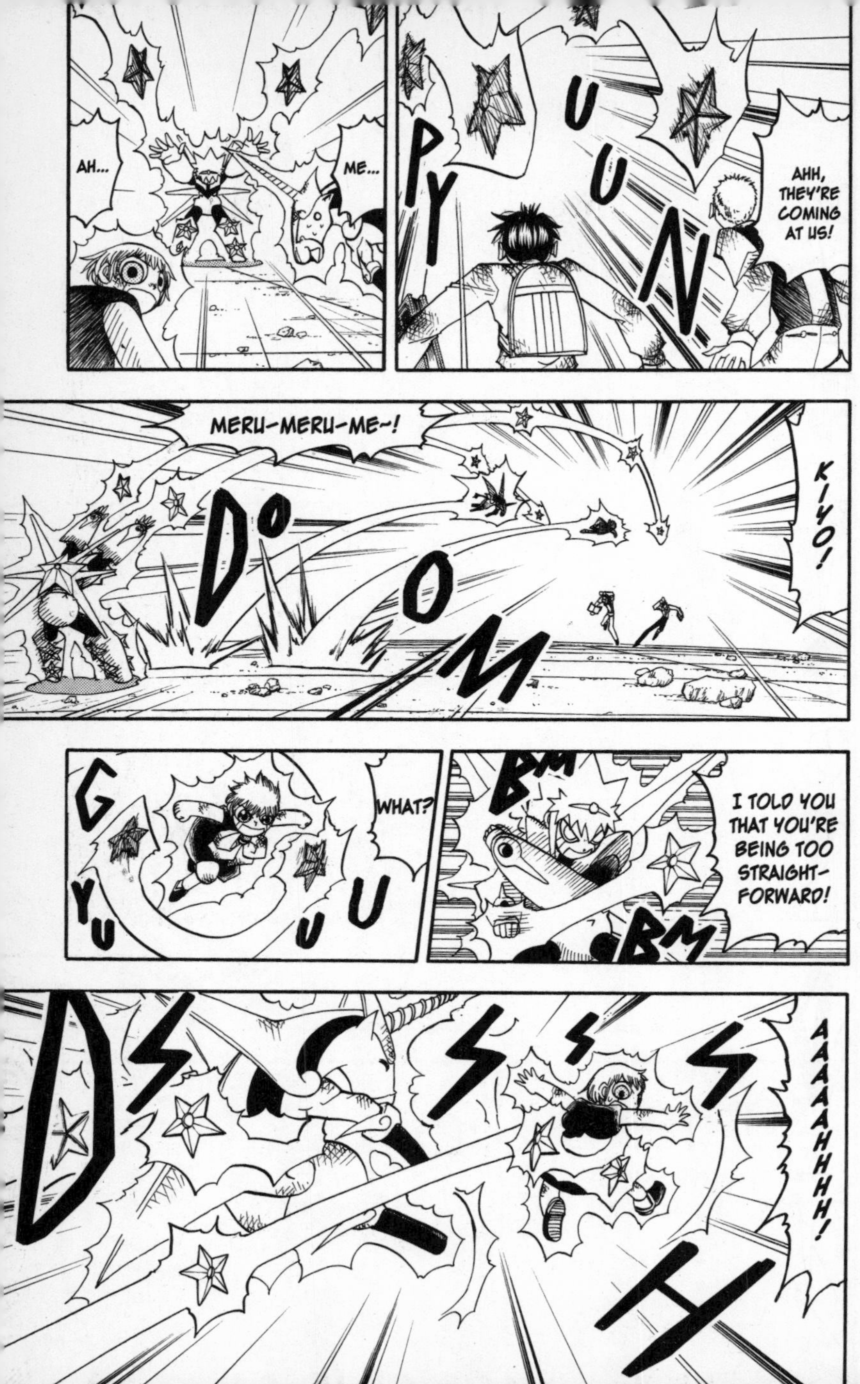
PYUUN
AHH, THEY'RE COMING AT US!
ME...
AH...
KIYO!
MERU-MERU-ME~!
DOOM
BM
I TOLD YOU THAT YOU'RE BEING TOO STRAIGHT-FORWARD!
BM
WHAT?
GYUUU
AAAAAHHHHH!
DSSSSH

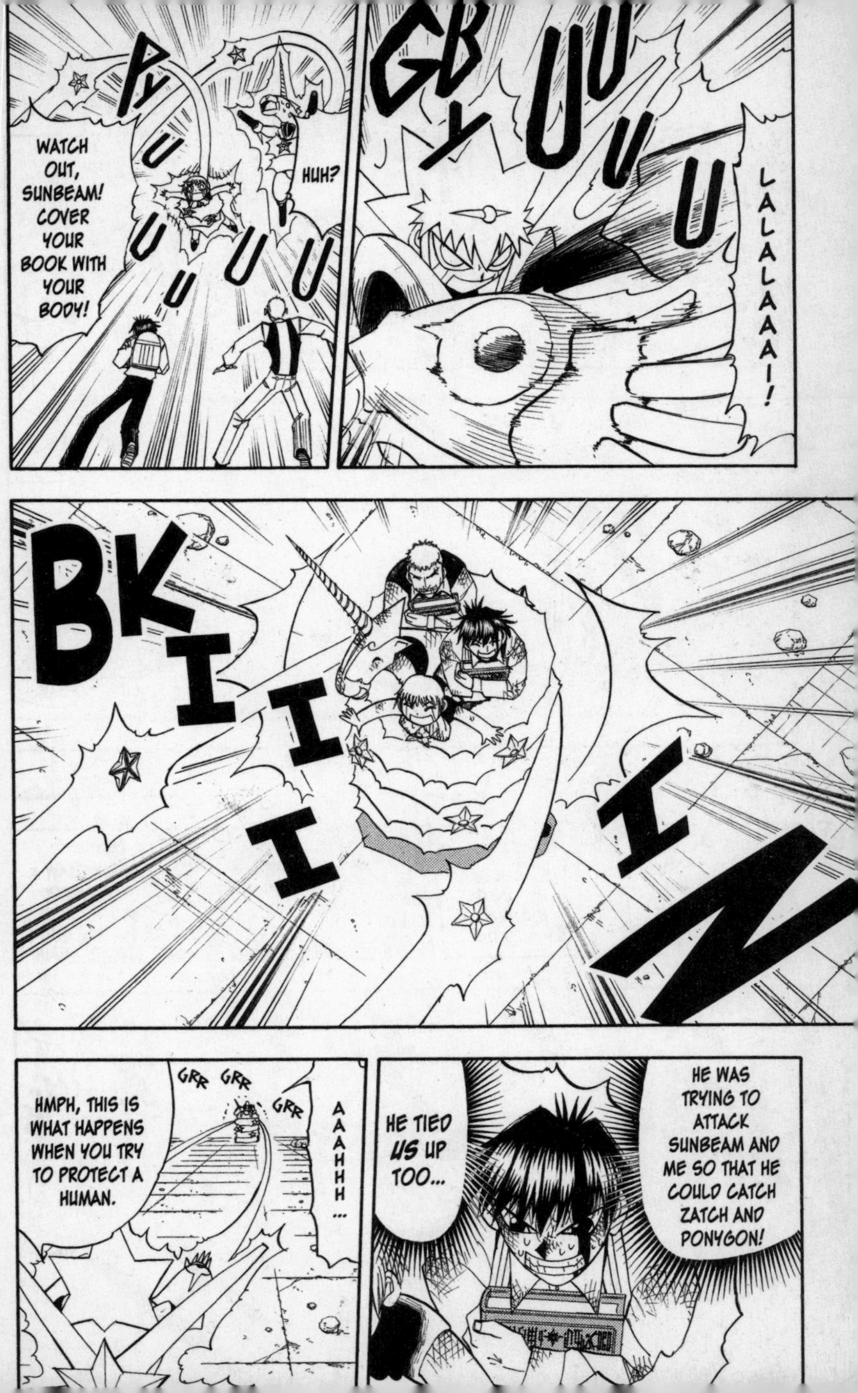
GBYUUUUUU
LALALAAAAI!
PYUUUUUU
HUH?
WATCH OUT, SUNBEAM! COVER YOUR BOOK WITH YOUR BODY!
BKIIIIN
HE WAS TRYING TO ATTACK SUNBEAM AND ME SO THAT HE COULD CATCH ZATCH AND PONYGON!
HE TIED US UP TOO...
AAAHHH...
GRR GRR GRR
HMPH, THIS IS WHAT HAPPENS WHEN YOU TRY TO PROTECT A HUMAN.

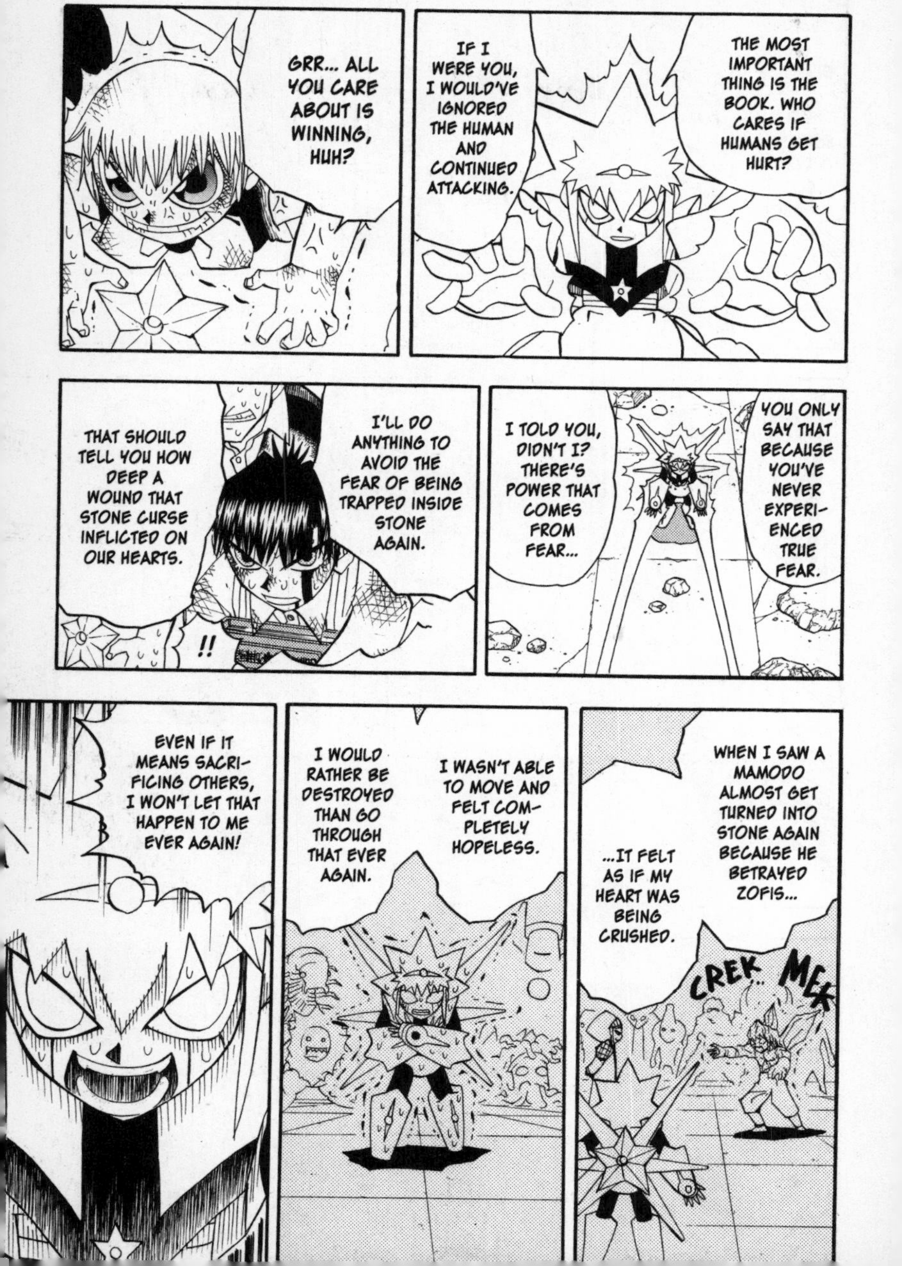
THE MOST IMPORTANT THING IS THE BOOK. WHO CARES IF HUMANS GET HURT?
IF I WERE YOU, I WOULD'VE IGNORED THE HUMAN AND CONTINUED ATTACKING.
GRR... ALL YOU CARE ABOUT IS WINNING, HUH?
YOU ONLY SAY THAT BECAUSE YOU'VE NEVER EXPERI-ENCED TRUE FEAR.
I TOLD YOU, DIDN'T I? THERE'S POWER THAT COMES FROM FEAR...
I'LL DO ANYTHING TO AVOID THE FEAR OF BEING TRAPPED INSIDE STONE AGAIN.
THAT SHOULD TELL YOU HOW DEEP A WOUND THAT STONE CURSE INFLICTED ON OUR HEARTS.
!!
WHEN I SAW A MAMODO ALMOST GET TURNED INTO STONE AGAIN BECAUSE HE BETRAYED ZOFIS...
...IT FELT AS IF MY HEART WAS BEING CRUSHED.
CREK... MEK
I WASN'T ABLE TO MOVE AND FELT COM-PLETELY HOPELESS.
I WOULD RATHER BE DESTROYED THAN GO THROUGH THAT EVER AGAIN.
EVEN IF IT MEANS SACRI-FICING OTHERS, I WON'T LET THAT HAPPEN TO ME EVER AGAIN!

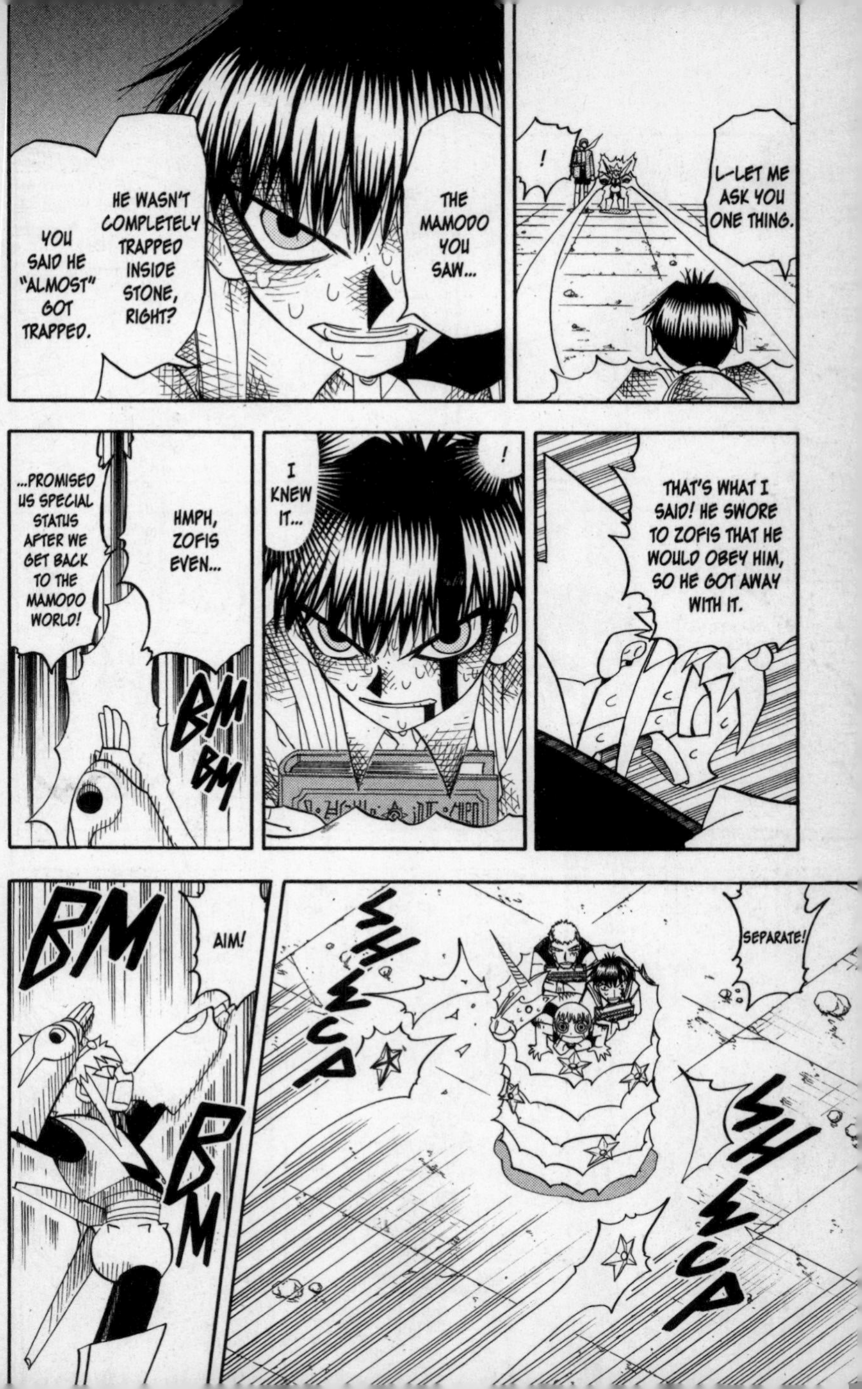
!
L-LET ME ASK YOU ONE THING.
THE MAMODO YOU SAW...
HE WASN'T COMPLETELY TRAPPED INSIDE STONE, RIGHT?
YOU SAID HE "ALMOST" GOT TRAPPED.
THAT'S WHAT I SAID! HE SWORE TO ZOFIS THAT HE WOULD OBEY HIM, SO HE GOT AWAY WITH IT.
!
I KNEW IT...
HMPH, ZOFIS EVEN...
...PROMISED US SPECIAL STATUS AFTER WE GET BACK TO THE MAMODO WORLD!
BM BM
SEPARATE!
SHWUP
SHWUP
AIM!
BM
BM

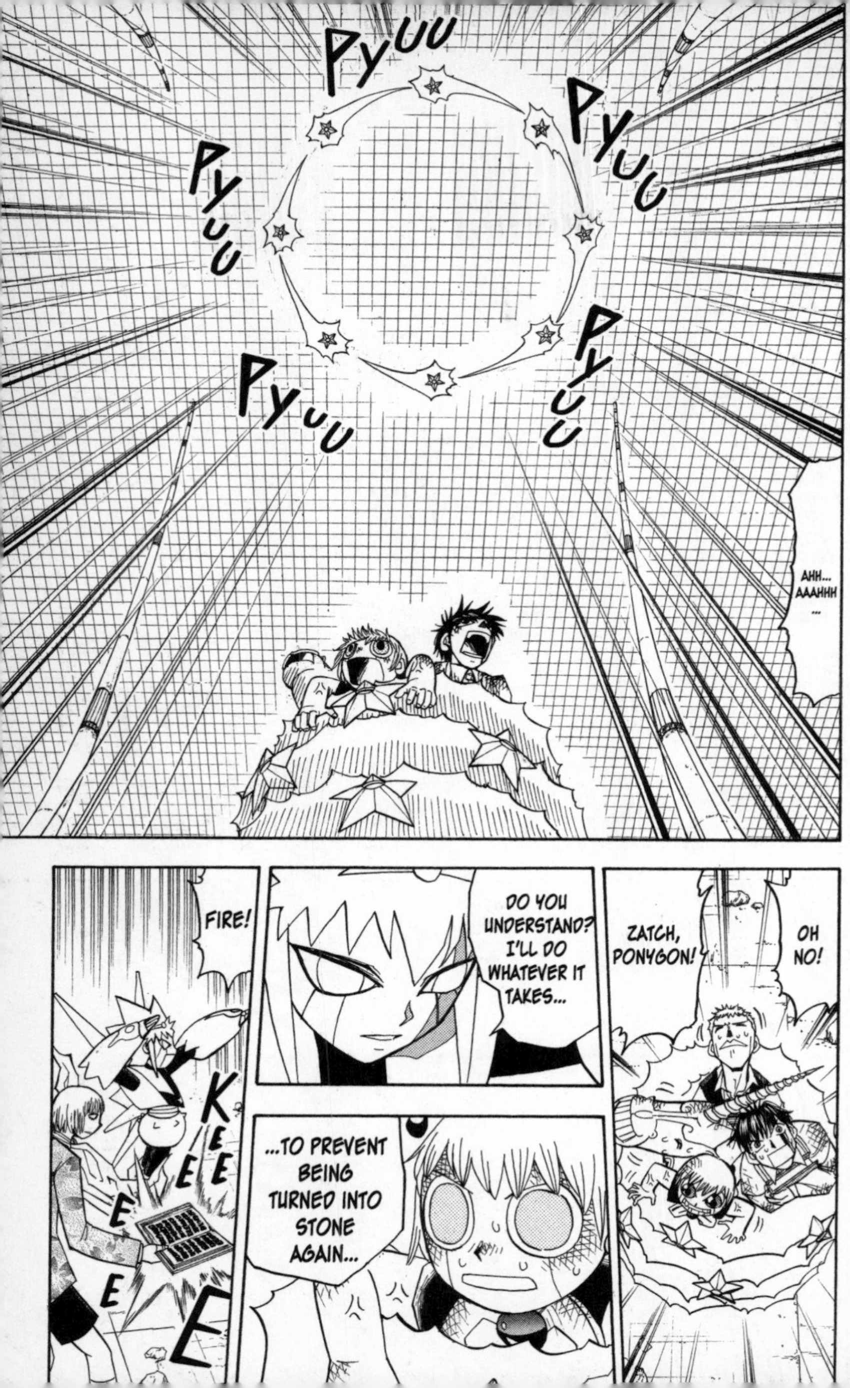
Pyuu
Pyuu
Pyuu
Pyuu
Pyuu
AHH... AAAHHH ...
OH NO!
ZATCH, PONYGON!
DO YOU UNDERSTAND? I'LL DO WHATEVER IT TAKES...
...TO PREVENT BEING TURNED INTO STONE AGAIN...
FIRE!
KEEEEEE

DIOGA
FARIZDON!

AH...

AAAAHHHHH!

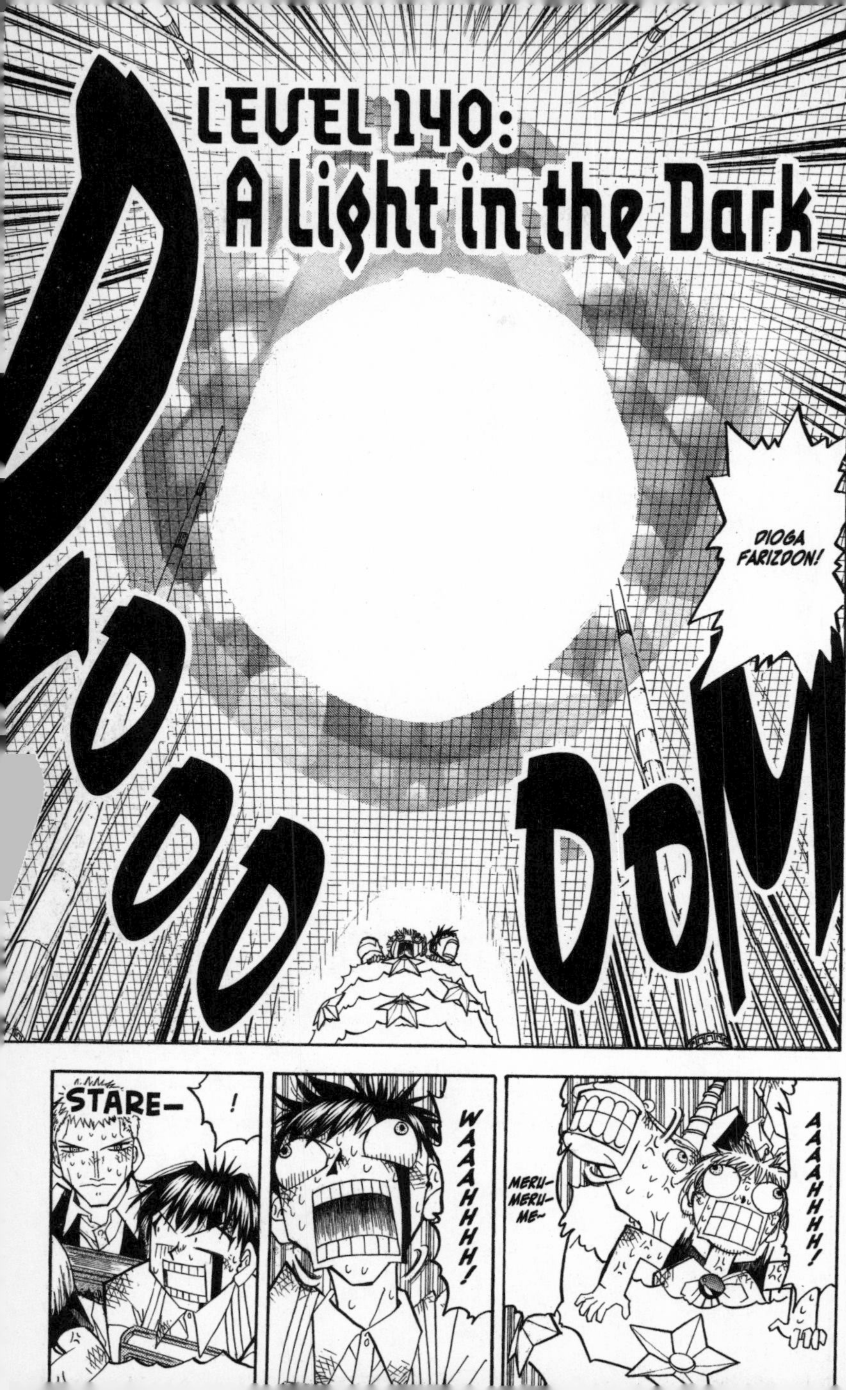
LEVEL 140:
A Light in the Dark
DIOGA FARIZDON!
DOOOO DOOM
MERU-MERU-ME~
AAAAAHHHHH!
WAAAAHHHHH!
STARE-
!

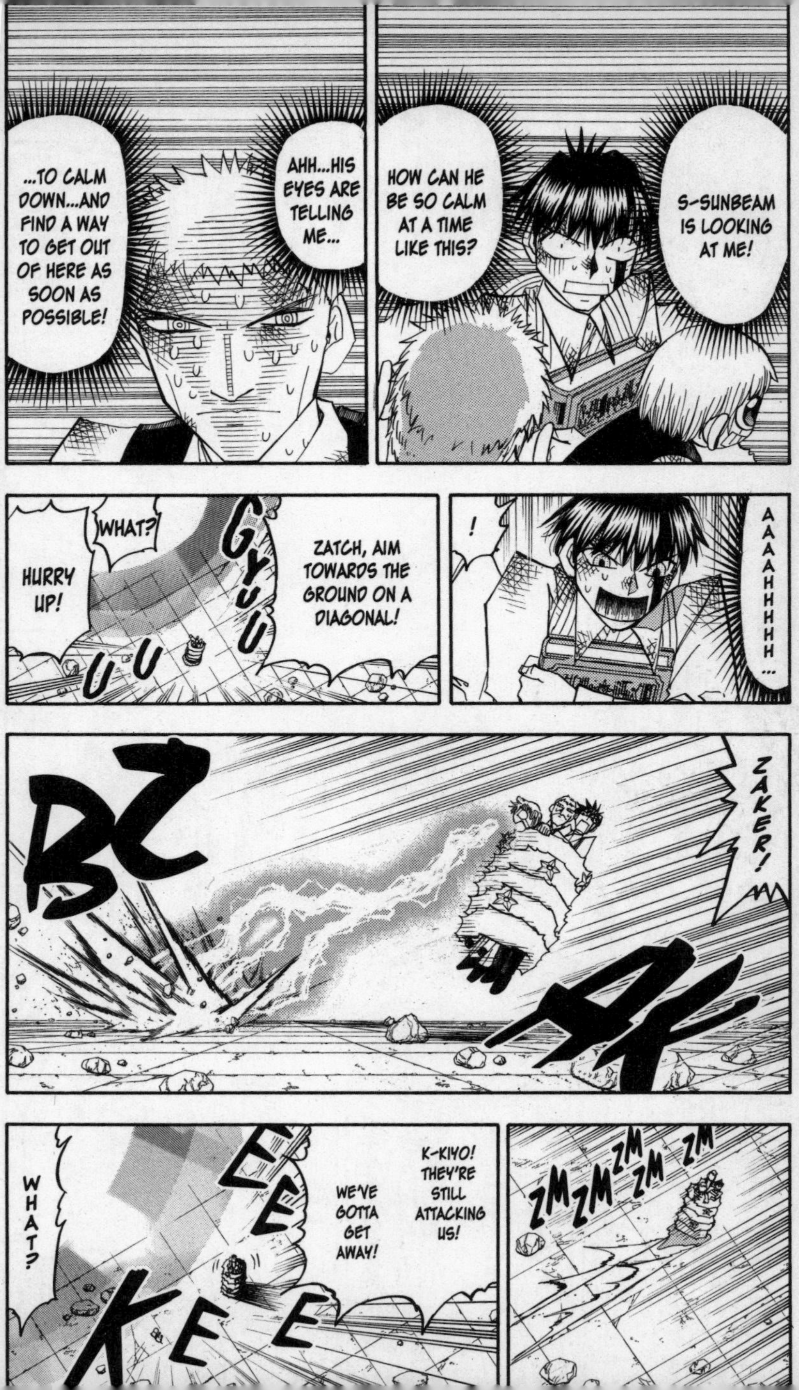
S-SUNBEAM IS LOOKING AT ME!
HOW CAN HE BE SO CALM AT A TIME LIKE THIS?
AHH...HIS EYES ARE TELLING ME...
...TO CALM DOWN...AND FIND A WAY TO GET OUT OF HERE AS SOON AS POSSIBLE!
AAAAAHHHHHH...
!
ZATCH, AIM TOWARDS THE GROUND ON A DIAGONAL!
GYUUUU
WHAT?
HURRY UP!
ZAKER!
BZ
AK
ZM ZM ZM ZM ZM ZM
K-KIYO! THEY'RE STILL ATTACKING US!
WE'VE GOTTA GET AWAY!
EEE
KEE
WHAT?

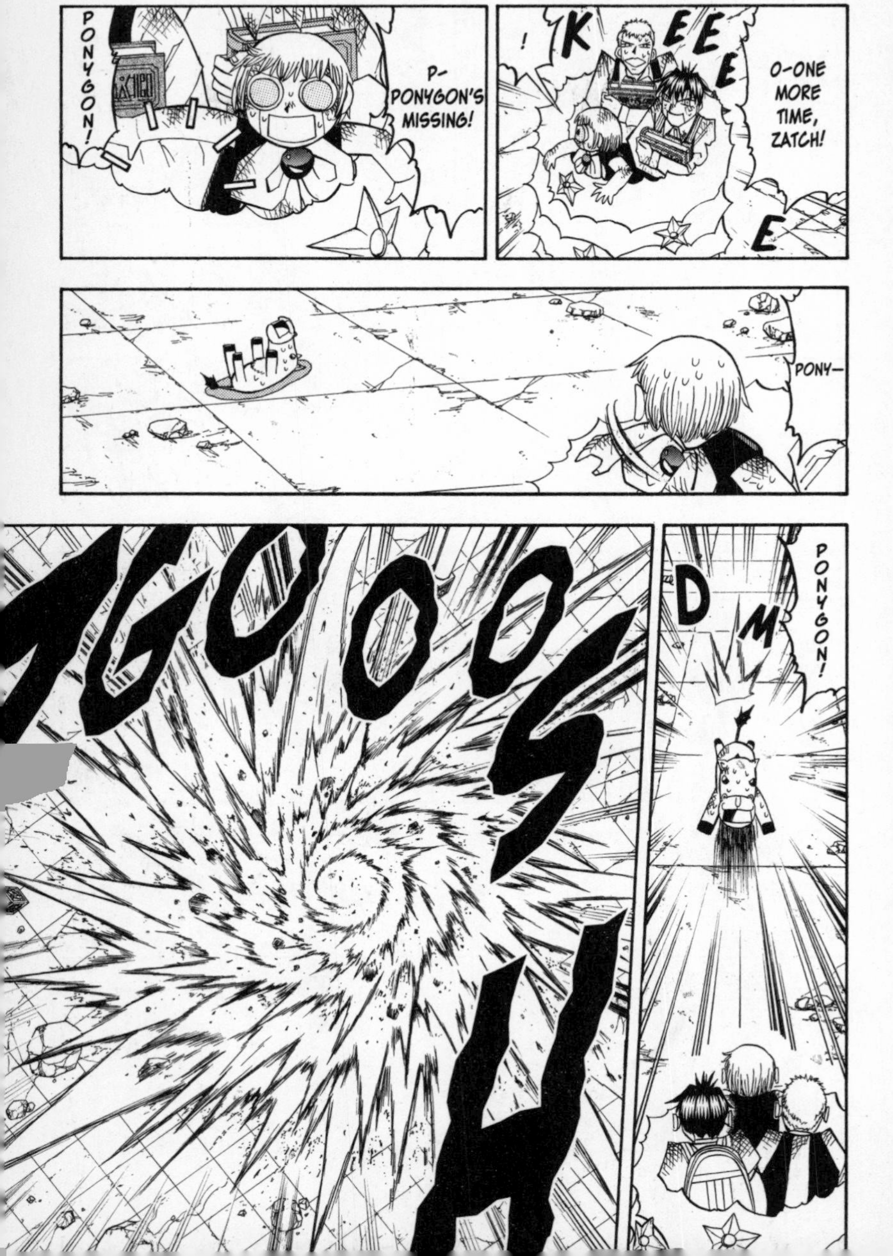
O-ONE MORE TIME, ZATCH!
KEEEEE
!
P-PONYGON'S MISSING!
PONYGON!
PONY-
PONYGON!
DM

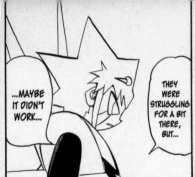

FSSSSSS
THEY WERE STRUGGLING FOR A BIT THERE, BUT...
...MAYBE IT DIDN'T WORK...
EEEEE
AAHH...
WE WERE LUCKY THAT SPELL WORE OFF AND PONYGON'S SIZE WENT BACK TO NORMAL, BUT...
SHOOP
...WITHOUT THE EFFECT OF THE SPELL, PONYGON WASN'T ABLE TO...
...CARRY US TOO FAR.
WE TOOK A LOT OF DAMAGE...
KIYO...
!
ZATCH, DO YOU STILL HAVE ENERGY?
GG GGG
KIYO... LET'S USE RAUZARUK...

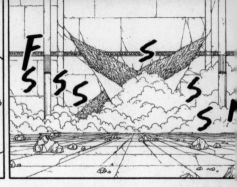

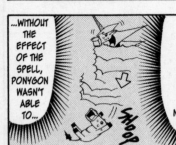

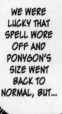

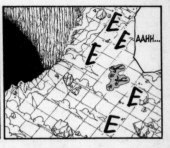

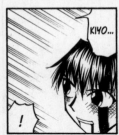

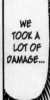

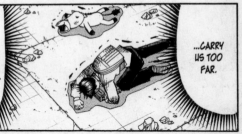

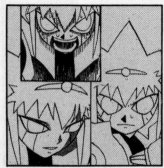

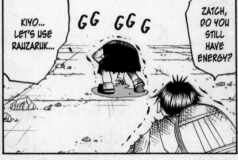

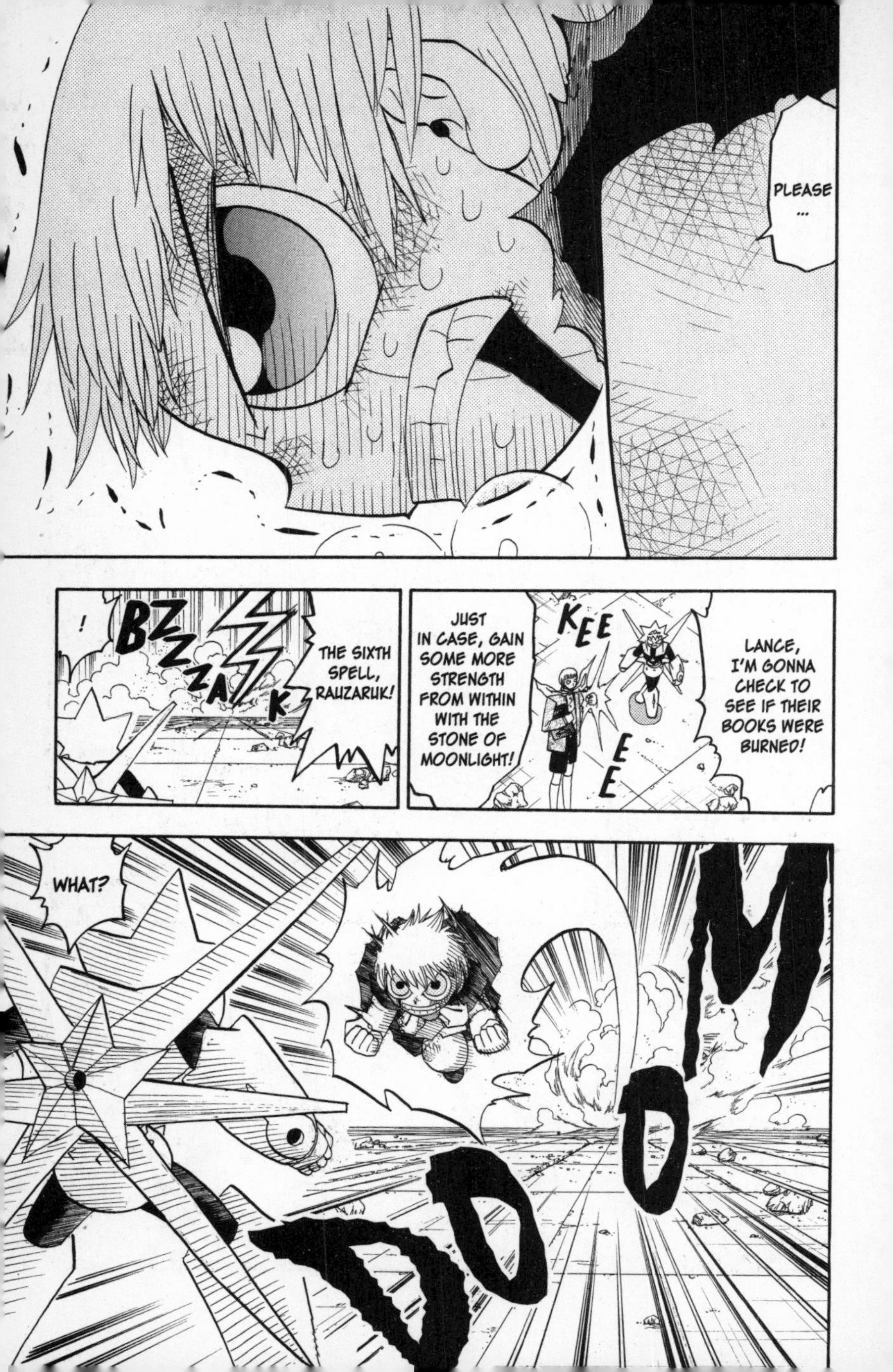
PLEASE ...
LANCE, I'M GONNA CHECK TO SEE IF THEIR BOOKS WERE BURNED!
KEEEEE
JUST IN CASE, GAIN SOME MORE STRENGTH FROM WITHIN WITH THE STONE OF MOONLIGHT!
THE SIXTH SPELL, RAUZARUK!
BZZZAK
!
WHAT?
DOM

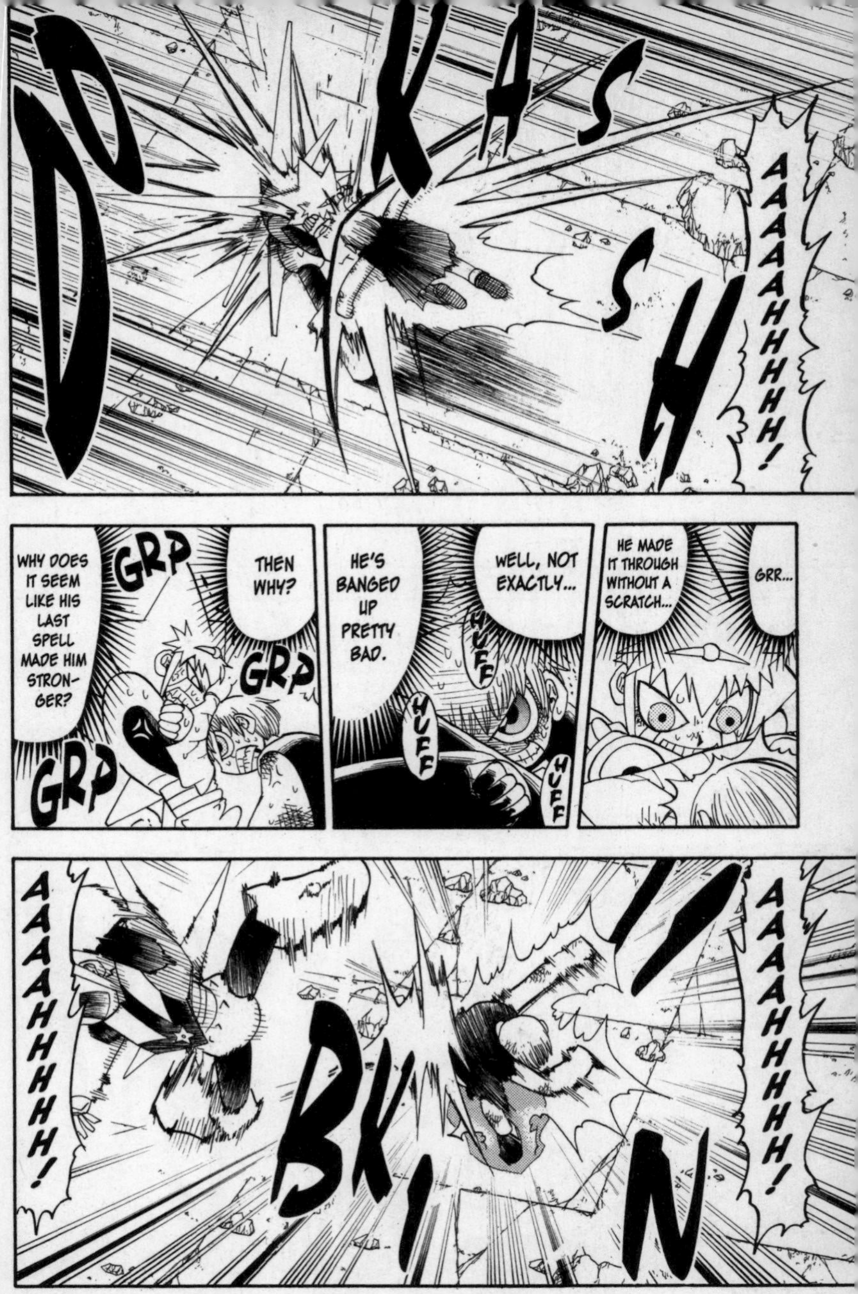
AAAAAHHHHHH!
DKASH
GRR...
HE MADE IT THROUGH WITHOUT A SCRATCH...
WELL, NOT EXACTLY...
HUFF
HUFF
HUFF
HE'S BANGED UP PRETTY BAD.
THEN WHY?
GRP
GRP
GRP
WHY DOES IT SEEM LIKE HIS LAST SPELL MADE HIM STRONGER?
AAAAHHHHHH!
BKIN
AAAAHHHHHH!

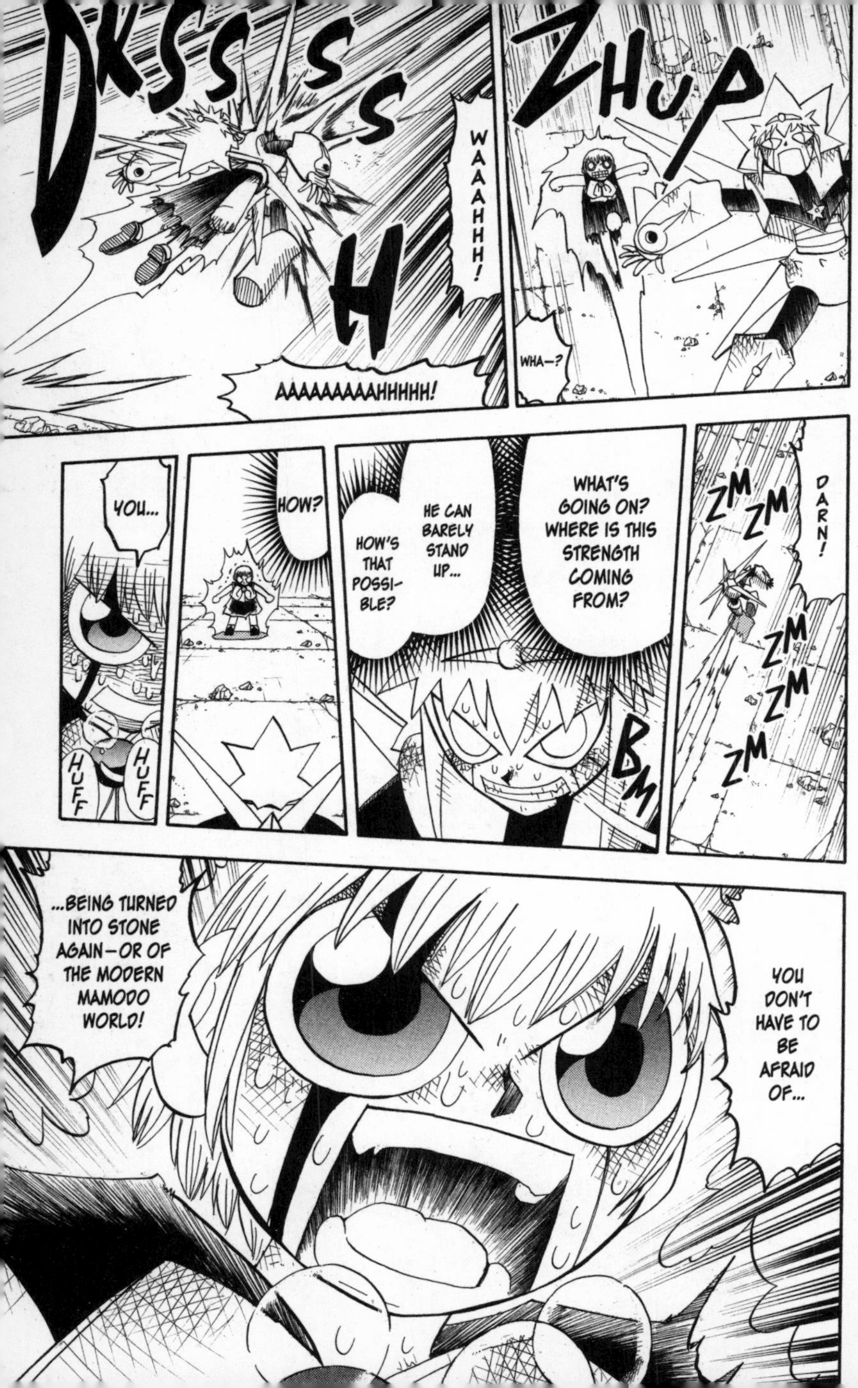
ZHUP
WHA—?
DKSSSSSH
WAAAAHHHH!
AAAAAAAAAHHHHH!
ZM ZM
DARN!
ZM ZM ZM ZM
WHAT'S GOING ON? WHERE IS THIS STRENGTH COMING FROM?
HE CAN BARELY STAND UP...
HOW'S THAT POSSIBLE?
BM
HOW?
YOU...
HUFF HUFF
YOU DON'T HAVE TO BE AFRAID OF...
...BEING TURNED INTO STONE AGAIN—OR OF THE MODERN MAMODO WORLD!

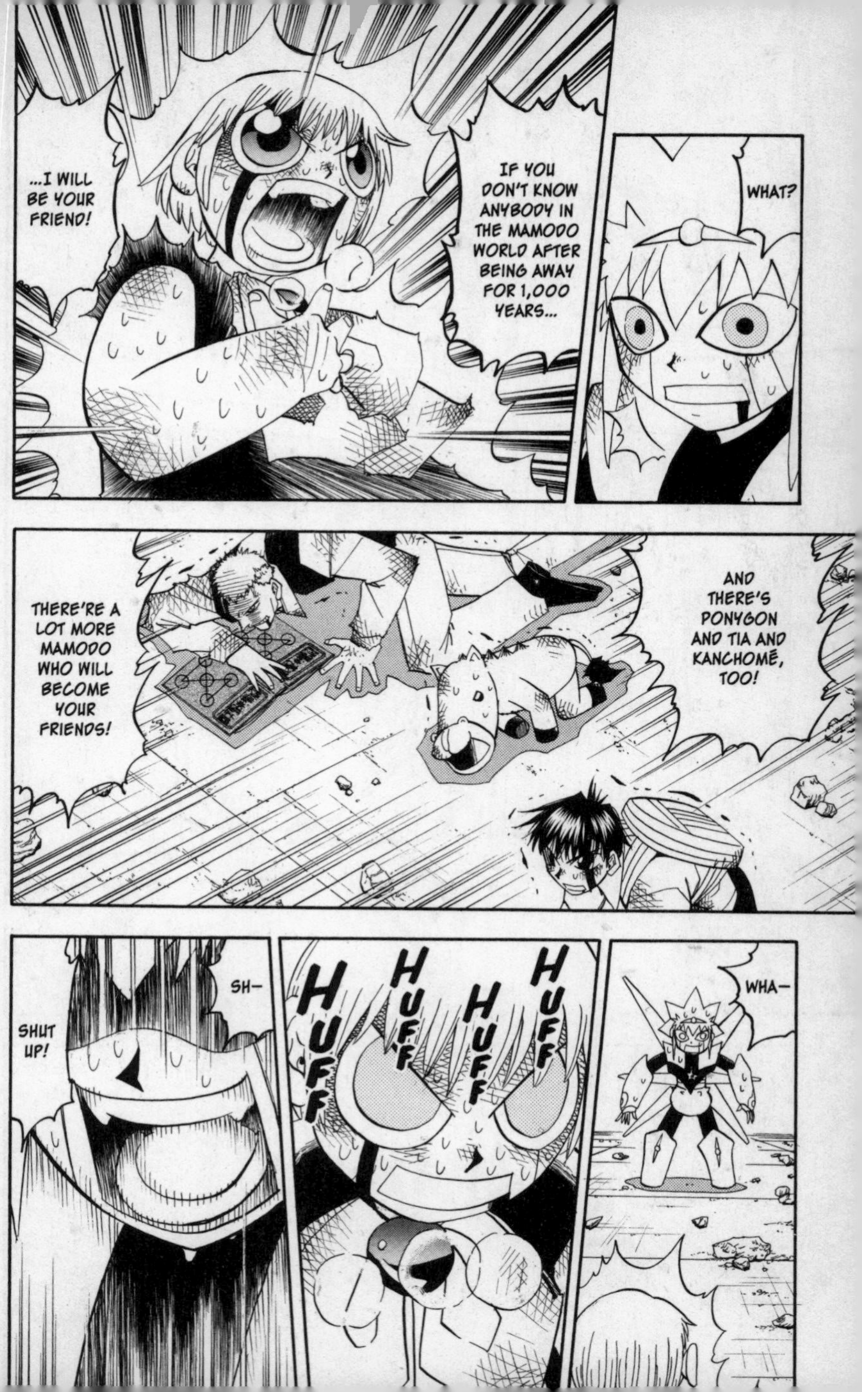
WHAT?
IF YOU DON'T KNOW ANYBODY IN THE MAMODO WORLD AFTER BEING AWAY FOR 1,000 YEARS...
...I WILL BE YOUR FRIEND!
AND THERE'S PONYGON AND TIA AND KANCHOMÉ, TOO!
THERE'RE A LOT MORE MAMODO WHO WILL BECOME YOUR FRIENDS!
WHA-
HUFF
HUFF
HUFF
HUFF
SH-
SHUT UP!

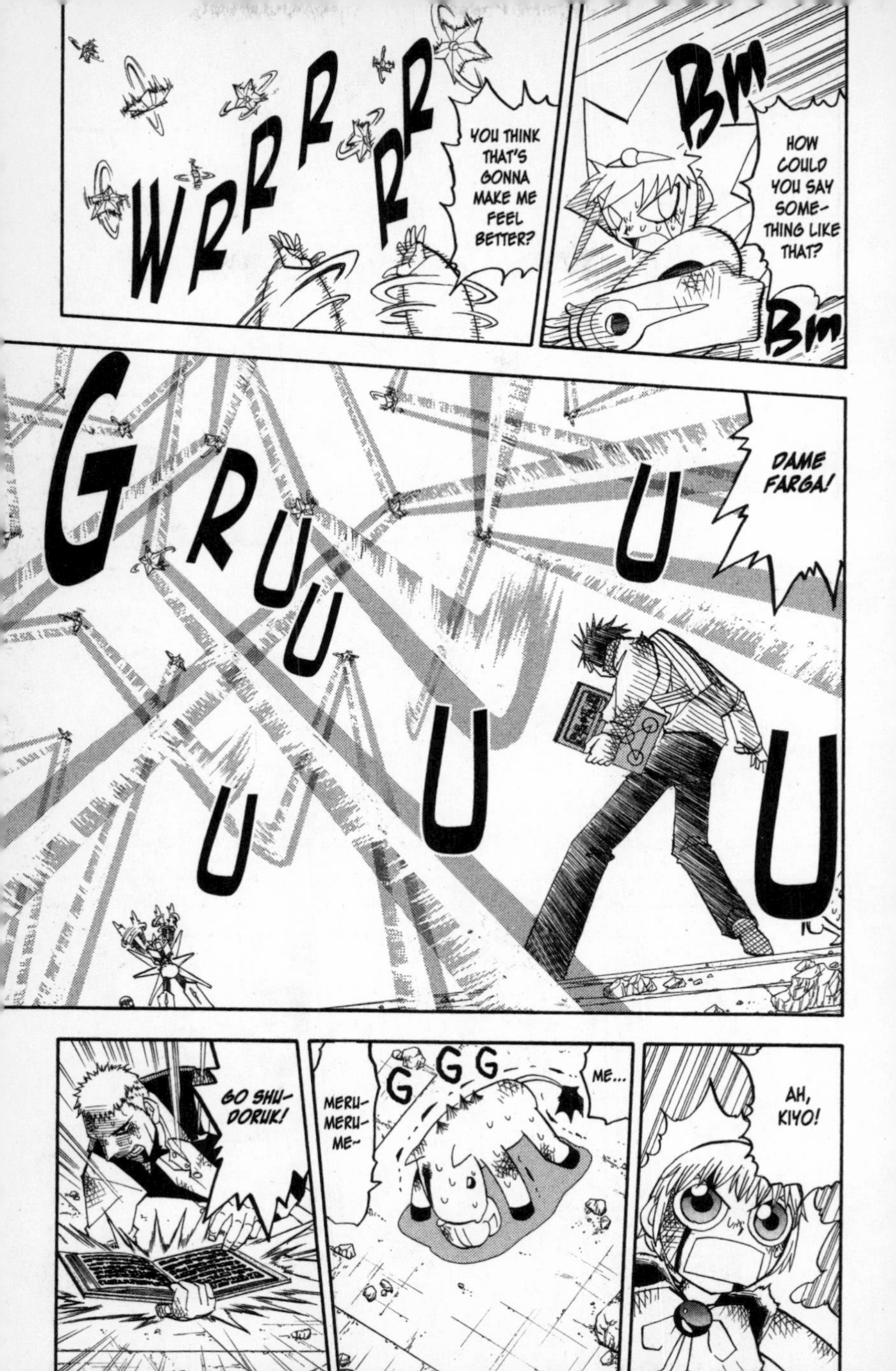
Bm
HOW COULD YOU SAY SOME-THING LIKE THAT?
Bm
YOU THINK THAT'S GONNA MAKE ME FEEL BETTER?
WRRRRR
DAME FARGA!
GRUUUUUUU
AH, KIYO!
ME...
GGG
MERU-MERU-ME~
GO SHU-DORUK!

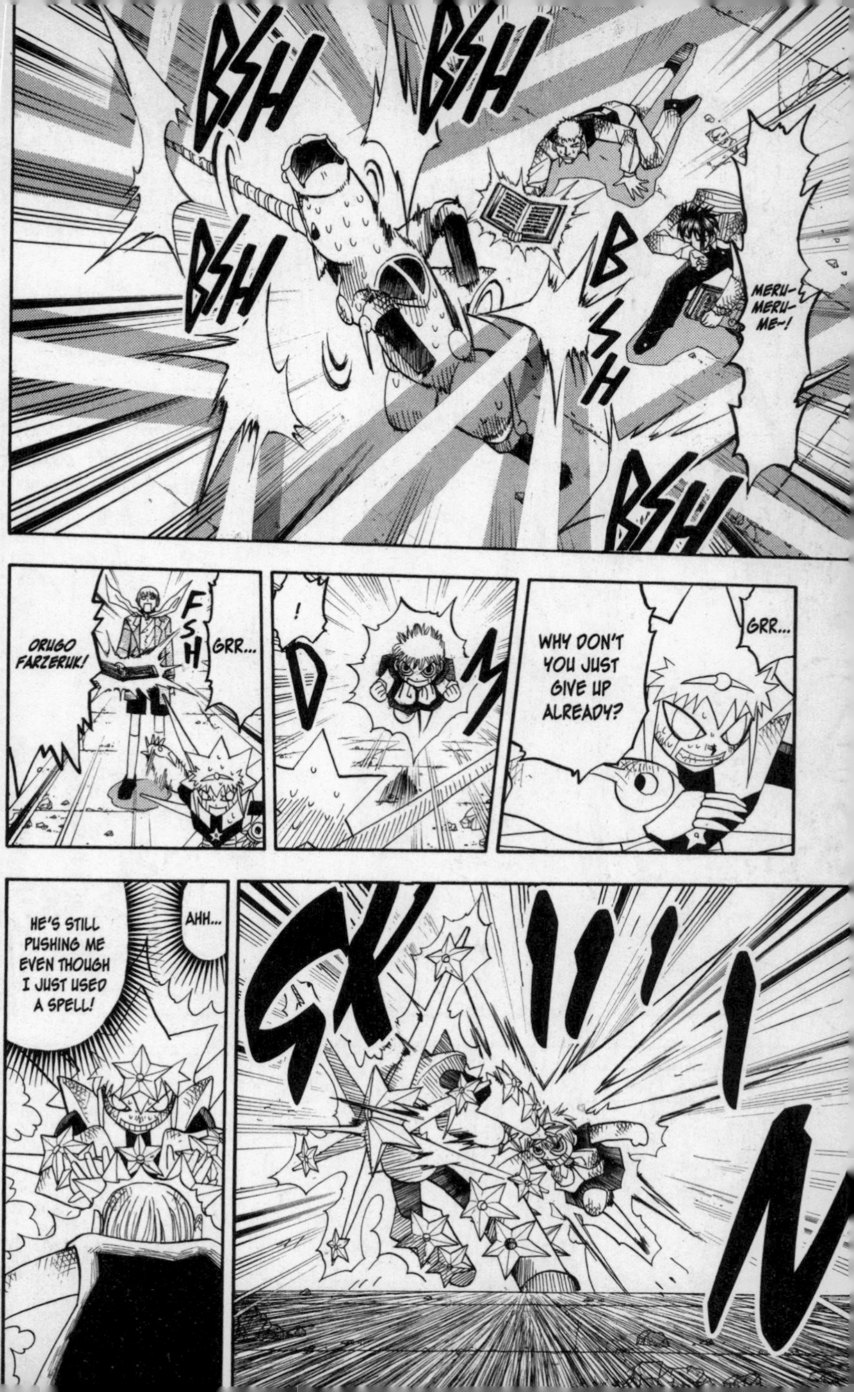
MERU-MERU-ME~!
BSH
BSH
BSH
BSH
BSH
GRR...
WHY DON'T YOU JUST GIVE UP ALREADY?
!
GRR...
FSH
ORUGO FARZERUK!
AHH...
HE'S STILL PUSHING ME EVEN THOUGH I JUST USED A SPELL!

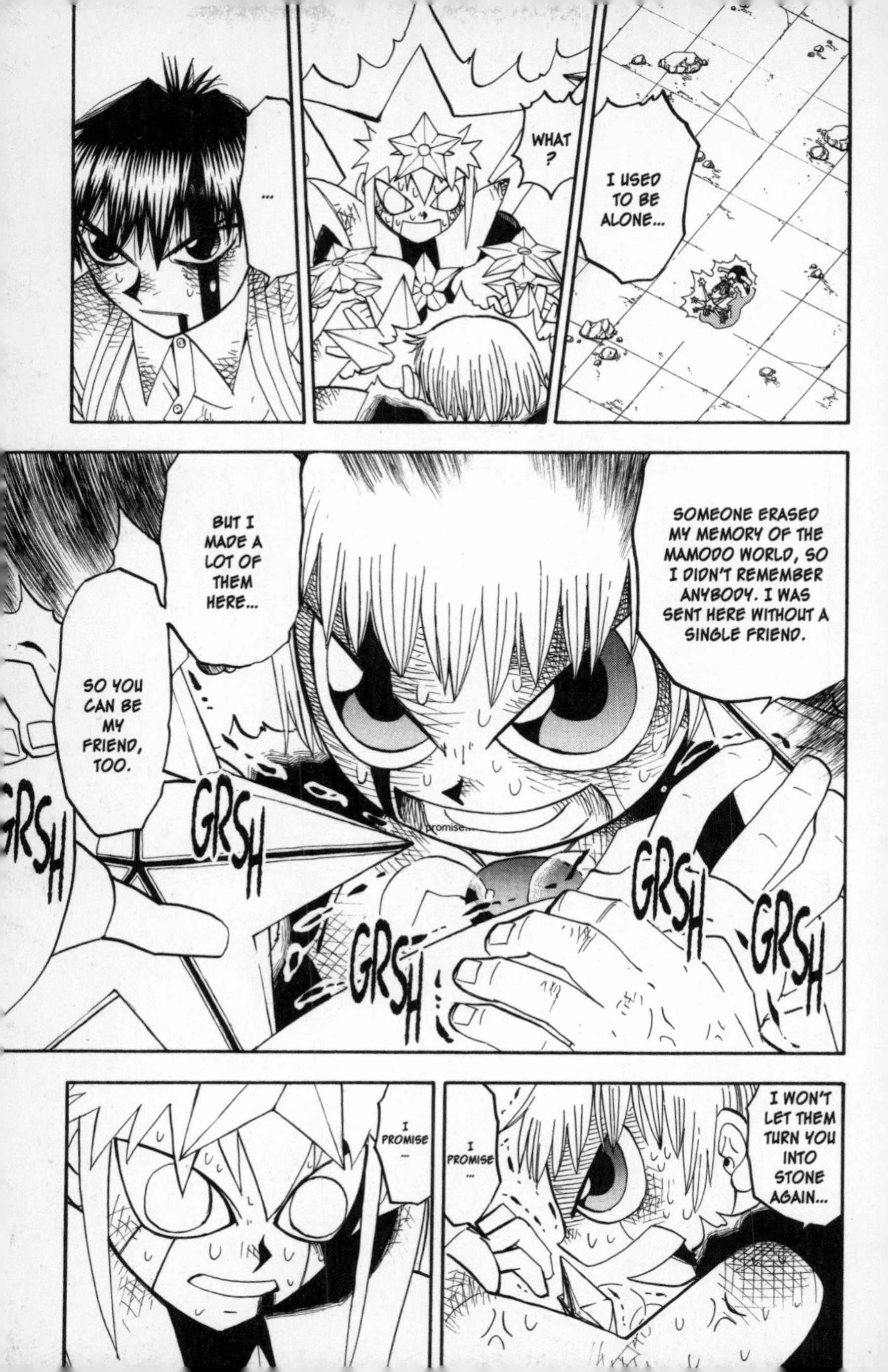
I USED TO BE ALONE...
WHAT?
...
SOMEONE ERASED MY MEMORY OF THE MAMODO WORLD, SO I DIDN'T REMEMBER ANYBODY. I WAS SENT HERE WITHOUT A SINGLE FRIEND.
BUT I MADE A LOT OF THEM HERE...
SO YOU CAN BE MY FRIEND, TOO.
GRSH
GRSH
GRSH
GRSH
GRSH
promise...
I WON'T LET THEM TURN YOU INTO STONE AGAIN...
I PROMISE...
I PROMISE...

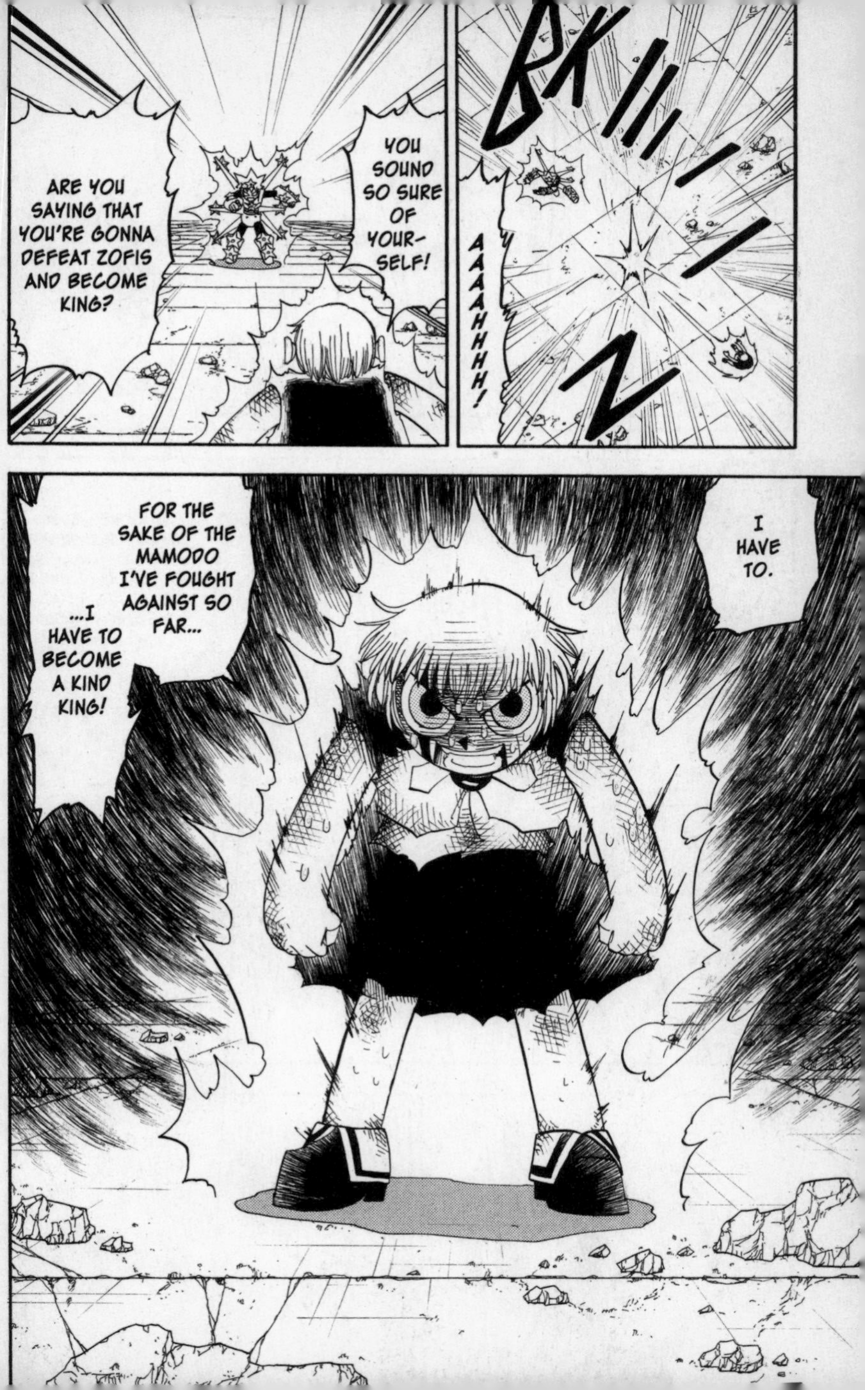
BKIIIIIIN
AAAAAHHHH!
YOU SOUND SO SURE OF YOUR-SELF!
ARE YOU SAYING THAT YOU'RE GONNA DEFEAT ZOFIS AND BECOME KING?
I HAVE TO.
FOR THE SAKE OF THE MAMODO I'VE FOUGHT AGAINST SO FAR...
...I HAVE TO BECOME A KIND KING!

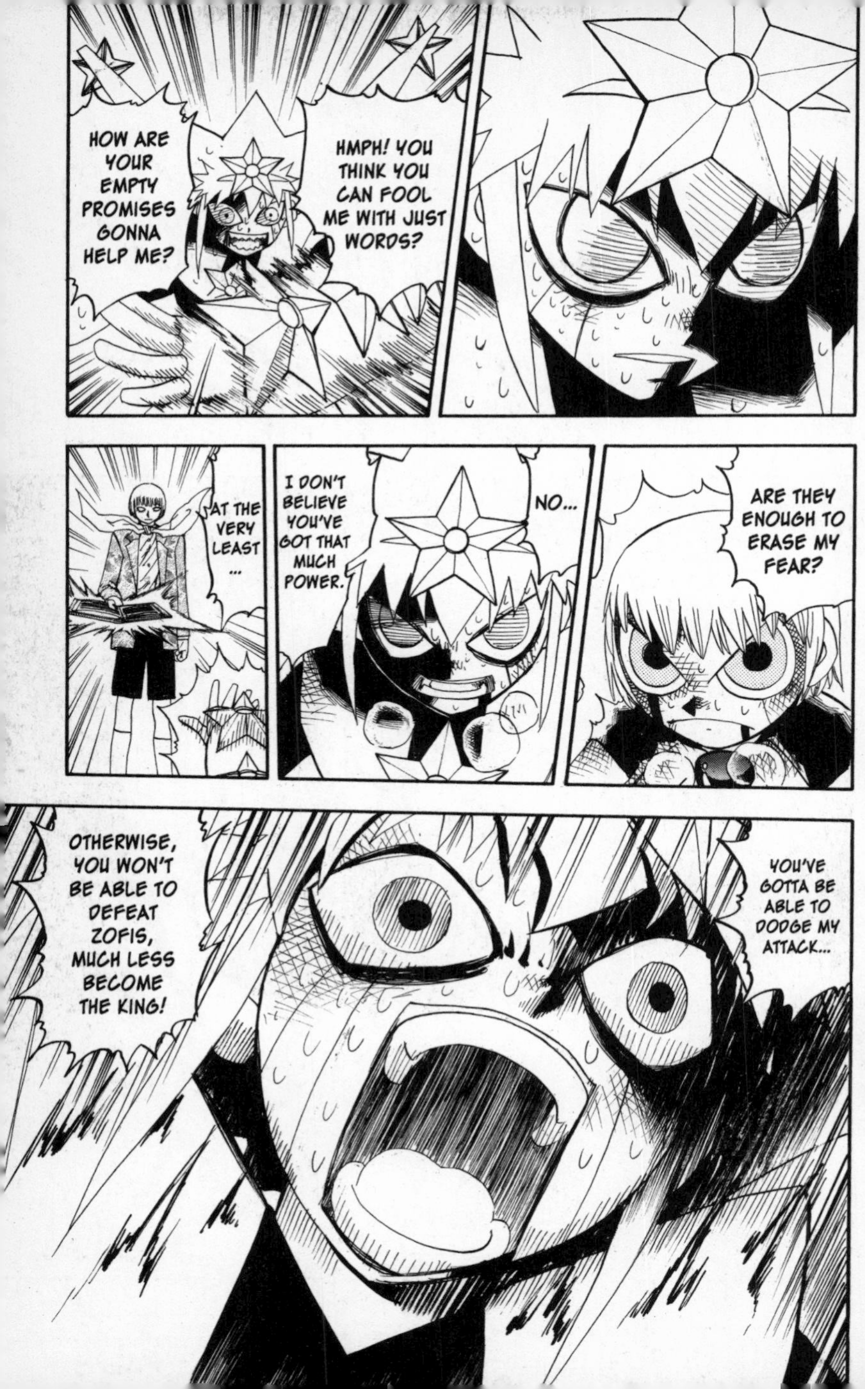
HMPH! YOU THINK YOU CAN FOOL ME WITH JUST WORDS?
HOW ARE YOUR EMPTY PROMISES GONNA HELP ME?
ARE THEY ENOUGH TO ERASE MY FEAR?
NO...
I DON'T BELIEVE YOU'VE GOT THAT MUCH POWER.
AT THE VERY LEAST ...
YOU'VE GOTTA BE ABLE TO DODGE MY ATTACK...
OTHERWISE, YOU WON'T BE ABLE TO DEFEAT ZOFIS, MUCH LESS BECOME THE KING!

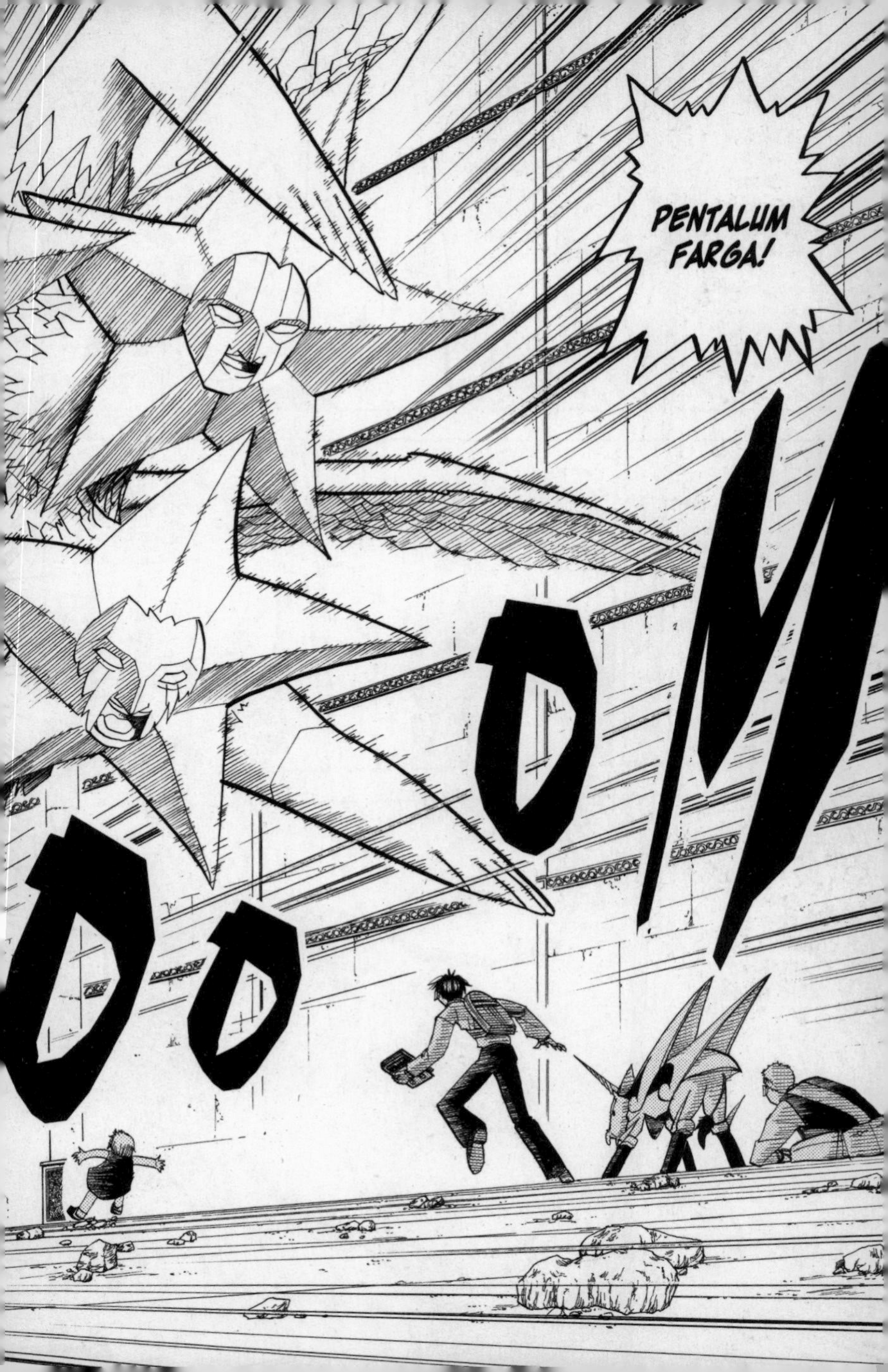
PENTALUM FARGA!
DOOOM

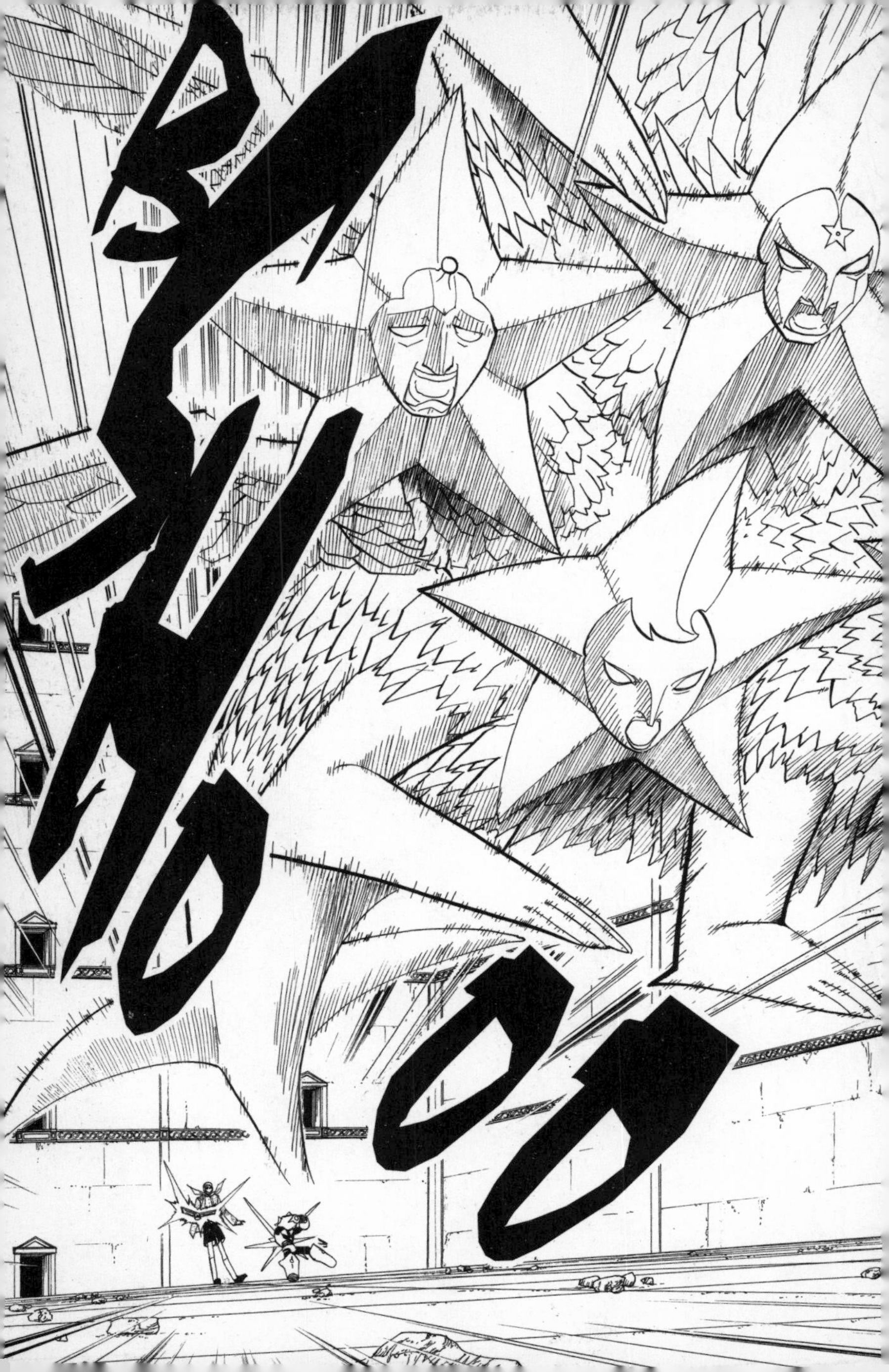

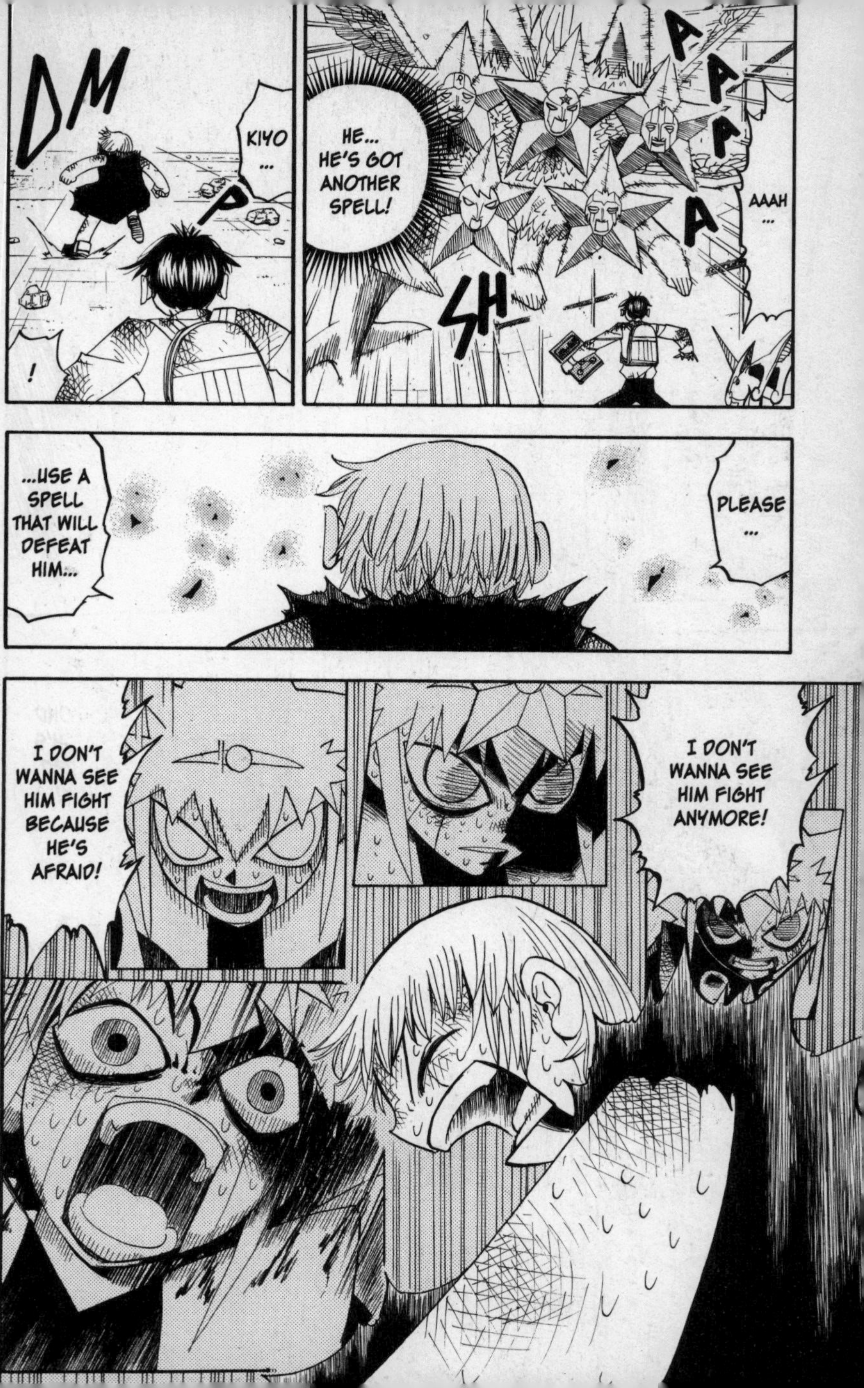
PAPAPA
HE... HE'S GOT ANOTHER SPELL!
AAAH ...
SH
DM
P
KIYO ...
!
PLEASE ...
...USE A SPELL THAT WILL DEFEAT HIM...
I DON'T WANNA SEE HIM FIGHT ANYMORE!
I DON'T WANNA SEE HIM FIGHT BECAUSE HE'S AFRAID!

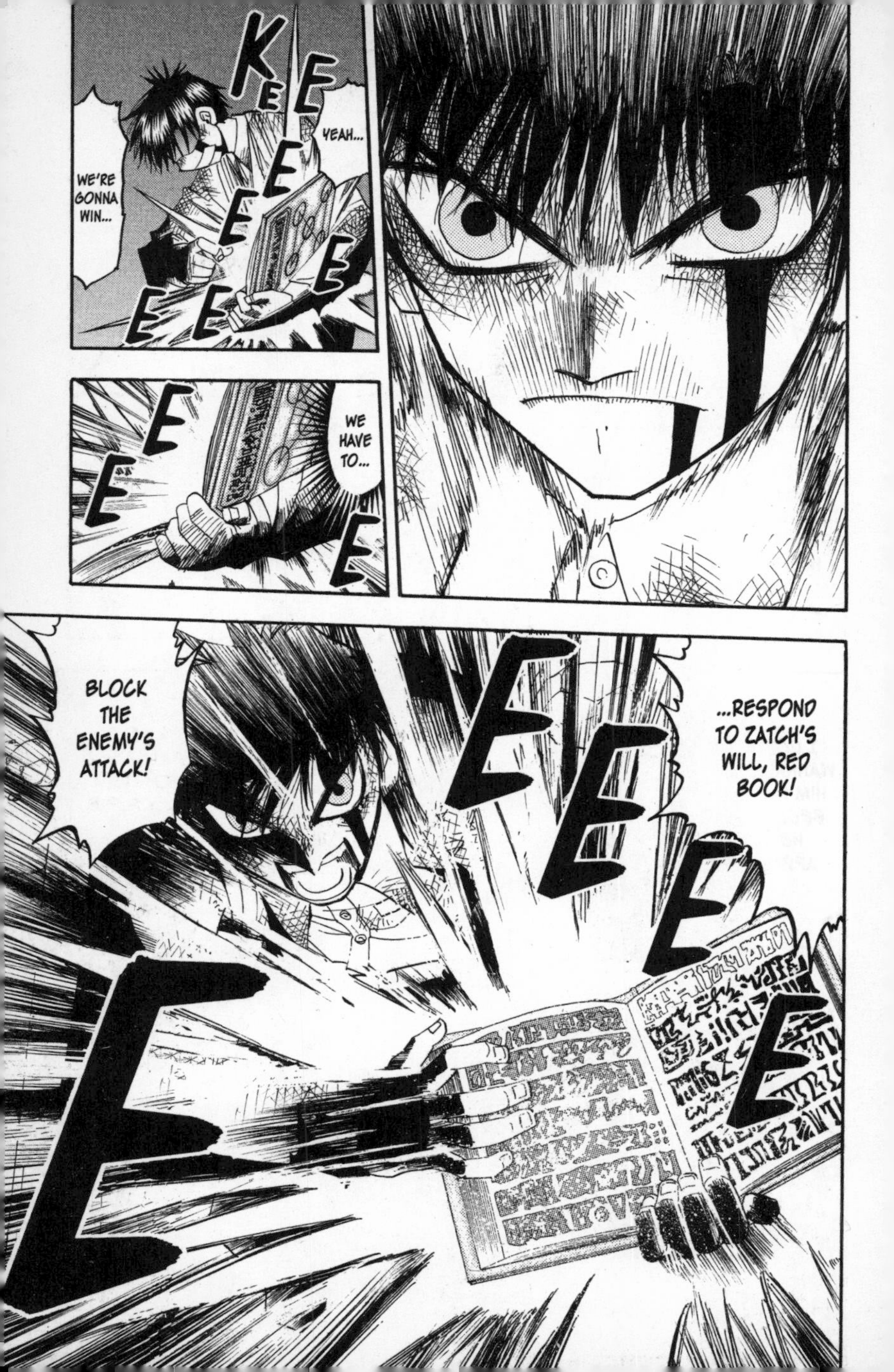
KEEEEEEEE
YEAH...
WE'RE GONNA WIN...
EEEE
WE HAVE TO...
EEEEEEE
...RESPOND TO ZATCH'S WILL, RED BOOK!
BLOCK THE ENEMY'S ATTACK!

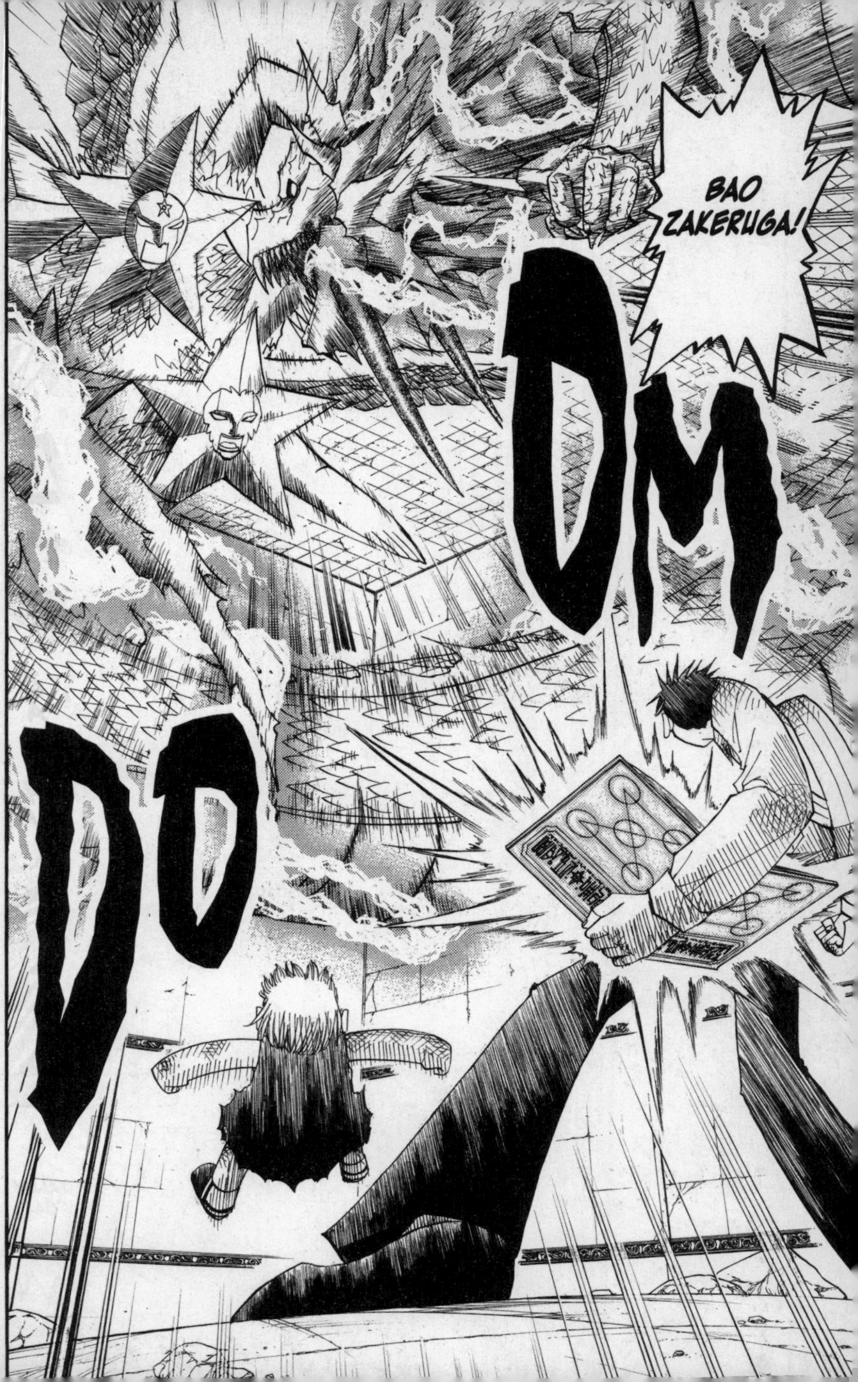
BAO ZAKERUGA!
DOM
DO

LEVEL 141: Another Face

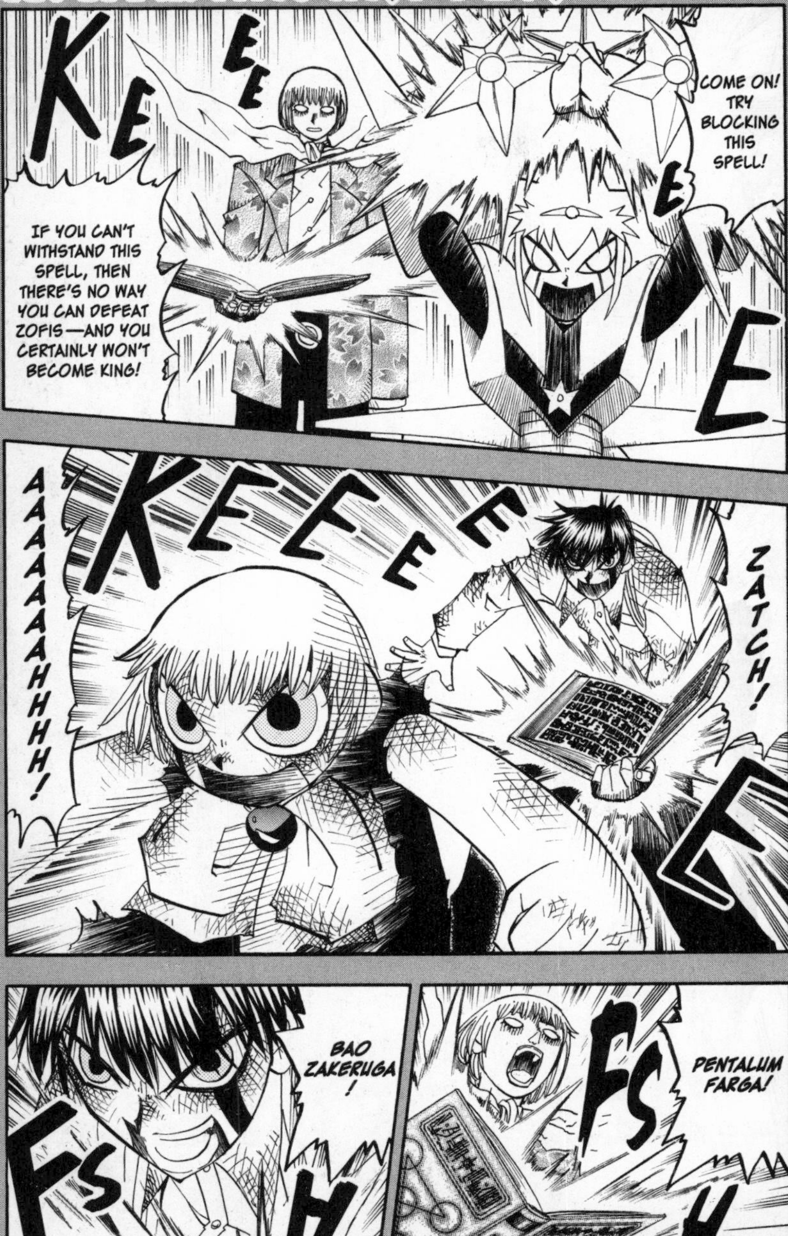
COME ON! TRY BLOCKING THIS SPELL!
IF YOU CAN'T WITHSTAND THIS SPELL, THEN THERE'S NO WAY YOU CAN DEFEAT ZOFIS—AND YOU CERTAINLY WON'T BECOME KING!
KEEEEEE
ZATCH!
AAAAAAAAAHHHHH!
KEEEEEE
PENTALUM FARGA!
FSSH
BAO ZAKERUGA!
FSSH

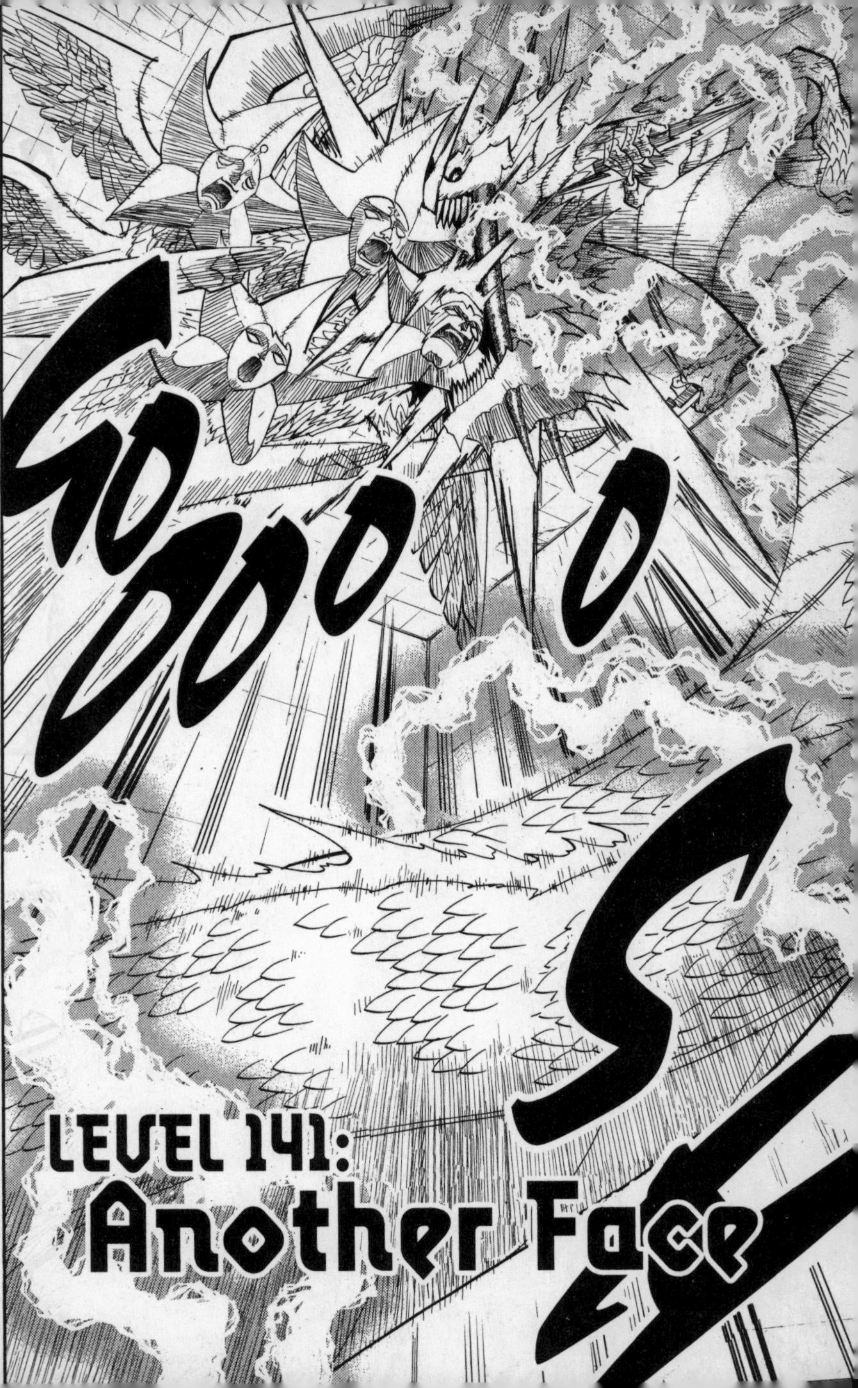
GOOOOOSH
LEVEL 141:
Another Face

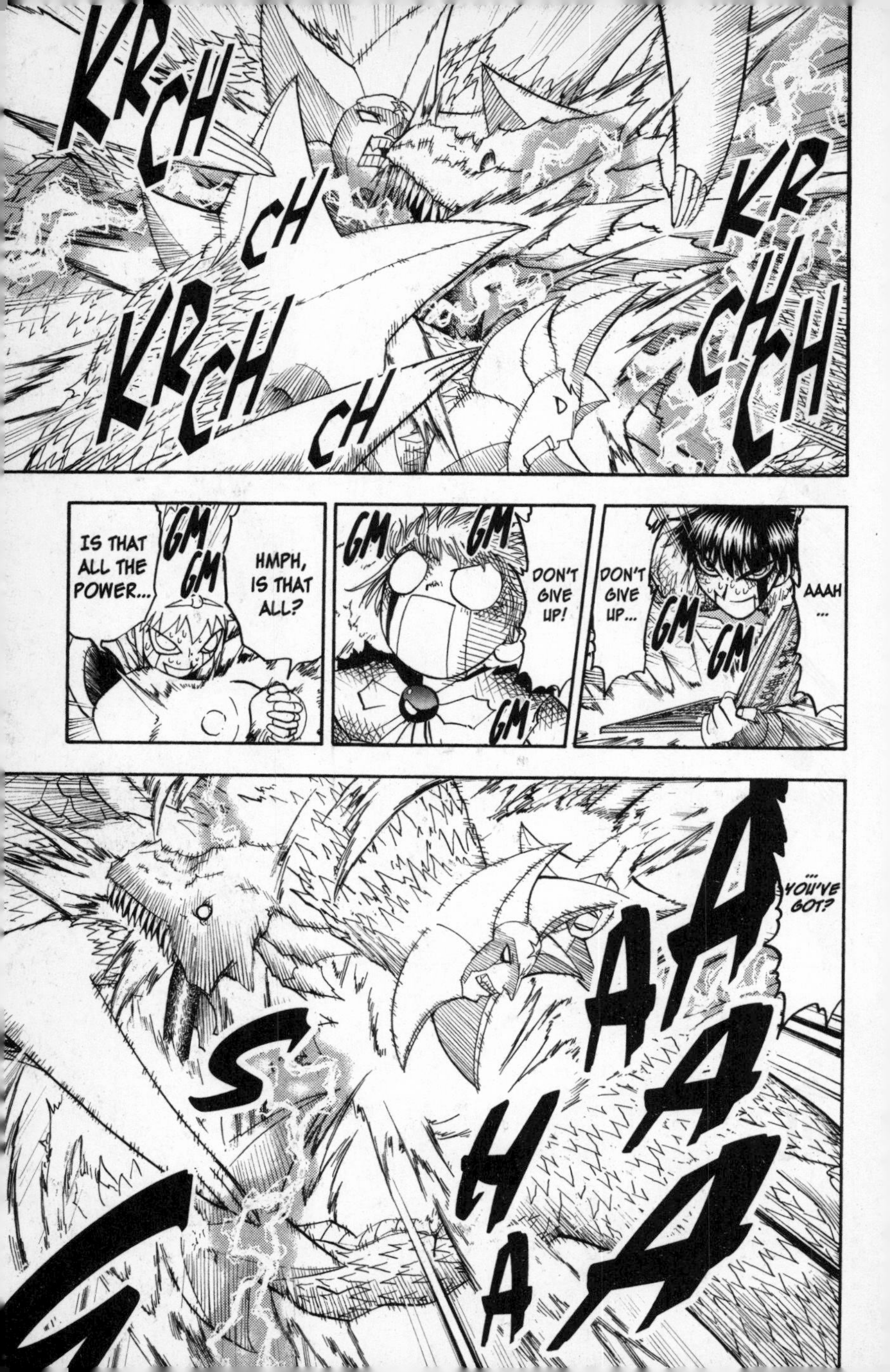
KR
CH
CH
CH
KRCH
CH
KRCH
CH
DON'T GIVE UP...
AAAH ...
GM
GM
GM
GM
DON'T GIVE UP!
GM
HMPH, IS THAT ALL?
IS THAT ALL THE POWER...
GM
GM
... YOU'VE GOT?

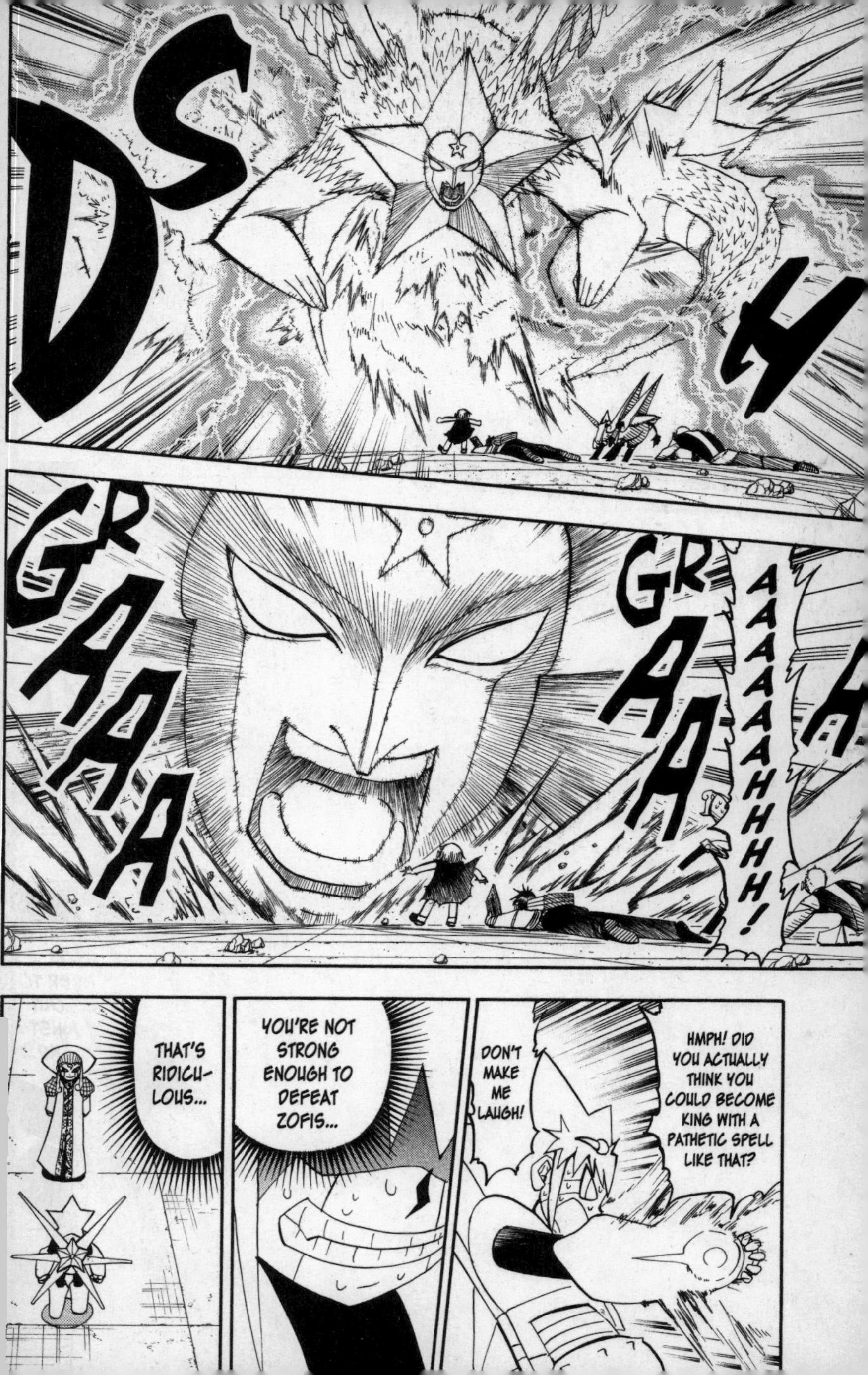
DSH
GRAAA
AAAAAAHHHH!
GRAAAA
HMPH! DID YOU ACTUALLY THINK YOU COULD BECOME KING WITH A PATHETIC SPELL LIKE THAT?
DON'T MAKE ME LAUGH!
YOU'RE NOT STRONG ENOUGH TO DEFEAT ZOFIS...
THAT'S RIDICU-LOUS...

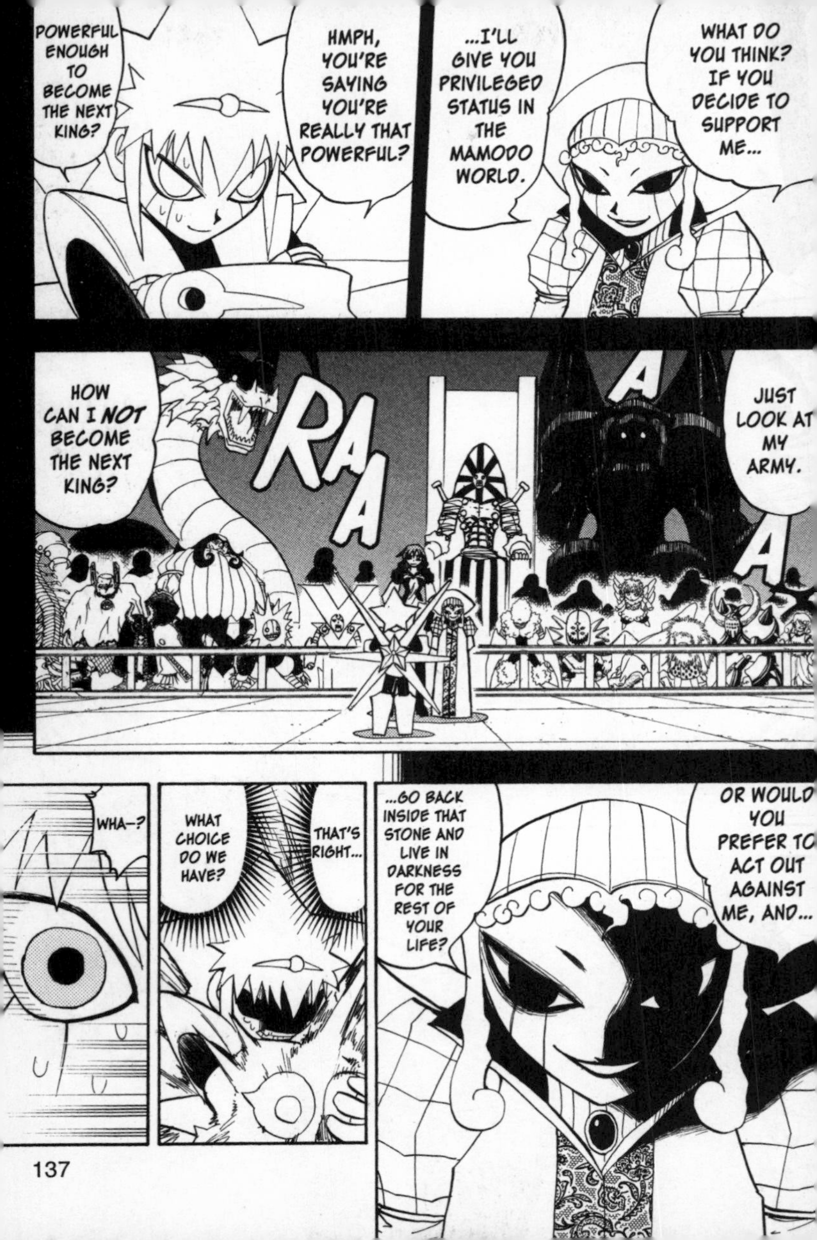
WHAT DO YOU THINK? IF YOU DECIDE TO SUPPORT ME...
...I'LL GIVE YOU PRIVILEGED STATUS IN THE MAMODO WORLD.
HMPH, YOU'RE SAYING YOU'RE REALLY THAT POWERFUL?
POWERFUL ENOUGH TO BECOME THE NEXT KING?
JUST LOOK AT MY ARMY.
RAAAA
HOW CAN I NOT BECOME THE NEXT KING?
OR WOULD YOU PREFER TO ACT OUT AGAINST ME, AND...
...GO BACK INSIDE THAT STONE AND LIVE IN DARKNESS FOR THE REST OF YOUR LIFE?
THAT'S RIGHT...
WHAT CHOICE DO WE HAVE?
WHA-?

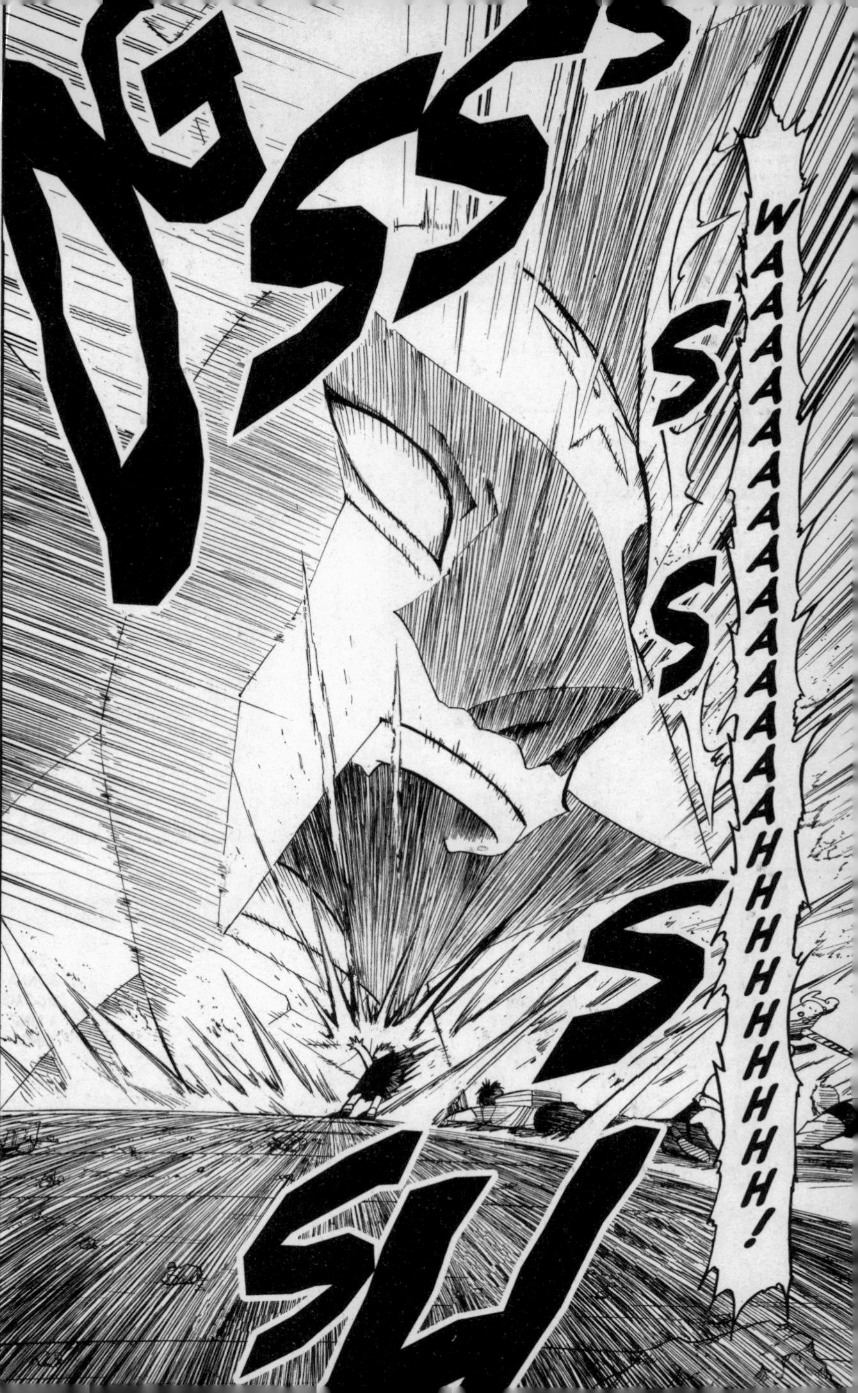
WAAAAAAAAAAAAAHHHHHHHHH!

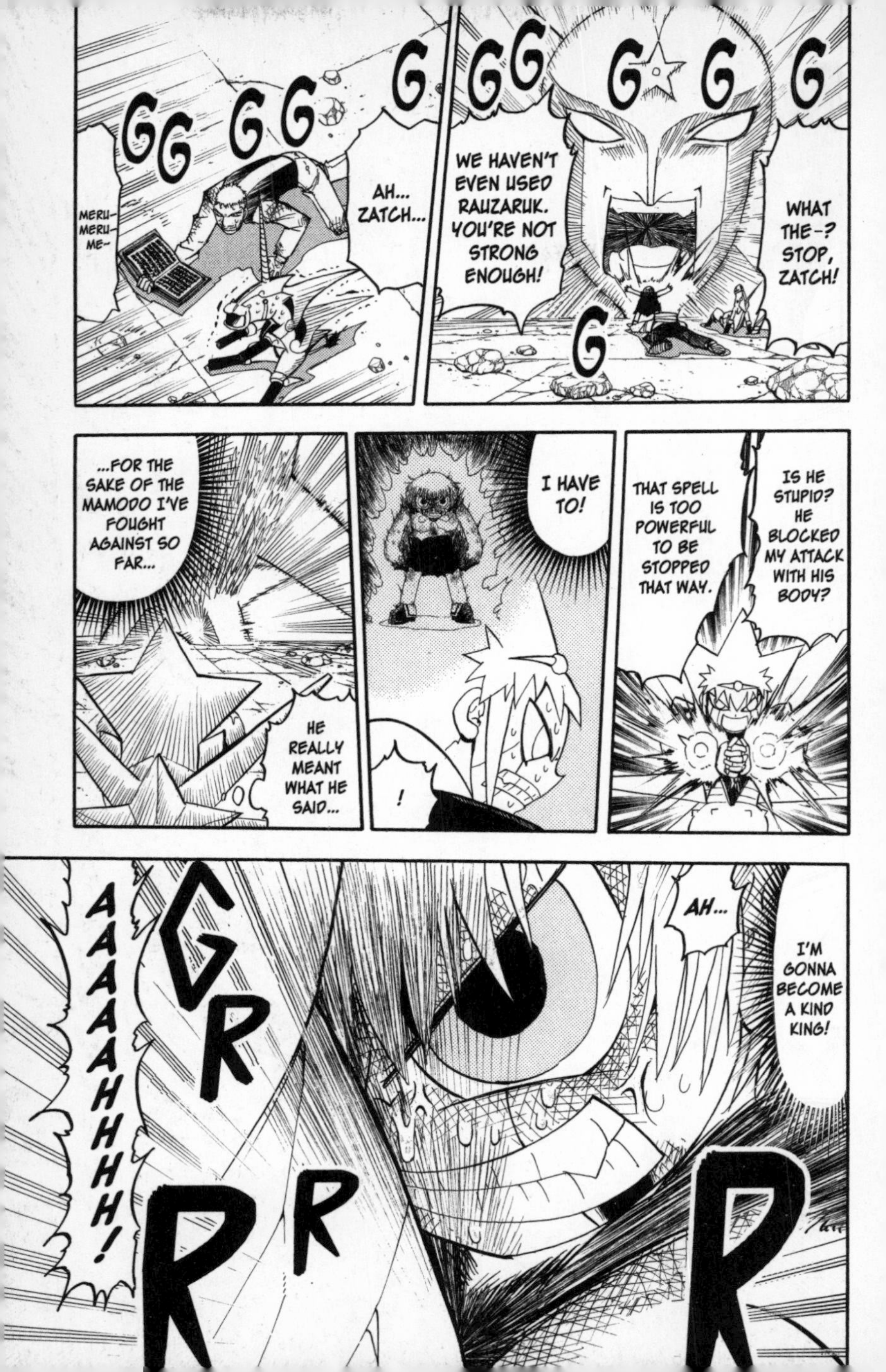
G G G G G G G
WHAT THE-? STOP, ZATCH!
WE HAVEN'T EVEN USED RAUZARUK. YOU'RE NOT STRONG ENOUGH!
G
G
AH... ZATCH...
MERU-MERU-ME~
G G G G G
IS HE STUPID? HE BLOCKED MY ATTACK WITH HIS BODY?
THAT SPELL IS TOO POWERFUL TO BE STOPPED THAT WAY.
I HAVE TO!
!
...FOR THE SAKE OF THE MAMODO I'VE FOUGHT AGAINST SO FAR...
HE REALLY MEANT WHAT HE SAID...
AH...
I'M GONNA BECOME A KIND KING!
GRRRR
AAAAAHHHH!

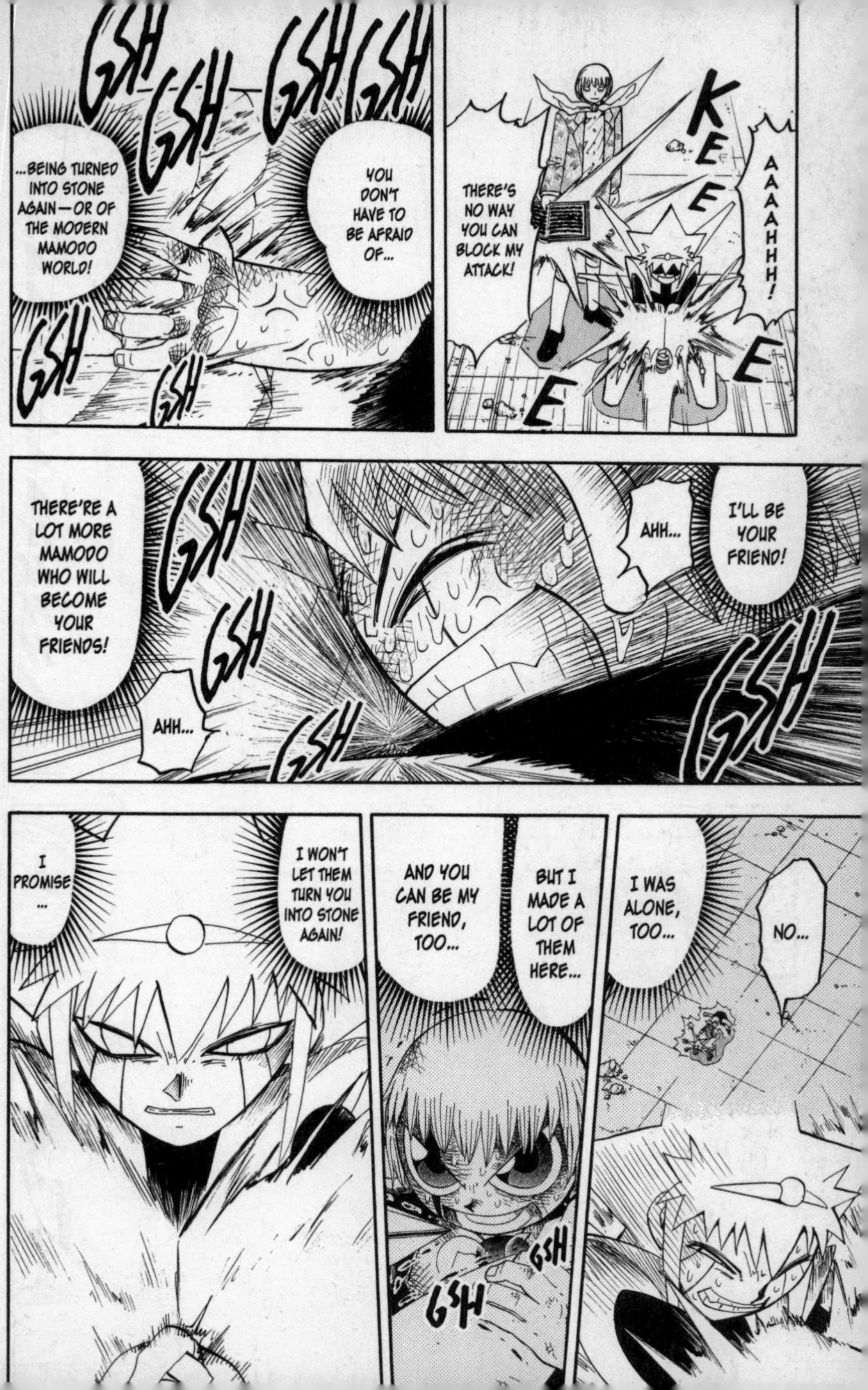
KEEEE
AAAAAHHH!
THERE'S NO WAY YOU CAN BLOCK MY ATTACK!
GSH GSH GSH GSH
YOU DON'T HAVE TO BE AFRAID OF...
...BEING TURNED INTO STONE AGAIN—OR OF THE MODERN MAMODO WORLD!
GSH GSH
I'LL BE YOUR FRIEND!
AHH...
GSH
GSH GSH GSH
THERE'RE A LOT MORE MAMODO WHO WILL BECOME YOUR FRIENDS!
AHH...
NO...
I WAS ALONE, TOO...
BUT I MADE A LOT OF THEM HERE...
AND YOU CAN BE MY FRIEND, TOO...
GSH GSH
I WON'T LET THEM TURN YOU INTO STONE AGAIN!
I PROMISE...

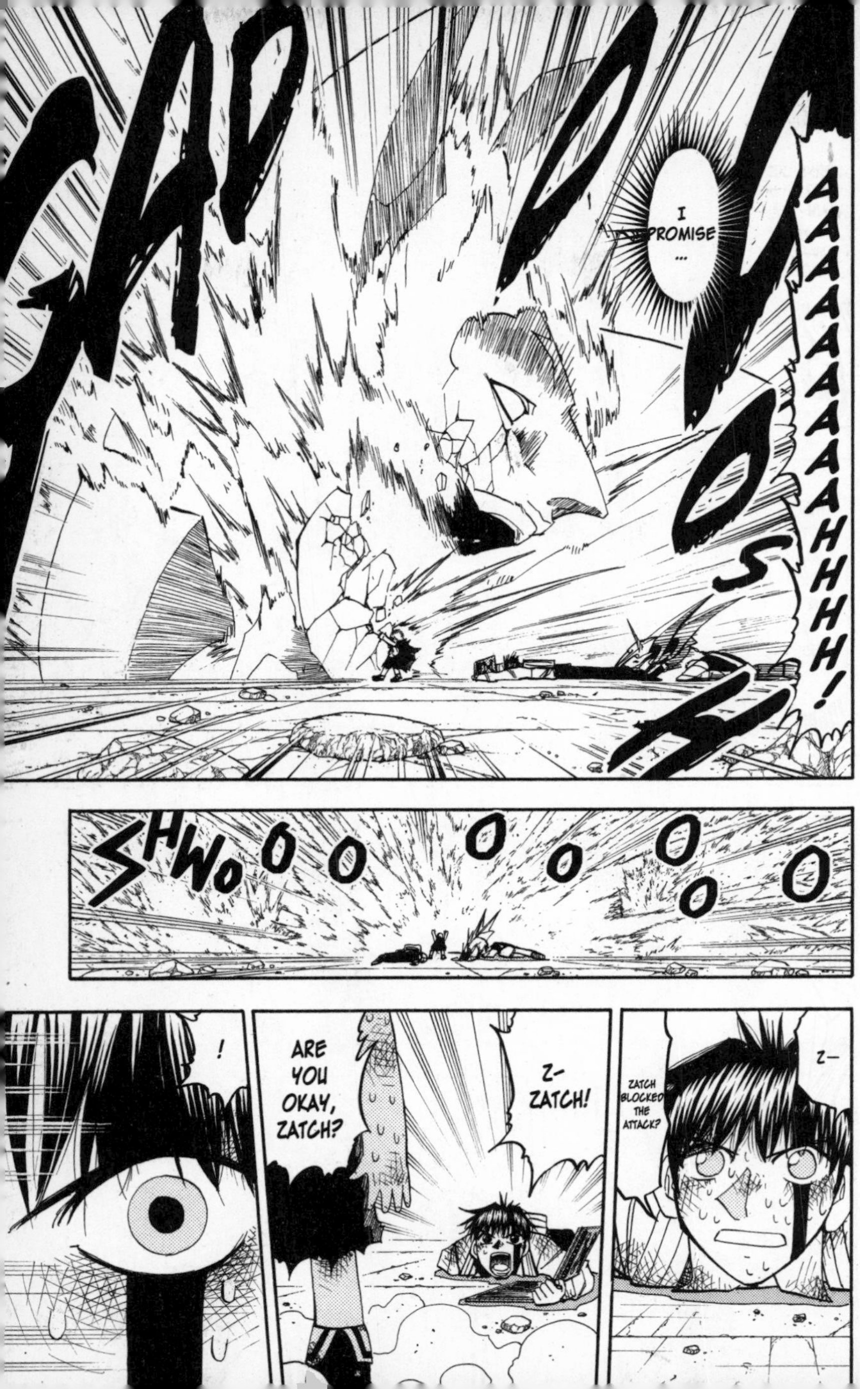
AAAAAAAAAHHHH!
I PROMISE...
SHWOOOOOOO
Z—
ZATCH BLOCKED THE ATTACK?
Z- ZATCH!
ARE YOU OKAY, ZATCH?
!

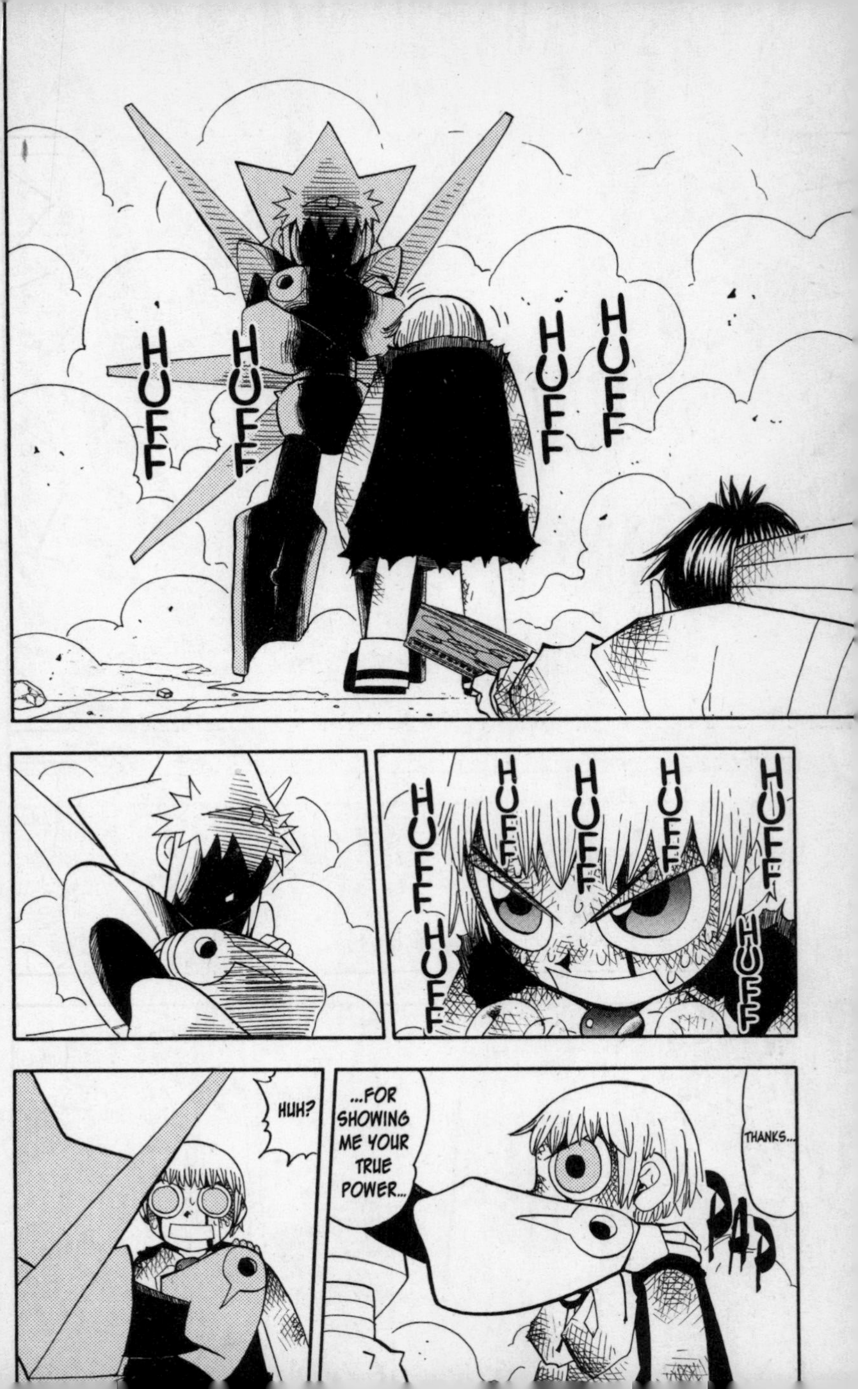
HUFF HUFF
HUFF HUFF
HUFF HUFF
HUFF HUFF
HUFF HUFF
HUFF HUFF
THANKS...
...FOR SHOWING ME YOUR TRUE POWER...
PAP
HUH?

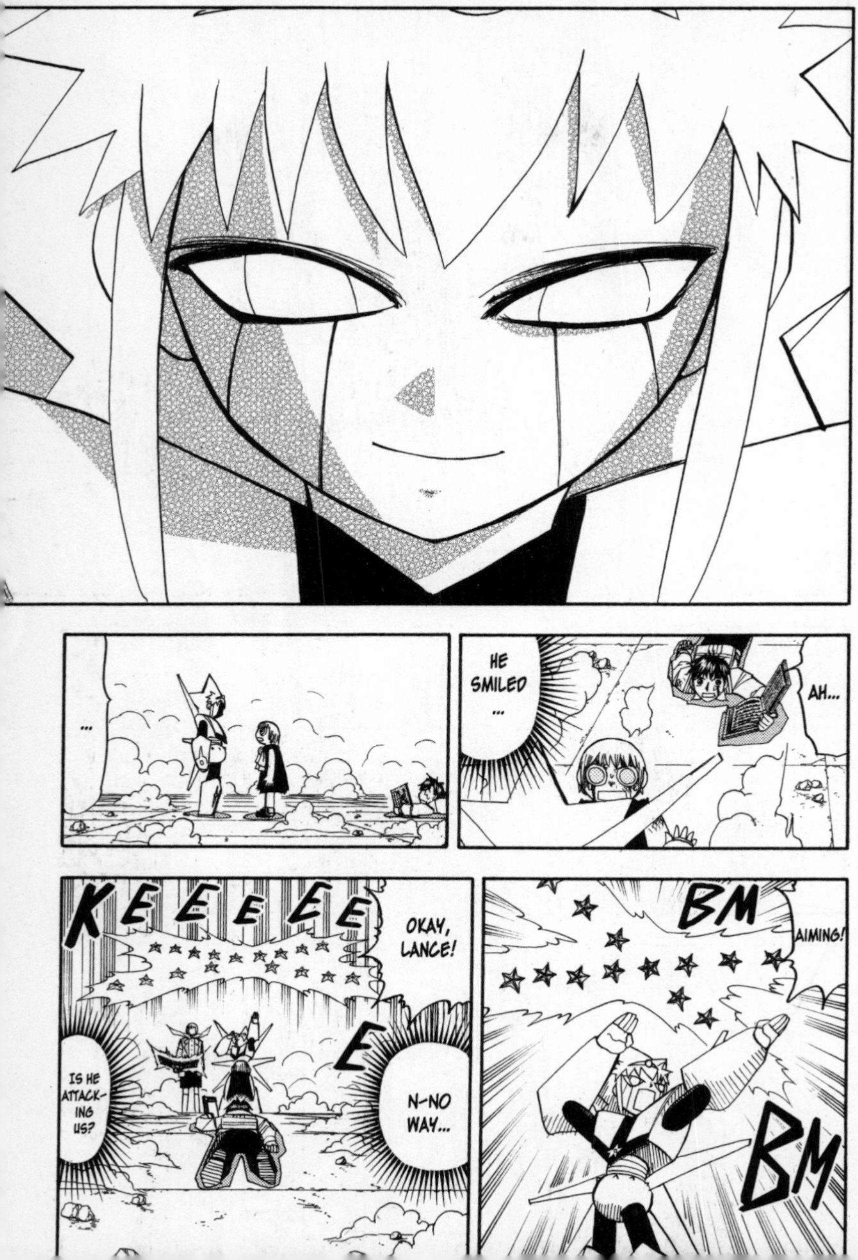
AH...
HE SMILED ...
...
BM
AIMING!
BM
KEEEEEE
OKAY, LANCE!
N-NO WAY...
IS HE ATTACK-ING US?

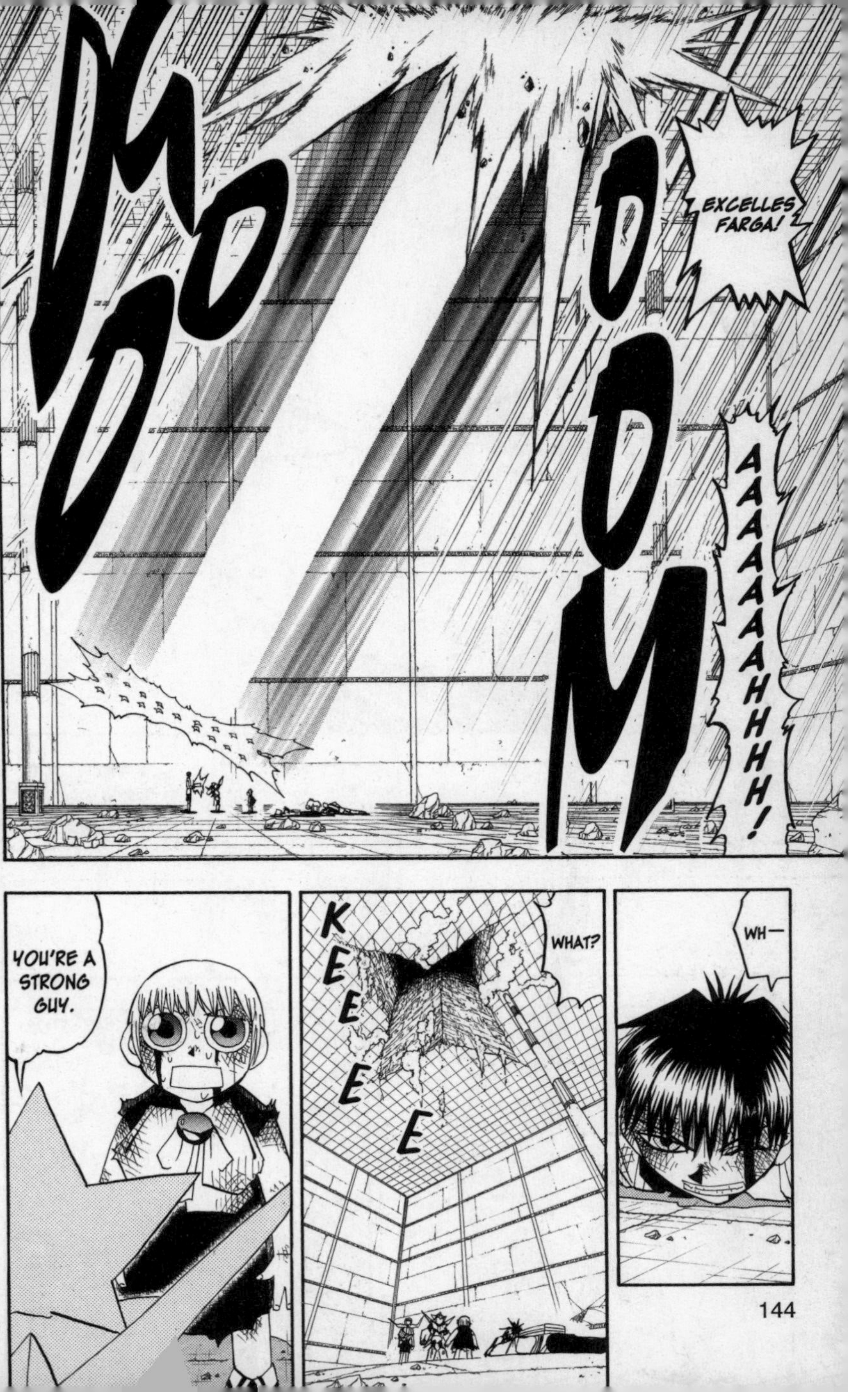
EXCELLES FARGA!
AAAAAAAAHHHHH!
WH—
WHAT?
KEEEEE
YOU'RE A STRONG GUY.

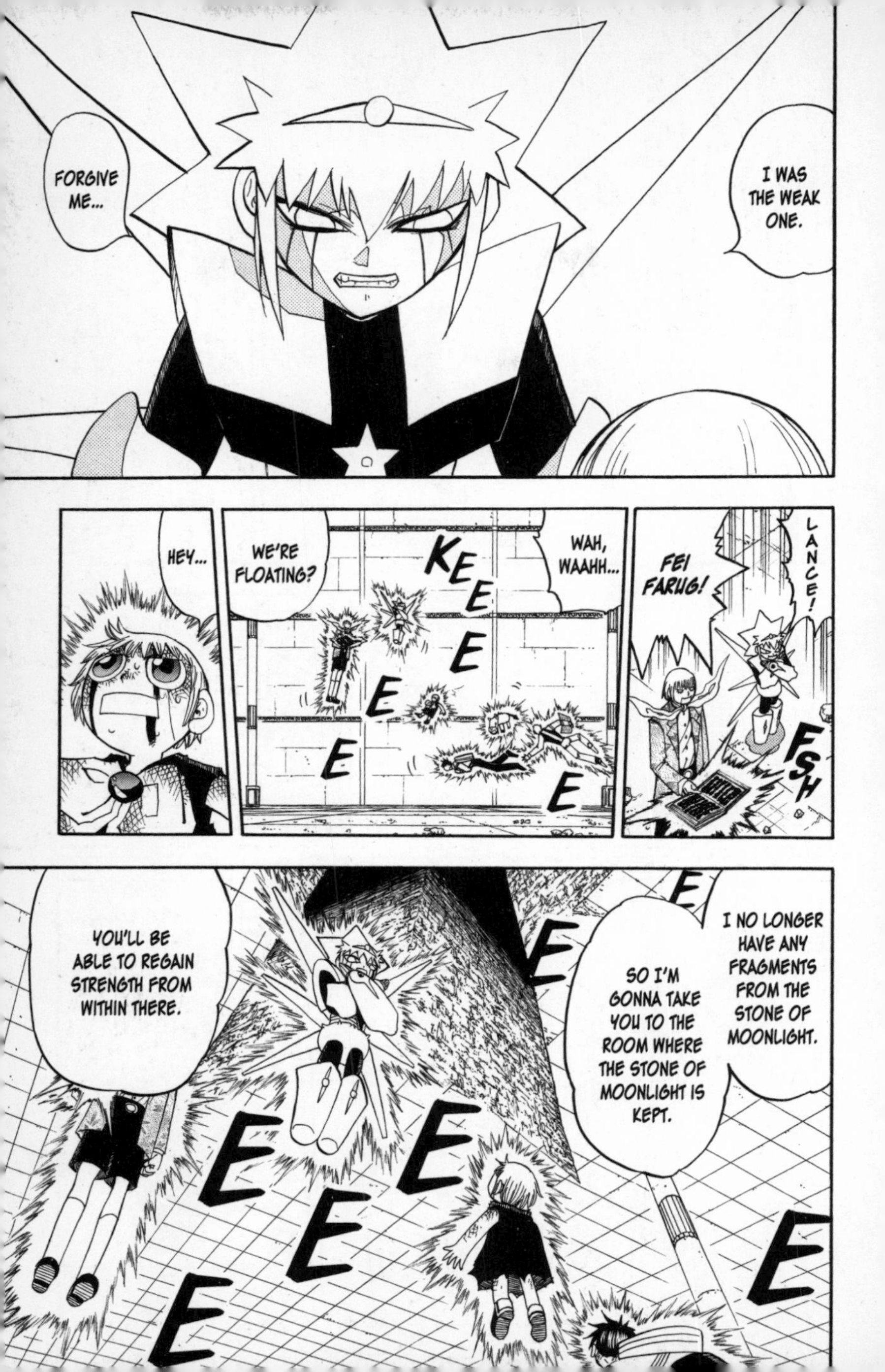
I WAS THE WEAK ONE.
FORGIVE ME...
LANCE!
FEI FARUG!
FSH
WAH, WAAHH...
KEEEEEEE
WE'RE FLOATING?
HEY...
I NO LONGER HAVE ANY FRAGMENTS FROM THE STONE OF MOONLIGHT.
SO I'M GONNA TAKE YOU TO THE ROOM WHERE THE STONE OF MOONLIGHT IS KEPT.
EEEEEEEE
YOU'LL BE ABLE TO REGAIN STRENGTH FROM WITHIN THERE.

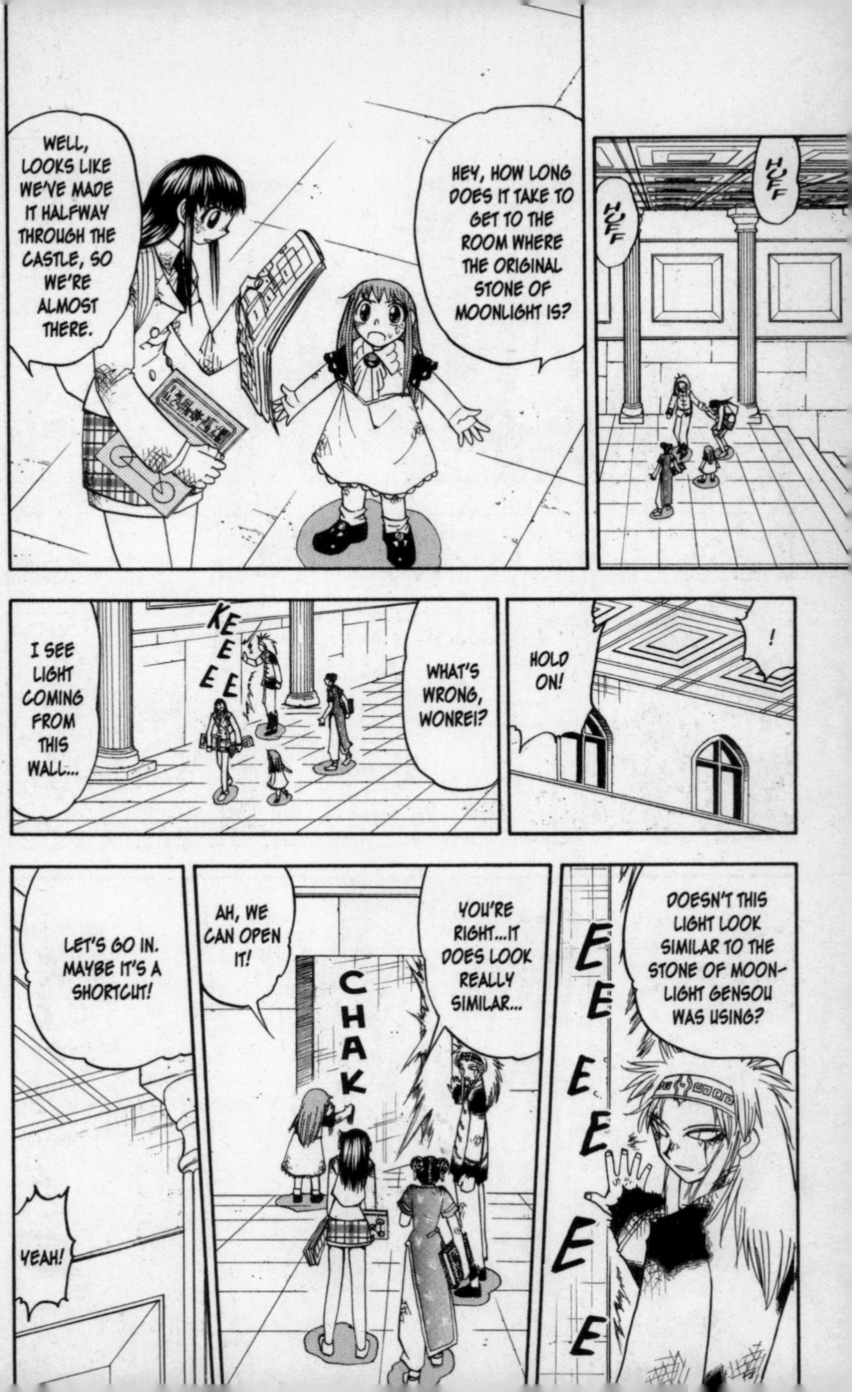
HUFF
HUFF
HEY, HOW LONG DOES IT TAKE TO GET TO THE ROOM WHERE THE ORIGINAL STONE OF MOONLIGHT IS?
WELL, LOOKS LIKE WE'VE MADE IT HALFWAY THROUGH THE CASTLE, SO WE'RE ALMOST THERE.
!
HOLD ON!
WHAT'S WRONG, WONREI?
KEEEE
I SEE LIGHT COMING FROM THIS WALL...
DOESN'T THIS LIGHT LOOK SIMILAR TO THE STONE OF MOON-LIGHT GENSOU WAS USING?
EEEEEE
YOU'RE RIGHT...IT DOES LOOK REALLY SIMILAR...
AH, WE CAN OPEN IT!
CHAK
LET'S GO IN. MAYBE IT'S A SHORTCUT!
YEAH!

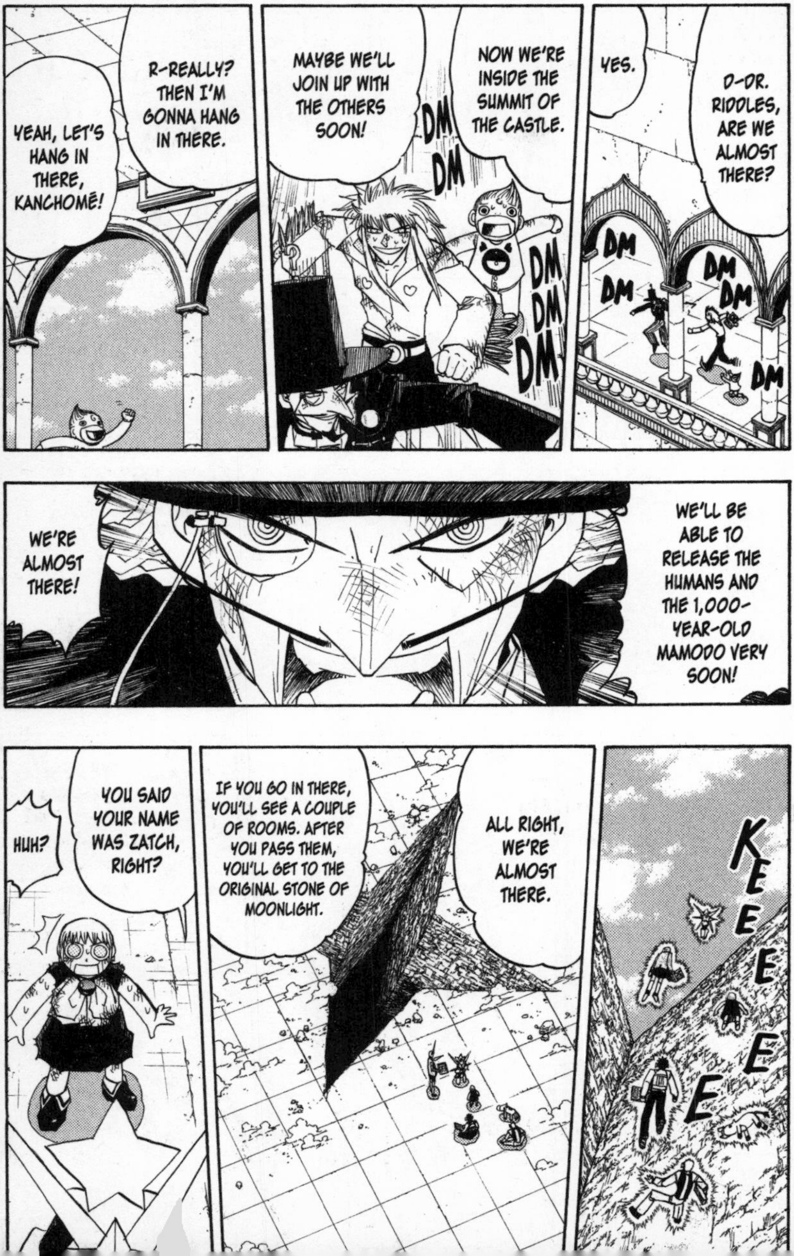
D-DR. RIDDLES, ARE WE ALMOST THERE?
YES.
DM DM DM DM DM
NOW WE'RE INSIDE THE SUMMIT OF THE CASTLE.
MAYBE WE'LL JOIN UP WITH THE OTHERS SOON!
DM DM
DM DM DM
R-REALLY? THEN I'M GONNA HANG IN THERE.
YEAH, LET'S HANG IN THERE, KANCHOMÉ!
WE'LL BE ABLE TO RELEASE THE HUMANS AND THE 1,000-YEAR-OLD MAMODO VERY SOON!
WE'RE ALMOST THERE!
KEEEEEE
ALL RIGHT, WE'RE ALMOST THERE.
IF YOU GO IN THERE, YOU'LL SEE A COUPLE OF ROOMS. AFTER YOU PASS THEM, YOU'LL GET TO THE ORIGINAL STONE OF MOONLIGHT.
YOU SAID YOUR NAME WAS ZATCH, RIGHT?
HUH?

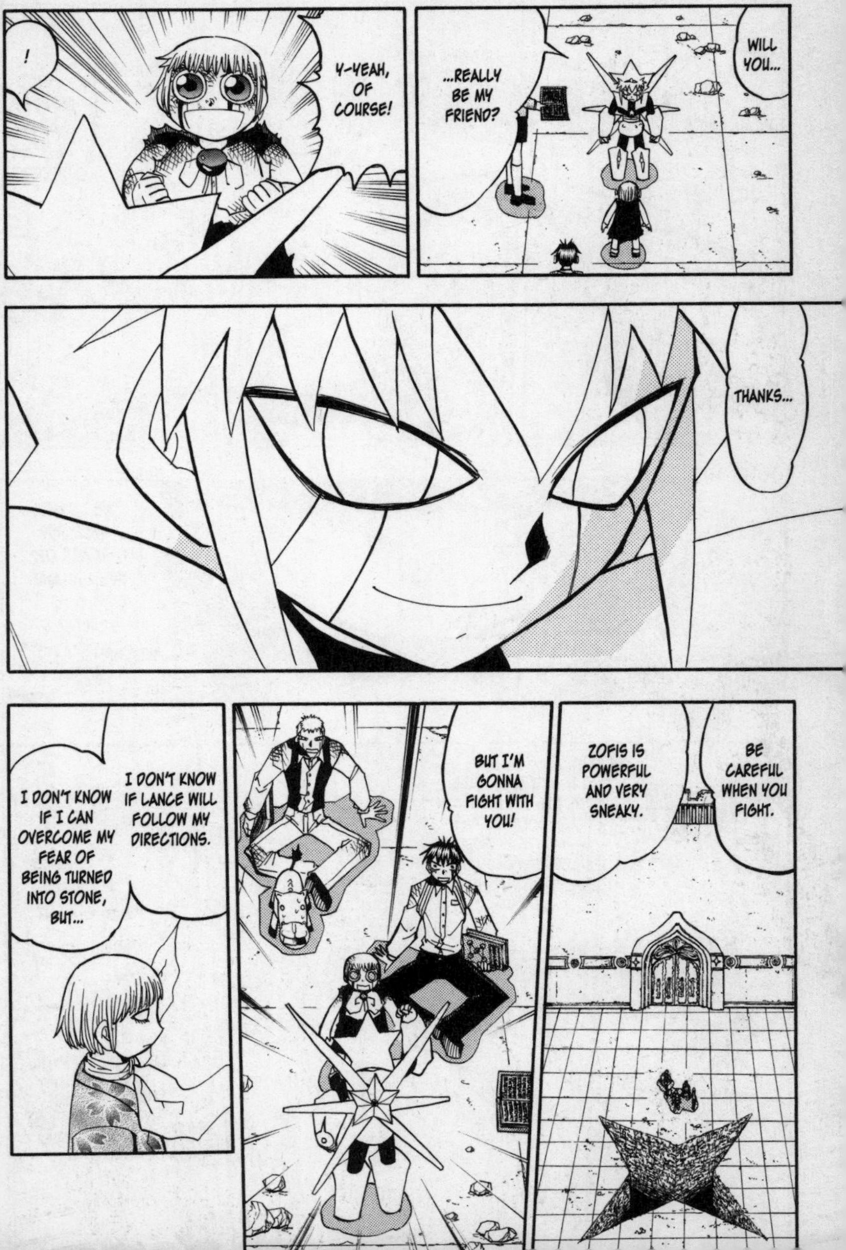
WILL YOU...
...REALLY BE MY FRIEND?
!
Y-YEAH, OF COURSE!
THANKS...
BE CAREFUL WHEN YOU FIGHT.
ZOFIS IS POWERFUL AND VERY SNEAKY.
BUT I'M GONNA FIGHT WITH YOU!
I DON'T KNOW IF LANCE WILL FOLLOW MY DIRECTIONS.
I DON'T KNOW IF I CAN OVERCOME MY FEAR OF BEING TURNED INTO STONE, BUT...

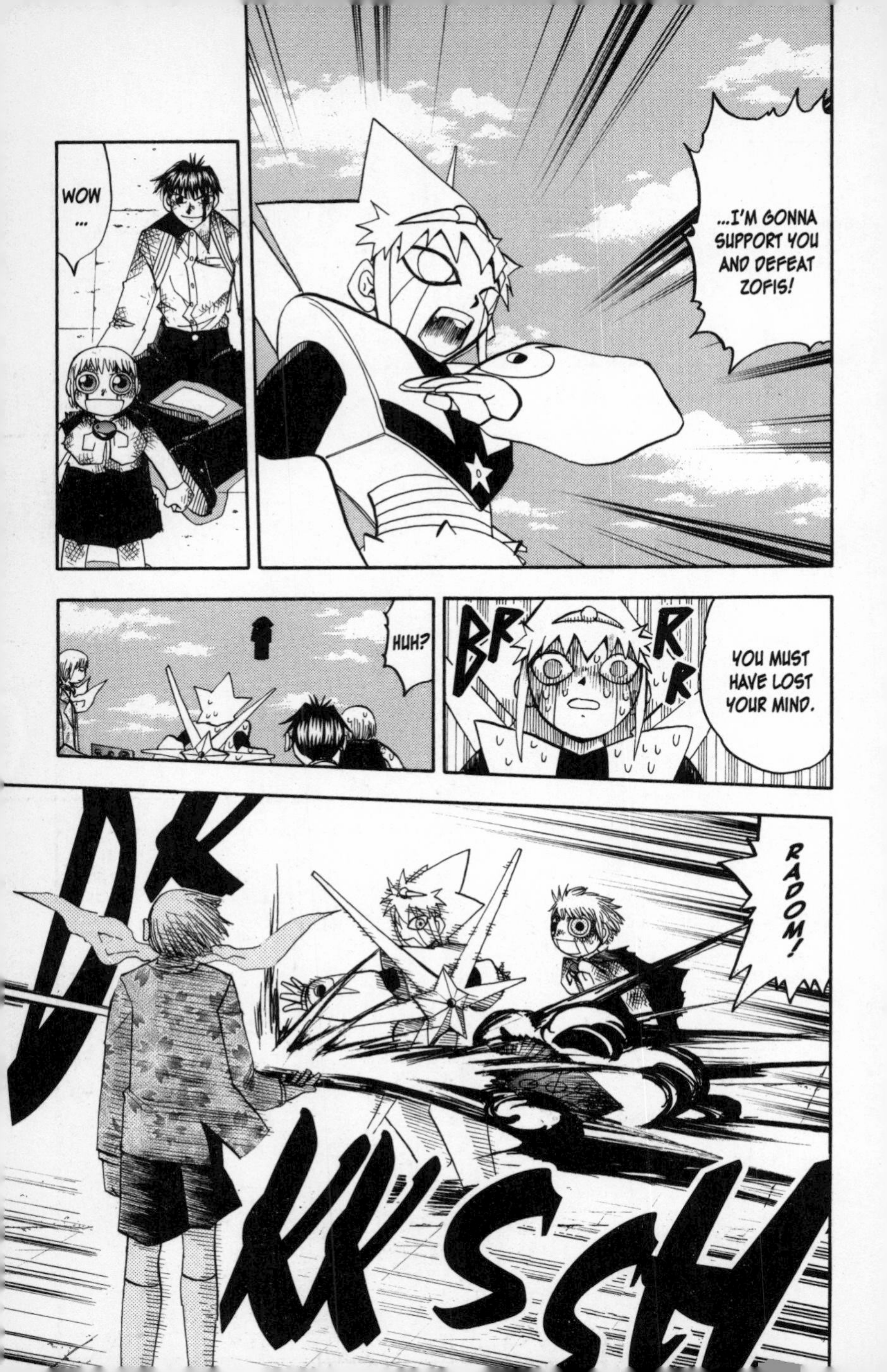
...I'M GONNA SUPPORT YOU AND DEFEAT ZOFIS!
WOW ...
BRRR
YOU MUST HAVE LOST YOUR MIND.
HUH?
RADOOM!

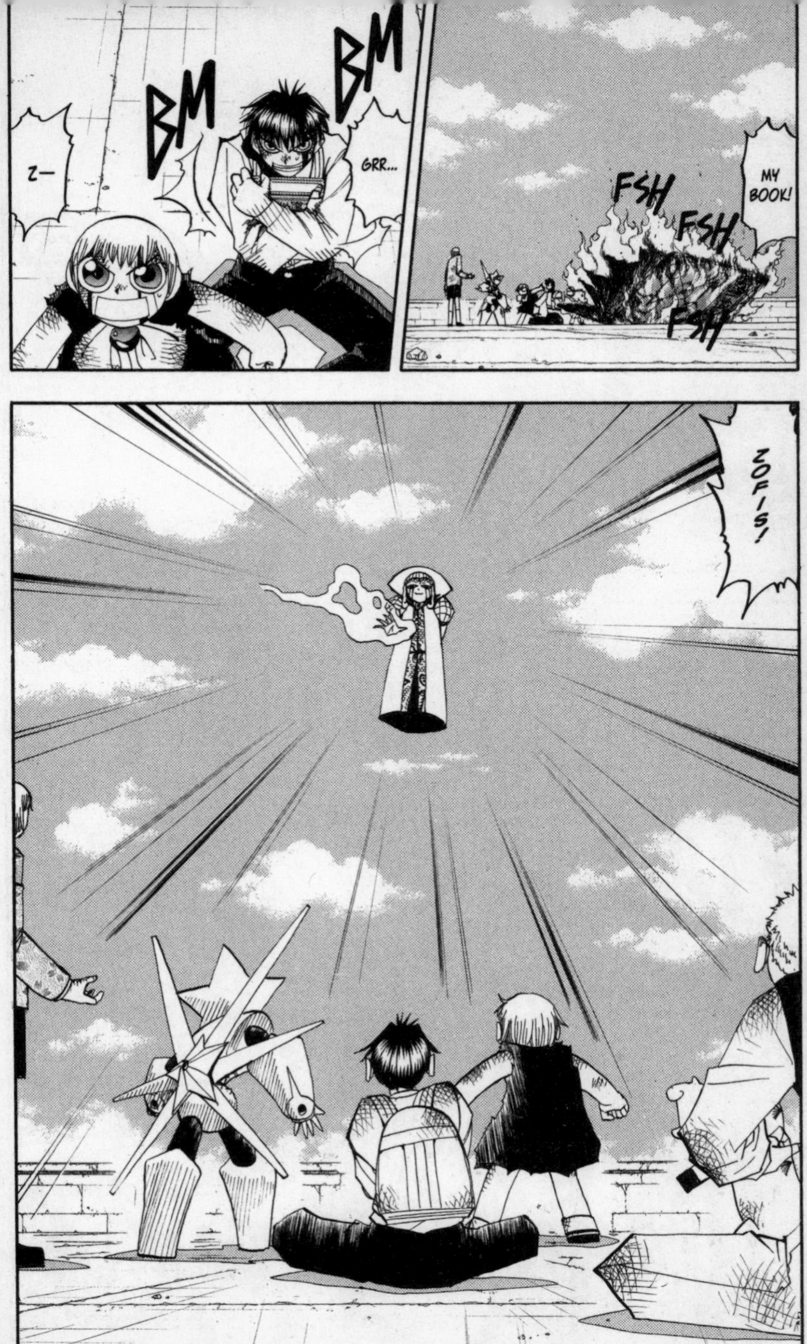
MY BOOK!
FSH
FSH
FSH
BM
BM
GRR...
Z—
ZOFIS!

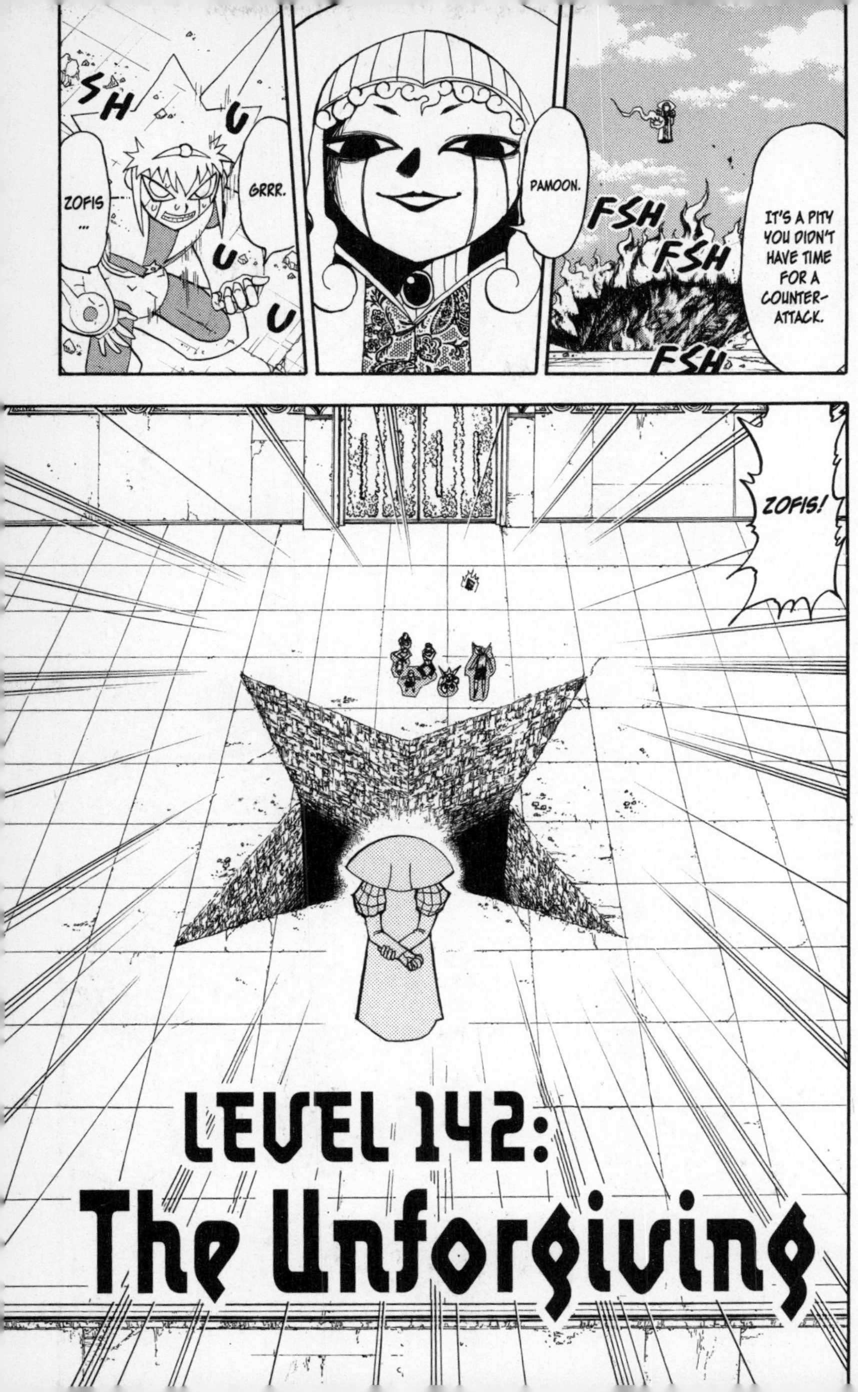
IT'S A PITY YOU DIDN'T HAVE TIME FOR A COUNTER-ATTACK.
FSH
FSH
FSH
PAMOON.
GRRR.
ZOFIS ...
SHUUUU
ZOFIS!
LEVEL 142:
The Unforgiving

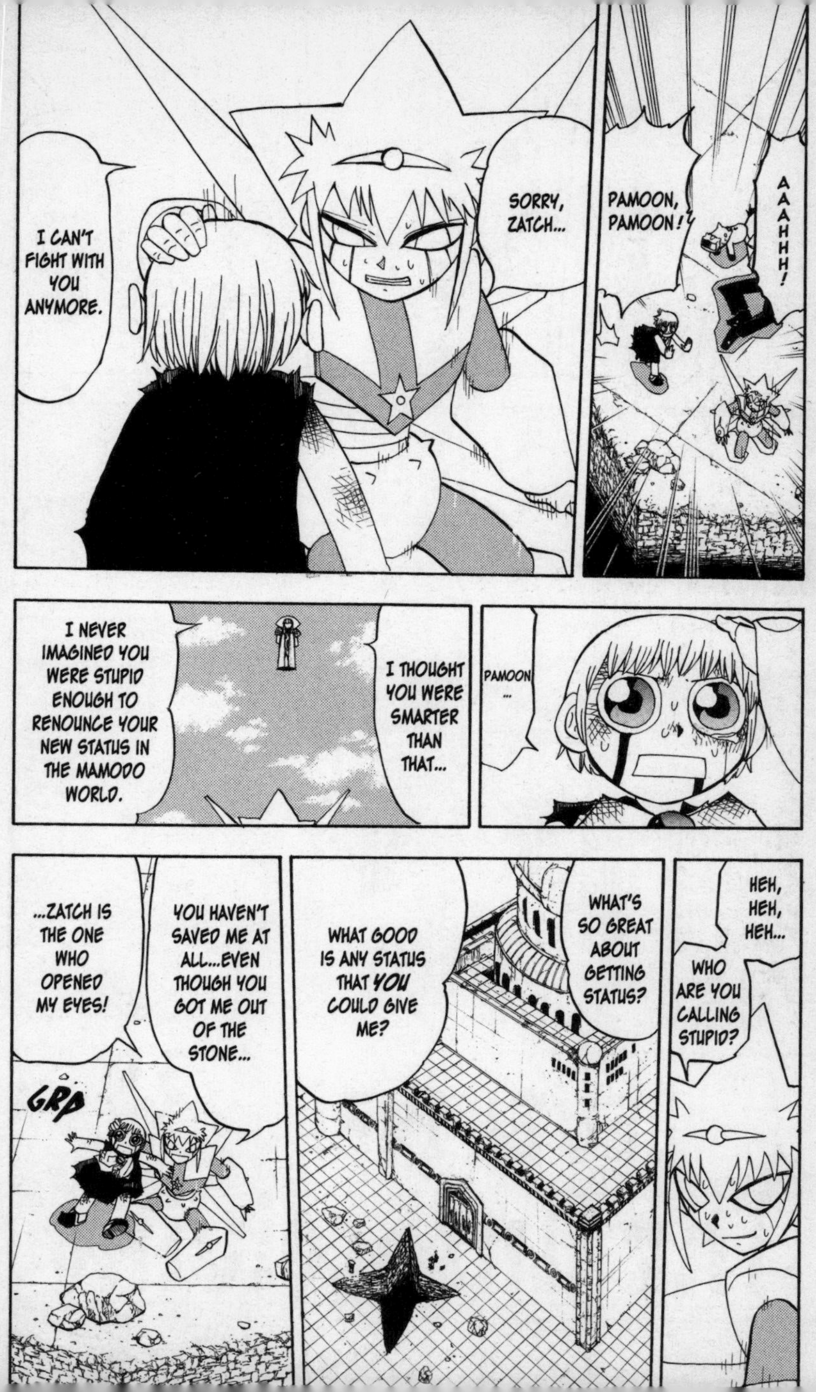
AAAHHH!
PAMOON, PAMOON!
SORRY, ZATCH...
I CAN'T FIGHT WITH YOU ANYMORE.
PAMOON...
I THOUGHT YOU WERE SMARTER THAN THAT...
I NEVER IMAGINED YOU WERE STUPID ENOUGH TO RENOUNCE YOUR NEW STATUS IN THE MAMODO WORLD.
HEH, HEH, HEH...
WHO ARE YOU CALLING STUPID?
WHAT'S SO GREAT ABOUT GETTING STATUS?
WHAT GOOD IS ANY STATUS THAT YOU COULD GIVE ME?
YOU HAVEN'T SAVED ME AT ALL...EVEN THOUGH YOU GOT ME OUT OF THE STONE...
...ZATCH IS THE ONE WHO OPENED MY EYES!
GRP

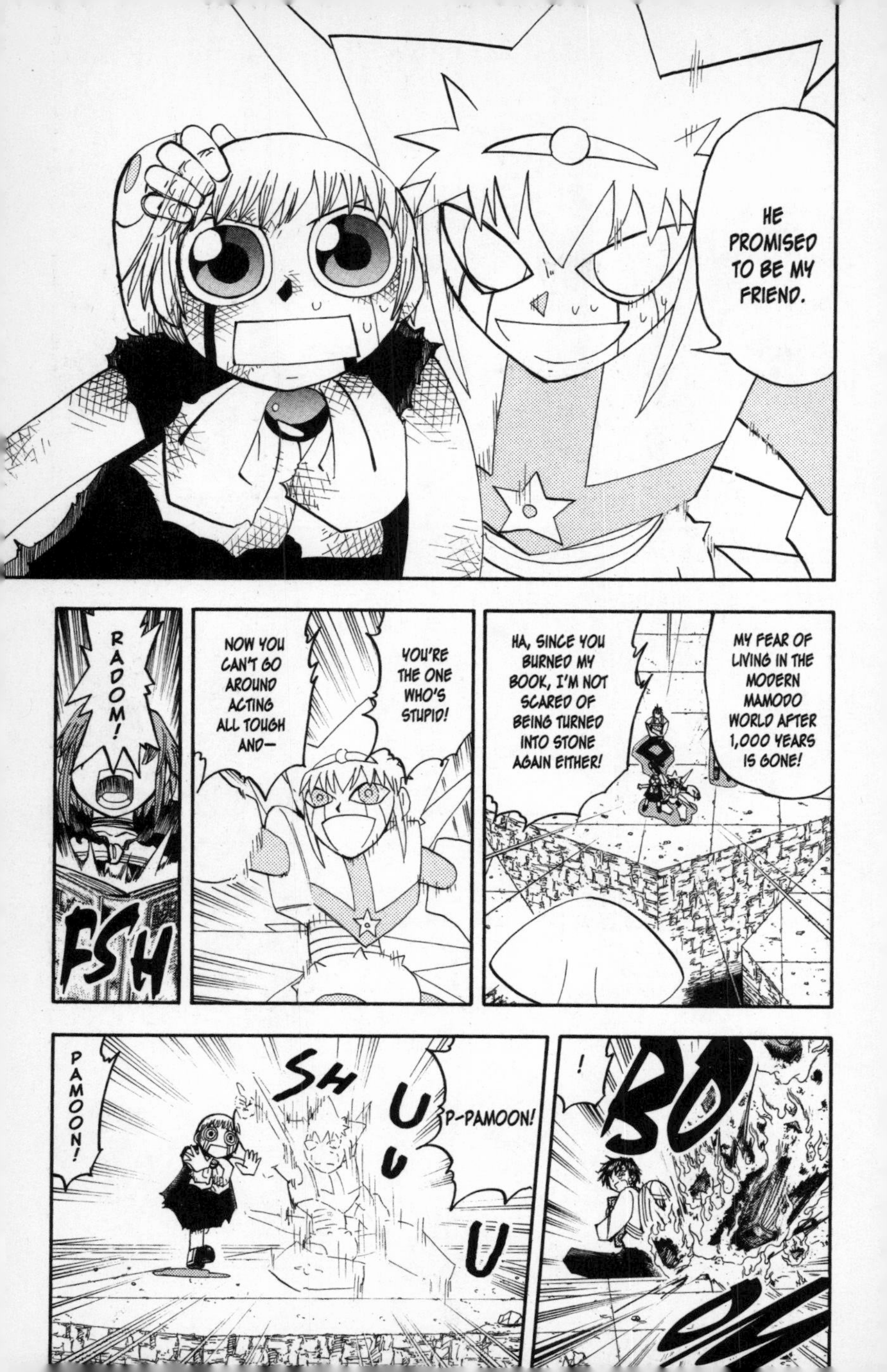
HE PROMISED TO BE MY FRIEND.
MY FEAR OF LIVING IN THE MODERN MAMODO WORLD AFTER 1,000 YEARS IS GONE!
HA, SINCE YOU BURNED MY BOOK, I'M NOT SCARED OF BEING TURNED INTO STONE AGAIN EITHER!
YOU'RE THE ONE WHO'S STUPID!
NOW YOU CAN'T GO AROUND ACTING ALL TOUGH AND—
RADOM!
FSH
!
P-PAMOON!
SHUUUU
PAMOON!

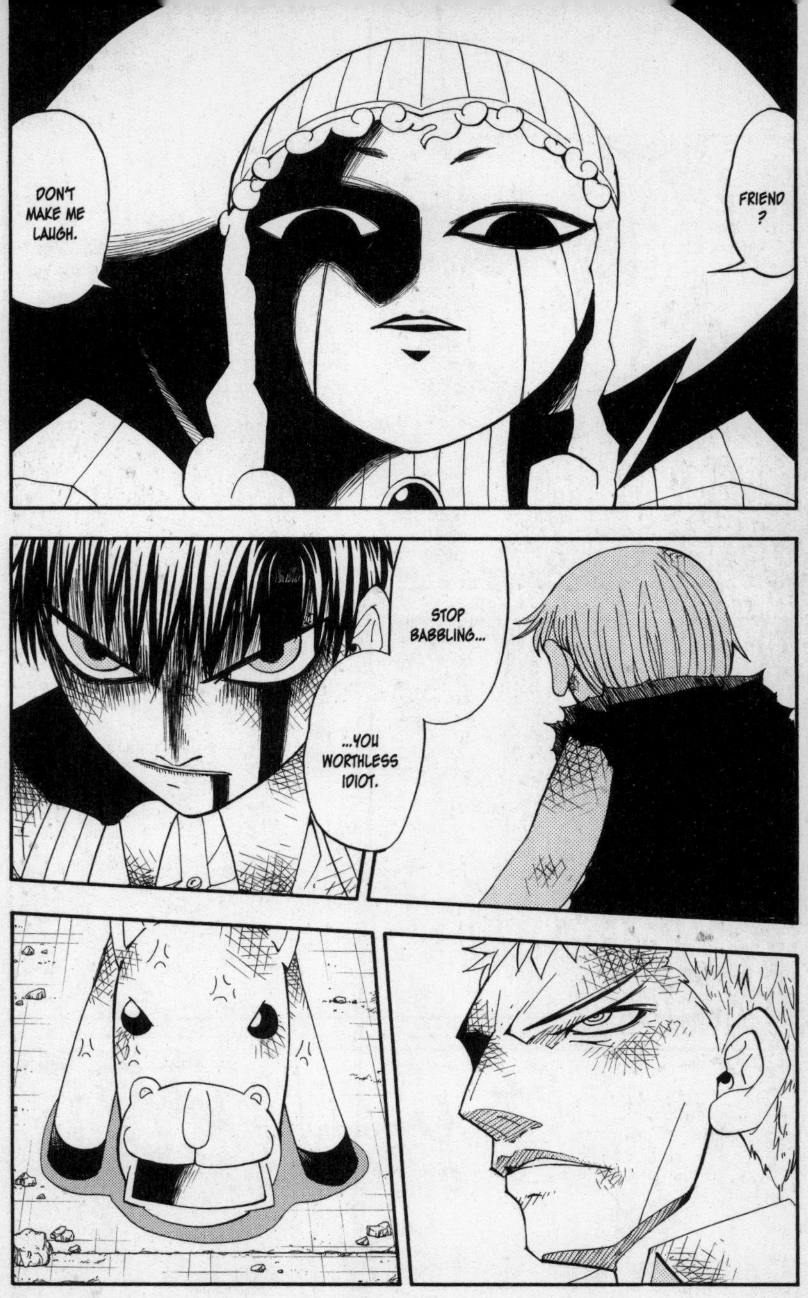
FRIEND?
DON'T MAKE ME LAUGH.
STOP BABBLING...
...YOU WORTHLESS IDIOT.

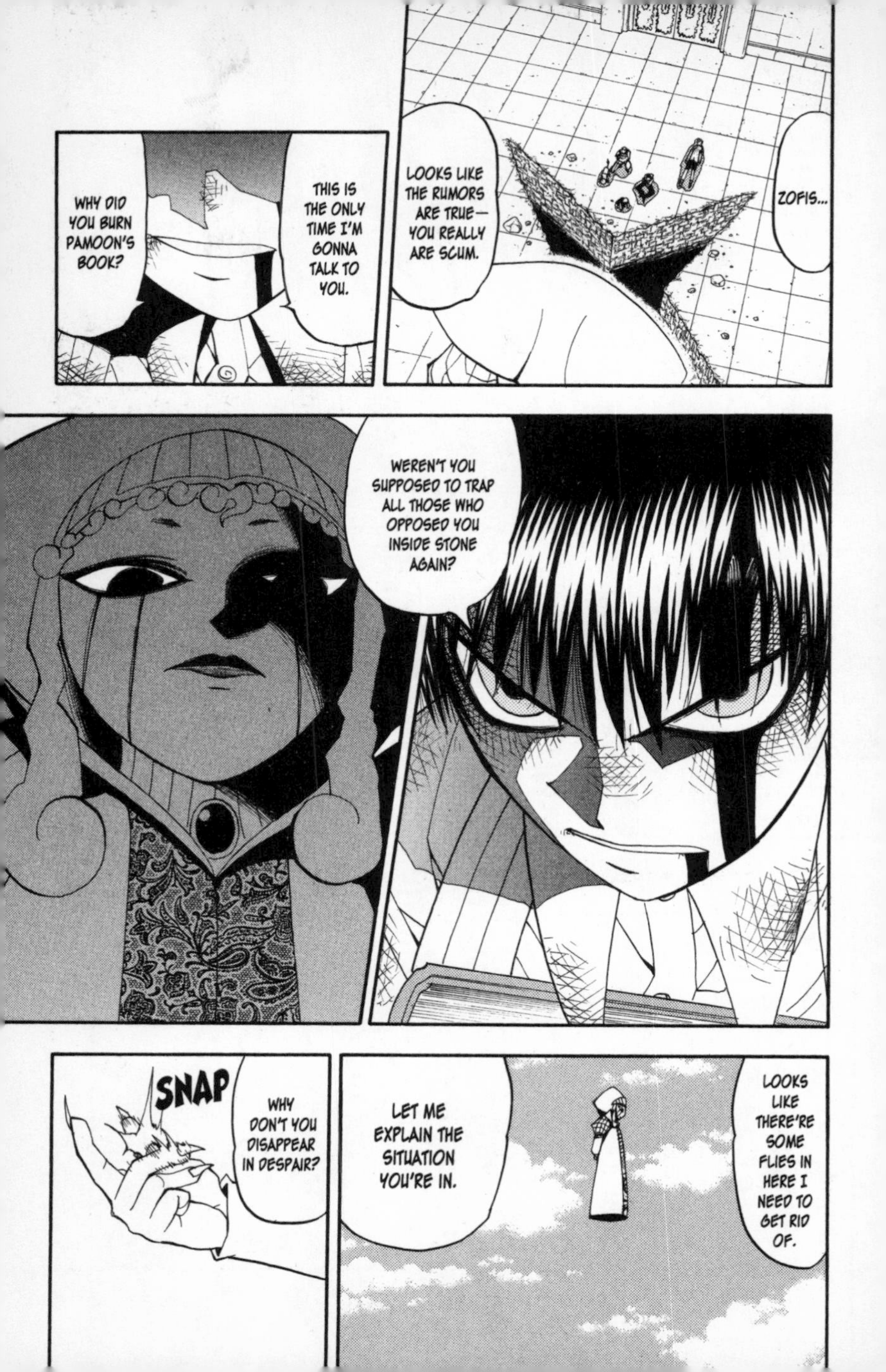
ZOFIS...
LOOKS LIKE THE RUMORS ARE TRUE— YOU REALLY ARE SCUM.
THIS IS THE ONLY TIME I'M GONNA TALK TO YOU.
WHY DID YOU BURN PAMOON'S BOOK?
WEREN'T YOU SUPPOSED TO TRAP ALL THOSE WHO OPPOSED YOU INSIDE STONE AGAIN?
LOOKS LIKE THERE'RE SOME FLIES IN HERE I NEED TO GET RID OF.
LET ME EXPLAIN THE SITUATION YOU'RE IN.
WHY DON'T YOU DISAPPEAR IN DESPAIR?
SNAP

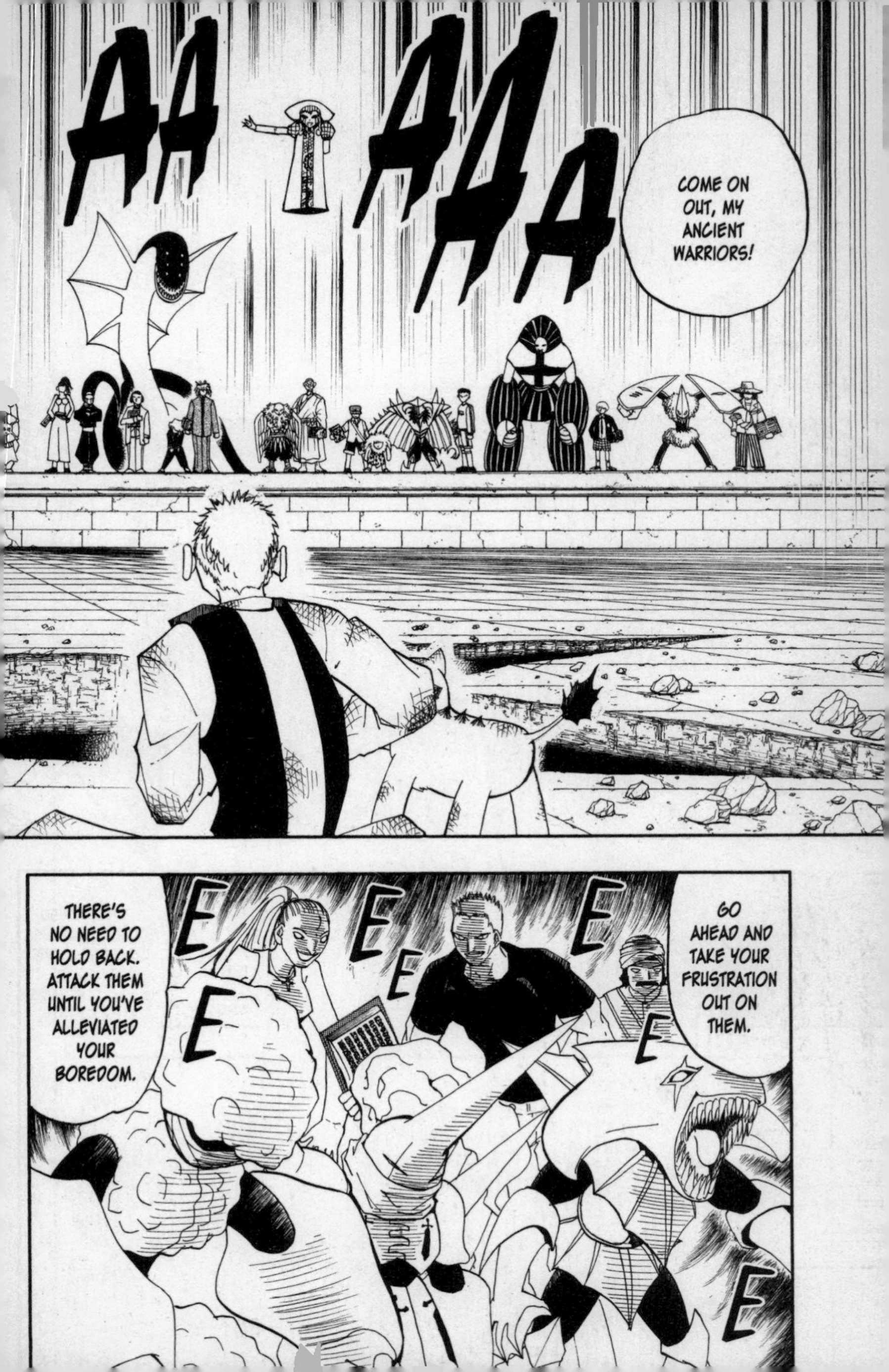
AAAAAA
COME ON OUT, MY ANCIENT WARRIORS!
GO AHEAD AND TAKE YOUR FRUSTRATION OUT ON THEM.
THERE'S NO NEED TO HOLD BACK. ATTACK THEM UNTIL YOU'VE ALLEVIATED YOUR BOREDOM.
EEEEEEEE

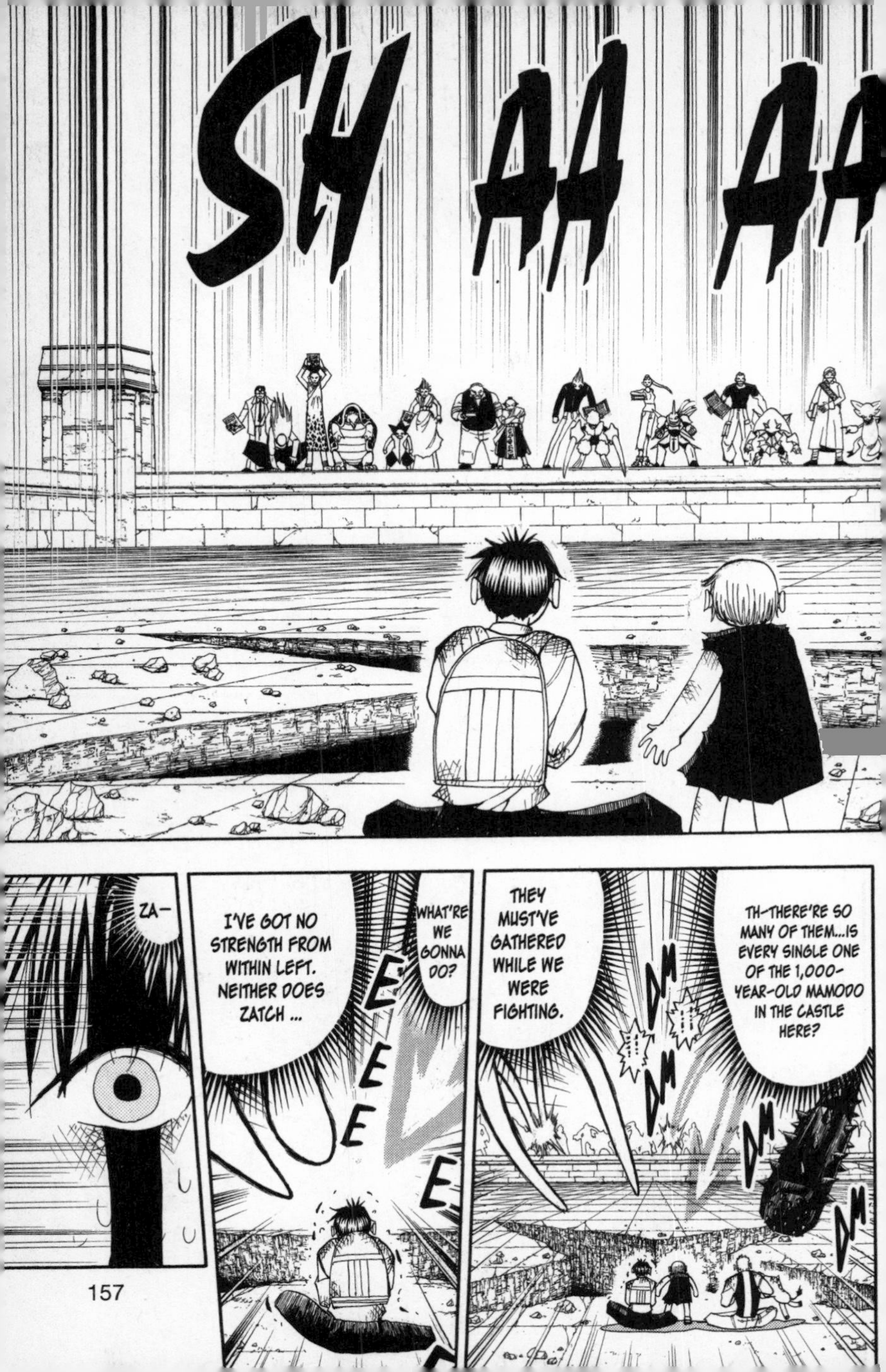
SHAAAA
TH-THERE'RE SO MANY OF THEM...IS EVERY SINGLE ONE OF THE 1,000-YEAR-OLD MAMODO IN THE CASTLE HERE?
THEY MUST'VE GATHERED WHILE WE WERE FIGHTING.
DMDMDMDM
WHAT'RE WE GONNA DO?
I'VE GOT NO STRENGTH FROM WITHIN LEFT. NEITHER DOES ZATCH ...
EEEEE
ZA-

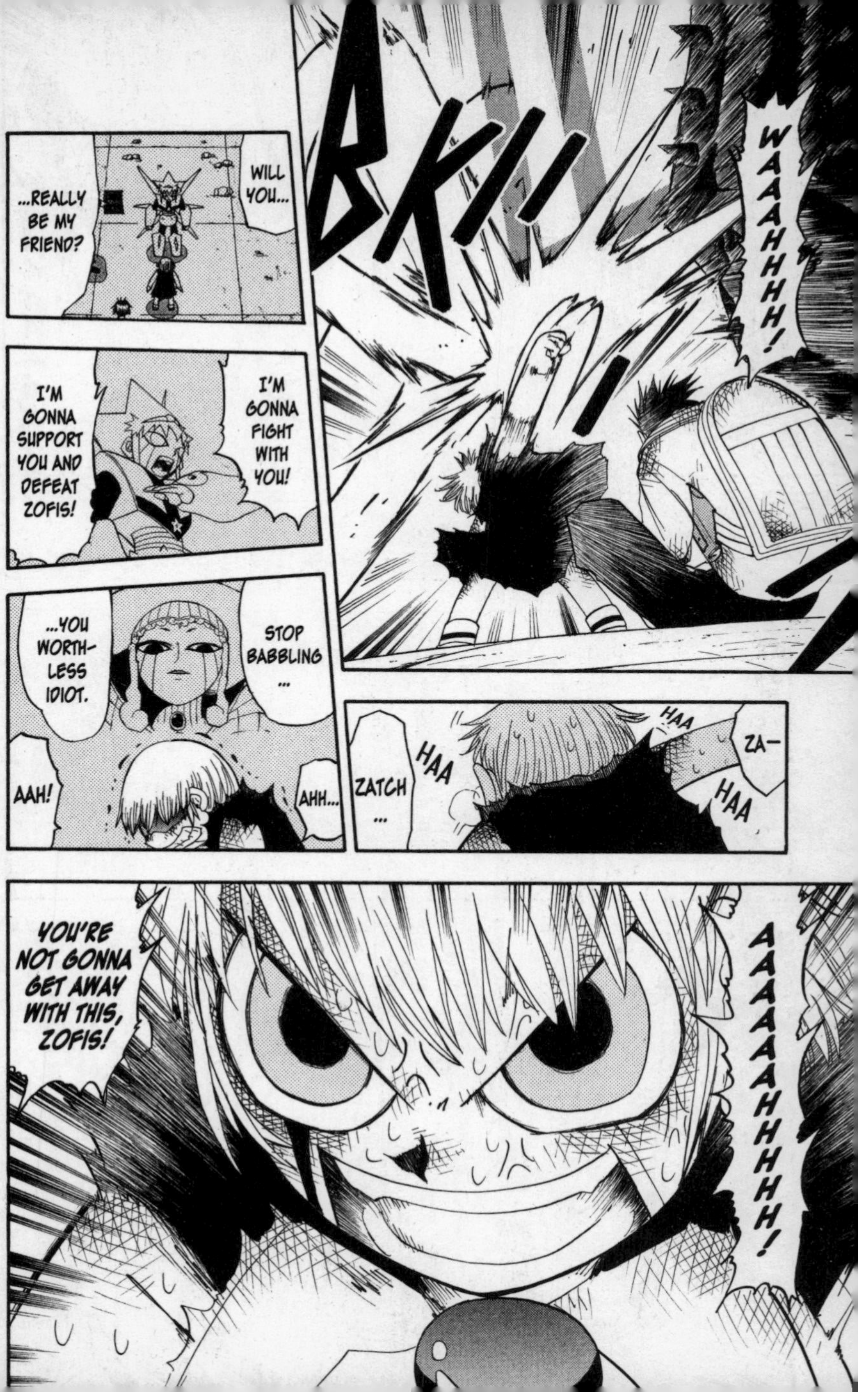
WAAAAHHHHH!
BKIII
ZA-
HAA
HAA
HAA
ZATCH...
WILL YOU...
...REALLY BE MY FRIEND?
I'M GONNA FIGHT WITH YOU!
I'M GONNA SUPPORT YOU AND DEFEAT ZOFIS!
STOP BABBLING...
...YOU WORTHLESS IDIOT.
AHH...
AAH!
AAAAAAAHHHHHH!
YOU'RE NOT GONNA GET AWAY WITH THIS, ZOFIS!

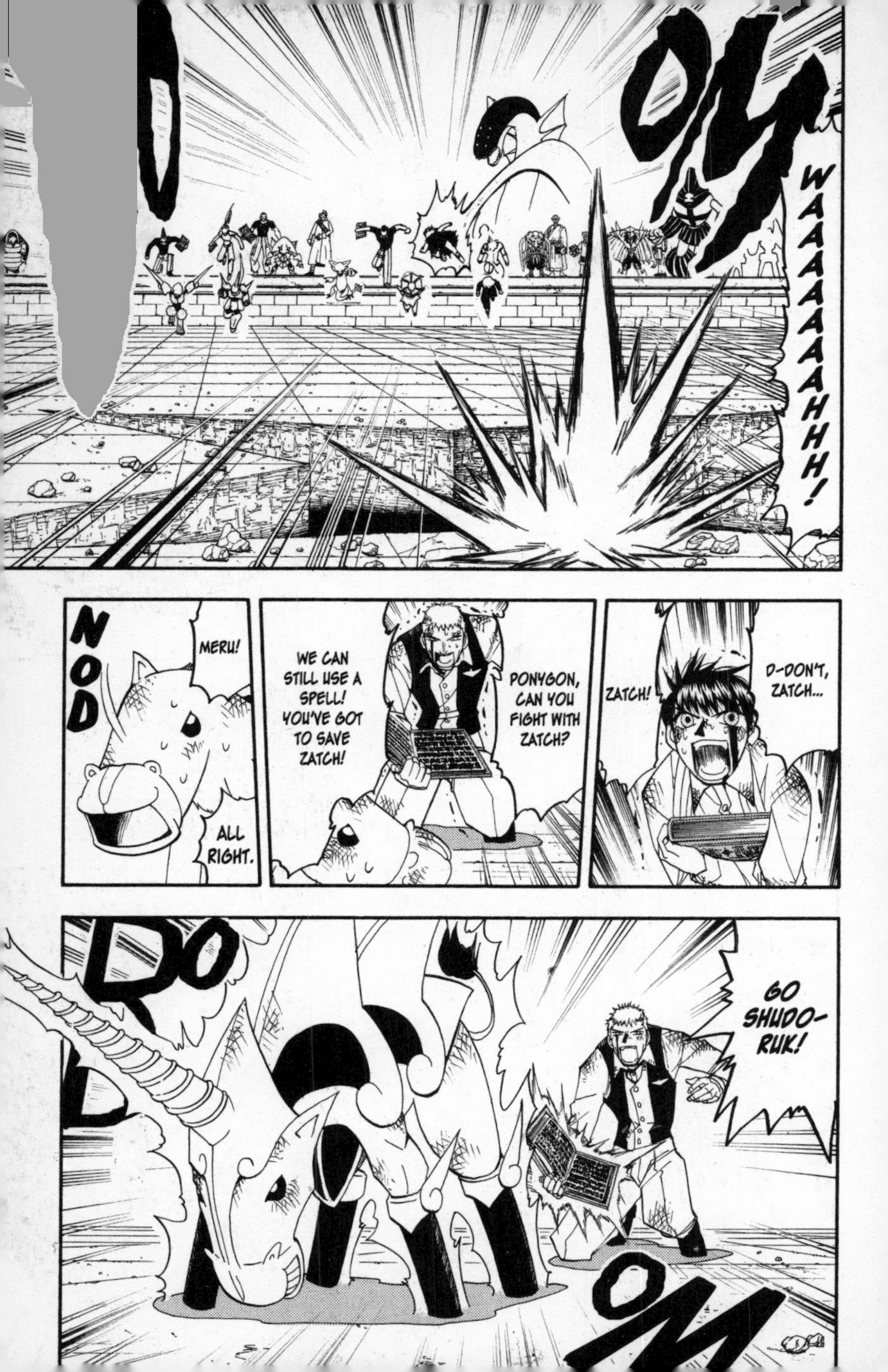
WAAAAAAAHHH!
D-DON'T, ZATCH...
ZATCH!
PONYGON, CAN YOU FIGHT WITH ZATCH?
WE CAN STILL USE A SPELL! YOU'VE GOT TO SAVE ZATCH!
MERU!
NOD
ALL RIGHT.
GO SHUDO-RUK!

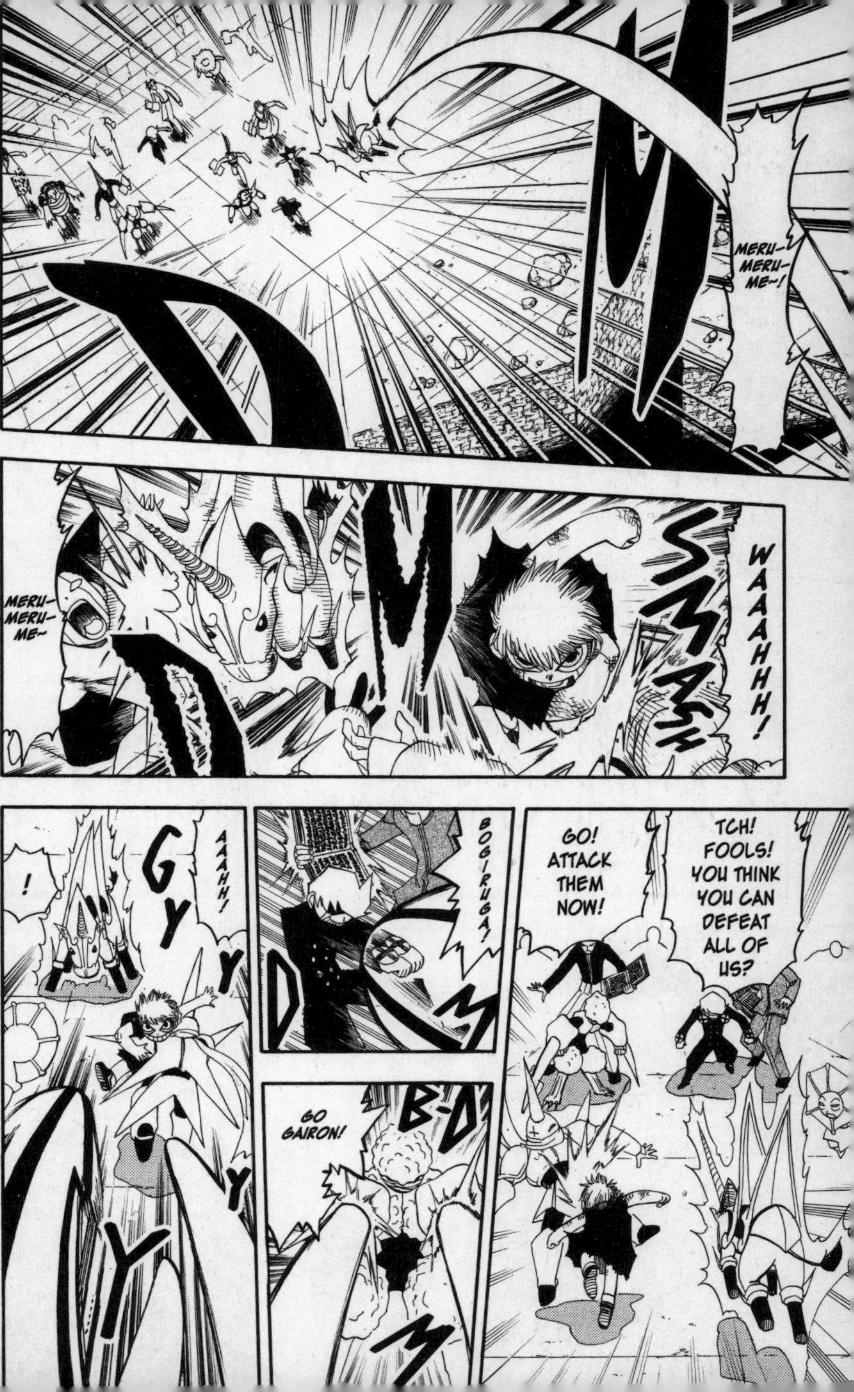
MERU-MERU-ME~!
WAAAAHHH!
SMASH
MERU-MERU-ME~
TCH! FOOLS! YOU THINK YOU CAN DEFEAT ALL OF US?
GO! ATTACK THEM NOW!
BOGIRUGA!
GO GAIRON!
AAAHH!
!
GYYY

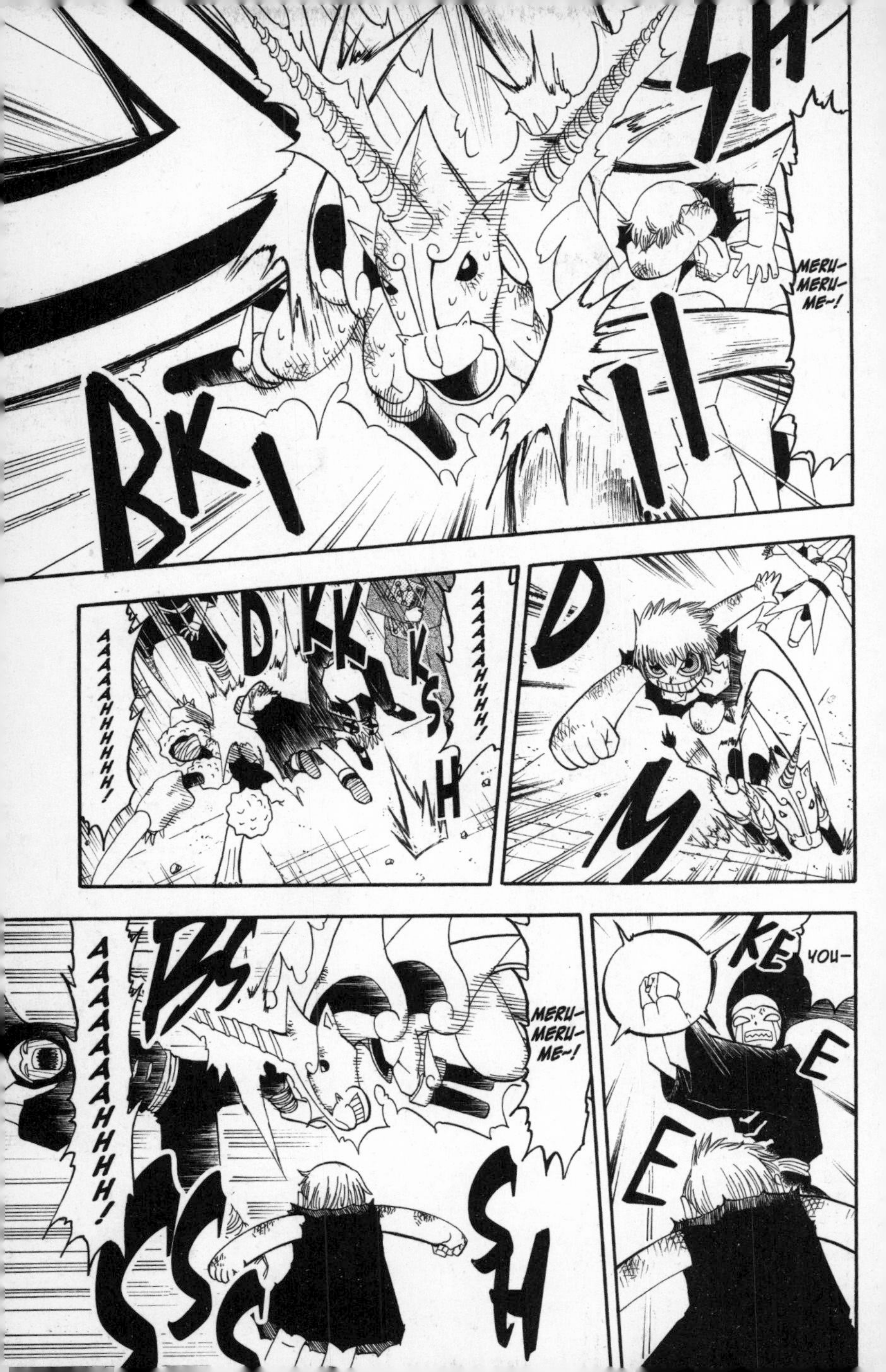
SH
MERU-MERU-ME~!
BKIII
DM
AAAAAAHHHH!
DKKKSH
AAAAAHHHHHH!
KEEE
YOU-
MERU-MERU-ME~!
BS
AAAAAAAAHHHHHH!
SSH

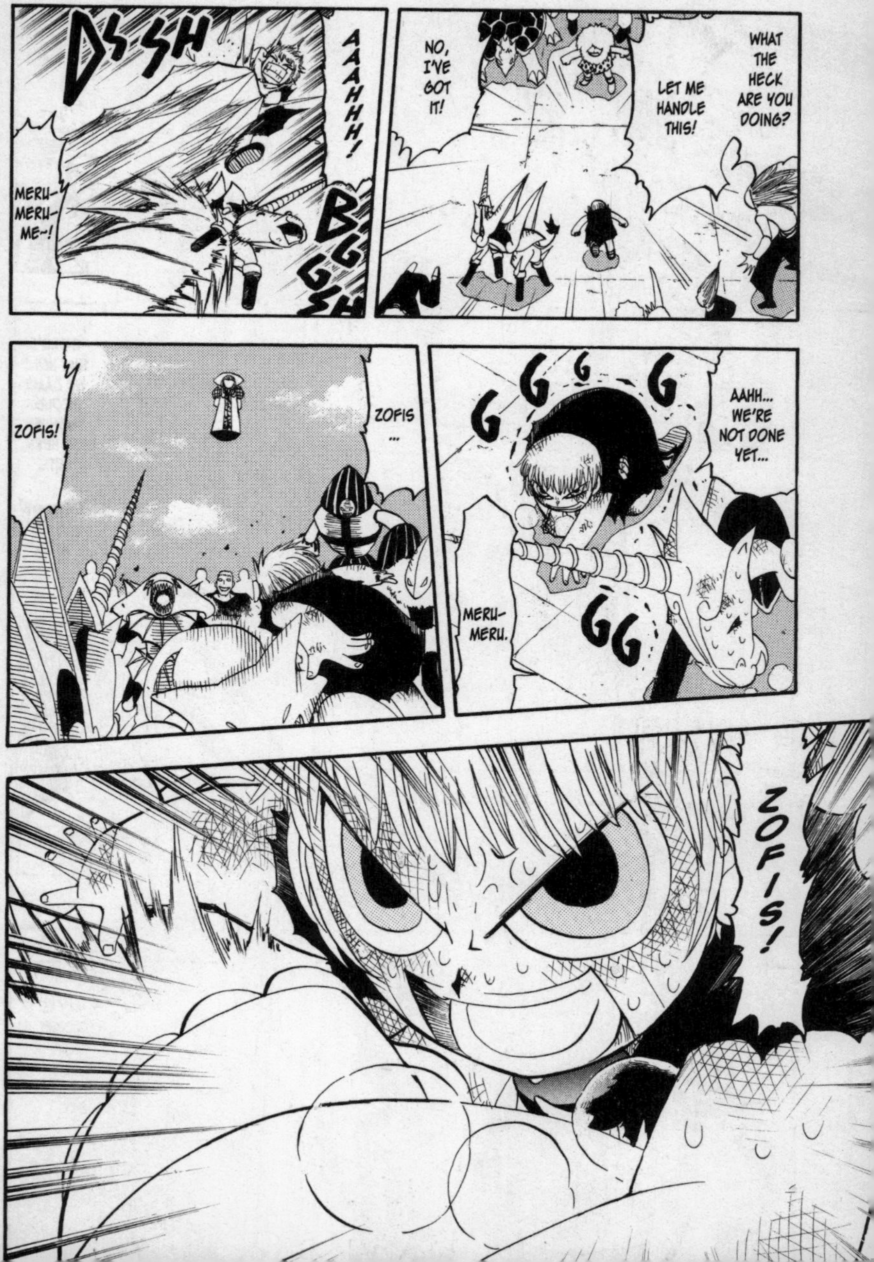
WHAT THE HECK ARE YOU DOING?
LET ME HANDLE THIS!
NO, I'VE GOT IT!
AAAHHHH!
DSSH
MERU-MERU-ME~!
BGGSH
AAHH... WE'RE NOT DONE YET...
GGGG
MERU-MERU.
GG
ZOFIS...
ZOFIS!
ZOFIS!

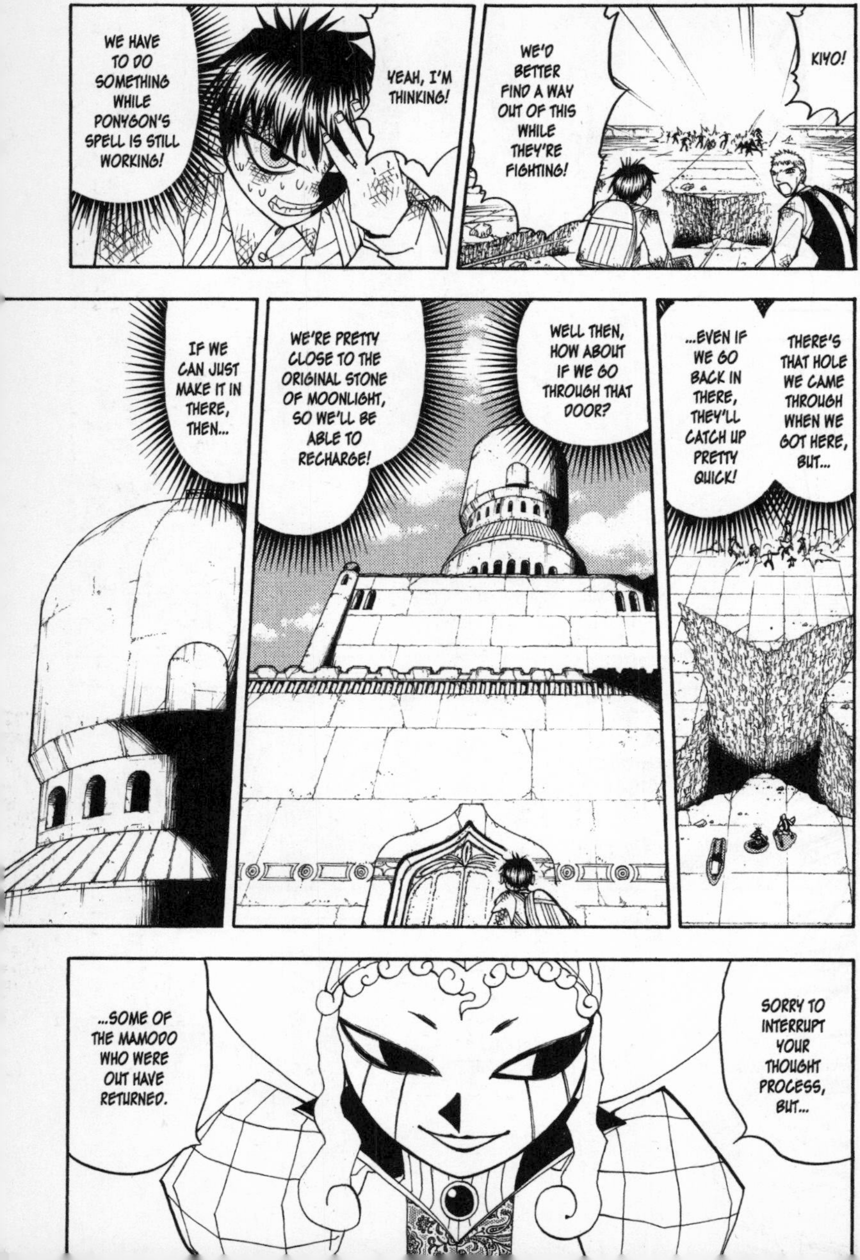
KIYO!
WE'D BETTER FIND A WAY OUT OF THIS WHILE THEY'RE FIGHTING!
YEAH, I'M THINKING!
WE HAVE TO DO SOMETHING WHILE PONYGON'S SPELL IS STILL WORKING!
THERE'S THAT HOLE WE CAME THROUGH WHEN WE GOT HERE, BUT...
...EVEN IF WE GO BACK IN THERE, THEY'LL CATCH UP PRETTY QUICK!
WELL THEN, HOW ABOUT IF WE GO THROUGH THAT DOOR?
WE'RE PRETTY CLOSE TO THE ORIGINAL STONE OF MOONLIGHT, SO WE'LL BE ABLE TO RECHARGE!
IF WE CAN JUST MAKE IT IN THERE, THEN...
SORRY TO INTERRUPT YOUR THOUGHT PROCESS, BUT...
...SOME OF THE MAMODO WHO WERE OUT HAVE RETURNED.

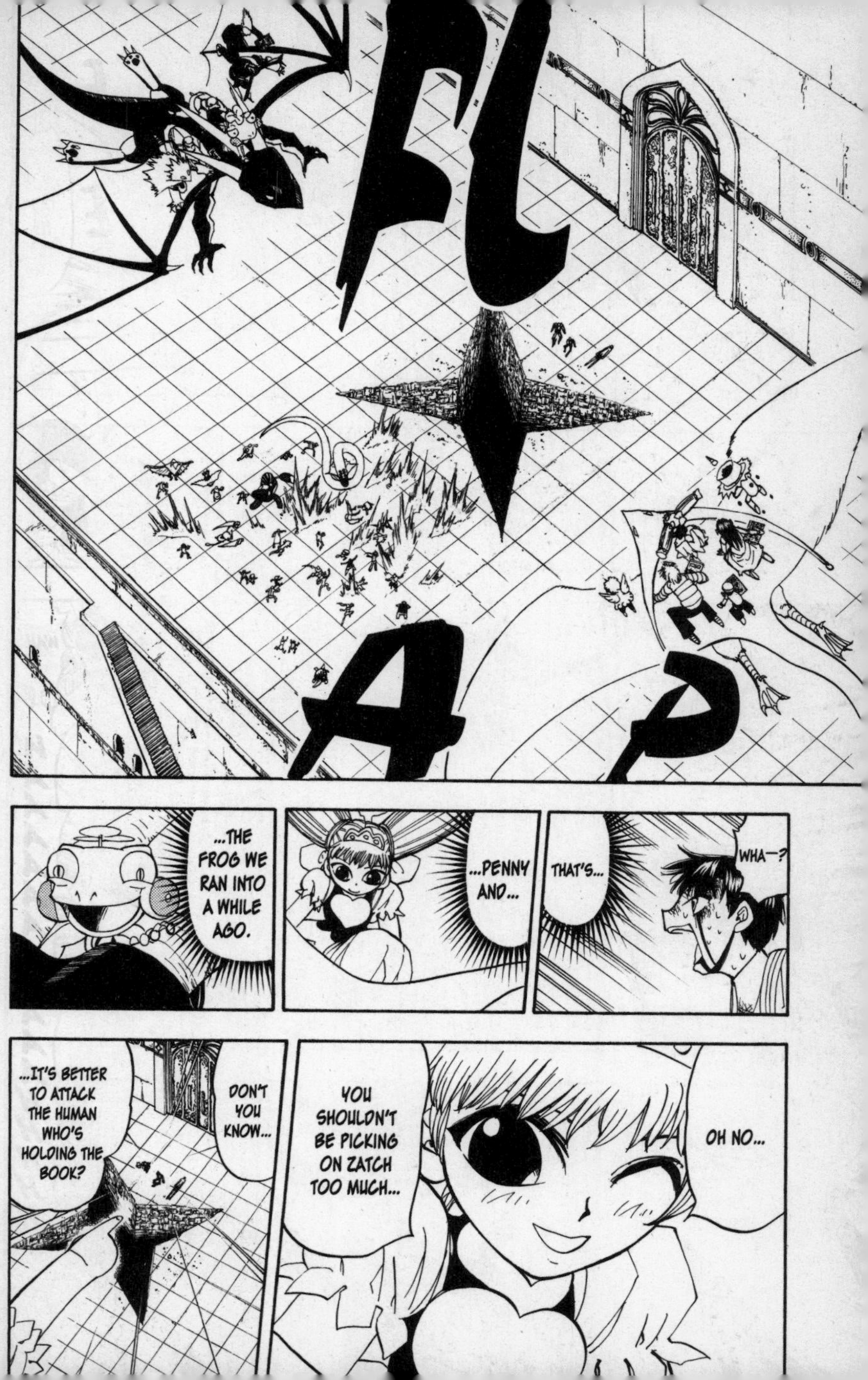
FLAP
WHA—?
THAT'S...
...PENNY AND...
...THE FROG WE RAN INTO A WHILE AGO.
OH NO...
YOU SHOULDN'T BE PICKING ON ZATCH TOO MUCH...
DON'T YOU KNOW...
...IT'S BETTER TO ATTACK THE HUMAN WHO'S HOLDING THE BOOK?

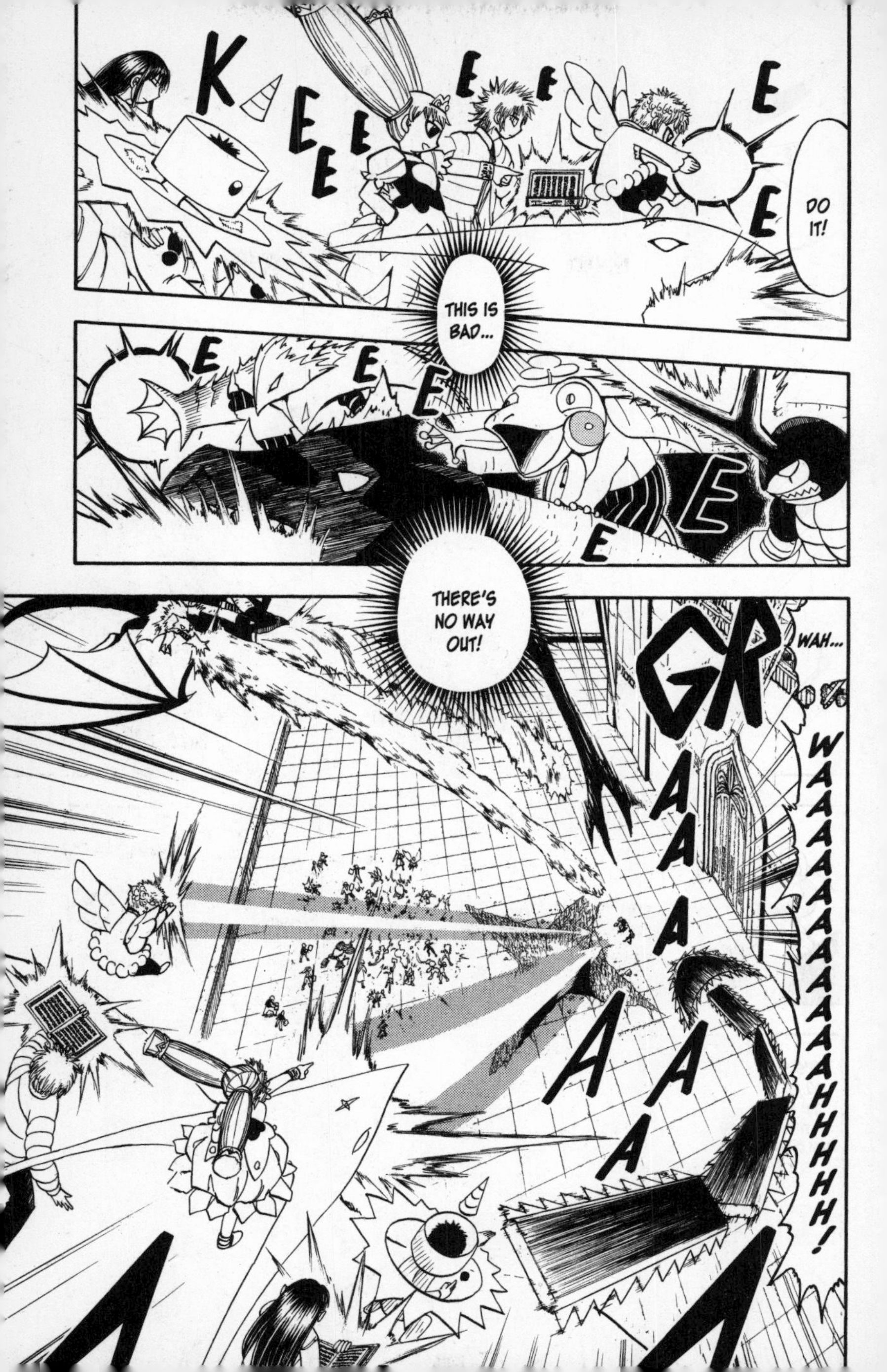
DO IT!
KEEEEEEEEE
THIS IS BAD...
EEEEEE
THERE'S NO WAY OUT!
WAH...
WAAAAAAAAAAAAAHHHHHH!
GRAAAAAAA

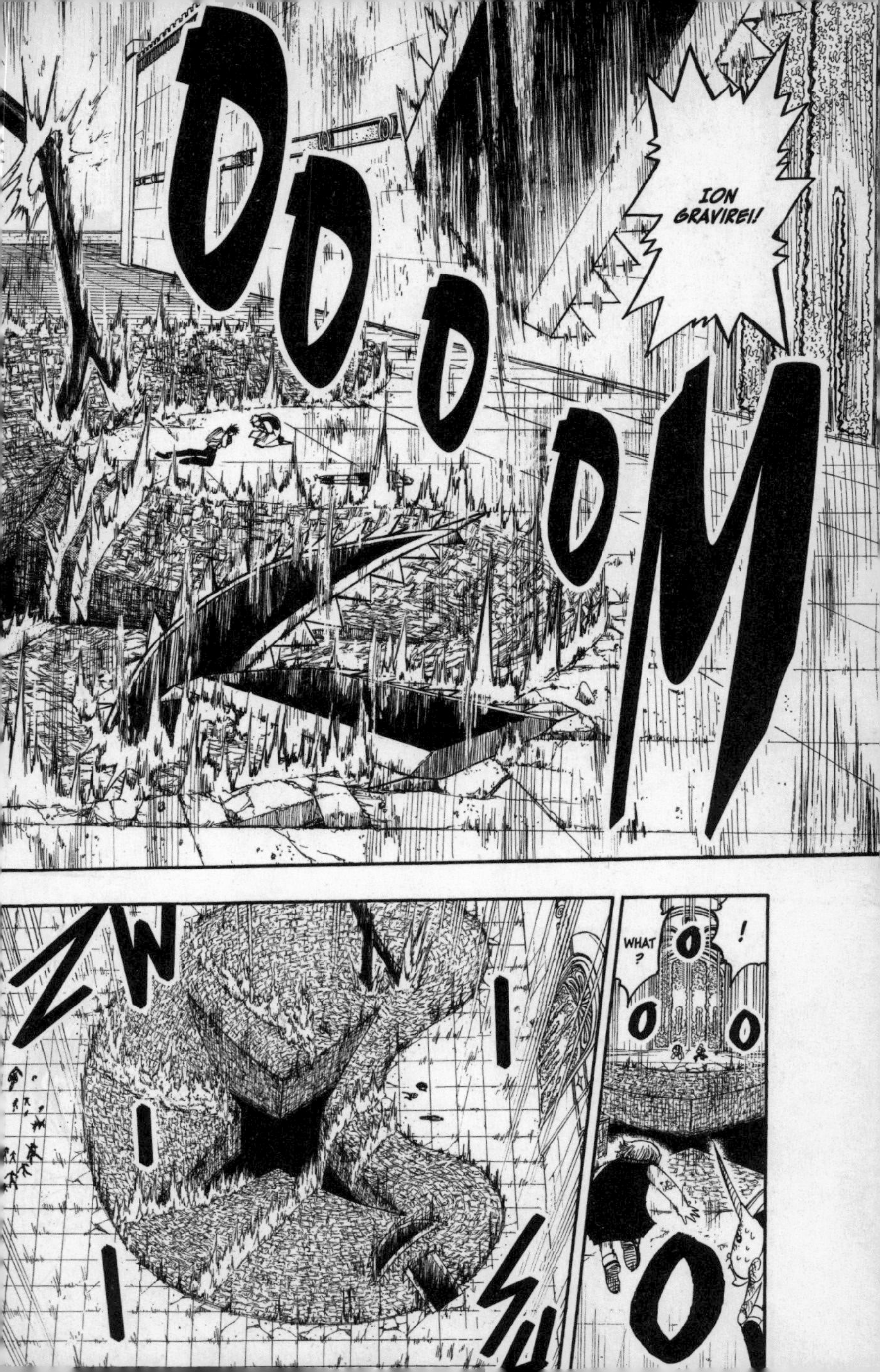
ION GRAVIREI!
DOOOOOM
WHAT?
!

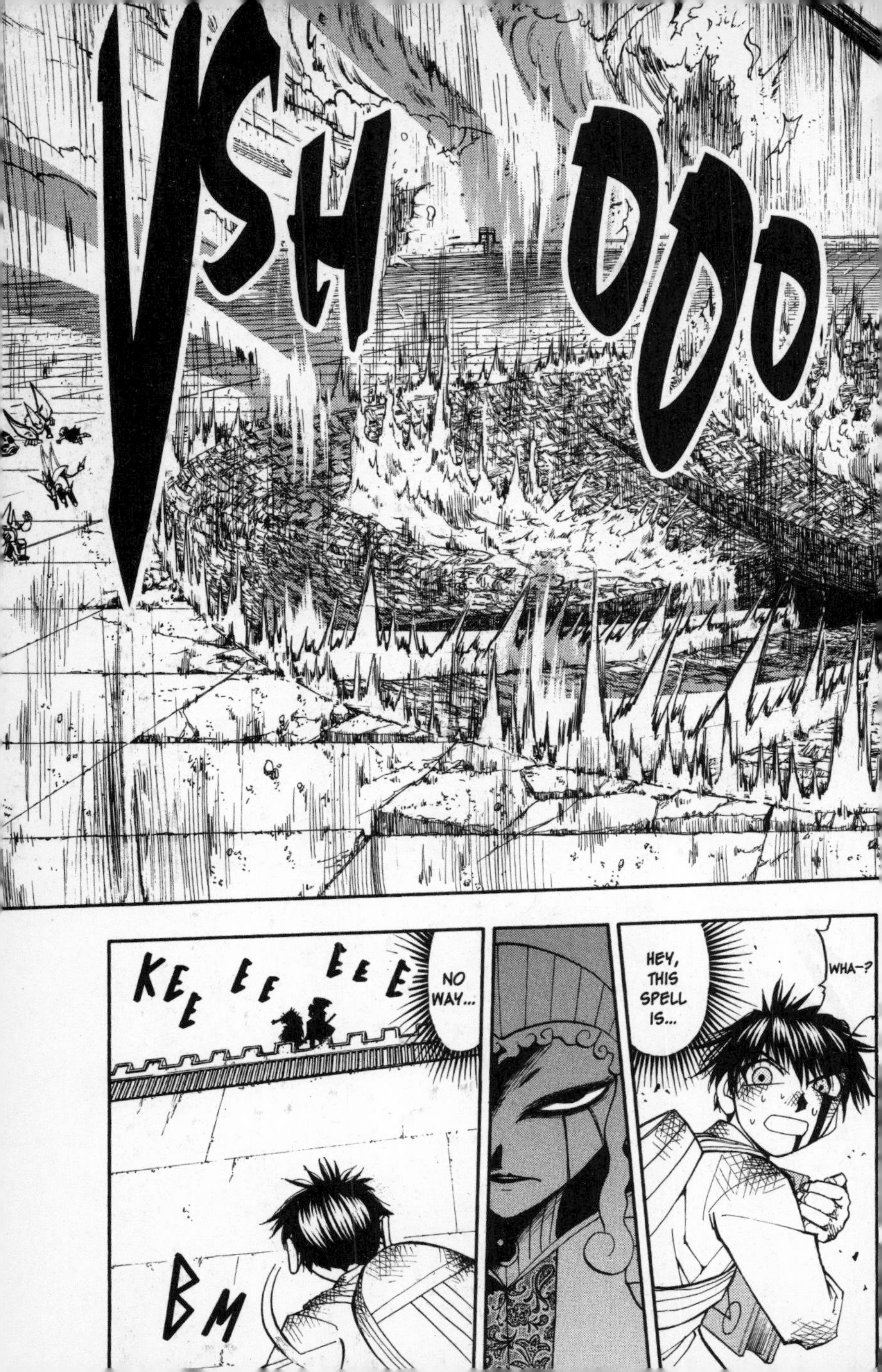
VSHOOOO
WHA-?
HEY, THIS SPELL IS...
NO WAY...
KEEEEEEE
BM

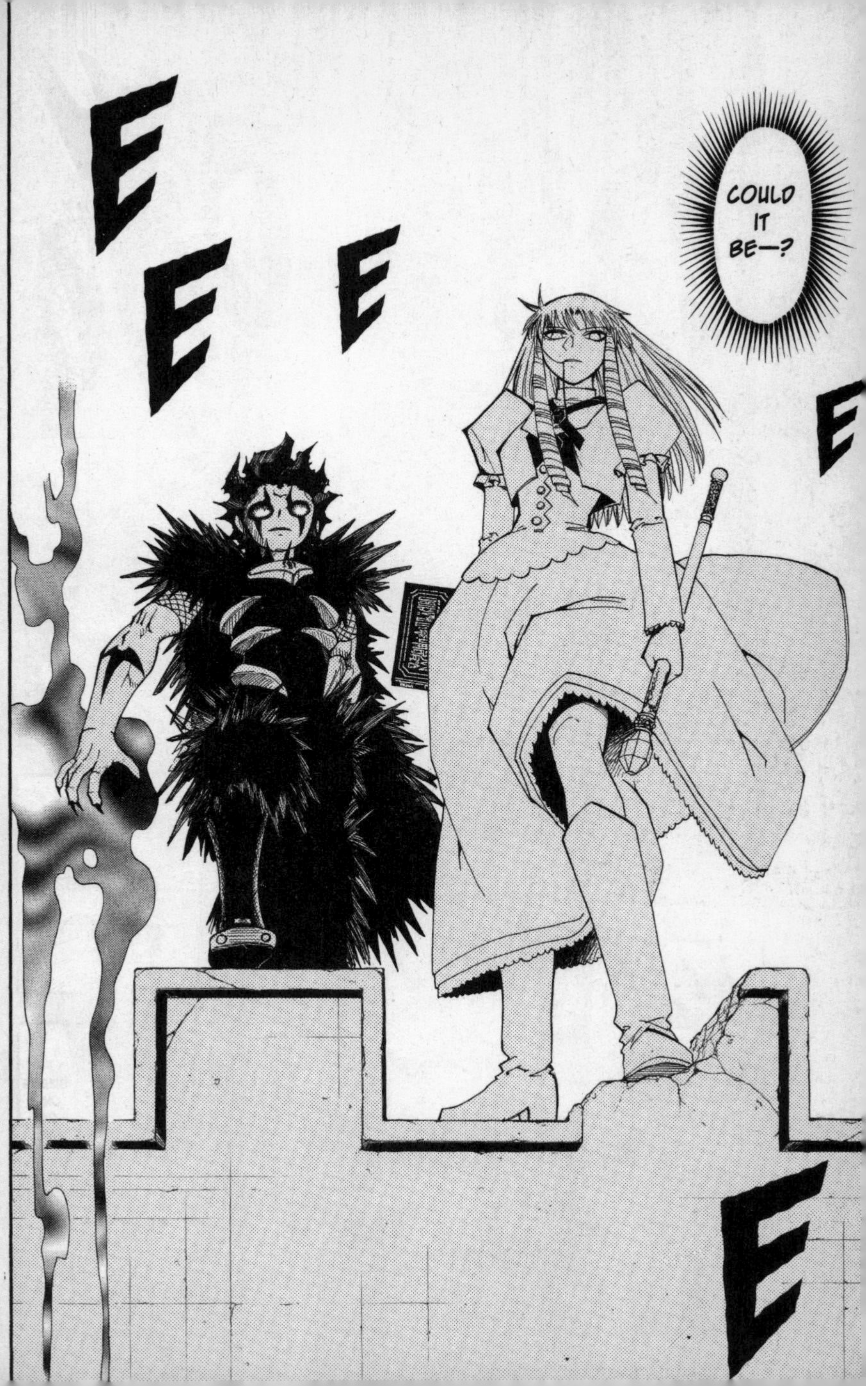
COULD IT BE—?
E E E E E

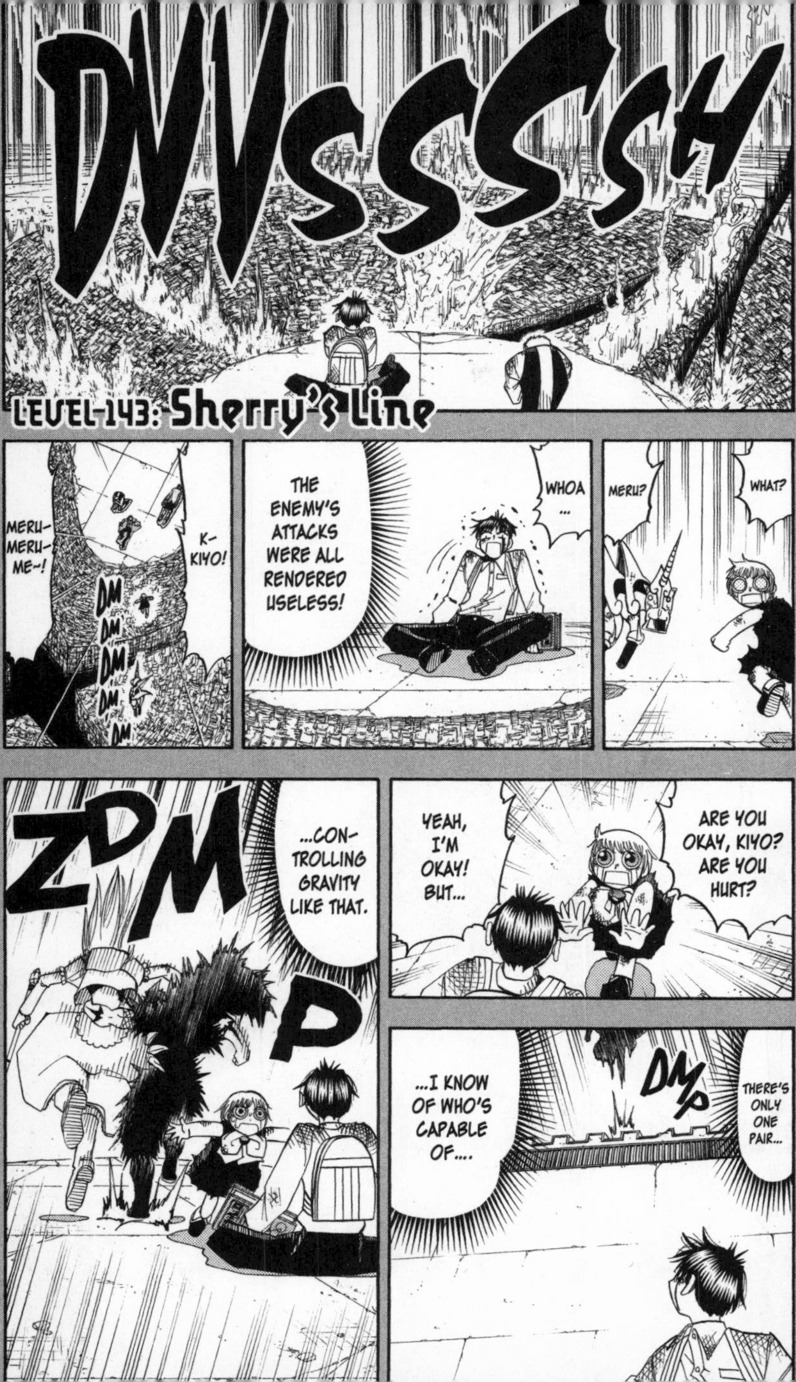
DVSSSSH
LEVEL-143: Sherry's Line
WHAT?
MERU?
WHOA ...
THE ENEMY'S ATTACKS WERE ALL RENDERED USELESS!
K-KIYO!
MERU-MERU-ME~!
DM DM DM DM DM
ARE YOU OKAY, KIYO? ARE YOU HURT?
YEAH, I'M OKAY! BUT...
THERE'S ONLY ONE PAIR...
DMP
...I KNOW OF WHO'S CAPABLE OF....
...CON-TROLLING GRAVITY LIKE THAT.
ZDMP

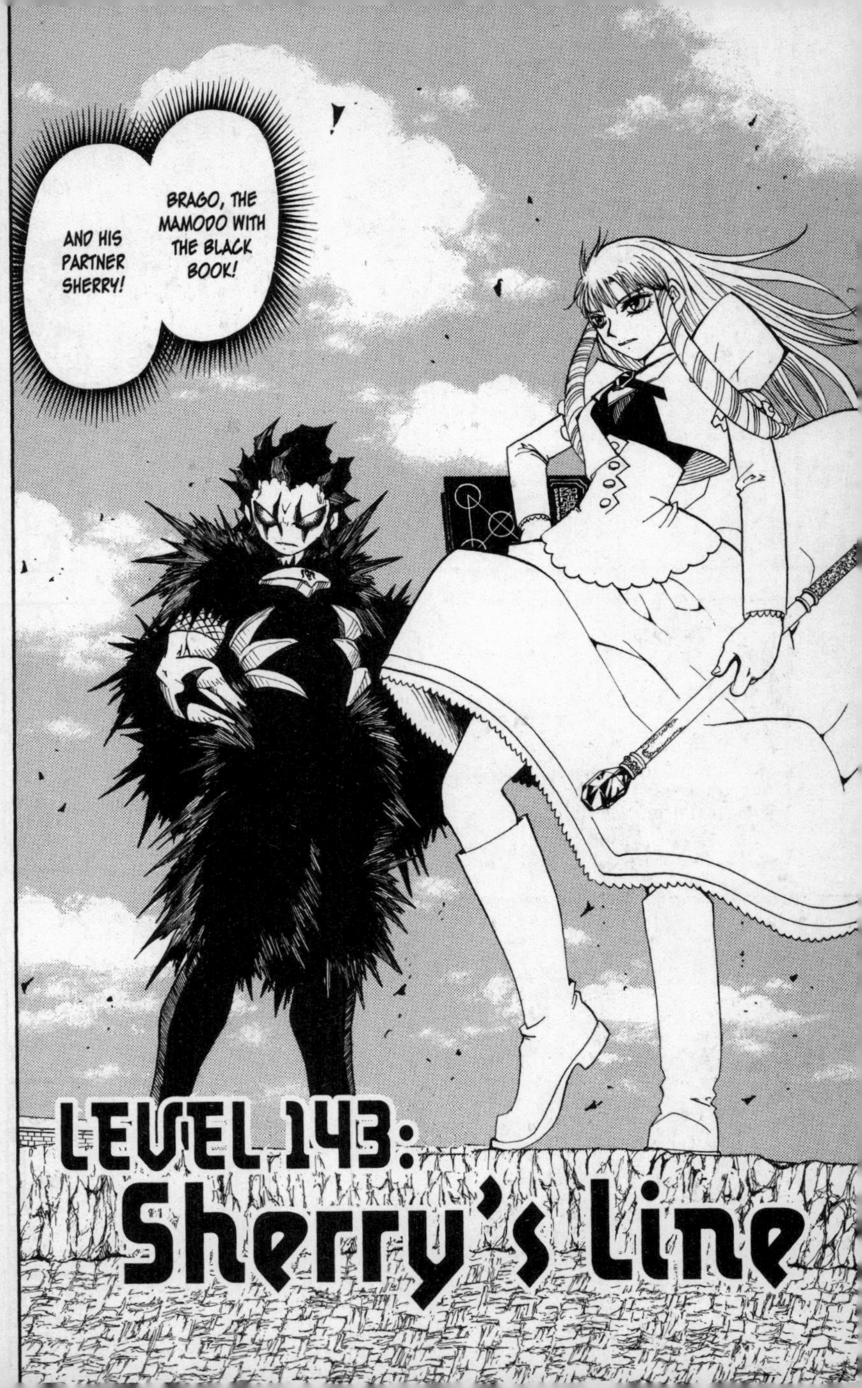
BRAGO, THE MAMODO WITH THE BLACK BOOK!
AND HIS PARTNER SHERRY!
LEVEL 143:
Sherry's Line

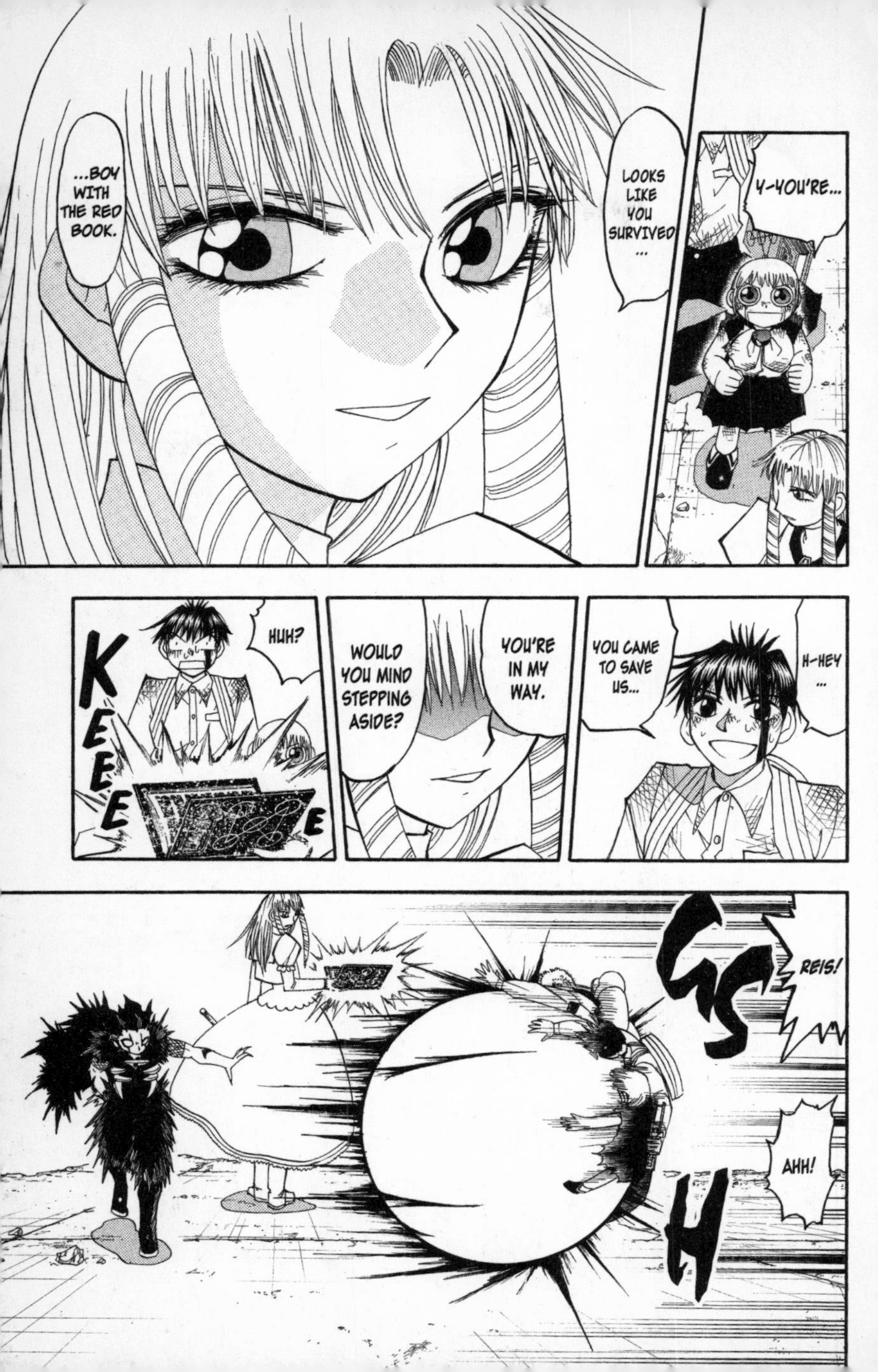
Y-YOU'RE...
LOOKS LIKE YOU SURVIVED...
...BOY WITH THE RED BOOK.
H-HEY...
YOU CAME TO SAVE US...
YOU'RE IN MY WAY.
WOULD YOU MIND STEPPING ASIDE?
HUH?
KEEEEE
REIS!
AHH!

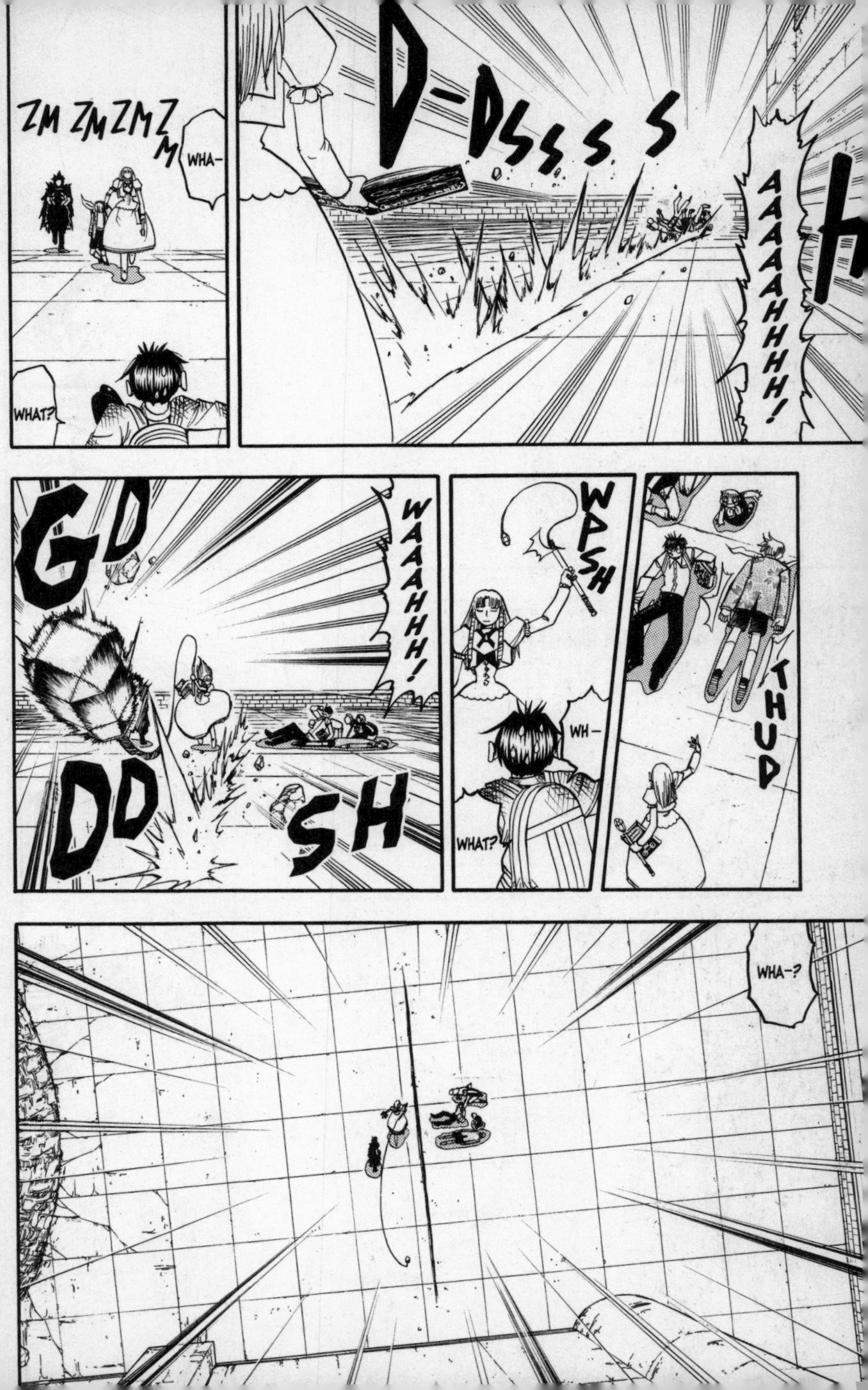
D-DSSS S
AAAAAHHHHH!
ZM ZMZMZ M
WHA-
WHAT?
THUD
WPSH
WH-
WHAT?
WAAAHHHH!
GD
DD
SH
WHA-?

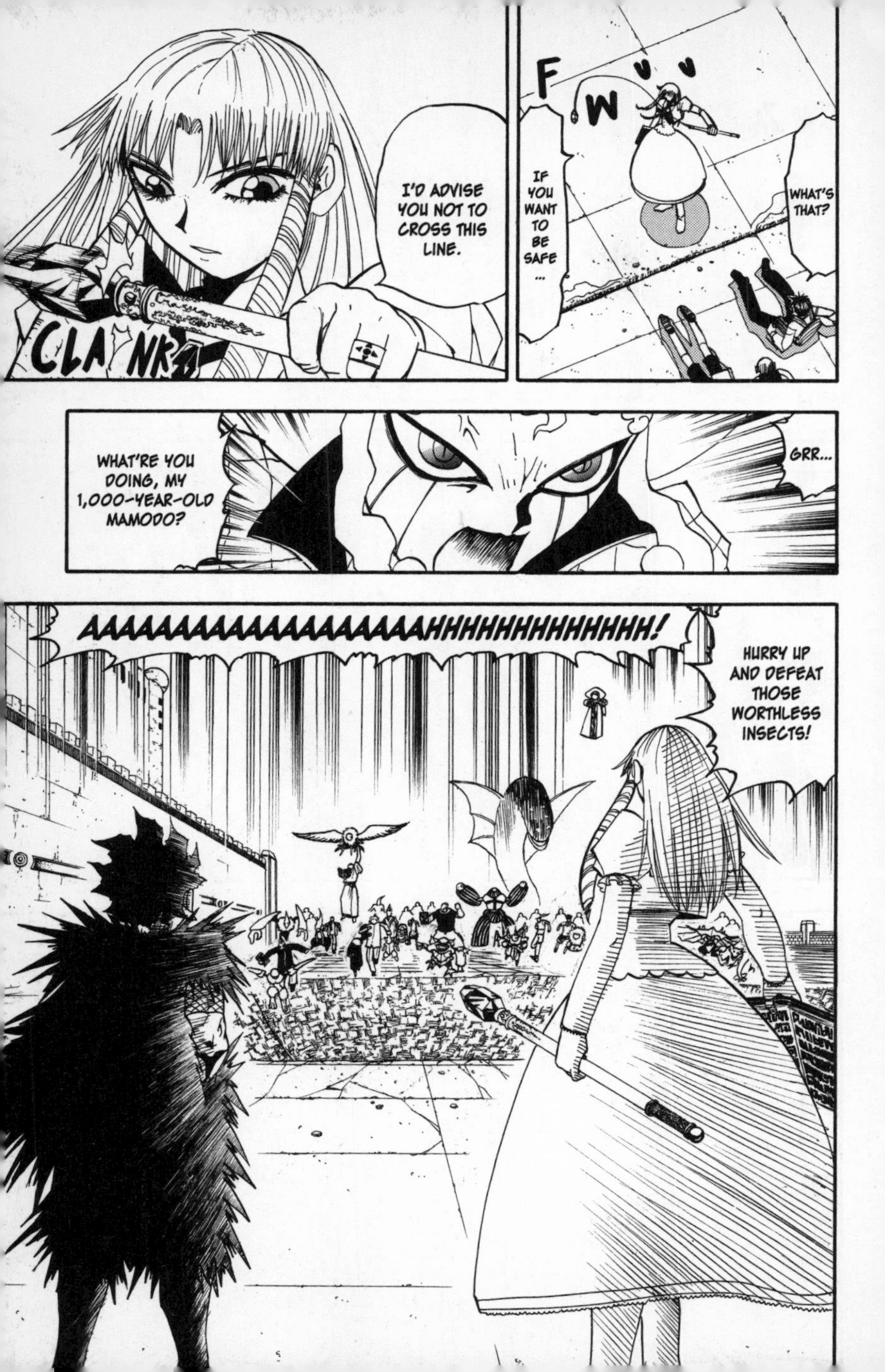
FWUU
WHAT'S THAT?
IF YOU WANT TO BE SAFE ...
I'D ADVISE YOU NOT TO CROSS THIS LINE.
CLANK
GRR...
WHAT'RE YOU DOING, MY 1,000-YEAR-OLD MAMODO?
HURRY UP AND DEFEAT THOSE WORTHLESS INSECTS!
AAAAAAAAAAAAAAAAAAAAHHHHHHHHHHHHHH!

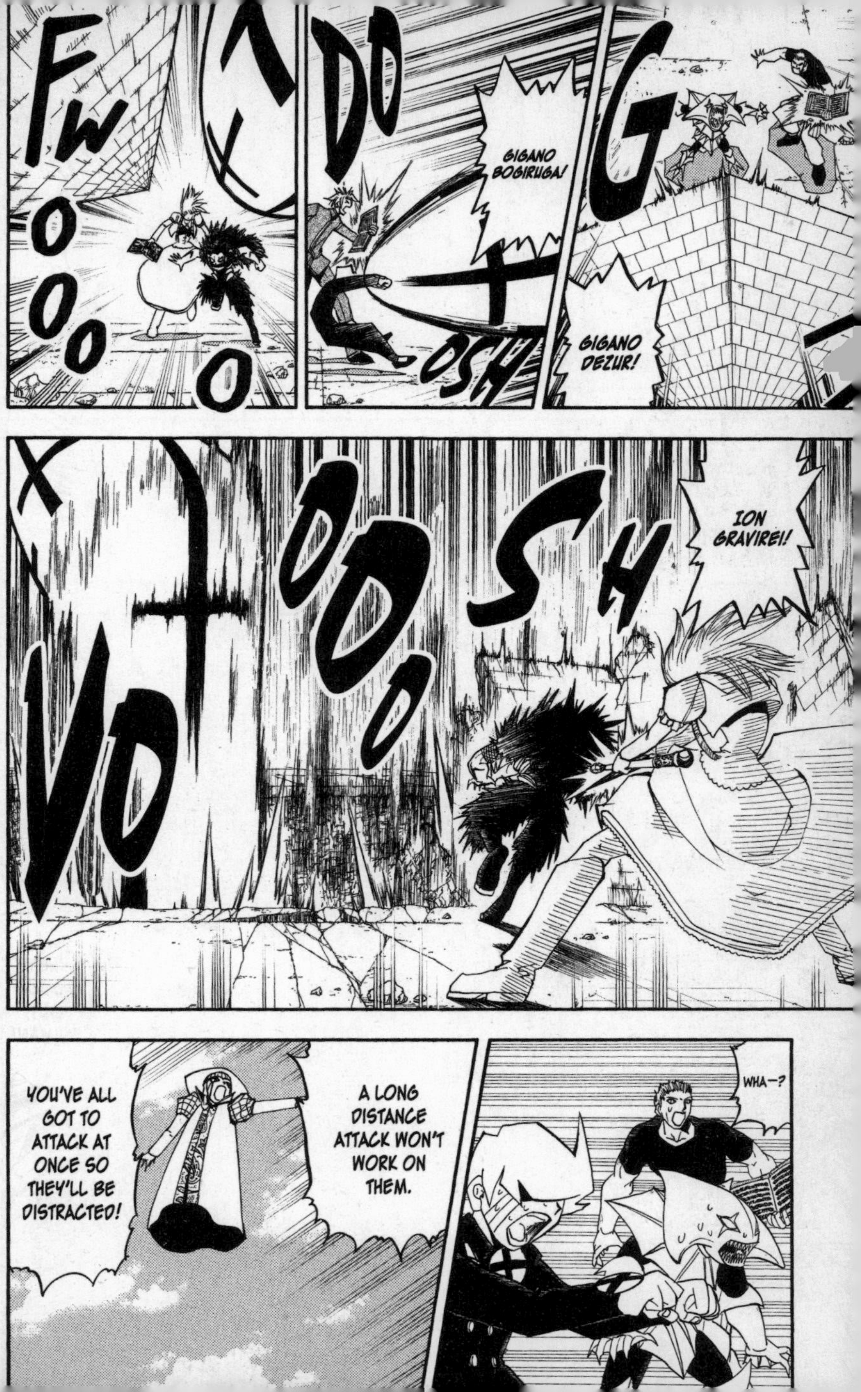
G
GIGANO DEZUR!
DO
GIGANO BOGIRUGA!
OSH
FWOOOOO
ION GRAVIREI!
SH
VO
WHA—?
A LONG DISTANCE ATTACK WON'T WORK ON THEM.
YOU'VE ALL GOT TO ATTACK AT ONCE SO THEY'LL BE DISTRACTED!

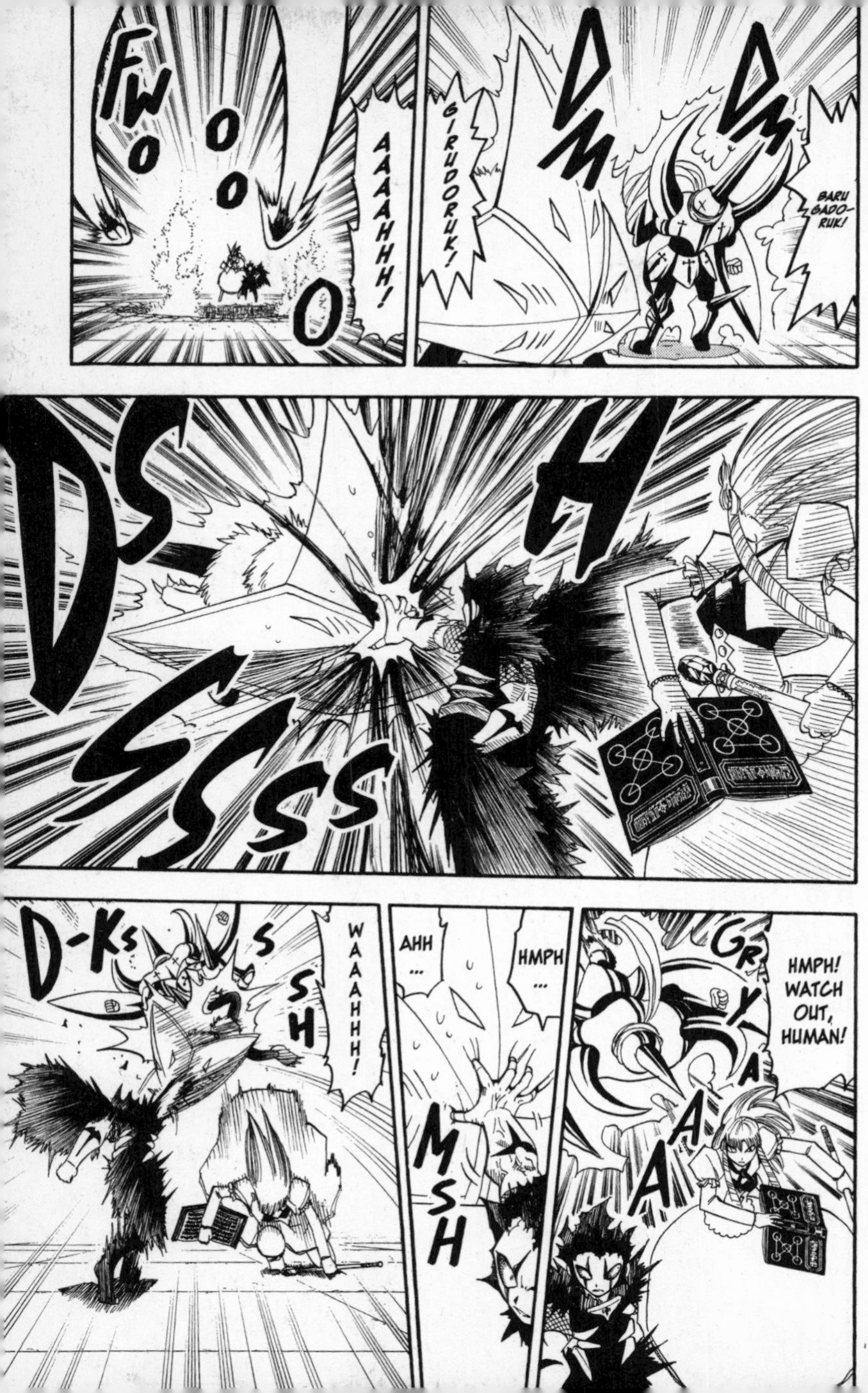
DM
BARU GADORUK!
DM
GIRUDORUK!
AAAAAHHH!
FWOOOO
DSSSSH
HMPH! WATCH OUT, HUMAN!
GRYAAA
HMPH...
AHH...
MSH
WAAAAHHH!
SSH
D-Ks

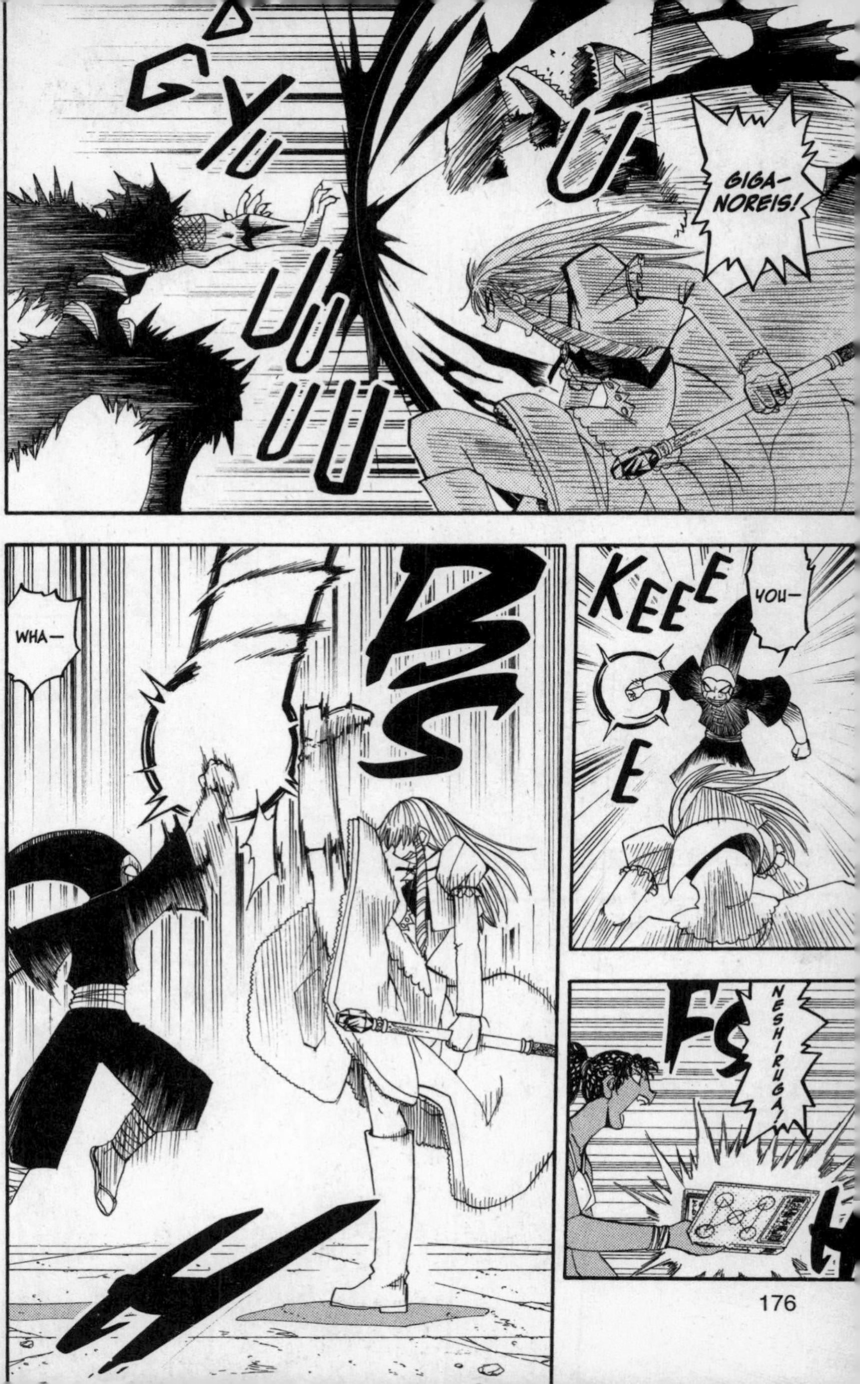

GIGA-NOREIS!
GYUUUUUUU
YOU—
KEEEE
NESHIRUGA!
WHA—

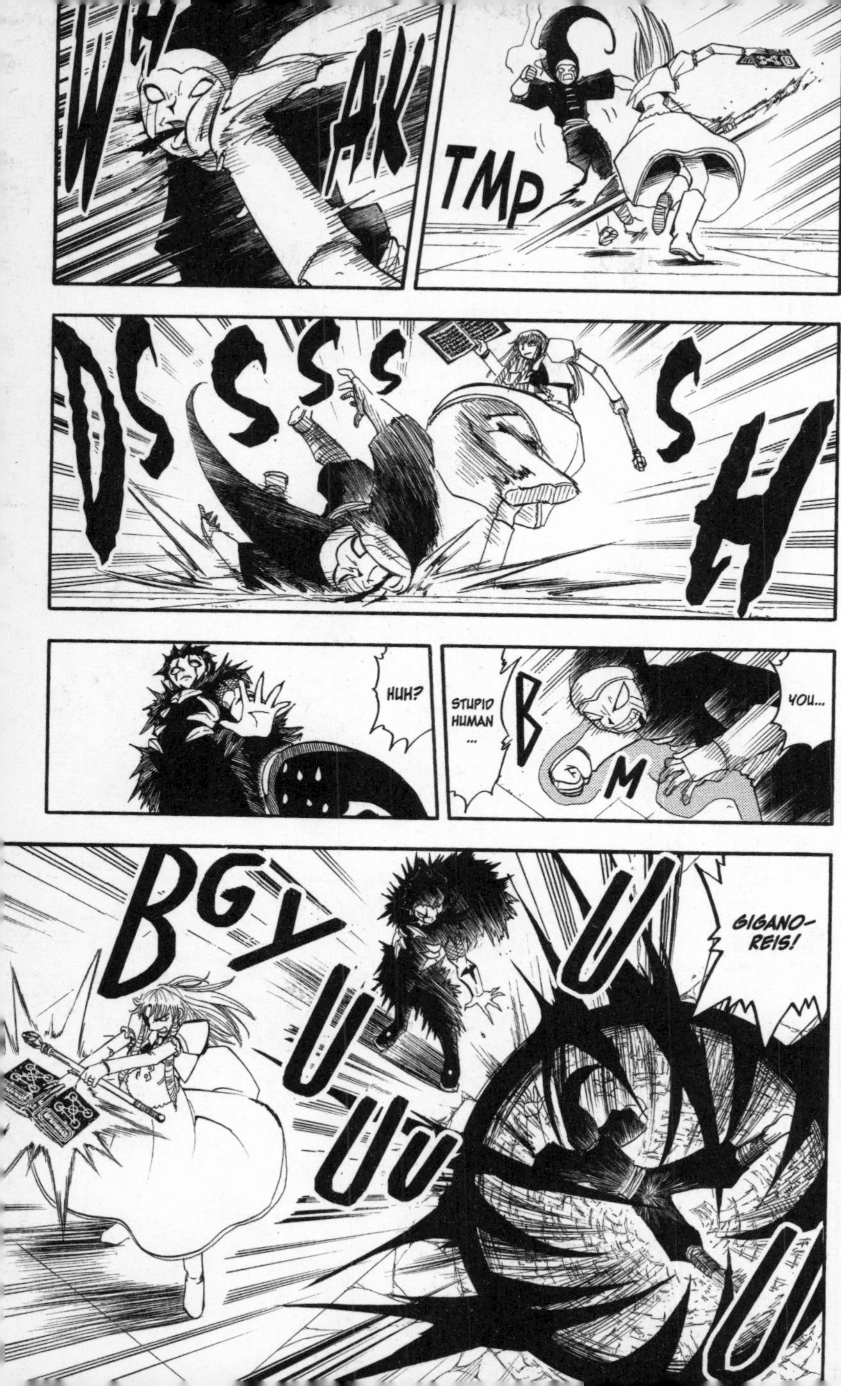
TMP
WHAK
DSSSSH
YOU...
BM
STUPID HUMAN ...
HUH?
GIGANO-REIS!
BGYUUUUUU

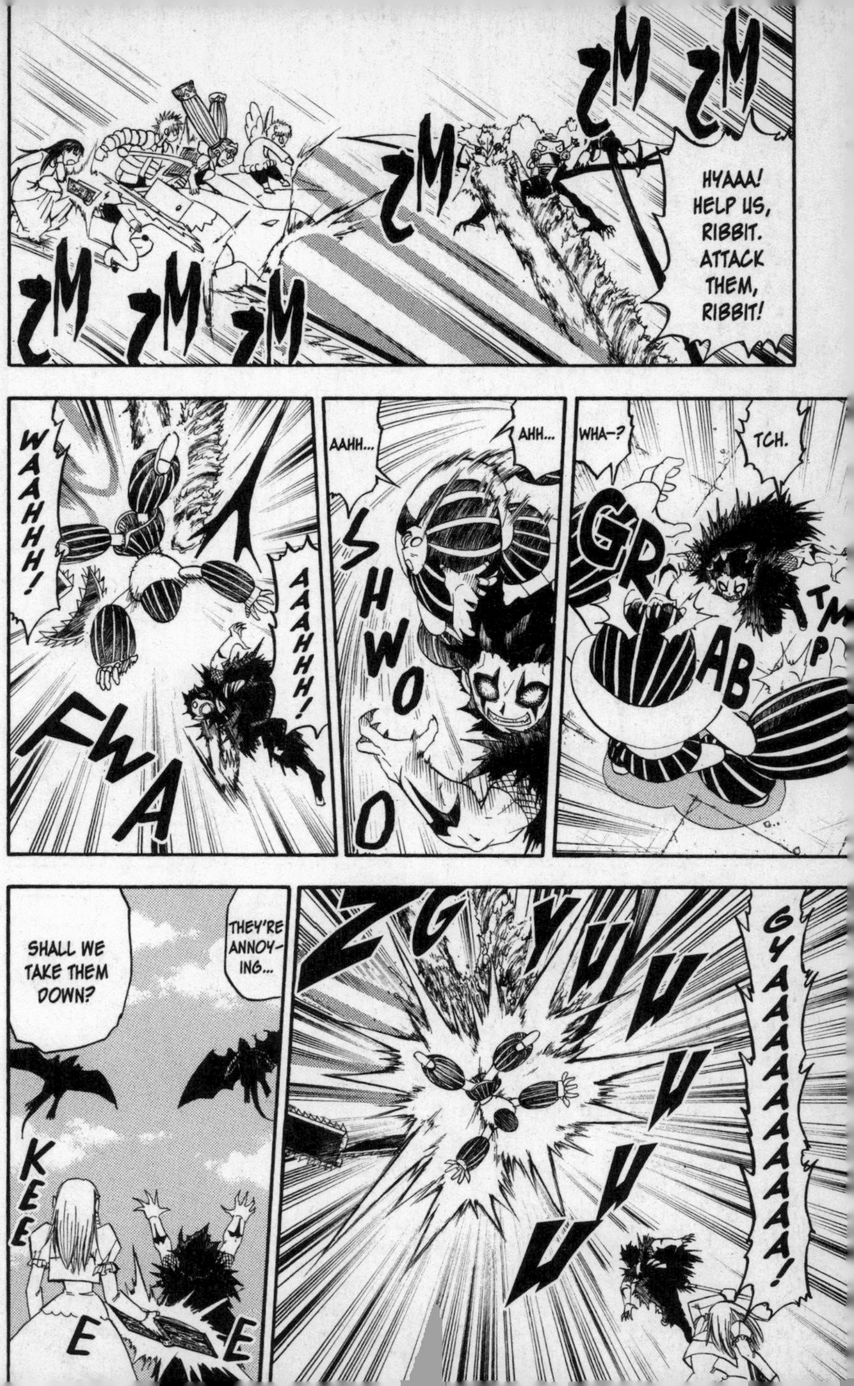
HYAAA! HELP US, RIBBIT. ATTACK THEM, RIBBIT!
TCH.
WHA–?
GRAB
TMP
AHH...
AAHH...
SHWOO
AAAHHH!
WAAHHH!
FWA
GYAAAAAAAAAAA!
ZGYUUUUU
THEY'RE ANNOY-ING...
SHALL WE TAKE THEM DOWN?
KEEEE

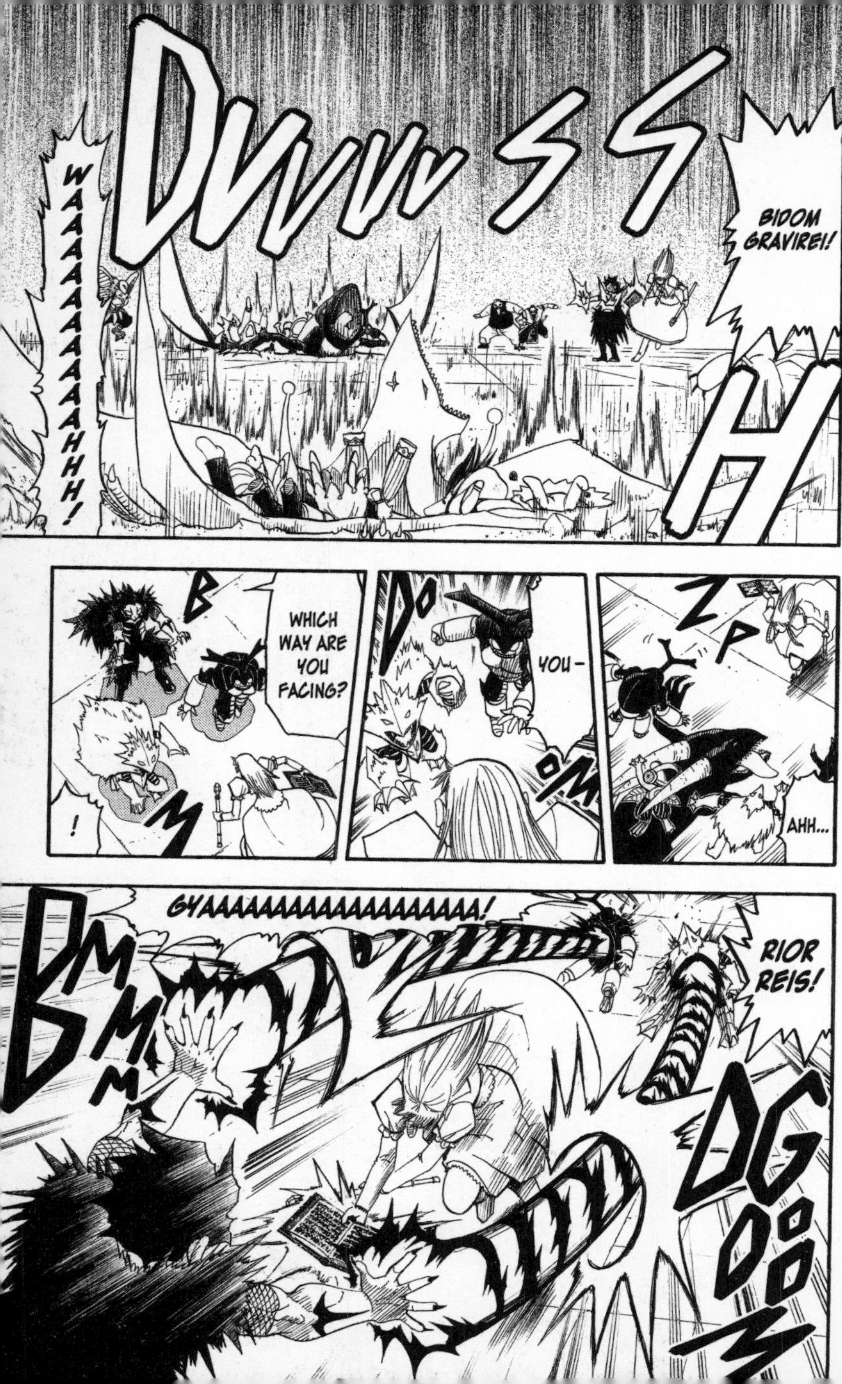
BIDOM GRAVIREI!
DVVVVSSH
WAAAAAAAAAAHHH!
ZP
AHH...
DO
YOU–
OM
B
WHICH WAY ARE YOU FACING?
M
!
RIOR REIS!
GYAAAAAAAAAAAAAAAAAAA!
DGOOOM
BMMMM

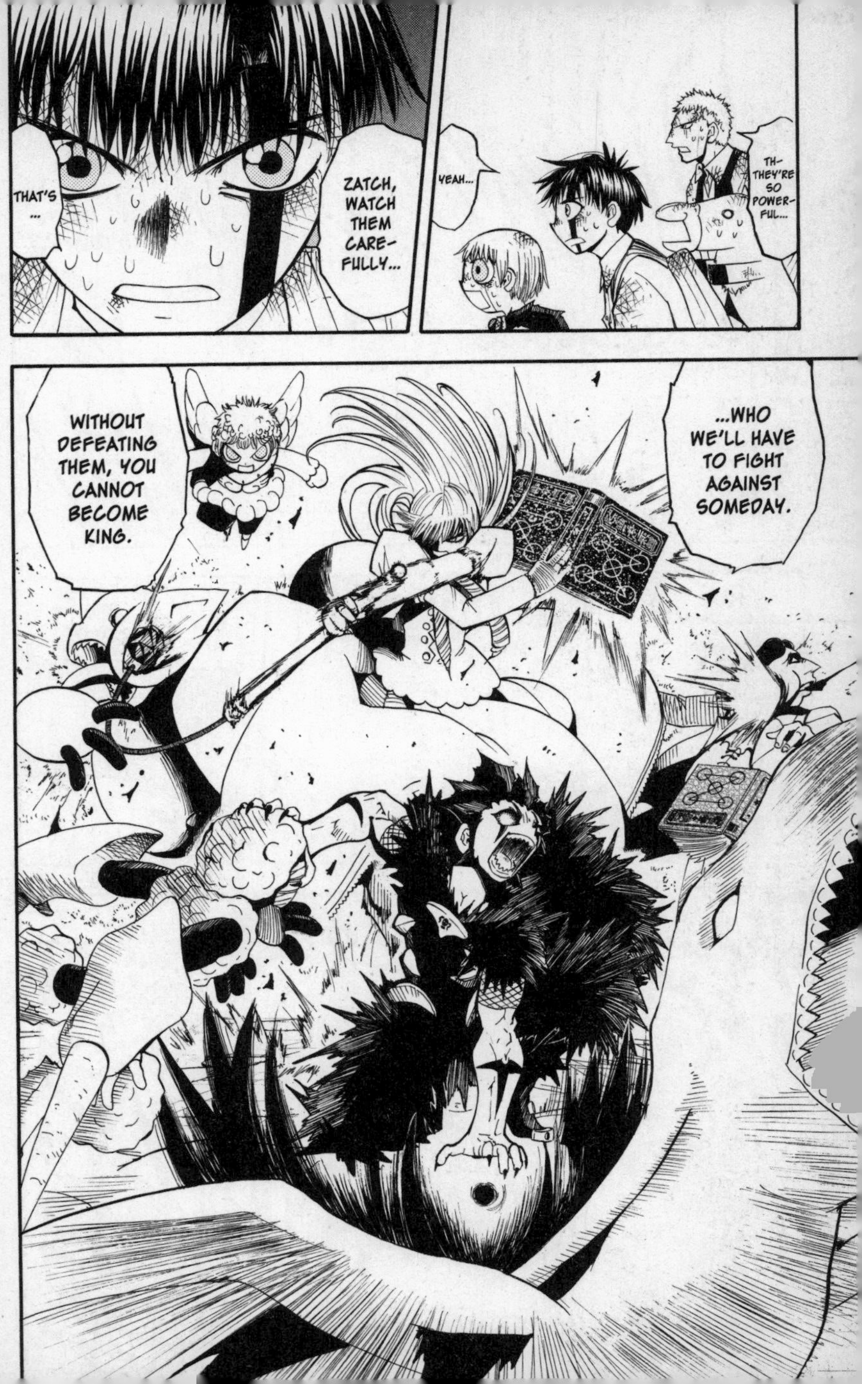
TH-THEY'RE SO POWERFUL...
YEAH...
ZATCH, WATCH THEM CAREFULLY...
THAT'S ...
...WHO WE'LL HAVE TO FIGHT AGAINST SOMEDAY.
WITHOUT DEFEATING THEM, YOU CANNOT BECOME KING.

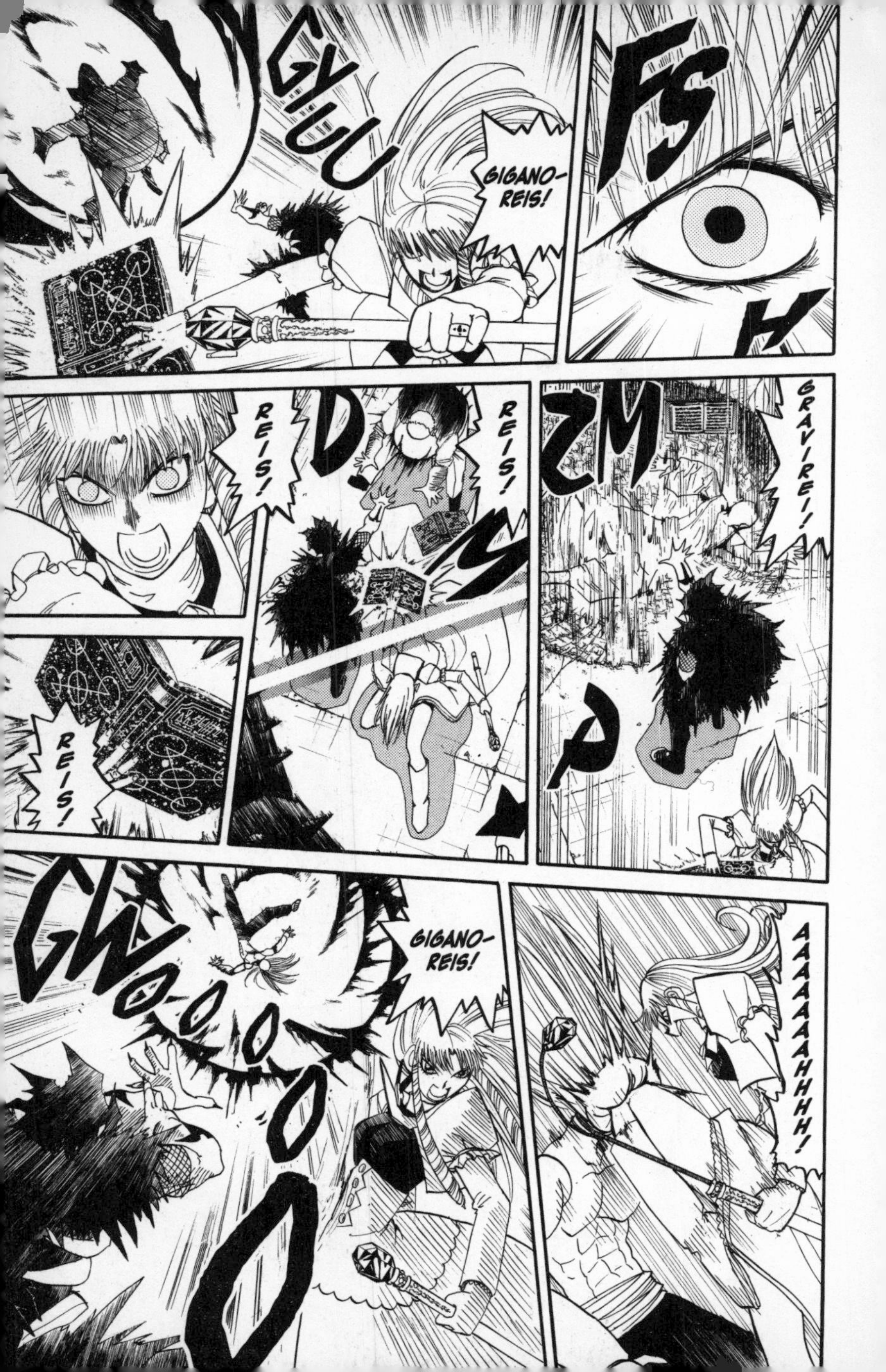
FSH
GYUU
GIGANO-REIS!
GRAVIREI!
ZMP
REIS!
DM
REIS!
REIS!
AAAAAAAHHHH!
GIGANO-REIS!
GWOOOOO

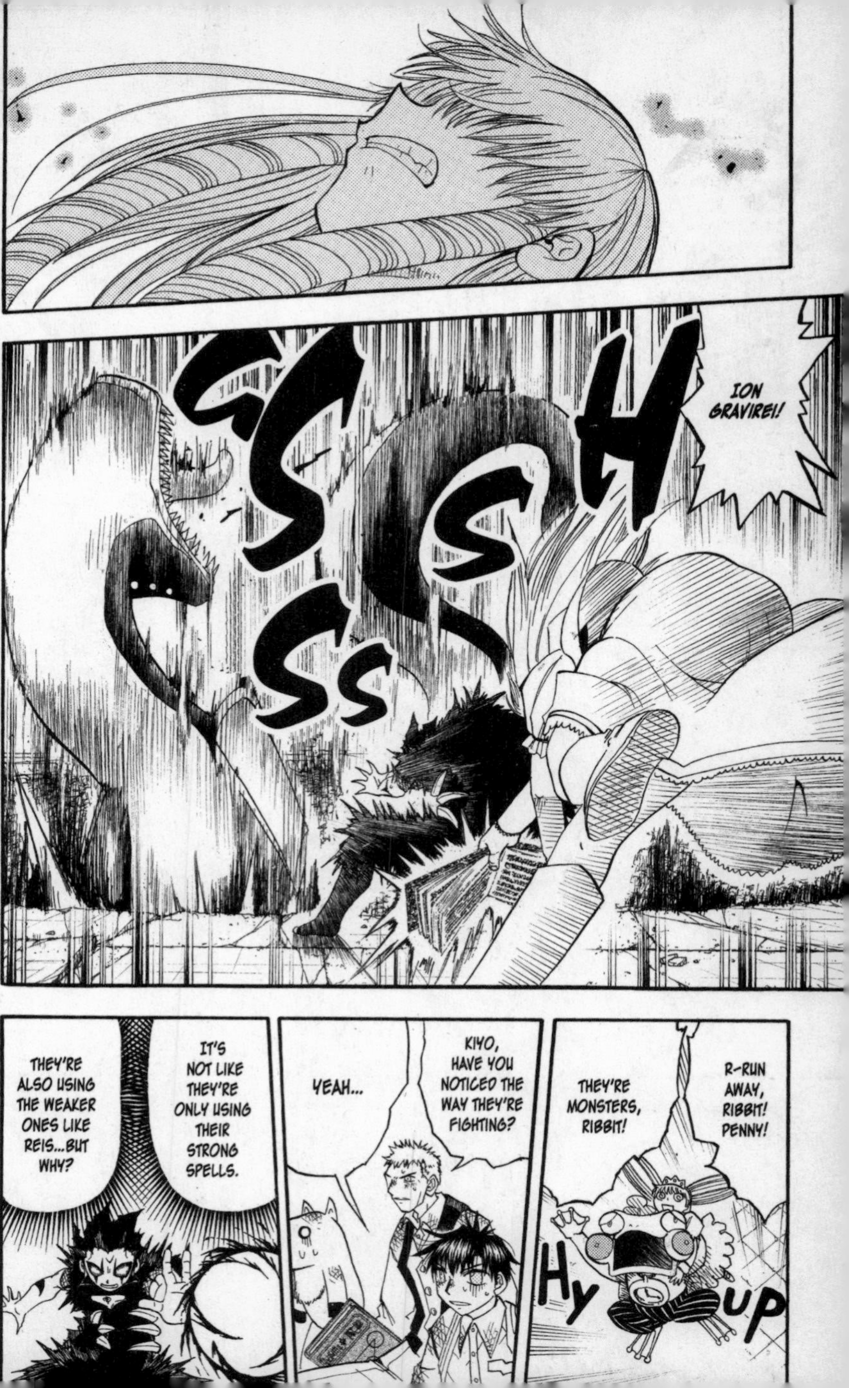
ION GRAVIREI!
GSSH
SSs
R-RUN AWAY, RIBBIT! PENNY!
THEY'RE MONSTERS, RIBBIT!
Hy UP
KIYO, HAVE YOU NOTICED THE WAY THEY'RE FIGHTING?
YEAH...
IT'S NOT LIKE THEY'RE ONLY USING THEIR STRONG SPELLS.
THEY'RE ALSO USING THE WEAKER ONES LIKE REIS...BUT WHY?

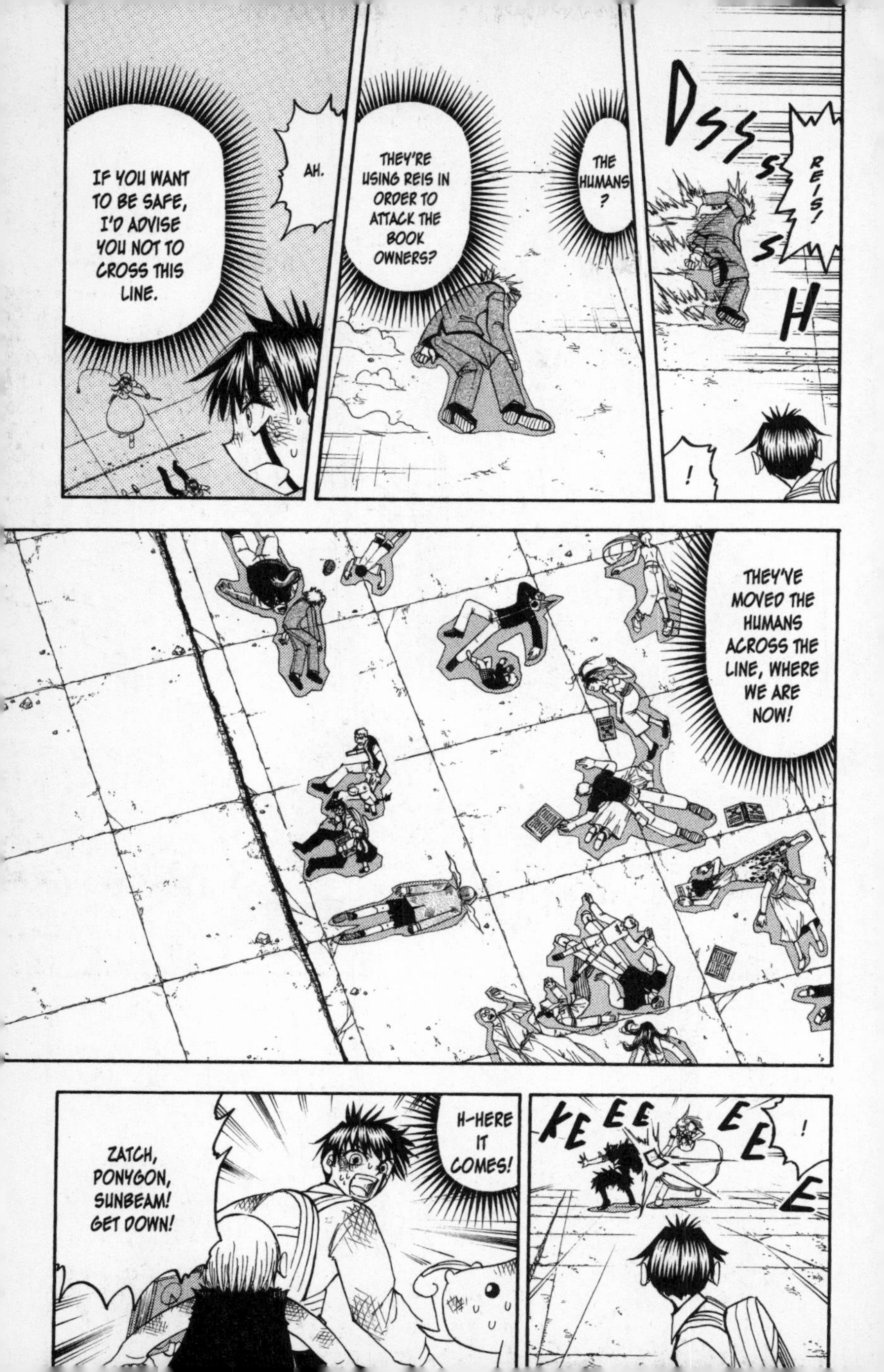
DSSSSH
REIS!
!
THE HUMANS?
THEY'RE USING REIS IN ORDER TO ATTACK THE BOOK OWNERS?
AH.
IF YOU WANT TO BE SAFE, I'D ADVISE YOU NOT TO CROSS THIS LINE.
THEY'VE MOVED THE HUMANS ACROSS THE LINE, WHERE WE ARE NOW!
KEEEEEE
!
H-HERE IT COMES!
ZATCH, PONYGON, SUNBEAM! GET DOWN!

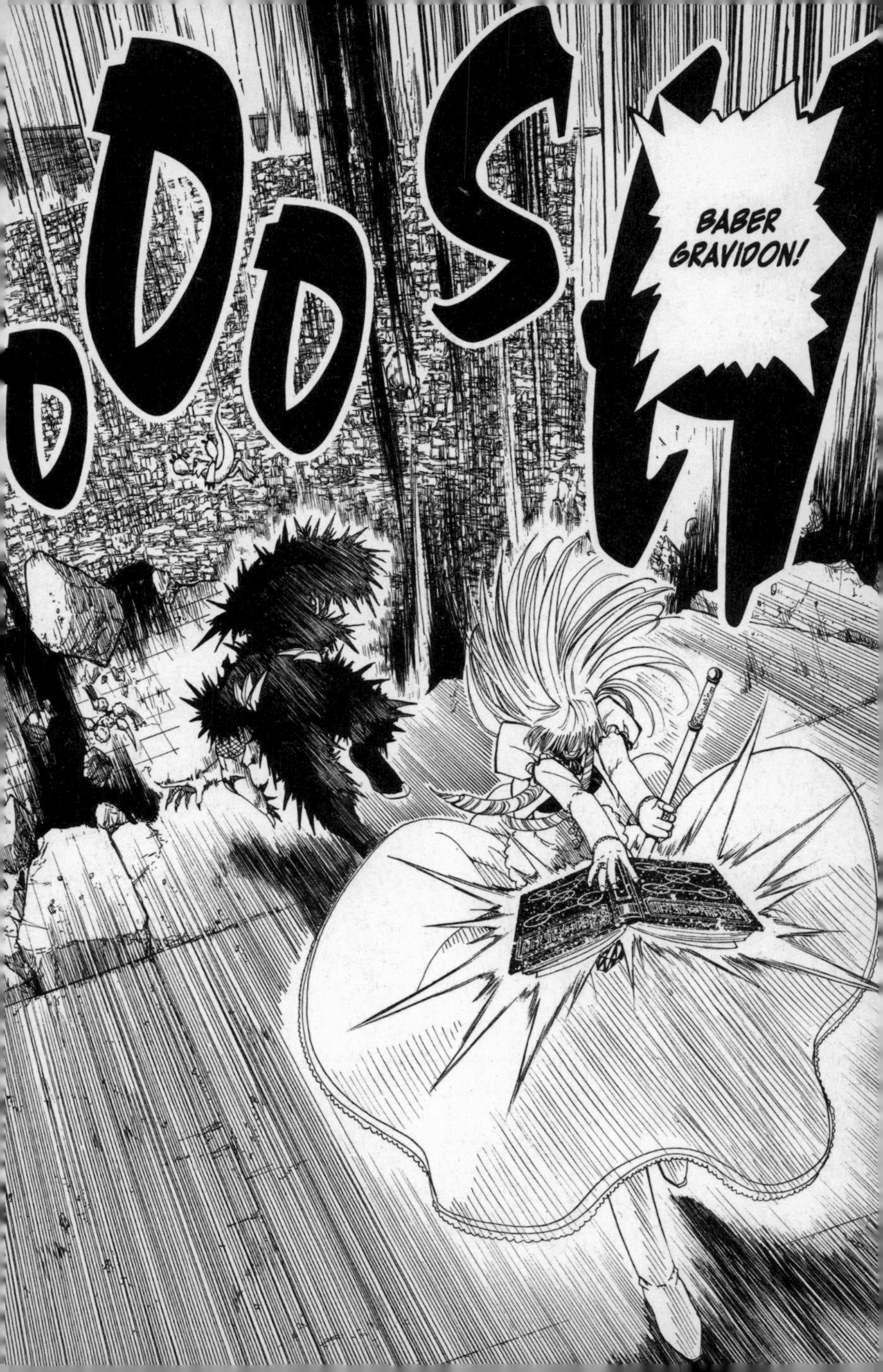
BABER GRAVIDON!

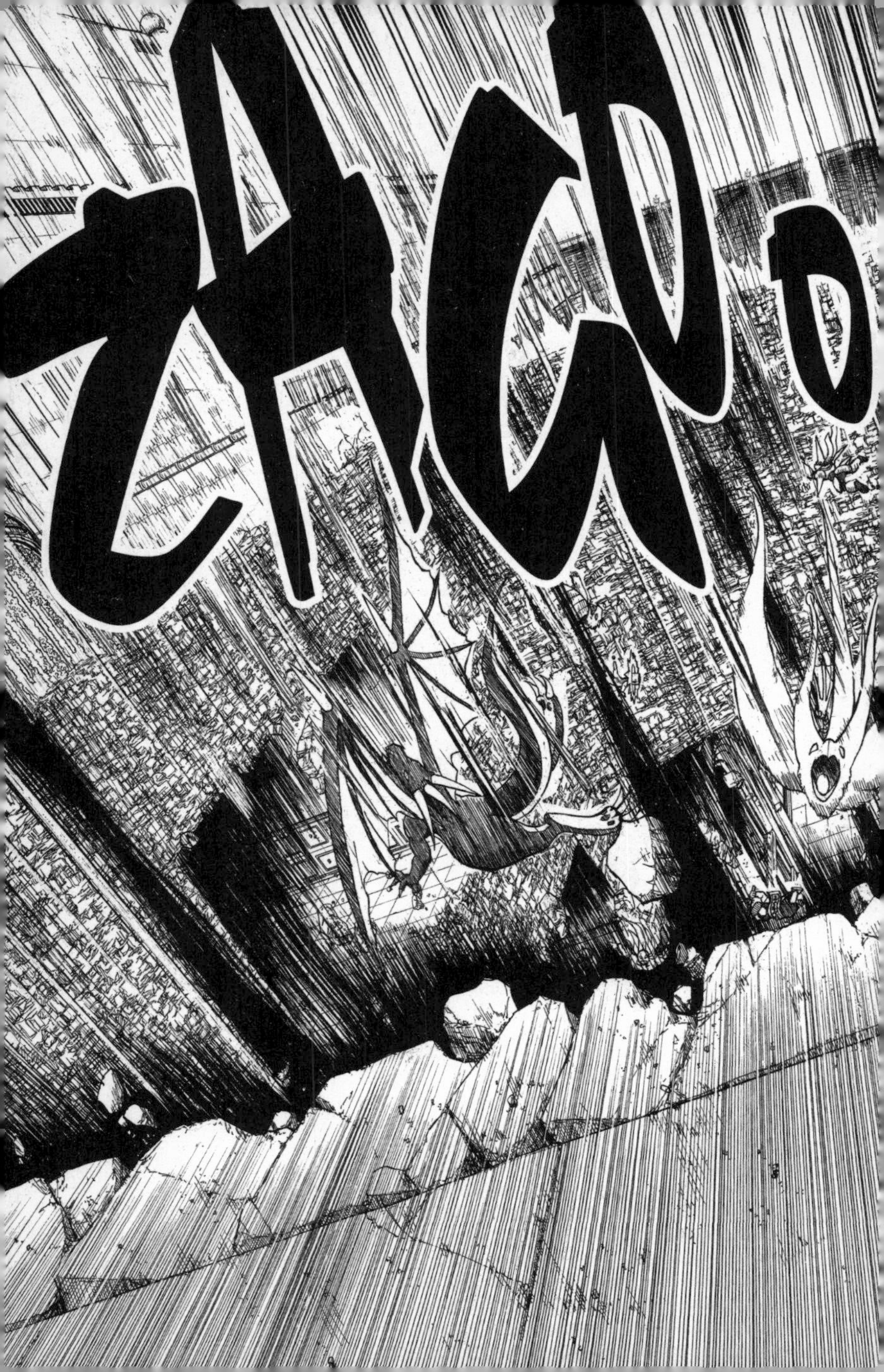

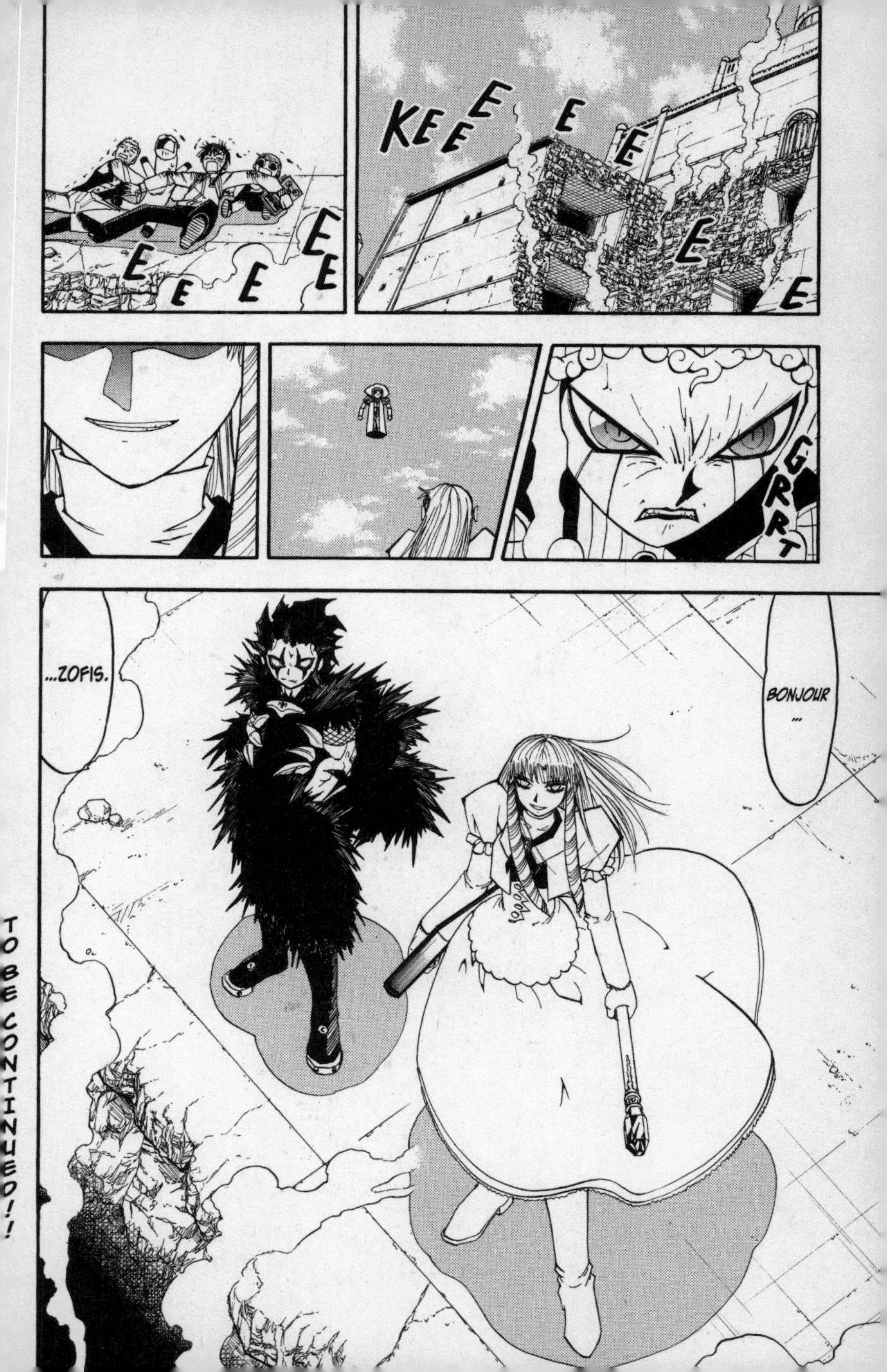
KEEEEEEEE
EEEEE
GRRRT
BONJOUR ...
...ZOFIS.
TO BE CONTINUED!!

ZATCH & SUZY
BY MAKOTO RAIKU
2x1=2 2x2=4 2x3=6 2x4=8
FWUUU
HEY, SUZY. WE'RE IN TROUBLE!
HUH? HOW MUCH TROUBLE ARE WE IN?
FWUUU
REMEMBER THAT TIME WHEN YOU WERE IN SECOND GRADE? IT'S LIKE THAT.
WHEN I WAS IN SECOND GRADE?
I CAN'T DO MY MULTIPLI-CATION TABLES.
HA, HA! THEN YOU'LL HAVE TO STAY AFTER CLASS!
I DON'T REMEMBER MY FOUR-SIES!
N-NO...
NOOOOOO!

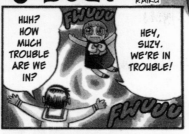

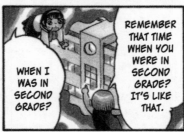

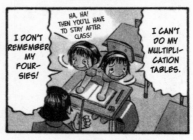

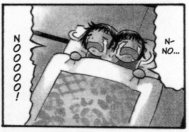

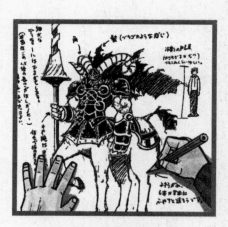

MAKOTO RAIKU

Zatch is gonna be an animated movie. Zatch'll be running around on the big screen. Helping out with the character designs is getting me really excited. Heh, heh, heh, it's gonna be amazing. They've finally made it...heh, heh, heh, heh...

ZATCH BELL!
Vol. 15

STORY AND ART BY
MAKOTO RAIKU

Translation/David Ury
Touch-up Art & Lettering/Gabe Crate
Design/Izumi Hirayama
Special Thanks/Jessica Villat, Miki Macaluso,
Mitsuko Kitajima, and Akane Matsuo
Editor/Kit Fox

Editor in Chief, Books/Alvin Lu
Editor in Chief, Magazines/Marc Weidenbaum
VP of Publishing Licensing/Rika Inouye
VP of Sales/Gonzalo Ferreyra
Sr. VP of Marketing/Liza Coppola
Publisher/Hyoe Narita

Printed in the U.S.A.

Published by VIZ Media, LLC
P.O. Box 77010
San Francisco, CA 94107

10 9 8 7 6 5 4 3 2 1
First printing, October 2007

www.viz.com
store.viz.com

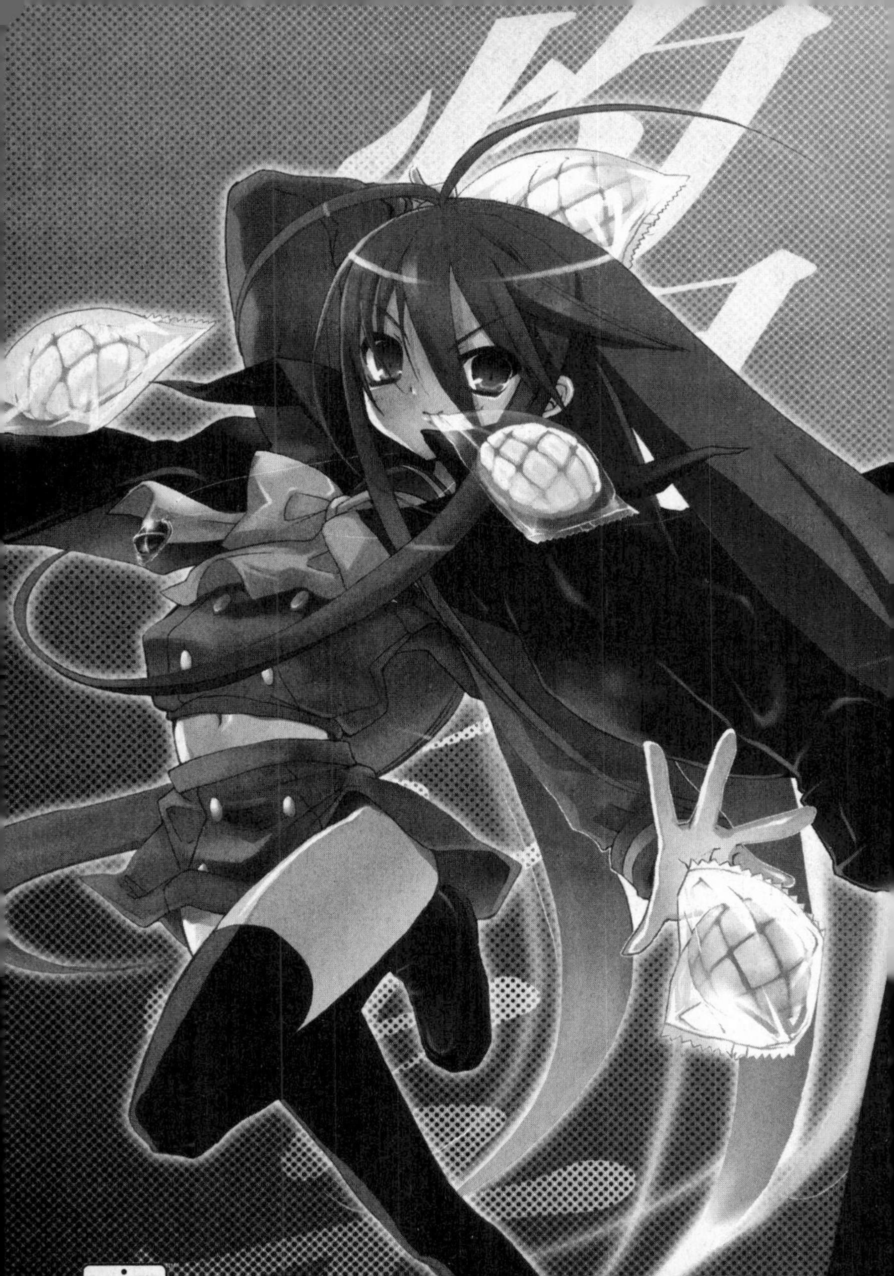